The Wagner Operas

Volume I

The Wagner Operas

Volume I

BY

ERNEST NEWMAN

HARPER COLOPHON BOOKS
HARPER & ROW, PUBLISHERS
NEW YORK, CAMBRIDGE, PHILADELPHIA, SAN FRANCISCO
LONDON, MEXICO CITY, SAO PAULO, SYDNEY

This work was originally published in one hardcover volume: in Great Britain under the title *Wagner Nights*; and in the United States by Alfred A. Knopf, Inc. It is here reprinted by arrangement with Alfred A. Knopf, Inc.

First HARPER COLOPHON edition published 1983.

Library of Congress Cataloging in Publication Data

Newman, Ernest, 1868-1959.
  The Wagner operas.

  Reprint. Originally published: New York : A. A. Knopf, 1981.
  Includes index.
  1. Wagner, Richard, 1813-1883. Operas. 2. Operas—Analysis, appreciation. I. Title.
MT100.W2N53 1983   782.1'092'4   83-47569
ISBN 0-06-091073-9 (v. 1)   83 84 85 86 87 10 9 8 7 6 5 4 3 2 1
ISBN 0-06-091074-7 (v. 2)   83 84 85 86 87 10 9 8 7 6 5 4 3 2 1

TO

VERA

Contents

WAGNER: THE LAST PHOTOGRAPH

Overture

WHEN the first volume of this series was published in England — the *Opera Nights* of 1943 — those great and good men the reviewers, from whose lynx-eyes nothing can remain hidden for long, reproached me tenderly for what they regarded as my arbitrary choice of operas. *Falstaff,* for instance, was there, but not *Otello* or *Aïda, Turandot* and *Gianni Schicchi* but not *Tosca* or *La Bohème, Così fan tutte* but not *Don Giovanni* or *Figaro,* and so forth. Berlioz and Tchaikovski and Johann Strauss were among the chosen composers, but not Weber or Rossini or Wagner and a few others in whose company the music lover looks to spending an occasional night at the opera. In their grieved perplexity at this seeming aberration on my part there went up a wail from the English reviewers like that of Mr. Wodehouse's Monty Bodkin when Miss Butterwick broke off the engagement — "Gertrude, your conduct is inexplicable." My own conduct, however, can be explained.

A good many years ago I dashed off, at the request of an English firm of publishers, a fortnightly series of analyses, in popular style, of some of the best-known operas, together with brief biographies of the composers. Although this matter did not, in my opinion, in any sense constitute a "book", it was issued as such, in three volumes, under the general title of *Stories of the Great Operas,* in the United States, where, if hearsay is to be trusted, it had a considerable sale. As the English copyright was mine, Messrs. Putnam and Co. suggested, during the late war, that the American volumes should be reprinted in London. From this suggestion I recoiled in horror. In the first place I saw no sense in reprinting the elementary biographies, while in the second place I felt that if the opera analyses were to be collected in volume form I would prefer to revise them all thoroughly, enlarge the scale of treatment, and altogether try to make a better job of it. On these terms agreements were ultimately made with Messrs. Putnam on my side of the Atlantic and Mr. Alfred Knopf on the other.

While these negotiations were proceeding I arranged with Mr. Knopf for a volume dealing with twenty-nine operas that had not been included in the fortnightly series to which I have referred. This entirely new volume appeared in England in 1943 under the title of *Opera Nights;* but as the analyses of twenty-odd years ago had been issued in the U.S.A. under the title of *Stories of the Great Operas,* Mr. Knopf brought out the new volume as *More Stories of Famous Operas,* a procedure calculated, I am afraid, to give a little trouble one of these days to library cataloguers and bibliographers. However, that was no concern of mine. I then set to work to rewrite all the original analyses (*Stories of the Great Operas*), one volume to be devoted to Wagner, the other to deal with all the famous works by other composers not included in *Opera Nights* (*More Stories of Famous Operas*). The present volume is the first stage in this process of reincarnation. It has no connection whatever with the Wagner volume of *Stories of the Great Operas;* it is an entirely new work from cover to cover. A further volume, similarly rewritten, dealing with the standard works of Mozart, Verdi, Puccini, Gounod, Rossini etc. not included in *Opera Nights,* will follow, I hope, before long.

At first sight there may appear to be no great necessity today for yet another book on the Wagner operas. Sooner or later, however, such a work would have had to be written by someone or other, for our knowledge of Wagner has been so vastly increased during the last few years that the close student of him has a score of lights on him that were denied to our fathers. The recent publication in Germany of his full-length prose sketches for some of his works has taught us a great deal we had never suspected before about him and them; for example, we are now able for the first time to trace every smallest step of his that led, over so many years, to the building up of the present *Ring.* We see how drastically his original scheme was changed in the course of time, and not always, perhaps, for the better; we see, too, that, as was the case with Vergil and the *Aeneid,* he has sometimes made an alteration in his plan without noticing that the new feature is inconsistent with something he has left in its first form elsewhere in the poem.

My own study of him has convinced me that it is impossible to understand fully the works of his maturity without having traversed on our own account the extensive and often difficult country over which he himself had to travel before he reached his distant goal. Often a point that is obscure or even inconsistent in the opera poem is elucidated for us by his sketches. Sometimes the psychological motivation of an episode becomes clear to us only in the light of our knowledge of the mediaeval legend that was his starting-point. Sometimes, in the *Ring*, the clue to his procedure is unexpectedly discovered in such works as the *Deutsche Mythologie* of the brothers Grimm, which we know him to have studied closely in the late 1840's.

I venture to lay it down, then, that a clear picture of Wagner's mind-processes during the conception and realisation of a work is to be obtained only by following him step by step through the literature, ancient and modern, out of which it grew. It may be objected that a work of art should be its own sufficient explanation. But there are cases, some of them the most notable in literary history, in which that simple proposition obviously does not hold good. The *Aeneid* is one of them; the *Divina Commedia* is another. No student of today can hope to get quite inside the mind of Dante by a mere reading of his text; he requires to be told a great deal about many things which are implicit in the text but not self-revelatory in it, such as the mediaeval conception of the universe, the mediaeval attitude towards religion, the contemporary characters who figure in the poem, and so on. Coming down to our own epoch, Albert Thibaudet, in his searching study of Flaubert, has told us that in *Salammbô* the great novelist "has for the most part followed the history of Polybius, and the reader assuredly needs to be acquainted with this." So it is again with Henry James: his own retracing, in the prefaces to one of the later editions of his works, of his mental processes when he was working out the characters and the situations of this novel or that is of fundamental importance to the serious student of him; after reading one of these prefaces we re-read the novel itself in quite a new way, with many a new and revealing light on things.

It would be surprising, indeed, if the case were otherwise: since the whole mind of a great artist has gone into the making of one of his major works, the more we know about the nature and the operations of that mind the more profound will be our understanding of the work; and since the inner world from which it came was built up by the slow unconscious coalescence within the man of influences and impulses from many quarters, it is of the first importance that we, for our part, shall re-live, to the best of our ability, his own inner life during the years when the work was shaping itself within him.

I have accordingly devoted a considerable amount of space not only to Wagner's prose sketches for some of his works but to the mediaeval poems that were the prime generators of them; we listen to *Tristan* and *Parsifal,* for instance, in a new way — and I venture to say, a way that is more like Wagner's than any opera house ever conveys to us — after we have read Gottfried of Strassburg and Wolfram von Eschenbach. The *Ring* is a peculiar case. The Wagnerian mental complex that went to the making of the great tetralogy was built up slowly out of not only the Nibelungenlied and the Volsunga and other sagas but also out of the storehouse of facts relating to the Teutonic past that was thrown open to Wagner by the Grimms and other scholars of the first half of the nineteenth century. For this reason, among others, I have gone at considerable length into the history of Wagner's prose sketches for the *Ring.* The reader need not necessarily plough doggedly through all this right away, for its complexities may sometimes discourage him: he will probably find it more convenient to keep these pages for reference after he has worked at the poems and the scores and read the present analyses. Some knowledge of it all is indispensable to a full understanding of the *Ring;* and a reader or two here and there may at any rate be grateful to me for having spared him the labour of hacking his way through the jungle on his own account.

The need for a clearer view on our part of the Wagner operas as Wagner himself saw them is all the greater because it is the sad lot of the ordinary opera-goer, who is almost entirely dependent for his impressions of them on what he sees and hears in the theatre, to have them put before him, in even the best of present-day performances, in a way that often does them the minimum of justice. In the Overture to *Opera Nights* I pointed out how much worse off the opera-lover is than the ordinary theatre-goer in the matter of casting. Care is taken when casting Hamlet, for instance, that by the grace of the gods there is some correspondence between the actor's own appearance and build and voice and mentality and those we associate with the character; whereas in the opera house a woman with neither the face nor the figure nor the mind for a Gilda or a Lakmé is set down to play the fragile part merely because she has the right range and timbre of voice and the coloratura technique for it; or a man who physically and intellectually might have made the ideal Des Grieux or Parsifal is forced to play the Conte di Luna or Germont *père* merely because nature has stupidly seen fit to make him a baritone instead of a tenor.

Seldom indeed do we find a Wagnerian part played by a man or woman who looks and thinks — or mimics the apparatus of thinking — like the character he or she is supposed to be representing. Wagner himself, after working himself to death trying to knock some understanding of a part into one of his male singers, asked the gods piteously by what primal curse laid upon him it came about that he had to allot his most intellectual parts to a tenor. Think of the young Siegfried as Wagner imagined him, the incarnation of youthful health and beauty and active joy in life, or the metaphysical Tristan, or the spiritual Parsifal, and then recognise these creations, if you can, in some amphora [1] Heldentenor or other who looks and behaves like an overgrown Boy Scout, and gives the spectator the impression of a man whose mental development was arrested at the age of twelve and has been in custody ever since. Or take the case of Brynhilde. "That is no man!" Siegfried ejaculates when he has removed the breastplate from the form of the sleeping Valkyrie; and a smile goes round the house, for what we see is a matron who could serve anywhere for a demonstration of the physical possibilities of the higher mammalia. And only the other day I found a French critic complaining that while some German lady or other had sung beautifully in *Lohengrin* her Elsa "manquait de virginité". Well, one can't have everything.

My main object in the present volume has been to help the opera-goer to see the Wagnerian works as nearly as possible as Wagner must have seen them, and so to get more value out of his

---

[1] An amphora is defined by the classical dictionaries as "a two-handled, big-bellied vessel, usually of clay, with a longish or shortish neck and a mouth proportioned to the size, sometimes resting firmly on a foot, but often ending in a blunt point . . ."

listening in the theatre and by radio. It is unfortunately impossible to make an analysis of them clear except by frequent reference to the leading motives. But I have tried to reduce that reference to the minimum, for two reasons: in the first place, if there is too much of it one's text comes to resemble a series of mathematical formulae; in the second place, it is a cardinal error to suppose either that the musical tissue of a Wagner opera is made up simply of a pinning together of motives, or that, in most cases, any one label can be found that will cover all the uses and meanings of any one motive. The practice of the commentators has been to make out the label in terms of the words that have accompanied a given motive at its first appearance in the score. But that is pure fallacy: for Wagner himself his motives had no such fixity or limitation of meaning, a point which the reader will find insisted upon again and again in the course of these analyses.

I have made the *Flying Dutchman* my starting-point because the central purpose of the volume is to be practically helpful, and the reader is hardly likely ever to see a performance of *Die Feen, Das Liebesverbot* or *Rienzi*.

As often as was possible I have allowed Wagner the poet to speak for himself, using my own translations in the Breitkopf and Härtel edition of the operas. (The one exception is *Lohengrin,* which I never translated).

E. N.

The Wagner Operas

Volume I

The Flying Dutchman

CHARACTERS

DALAND, A NORWEGIAN MARINER	*Bass*
SENTA, HIS DAUGHTER	*Soprano*
ERIK, A HUNTER	*Tenor*
MARY, SENTA'S NURSE	*Mezzo-soprano*
DALAND'S STEERSMAN	*Tenor*
THE DUTCHMAN	*Baritone*

Scene: The Norwegian Coast

1

THE STORY of the Flying Dutchman may be a modern variant of the ancient one of the Wandering Jew; but when it first took its present form we do not know. In *Blackwood's Magazine* for May 1821 there appeared an anonymous short story entitled *Vanderdecken's Message Home; or, The Tenacity of Natural Affection,* which, on the face of it, could be taken for an episode detached from a novel. The narrator is on a vessel that has just left the Cape of Good Hope. The conversation on board turns to the story of the Flying Dutchman, which is assumed to be known, more or less, to everyone present. Seventy years earlier, it appears, one Vanderdecken, captain of an Amsterdam ship, had sworn to round Table Bay in spite of wind and weather, "though I should beat about here until the day of judgment"; and beating about those seas he is still, always bringing foul weather to any ship that sights him. He has an embarrassing habit of hailing other vessels, sending out his jolly-boat to them, and asking them, if they are homeward bound, to take charge of a bundle of letters for delivery to his friends and relatives in Holland; "but no good", says one of the seamen who are discussing the matter, "comes to them who have communication with him".

Soon the Flying Dutchman's ship comes into sight, its boat is lowered, and a sailor appears with letters from the captain for Holland; but he is considerably put out when the crew of the English ship, after glancing at the letters, inform him that this and that addressee — including the wife of Vanderdecken — has long been dead, such-and-such a banking house went bankrupt forty years ago, and so on. He insists on leaving the letters on the deck, however, though none of the English seamen will touch them. In the end, to everyone's relief, a gust of wind blows them into the sea; "there was a cry of joy among the sailors, and they ascribed the favourable change which soon took place in the weather to our having got quit of Vanderdecken".

The writer, as has just been said, seems to take it for granted that his readers have already heard of the Flying Dutchman. But there is nothing elemental or eerie in the story as he tells it — no compact with the Devil, no landing of Vanderdecken every few years to find, if he can, some woman whose love will lift the burden of the curse from him. All the *Blackwood's Magazine* writer is concerned with is the touching evidence of "the tenacity of natural affection" afforded by Vanderdecken's still writing home to wife and friends after seventy years.

2

We next meet with the story, so far as England is concerned, in a play by an industrious theatrical man-of-all-work of the period, calling himself Edward Fitzball, which was produced at the Adelphi Theatre, London, under the title of *The Flying Dutchman, or the Phantom Ship, a Nautical Drama in three acts*, on the 4th December 1826. We need not have concerned ourselves with Fitzball at all had it not been conjectured at one time that Heine may have seen the play in London in 1827 and derived from it some hints for his story of a play in his *Memoirs of Herr von Schnabelewopski*, to which we shall come shortly. No one who had ever read Fitzball's farcical tragedy could have entertained such a notion. The drama has the minimum of connection with the Flying Dutchman story as we all know it now, and that minimum it derives from the fact that, as the author tells his readers in a foreword to the play, it was founded on the *Blackwood's* article of 1821.

Evidence of the currency of the legend just then is afforded by a passage in De Quincey's *Murder as a Fine Art,* which appeared in 1827. Speaking of the cool intrepidity by which the philosopher Descartes was said to have saved himself, in 1621, from the seamen who were plotting to kill him, De Quincey says that "he could not possibly have brought the vessel to port after murdering the crew; so that he must have continued to cruise for ever in the Zuyder Zee, and would probably have been mistaken for the Flying Dutchman, homeward bound." The casual nature of the reference implies that knowledge of the legend on the ordinary reader's part can be taken for granted.

3

Captain Marryat's full-length novel *The Phantom Ship,* which is still a capital yarn of the sea, appeared in 1839. Here again the Dutch captain bears the name of Vanderdecken, but there is still no suggestion either of the periodical permission of the mariner to seek salvation on shore or of the Devil having had a hand in the business. It is the celestial, not the infernal powers that pounce upon the Dutchman's oath and take the bold blasphemer at his word. His vow to round the Cape even if he had to beat about until the Day of Judgment "was registered", he writes to his wife in Amsterdam, "in thunder and in streams of sulphurous fire. The hurricane burst upon the ship, the canvas flew away in ribbons; mountains of seas swept over us, and in the centre of a deep o'erhanging cloud, which shrouded all in darkness, were written in letters of vivid flame these words — UNTIL THE DAY OF JUDGMENT!" He had sworn his impious oath by a sacred relic, a fragment of the Holy Cross, which his wife was accustomed to wear on her neck; and the only thing that can put an end to his sufferings is a sight of this, if it can be brought to him. His son Philip brings it to him after many marvellous adventures by sea and land; at the moment of reunion his vessel breaks into fragments, father and son sink beneath the waves, and "all nature smiled as if it rejoiced that a charm was dissolved for ever, and that THE PHANTOM SHIP WAS NO MORE."

Marryat has an uncanny character of the name of Schriften,

a little wizened old sailor who turns up like a bad penny wherever Philip Vanderdecken junior goes, always bringing disaster to him and the ship on which he happens to be, but always being miraculously saved from death himself. It appears that when Vanderdecken senior was persisting in his blasphemous resolve to round the Cape he was remonstrated with by his pilot, whom the captain knocked overboard in a scuffle and left presumably drowned. Schriften was this pilot: like the Flying Dutchman, he is deathproof, and he lives only for the exquisite revenge of enticing the son to destruction and so preventing the father from ever getting a sight of the holy relic. Just before the final catastrophe to Vanderdecken and Philip, however, Schriften is redeemed and released from his own particular curse by the magnanimous forgiveness of the son.

Though Wagner makes no use of this Schriften, a character corresponding to him comes into the Wagnerian record later in a curious way. The reader will know that while Wagner was working at his *Flying Dutchman* in Paris in 1841 he tried to get the work accepted at the Opéra. The Director, Léon Pillet, would not promise this; but he liked the scenario so much that he offered to buy it from Wagner, meaning to have it made into a libretto for one of the composers on the Opéra's waiting-list. As Wagner could claim no proprietary rights in the story itself he wisely, though much against the grain, accepted Pillet's offer; he was not in a position at that time to turn his back contemptuously on a few hundred francs. A new text was therefore put together by two theatre hacks of the day, Benedict-Henri Révoil and Paul Foucher; it was set to music by Pierre Dietsch, and the opera, which proved a dismal fiasco, was produced in 1842. The French librettists altered Wagner's plan so radically that the two plots are hardly the same. It is interesting to note, however, that in their version the phantom seaman — not Vanderdecken and a Dutchman now but a Norwegian of the name of Troïl — has added to the sin of impiety the crime of killing the pilot when the latter tried to persuade him not to persist in his mad purpose. Now this pilot motive, as we may call it, is not found either in Wagner or in Heine, who was Wagner's source for at any rate part of the story. It appears, however, as we have seen, in Marryat, so that it looks as if Révoil and Foucher may have read *The Phantom Ship;*

as a matter of fact their opera was entitled not *The Flying Norwegian* but *Le vaisseau fantôme*. (The pilot motive, of course, may have existed already in some popular version of the legend, unknown to us today, that was in circulation at the time).

4

In view of the fact that Marryat, De Quincey and the *Blackwood's* writer all imply that the legend of the Flying Dutchman was known to their readers we can take it for granted that a popular version of it was already current to some extent. We find the same implication again in the next literary form of the story that comes within the scope of our enquiry.

In 1834 Heine published in his *Salon* a series of papers with the title of *Memoirs of Herr von Schnabelewopski*. In Chapter VI the supposed memoirist tells how in Hamburg he saw one night "a big ship looking like a sombre giant in a great scarlet cloak. Was it the Flying Dutchman?" he asks. "This fable of the Flying Dutchman", he continues, "you surely know." After leaving Hamburg the itinerant Herr von Schnabelewopski had gone to Amsterdam; and in his next chapter he tells how he there saw "the dread Mynherr", as he calls him, on the stage. Heine outlines the action of the play thus. The Dutch captain had sworn by all the devils in hell that he would round a certain cape if he had to keep on sailing until the Day of Judgment. "The Devil took him at his word; he would have to sail the seas until the Last Judgment, unless he was redeemed by the fidelity of a woman's love. Donkey as the devil is, he doesn't believe in female constancy; so he allows the accursed captain to land once every seven years, take a wife, and thus achieve his salvation. Poor Dutchman! Time after time he is glad enough to be saved from matrimony itself and escape from his saviour, so back he goes to his ship again."

Heine continues with the action of the play up to the point where the Dutchman has met Katharina, the daughter of a Scottish skipper, and received her promise to be "true unto death". Then Herr von Schnabelewopski's attention is diverted to a pretty blonde in the audience. He makes her acquaintance: she is of an obliging disposition, and by the time the pair return to the theatre the drama is in its final stage, with the Dutchman generously warning Katharina of the doom that awaits her if she links her fate with his, Frau Flying Dutchman, as Heine calls her, leaping into the sea, true to death, the accursed seaman being well and truly redeemed at last, and the spectral ship being engulfed by the waves. "The moral of the piece", Heine concludes, "is, for women, to be careful not to marry Flying Dutchmen, while we men may learn from it how even at the best we founder through women."

As this important motive of redemption by a woman is found only in Heine, it has been universally assumed that it was from him that Wagner derived the idea of an opera on the Dutchman theme. Wagner, of course, had read the *Memoirs of Herr von Schnabelewopski,* and never made any secret of that fact. But that does not necessarily mean that he made his first acquaintance with the story itself through Heine; from his own various accounts of the matter it is evident enough that he, like thousands of other people, was already familiar with the legend *as* a legend. Eight years before the publication of the Schnabelewopski memoirs Heine himself had referred to the story in a letter from the island of Nordeney which formed part of his *Travel Pictures*. He often strolls along the shore, he says, and turns over in his mind the yarns the sailors have told him. "One of the most attractive of these is that of the Flying Dutchman, whom one sees sailing by with sails spread, and who occasionally sends a boat out to a ship with a bundle of letters, which the men of the ship can do nothing with, however, for they are addressed to people who have long been dead." For the legend itself, then, Wagner need not have been indebted in any degree to Heine's account of the supposed play at Amsterdam.

5

The impression we receive from his autobiography is that he had conceived the idea of an opera on the subject even before he embarked on the "Thetis", in July 1839, on his famous voyage from Riga to London, *en route* to Paris, where he arrived in the following September. While the ship was passing through the Norwegian fjords to escape a storm, he says, "a feeling of indescribable contentment came over me when the enormous granite walls echoed with the hail of the crew as they cast anchor and furled the sails. The sharp rhythm of the call struck into me like a mighty consoling omen, and soon shaped itself into the theme of the sailors' song in my *Flying Dutchman,*[1] *the idea of which was already at that time continually in my mind;*[2] now, under the influence of these new impressions, it took on a definite poetic-musical colour." This was written about 1866. More than twenty years earlier, when writing his short *Autobiographical Sketch* in 1842, he had been equally definite. A storm, he said, had compelled the captain of the "Thetis" to put into a Norwegian haven: "The passage among the crags made a wonderful impression on my fancy; the legend of the Flying Dutchman, *as I heard it confirmed from the seamen's mouths,*[3] took on within me a distinct and peculiar colour, which only the sea-adventures I was experiencing could have given it." Once more, then, we gather that he had no need to go to Heine for an introduction to the legend. He knew it before he stepped on board the "Thetis". He did not even learn it from the seamen; he talked about it to them, and they "confirmed" it.[4]

That he had previously read Heine's account of the Amsterdam play is proved by a letter of his of July 1843 to Ferdinand Heine, the costume designer at the Dresden theatre. "When I wrote my *Flying Dutchman*", he said, "it was in the firm conviction that I could not proceed otherwise than I did. During my famous sea-voyage and amid the Norwegian cliffs the subject — already long known to me through your namesake — acquired for me a quite peculiar colour and individuality, gloomy, it is true, but deriving from the nature common to all of us, not at all from the speculations of a gloom-sick enthusiast. But the vast wild ocean, with the legends woven about it, is an element that does not lend itself obediently and willingly to being trimmed into a modern opera; and I saw that the whole story of the Flying Dutchman, filled as it is with the roar of the sea — which now took such complete possession of me that it cried out for artistic reproduction, — would have to be atrociously cropped and mangled to be made into an opera text with the piquant suspenses, surprises and so

---

[1] See musical examples Nos. 10, 14, 15, 16.
[2] Italics mine.
[3] Italics mine.
[4] Ashton Ellis, in his English translation of the *Autobiographical Sketch*, unwittingly kept this fact from the reader by omitting the important word "bestätigt" (confirmed).

forth which the modern taste demands. Therefore I preferred not to modify the material, just as it lay to my hand, to any further extent than is required by a dramatic action, leaving the full aroma of the legend entirely free to spread itself over the whole. Only in that way, I believed, could I cast upon the spectator the full spell of that strange mood in which anyone with a feeling for poetry can take to his heart this gloomiest of legends."

6

Wagner, it will be noticed, speaks of the "subject" as being "already long known to me through your namesake". Does this mean that he had never heard of it until he had read Heine? That is an unwarrantable assumption. The "subject" — *der Stoff*, the raw material — was of course to be found in Heine, as it had been in Marryat and the others. But this does not forbid our believing, on the strength of the evidence as a whole, that Wagner had met with this "material" independently, as the crew of the "Thetis" and the mariners with whom Heine had talked at Nordeney had manifestly done. The point to be observed in Wagner's letter to Ferdinand Heine is his threefold use of the term "legend". We meet with it again in a letter of his of January 1843 to one Philipp Samuel Schmidt of Berlin, who had asked him for particulars of the new opera, which had just had its third performance in Dresden. He is sending him, he says, a copy of the text-book, from which Schmidt will see for himself that his *Flying Dutchman* is in an entirely different genre from that of *Rienzi,* and how far it departs from the conventions expected of an opera composer by the public. "You will see that I have allowed the simple legend to tell itself purely in its own way, without adding this or that modern accessory to make it 'operatic' in the sense which everyone deems necessary nowadays;" and he goes on to speak of the way in which "the marvellous fragrance of the legend" has been completely destroyed in the French perversion of the subject by Foucher and Dietsch, where "effective" episodes of the kind without which no French opera is considered complete have been introduced.

Liszt, in an article on *The Flying Dutchman* written in 1854, told his readers that "during a sea voyage Wagner read Heine's

version of the legend of the Flying Dutchman: the coincidence
of this reading with a violent storm aroused in him, swept as he
was himself by so many inner tempests, the idea of a dramatic
treatment of the material. He worked this out without making any
essential changes in Heine's moving narration." This account of
the genesis of the opera is not strictly accurate: from Wagner's
own testimony, both at the time and later, it is clear that not only
had he known the Schnabelewopski story before sailing from Riga
but he had already formed the idea of turning the subject into an
opera; his experiences in the Norwegian fjords had merely quick-
ened his interest in the theme. All this, however, is of minor importance; the point vital to our present discussion is that Liszt,
like Wagner, distinguishes between the "legend" — which, he
says, is well known — and Herr von Schnabelewopski's account
of the play he alleged he had seen in Amsterdam.

7

One other source may possibly have contributed a trifle to
Wagner's poem. In Wilhelm Hauff's *Die Karawane* — the story
of an Oriental caravan the members of which entertain each other
with adventures in their own lives — one of them, Achmet, contributes "The Story of the Phantom Ship". During a voyage he
had made in his youth his own ship had sighted a ghostly vessel
from which came sounds of uncanny merriment, although a storm
was threatening. "The captain, who was standing by my side,
went deathly white. 'My ship is lost', he cried; 'there sails
Death!';" and sure enough they were wrecked that night, only
Achmet and his old servant Ibrahim being saved. The stranger
ship comes clearly into sight, and they recognise it as the spectral
one they had seen just before the storm. They board it and find it
manned only by dead men; the decks are red with blood; the captain, sword in hand, is nailed through the head to the mast. Achmet and Ibrahim cannot sleep o' nights because the captain and
the crew have an unpleasant habit of coming to life again then
and going about their ordinary ship's occasions, while in the day-
time they are once more as dead as when Achmet first set eyes on
them. In the end, with the assistance of a magician, the ghostly
crew are taken ashore and buried, while the captain, after earth

has been placed on his head, comes to life again long enough to tell them his story. Fifty years ago he had been a pirate operating from Algiers. On one of the ships he had captured was a holy dervish who annoyed him by trying to get him to see the error of his ways. He plunged his dagger into the breast of the good but pestiferous old man, who thereupon cursed him and his ship with his last breath: he and his crew should henceforth neither die nor live until their heads were laid in earth. That same night his crew began to massacre each other; soon they were all dead men by day and live men again by night; and so it had gone on for fifty years, for how, in circumstances such as these, could the ship ever reach land?

Obviously this is one more variant of the Flying Dutchman legend. Wagner, who was an omnivorous reader and had a most retentive memory, must have read Hauff's popular story in his youth; and perhaps a few phrases from it may have sunk into what Henry James called "the deep well" of his subconsciousness, to come to the surface later in the way that so many fragments from Coleridge's multifarious reading emerged to make up the story and even the wording of *The Rime of the Ancient Mariner.* "With insane joy", says the captain to Achmet when telling him the story of his crime and its punishment, "we would plunge again and again, with sails full set, into the teeth of a storm, hoping we might be dashed to pieces on some cliff or other and so lay our heads on earth." Did some dim memory of all this re-emerge in Wagner when he made his Dutchman soliloquise thus when he sets foot on land once more after another seven years?:

> *How oft in ocean's seething deep*
> *Death have I sought, eternal sleep: —*
> *Yet ah! sweet death, I found it ne'er!*
> *Upon the cliffs my ship I drave,*
> *In hope to find the longed-for grave:*
> *But ah! no grave for me was there.*
> *In scorn on pirates would I fling me,*
> *Their utmost fury I would dare:*
> *"Here", cried I, "bitter death come bring me,*
> *My ship is filled with treasure rare!"*
> *But ah! the scourge of every sea*
> *Would cross himself, and shrink and flee!*

Stranger things have happened in the creative subconsciousness than that Hauff's captain's talk about pirates and driving his ship on to the cliffs in the hope of finding a grave in earth should have suggested the above lines to Wagner. We may further note the passage in Hauff in which sounds of uncanny merriment are heard coming from the phantom ship just before the storm breaks. This has its direct counterpart in the grisly episode at the end of the first scene of the third act of the opera, where the crew of the Dutchman's vessel, after their long silence, terrify the Norwegian sailors by breaking into a grim chorus as the storm begins to shake their ship. There cannot be much doubt that Wagner had read Hauff.

8

We can now address ourselves to the vexed question of the extent of Wagner's indebtedness to Heine. The motive of redemption by female fidelity, as we have seen, appears only in the poet's story of the Amsterdam play. Was there really such a play, or was the motive Heine's own invention, the "play" being only a fictive way of introducing it?

If the reader will turn to the relevant passage in Wagner's *Autobiographical Sketch* (written not long after he had returned from Paris, where he had met Heine), he will find the following account of the processes by which the *Flying Dutchman* came into being:

"I had already provided myself with a scenario for this emergency [i.e. the possibility that Pillet might commission an opera from him]. The Flying Dutchman, whose intimate acquaintance I had made on the ocean, fascinated my imagination unceasingly. In addition I made the acquaintance of Heine's particular version of this legend in a section of his *Salon;* and it was especially his treatment — borrowed from a Dutch play bearing the same title — of the redemption of this Ahasuerus of the sea that furnished me with all I needed to turn the story into a subject for opera. I came to an understanding [the German may mean also "an arrangement", or "terms"] with Heine himself on this matter, drafted a sketch, and gave it to M. Léon Pillet."

While making it clear, then, as he did in various other places at various other times, that the idea of his opera was born of his fascination with the legend, he acknowledged that it was the redemption motive that enabled him to round off his plan, and that he had found that motive in Heine, who had "borrowed" it from a Dutch play.

But this *was not the original wording of the passage* in the *Autobiographical Sketch* as it appeared in the *Zeitung für die elegante Welt* of February 1843. There the sentence relevant to our enquiry had run thus: "Heine's truly dramatic treatment — his own invention — of the redemption of this Ahasuerus of the sea gave me all I needed to utilise the legend for an opera subject." Originally, then, Wagner had given Heine credit for having "invented" (*erfundene*) that motive; later he said that it had only been borrowed (*entnommene*) by the poet. It may be added that before the publication of the *Sketch* in the *Zeitung für die elegante Welt* there had appeared in the first number of that journal a despatch from its Dresden correspondent, giving its readers some advance information — which could only have been derived from an interview with Wagner — about the young composer who had so suddenly sprung into fame. "A second opera by Richard Wagner, who has become famous overnight through his *Rienzi,* is being energetically rehearsed for production this month. [December 1842: actually the production did not take place until the 2nd January 1843]. It is entitled *The Flying Dutchman,* and Wagner has combined Heine's fantastic story *and the English narrative,*[1] with some additions of his own." Once more, then, we see that for the legend in general Wagner had had other sources open to him than Heine. What "the English narrative" may have been we can hardly even conjecture: from the casual way the words flow from the Dresden writer's pen, and the fact that he speaks not of *an* but of *the* English narrative, it looks as if either the *Blackwood's* story or the Marryat novel may have been translated into German; the journalist appears to be speaking of something which he takes it for granted his readers will understand without explanation. But neither *Blackwood's* nor *The Phantom Ship* can be seen to have contributed anything to Wagner's scenario, which makes the situation still more puzzling. What is in neither of the English stories, but is in both Heine and Wagner, is the motive of redemption through a woman's love; and in 1842/3 Wagner credited the "invention" of this motive to the poet.

[1] Italics mine.

9

All the modern reprints of the *Autobiographical Sketch* reproduce the text as it appeared in the first edition of Wagner's Collected Writings, issued by himself from 1871 onwards. Why did he make at that time the radical alteration in his original text of 1843 to which I have drawn attention above, and further omit all reference to Heine's supposititious contribution to the *Dutchman* plan in *My Life* — the large-scale autobiography on which he was engaged at that time? The customary and most facile explanation of his cold-shouldering of Heine in *My Life* is that Wagner was giving way to a prejudice against him both as a personality and as a Jew. But we may reasonably doubt whether that is a correct explanation; while it is a still more dubious explanation of his substituting "borrowed" for the original "invented" when reprinting the Sketch of 1842/3 in 1871.

Had his object been to edge Heine out of the picture he would surely have expunged all reference to him in his account of the genesis of the *Flying Dutchman*. But he does not do so. Even here he makes no secret of the fact that it was his reading of the *Memoirs of Herr von Schnabelewopski* that had furnished him with the ideal motive for rounding off the dramatic action of the opera upon which he had long been brooding. All he does in 1871 is to say that Heine did not invent but only borrowed that motive. What lies behind that change of wording?

Had he found reason in the after years to doubt Heine's originality in the matter? Do we not come upon at least a hint of that scepticism as early as 1851, when, in *A Communication to My Friends*, he once more set forth the genesis of his early works? Here he already as good as ruled Heine out as an *original* contributor to the Dutchman subject. All he said was this: "During this [Riga] period I first became acquainted with the story of the Flying Dutchman: Heine tells it incidentally when speaking of a performance he had seen in, I believe, Amsterdam." The point-blank declaration in 1871 that Heine had merely borrowed the redemption motive he had claimed to have invented is only a more emphatic nuance of what looks like the irony of the "seen, I believe" in the sentence of 1851.

I would suggest the following possible interpretation of the matter. In their conversations in Paris in 1840/1 Heine had told him that the alleged "Amsterdam play" was pure fiction on his part, and claimed in particular that the redemption motive, to which he could see that Wagner was attaching the greatest importance as a factor in his opera, was entirely his own invention. Only on some such hypothesis as this can we account for that sentence in the *Autobiographical Sketch* in which Wagner said that he "came to an understanding [or "arrangement", or "terms"] with Heine himself on this matter." What was there to come to an understanding about with Heine or anyone else? Certainly not the use of the Flying Dutchman subject in general, for that was well known and was no one's literary property. Nor even a redemption motive *per se;* for it was of the poetic essence of the legend that the Dutch skipper, who had everyone's sympathy, should be redeemed from the curse in some way or other at the finish; he had been so, in fact, in Marryat's novel — by the devotion and pious labours and sufferings of his son. The only feature of the Schnabelewopski story in which Heine could have claimed the shadow of a proprietary right in his conversations with Wagner was this little matter of having the Dutchman saved by "a woman true unto death". It seems, then, a workable hypothesis that Heine had demanded from Wagner an "understanding" or "arrangement" of a pecuniary kind with regard to that motive, and that Wagner had reason, or thought he had, to doubt, in later years, whether the poet had played quite straight with him on that point. Heine was rather given to levying a quiet kind of financial blackmail on his friends, as Meyerbeer and Liszt and others knew to their cost.

10

So the question arises, *did* he, as has been universally taken for granted, invent the redemption-by-a-woman motive, or had he really seen some play or other, or heard some version or other of the story of which it formed a part? Let us glance critically at his account of the matter.

He begins, as we have seen, by saying that his readers will already be familiar with the tale of the Flying Dutchman: it tells, he says, of a ship condemned to sail the seas for ever because its Dutch captain had sworn by all the devils that he would round a certain cape even if it took him until the Day of Judgment. The Devil had taken him at his word; his only chance of redemption from the curse would be by the love of a faithful woman. Whenever the phantom ship sights another vessel, Heine goes on to say, the Dutch crew send out a boat with letters which they desire to be carried to Holland; but these letters are always addressed to people who have long been dead.

Heine, then, is confessedly telling a story already known to his readers; and — a point of some importance — he makes no distinction between one item in the tale and another, or between the familiar legend and the play. The legend of the Flying Dutchman *per se* was widely current; the evidence as to that is copious. The "letters motive" had formed the core of the *Blackwood's* story of 1821; and Heine himself had included it in his summary, in the *Travel Pictures* of 1826, of the Dutchman legend as, according to him, it had been told to him by the seamen at Nordeney.[1] In the Schnabelewopski account of the Amsterdam play Heine makes no claim whatever that whereas all the other elements of the drama are already in general circulation the motive of redemption by a woman was peculiar to the play. He begins with the words "The legend of the Flying Dutchman will be known to you". He tells it from start to finish *as* a legend; and having done so he begins his next paragraph with the words "It was on this legend that the play was based which I saw in the theatre at Amsterdam." In face of these plain facts, what warrant is there for assuming that one feature of the play — the redemption motive — was not part of the legend but Heine's personal contribution to it?

And how does he handle this motive? He mentions it only to gibe at it as a piece of romantic tarradiddle. After having told his readers how, *in the legend,* the Devil had taken the impious seaman at his word and condemned him to sail the seas to all eternity unless he could find a woman faithful enough to redeem him, he speaks *in propria persona*. The Devil is not such a fool as to believe in female constancy, and the perennially disillusioned Dutchman is always glad to escape from his redeemer and go off to sea again.

---

[1] Years later, in chapter 6 of the Schnabelewopski *Memoirs,* he said that the legend had been told him of old by his grand-aunt. It is always difficult to distinguish between truth and fiction in Heine.

Next we have an account of the action of the play, beginning with the Dutchman's meeting with the daughter of a Scottish skipper who is willing to play the part of redemptress, and ending with the Dutchman's lament to her over his sad lot — life maltreats him and death rejects him; "his grief is as deep as the sea, his ship without an anchor, his heart without hope." "These", says Heine, "were virtually the words with which the bridegroom concluded" — a little touch which seems to suggest that he was in truth describing some play he had seen.

It is at this point, after Katharina has sworn eternal fidelity, that Heine tantalisingly breaks off to tell, with great gusto, that adventure of his with the light-o'-love in the audience that took him away from the theatre for a while — an episode which was probably the real reason for the writing of that chapter. When he returns the play is in its last moments, with the ending we all know so well. And now again Heine speaks *in propria persona;* the moral is for women not to marry Flying Dutchmen and for men to beware of women. Once more, it will be observed, he touches on the motive of redemption by a woman's fidelity only to drench it with the acid of his irony. Is it not making a rather heavy demand on our credulity to ask us to believe that he "invented" that motive only to deride it? As has been pointed out already, it was of the poetic essence of the legend that the curse should be lifted from the Dutchman some time or other. Marryat had found one way to do that. Another way — through the self-sacrificing devotion of a woman — was one so wholly in keeping with the romantic sentiment of that generation that even if it had not figured in some current version of the legend, even if it had not appeared in an Amsterdam or some other play, it was certain, we feel, to have occurred at some time or other to some German romantic or other. But no one, surely, after having been so fully sympathetic to the Dutchman as to depict his unending sufferings, would have invented that charitable ending merely to make ribald fun of it. One's final impression of it all is that the ribaldry alone was Heine's, that he was indulging his satirical bent at the expense of a romantic invention of some one else — that, in fact, he actually had met with that particular ending to the legend somewhere or other, and as likely as not in a play. And perhaps the explanation of Wagner's coolness towards Heine in 1851, and of his substitution of "borrowed" for "invented" in 1871, is that by then he had found good reason, or thought he had, for doubting the poet's claim to originality in the matter of the redemption motive, and felt that the "arrangement" of 1841 with him had really been unnecessary.

To complete the factual record it may be added that in one of his letters (to Ewald) about the French stage (1837), Heine had spoken of himself as homesick in Paris, "like the Flying Dutchman and his shipmates . . . Poor Vanderdecken!" He refers to the Dutch crew writing letters home to people long since dead, but does not say a word to suggest that in the *Schnabelewopski* of 1834 he himself had contributed any new feature to the well-known story. Finally, in one of his articles (March 26th 1843) for a German journal on "The [Paris] Musical Season of 1843" he refers to the failure of the Foucher-Dietsch opera in these terms: "Dietz's (*sic*) *Flying Dutchman* has suffered woeful shipwreck. I did not hear the opera, but I saw the libretto, and I was disgusted to see what a mess had been made in the French text of the beautiful story which a well-known author, Heinrich Heine, had imagined in a form completely suitable for the stage." Here he certainly appears to be implying that the "Amsterdam play" was his own invention. But even at that he only claims to have given a stage form to the "beautiful story" which everyone knows: he makes no claim whatever that the redemption motive was a contribution of his own, a crowning touch, to the legend.

11

The legend of the Flying Dutchman and the motive of redemption through love appealed so strongly to the buffeted young Wagner because he could read his own melancholy story into it: he too was a homeless wanderer on the face of the earth, he too longed for the sympathy and self-sacrifice of a woman who would understand and pity and comfort him. He shared the passion of most of his poetic compatriots of that romantic epoch, nourished as they were on Goethe, for idealising woman into the *Ewig-weibliche*. In *A Communication to My Friends* (1851) he described his "utter homelessness in Paris" between 1839 and 1842 and his "yearning for the German homeland" — not the political entity known at that time as Germany, however, but a new Germany of his dreams, "in connection with which I was certain only of one thing, that I would never find it here in Paris". "It was the longing of my Flying Dutchman for *the woman* — not . . . the wife who waited for Odysseus but the redeeming Woman whose traits I did not see in any definite outline but who only hovered before my vision as the element of Womanhood in general"; "the quintessence of womankind, and yet still the longed-for, the undreamed-of, the infinitely womanly Woman; let me say it in one word, *the Woman of the Future*."

Immature as it is, dramatically and musically, *The Flying Dutchman* foreshadows in various ways the Wagner of the later years. He himself was objectively critical of it even as early as 1851. There was much in the poem, he said, that "is as yet inchoate"; "the joinery of the situations is in the main so loose, the poetic diction and versification so often lack the stamp of individuality", that he would not be surprised to find the professional playwrights treating it all as "a piece of impudence that calls for severe castigation". But for all that he always had a soft spot in his heart in later life for this ardent if cubbish work of his prentice days, because he could see in it an aspiration, however imperfectly realised, towards the logically-knit musical drama — the antithesis of "opera" — that had haunted his imagination almost from the first. In the last months of 1864 he had to prepare a "model" production of it for King Ludwig in Munich; and on the 2nd September he wrote thus to the King: "It is by a good dispensation that it is this early, unassuming work — which, for all that, is in my true style — that constitutes the occasion for my renewing my connection with the queer world of the theatre."

For he had been conscious from the first that here he had made his first big step, small as it may seem to us now in the light of the *Ring* and *Tristan* and the *Meistersinger*, from opera to music drama. He was right when he said in later life that "so far as my knowledge goes I can find in the life of no artist so striking a transformation, in so short a time, as is evident between *Rienzi* and *The Flying Dutchman*, the former of which was hardly finished when the latter was begun." His creative imagination had seen the subject from the beginning in terms of a new plastic form; though he was not sure enough of himself as yet to build up his work without the usual apparatus of arias, duets, ensembles and so on, he had begun not with these for their own sake but with a central conception from which the whole drama was to evolve as an organism from a germ. This was Senta's ballad in the second act, which is not only the central psychological point of the action but the musical core of the work.[1]

The poem was written in Paris between the 18th and 25th May 1841. Wagner began the musical composition with the ballad; next came the song of the Norwegian sailors and the "Phantom Song" of the Dutchman's crew, then the Helmsman's song and the Spinning Chorus; and so possessed was he by the subject and so easily did his ideas flow that the whole score was completed in seven weeks, the overture being written last. According to Glasenapp the title-page bears the inscription "In Nacht und Elend ["In Night and Wretchedness"]. Per aspera ad astra. Gott gebe es! ["God grant it!"]" It has recently been established, however, that Glasenapp was in error on this point. After the Munich performance of the 4th December 1864, which was conducted by Wagner himself, he presented King Ludwig with the complete orchestral sketch of the work. His jottings on this give us a glimpse into the misery of soul in which the opera was conceived; he was generally on the verge of starvation in Paris, and it seems certain now that he spent a few days in confinement for debt. At the end of the second act he wrote: "13 August. Tomorrow the money difficulties start again!"; at the end of the third act, "Finis, Richard Wagner. Meudon, 22 August 1841"; and at the end of the overture, "Paris: 5 November 1841. Per aspera ad astra. Gott geb's!" The words "In Nacht und Elend" do not appear in the manuscript.

Wagner's intention had been from the first that the opera should be in one act only; by this means, he tells us in *My Life,* he hoped to be able to cut out all the conventional "operatic" accessories and concentrate on the psychological involutions and evolution of the two principal characters. But the practical exigencies of the German stage of the period compelled him to cast it into the

---

[1] In his letter of the 9th January 1843 to Schmidt he stressed the fact that he had worked out his opera without any "resounding, effective finales", trusting to his audiences, who expected that kind of thing as a matter of course, to get over their first disappointment after seeing the work a few times and realise that his simple treatment of the moving legend was the right one.

21

customary three acts, which fact no doubt accounts in part for the weakness of some of the more obviously padded parts of it. In later years he often thought of revising the opera and compressing it into a single act; he promised King Ludwig, indeed, in 1865 that he would do this, and had his life been prolonged for a few years after 1883 he would certainly have included a re-shaped *Flying Dutchman* in the Bayreuth programmes. As it was, the plan came to nothing. What he actually did in the way of revision was to tone down the original orchestration, which, in the inexperience of youth, he had made excessively noisy, and to re-write the ending of the last act and that of the overture, points with which we shall deal later.

12

The Flying Dutchman has been made to look so old-fashioned by Wagner's later works that it is difficult for us now to realise the many ways in which it leaped ahead of contemporary operatic thinking and the problems it created for the actors and stage managers and machinists. It was to assist all these people to present the opera more intelligently that he wrote in 1852 his *Remarks on Performing the Opera 'The Flying Dutchman'*, which singers and producers of today would do well to study. Every theatre specialist who came into contact with Wagner agreed that if he had had sufficient voice and stature he would have been the greatest German actor of his time; again and again at rehearsals he would not merely tell his singers how a given scene should be acted but show them in his own person how to do it. In the *Remarks* he devotes three pages of print to analysing the opening monologue of the Dutchman, describing every nuance of voice he expected of the singer, every gesture and posture he demanded of the actor. He warned the singer of Senta's part against turning her into a soft sentimental *ingénue* of the conventional stage kind; on the contrary, while she was to be naïve she was also to give the impression of a sturdy Northern maiden with the strength of the salt sea in her; her obsession with regard to the Dutchman whose story she had so often heard should be the monomania of a strong nature, not of a sickly one. And Erik, her lover, should not be a futile "sentimental whiner" but "tempestuous, vehement, sombre, like every solitary, especially in the highlands of the North. Whoever sings Erik's cavatina in the third act in sugary style does me a sad disservice; it ought to breathe sorrow and affliction". (Unfortunately the part is generally given to what is called a "light lyrical tenor", whose voice is incapable of the sombre tints that Wagner required, and whose notions of acting are rudimentary). Wagner insisted, too, that the part of Daland should not be played in the conventional key of the comic stage sailor. "He is a tough, blunt figure of everyday life, a seaman who defies tempests and dangers for the sake of gain, and with whom the sale — as it appears to be — of his daughter to a rich man would not seem at all reprehensible; he thinks and acts, like a hundred thousand others, without the least suspicion that he is doing anything wrong." Wagner, it will be seen, made heavy demands on the intelligence and the technique of his actors, especially those of the second line. It all seemed so easy to him because he had no difficulty in doing it himself: one singer who had watched him producing *Tannhäuser* in Vienna declared in later years that he had never afterwards seen a performance of the opera in which he was not constantly reminded of Wagner's acting in this or that situation — to the great disadvantage of the singers who were supposed to be representing this character or that.

To the staging of *The Flying Dutchman,* and more especially of the scenes in which the phantom ship appears, Wagner attached the greatest importance. He gives a good deal of attention to this matter in the *Remarks;* and there have recently been published in Germany some excerpts from his numerous jottings in the margin of the vocal score used for the production of the opera in Munich in 1864. (That score is still in the archives of the Munich Theatre). The notes were intended for the guidance of the stage designers and machinists; and it is interesting to see Wagner insisting on the sharpest differentiation between the appearance of the Dutchman's ghostly ship and that of Daland, and on it being made perfectly clear to the spectator that while the latter was calm at its moorings, the former seemed to be still tormented and tossed about by something evil and eerie in it, as if it carried the storms of the Cape about with it wherever it sought shelter.

13

The opera was first performed in Dresden, Wagner himself conducting, on the 2nd January 1843, with the following cast:

Senta	Wilhelmine Schröder-Devrient
The Dutchman	Michael Wächter
Daland	Karl Risse
Erik	Reinhold

(In Wagner's first sketch for the opera the heroine bore the name not of Senta but of Minna).

When the *Flying Dutchman* was being rehearsed in Munich in 1864 the conductor, Franz Lachner — a capable, sober routinier of the older school — used to grumble about "the wind that blew out at you wherever you opened the score". He was right: the *Flying Dutchman* was born on the sea and still has its home on it. The overture is the first real sea-picture in music, and to this day the best of its kind.

It opens with reiterated hollow fifths and octaves in the strings, against which, in the third bar, the stark motive always to be associated later with the Dutchman stands out challengingly in bassoons and horns. (It will be observed that it too consists simply of the tonic and dominant of the scale of D):

No. 1

We hear the whistle of the wind in the rigging and a roar from the depths of the sea, then another statement of the Dutchman motive. It all culminates in a great crescendo on a diminished seventh chord in the full orchestra:

No. 2

after which we hear, in the orchestral winds, a succession of calls that will always be associated later with the spirits of the ocean:

Then comes a hint of the motive of the Dutchman as perpetual wanderer over the seas:

followed by a descending sequence of those chords of the diminished seventh which even composers of the present day, however much they may affect to look down their noses at them, find extremely useful for the expression of horror and terror:

Gradually the fury of the wind and waves dies down into an exhausted muttering in the lower strings, with an occasional throb in the kettledrums; the tempo slows down to andante, and one of the main motives of the opera, that of the Redemption of which Senta is the predestined instrument, is heard in the wood wind, with the melody sung by the cor anglais:

It is the theme of the refrain of Senta's ballad in the second act. At this point in the overture, however, the melody, significantly enough, does not come to any kind of formal end, but, at the point where we would expect it to do so, shades off into a figure:

No. 7

that will be associated later with the Fate that eternally over-hangs the Dutchman.

This episode is a kind of inset in the great sea picture, marked off from that by both its tempo and its colouring. With a resumption of the original tempo we are back on the sea once more, with the motive of Wandering (No. 4), that of the ocean spirits (No. 3, with the figure of the restless sea shown in the bass of that quotation), the motive of Fate (No. 7), the characteristic theme of the Dutchman (No. 1), and a new motive, that of his Longing for Death:

No. 8

all woven into one symphonic web. In the course of this development we find No. 1 answered by a theme in the wood wind which Wagner has marked *espressivo*:

No. 9

This episode ends with a melody that will be recognised later as that of the sailors on the Norwegian ship:

No. 10

Then the storm picture is resumed, with the various motives associated with the Dutchman and Senta. No. 6 asserts itself more and more insistently until we come to the final vivace section, with No. 6 in a new and more exuberant form:

No. 11

Now, too, the Redemption motive is given for the first time the ardent ending it has when Senta sings her ballad in the second act:

No. 12

This Redemption motive dominates the remainder of the overture. Wagner, however, elaborated the final section considerably in later years, drawing more and more expression out of the repetitions and metamorphoses of No. 6; and he changed the coda completely. In the original edition of the score he had introduced the Dutchman's motive (No. 1) for the last time, in D major, at a point seventeen bars before the finish, rounding it all off rather conventionally with a scale passage and a few final emphatic chords. But his artistic sense must have told him later that logically the last word should be not with the Dutchman but with Senta; so now, after the thunderous re-statement of the Dutchman motive in D major in the brass, he suddenly switches for a moment into G major, tones the orchestral mass down to wood wind and harp, and finally reaches a restful D major in this way:

No. 13

The effect is the one of "transfiguration" with which Wagner was later to end *Tristan* and the *Twilight of the Gods.*[1]

14

The curtain rises on a sea coast with steep and rocky cliffs: those in the foreground form gorges on either side which from time to time give back echoes. A violent storm is raging; on the open sea the wind is lashing the waves, but between the rocks it is calmer, except for an occasional gust. Close to the shore lies a Norwegian ship, driven to take refuge here from the storm when already near home. It has just cast anchor, and the seamen are energetically occupied in furling sails, throwing out ropes, and so on, singing their "Hojohe! Halloho!" to typical sailors' calls of this kind:

and this:

and this:

the while the sea surges and the wind howls or mutters in the distance. The little figure shown in the second bar of No. 14 is echoed from time to time first by the cliff-hollows on one side, then by those on the other. For not only the stage action but the music of this scene Wagner drew upon his experiences in the "Thetis" during his voyage from Riga to London, when, as he tells

[1] The reader will find the *Flying Dutchman* overture in its first form in the Novello edition of the opera.

us, a violent storm in the Skagerrack had forced the captain to run for shelter into one of the Norwegian fjords.[1]

The captain, Daland, has gone ashore; he has climbed one of the cliffs and is gazing landwards, trying to recognise the locality. At last he descends to the shore again; the storm, he says, has blown them a good seven miles out of their course, just as they were hoping to make their own port. The steersman assures him that all is well with the ship, in spite of the buffeting it has had. "Sandwike it is", says Daland; "full well I know the bay." [Sandwike, as we have just seen, was the little fishing village in the fjord to which the "Thetis" had run for safety]. He breaks into one of those foursquare melodies, with the stresses falling in the same place in bar after bar, which Wagner himself was to recognise later, with a certain amount of amusement, as a mannerism of his melodies in his earlier years:

No. 17

Schon sah am U - fer ich mein Haus,
There 'fore my eyes my own home lay;

Sen - ta, mein Kind, glaubt' ich schon zu um - arm - en:
Sen - ta, my child, I thought should give me greet-ing:

There, before Daland's eyes, had actually lain his own house, where his daughter Senta was waiting to embrace him; then this

---

[1] See the quotation on pages 8/9. Four pages have survived of the pocket-book in which Wagner jotted down his day-to-day experiences during the voyage. There were evidently more storms than the one in the Skagerrack. Wagner's entries from the 27th July to the 11th August (1839) run thus: "27th in Skagerrack storm. 28 storm. 29 stormy west wind: had to run into a small Norwegian harbour near Arendal. Evening on shore with Minna. Marvellous rocks out at sea. Place, Sand-Wigke. On the 31st we tried to sail again; going out of the harbour the ship strikes an invisible rock: 2 shocks. Back again . . . 1 August safe on sea again. Sunday evening, 4th, stormy north wind: favourable. 6th, evening, contrary storm. Wednesday, the 7th, bad day: storm at its worst 2.30 in the afternoon. 8th, mild contrary wind. 9th, evening, off English coast at Southwold . . . Evening 10th to evening 11th, fierce storm from the west between the sandbanks . . ."

infernal storm had sprung up and driven him out of his course. "Who trusts in the wind trusts to the mercy of Satan!" he remarks sagely.

However, there is no help for it now, and a tempest of this ferocity cannot last long. At his bidding the crew go below; he himself goes into his cabin after telling the Steersman to take his watch for him that night and keep a sharp look-out, which the man promises to do. Left alone, the Steersman paces up and down the deck for a while: the storm has abated somewhat in the haven, but out on the open sea it is still rough. A fragment of what we shall discover later to be a dance-tune of the sailors:

No. 18

runs through his mind. He is tired; he sits down, yawns, and, by way of fighting down his desire for sleep, begins a song to the maiden of his fancy:

No. 19

Mit Ge - wit - ter und Sturm aus fern - em Meer, mein
Through the thun-der and storm, from dis - tant seas, My

Mä - del, bin dir nah!
maid - en, come I near!

with a prayer to the south wind to carry him soon to her:

No. 20

Mein Mä - del, wenn nicht Süd - wind wär, ich
My maid - en, if the south wind fails, no

nim-mer wohl käm' zu dir:
more can I come to thee:

30

He ends with a long "Halloho! Holloho!" Just then there is an ominous upward surge from the depths to the heights of the orchestra (the "Waves" motive seen in the bass of No. 3), as a bigger wave than ordinary mounts and hurls itself against the ship, shaking her violently. The Steersman looks round with a start; assuring himself that all is well with the vessel he sits down again and resumes his song. But it is broken by yawns which he cannot suppress, and before he can finish his "Hoyohe! Halloho!" cadenza he falls asleep from sheer weariness.

15

By now it has grown darker and the storm has increased: the Dutchman's motive (No. 1) is heard thundering through the whistling wind as another ship (that of the Flying Dutchman) is seen approaching. Its masts are black, its sails blood-red: it makes swiftly for the shore on the side opposite the Norwegian vessel and casts anchor with a tremendous crash that wakens the Steersman. But only for a moment, so tired is he; he glances at the helm, sees that all is right, begins the refrain of his song once more — and falls asleep again.

The spectral crew of the Dutch ship is now seen furling the sails in uncanny silence, while the orchestra gives out the sombre, fate-laden theme associated with the Dutchman's endless submission to the behest of Fate (No. 7). He steps on shore, a sinister figure in a black costume of Spanish type: the orchestra accompanies him with a phrase that is not used often enough in the work to be ranked as a motive, but which is heard several times in the course of the monologue that now follows; it symbolises his weariness of life:

In an expressive recitative he describes how, another seven years having passed, the author of his curse allows him to set foot on land again, in quest of a grace which he knows he will never find:

to the sea he is condemned to be true until its last wave is spent and it itself has been swallowed up. Then, over the undulating motive (No. 4) that symbolises the endless wandering to which he is doomed, he begins an aria — "How oft, in ocean's seething deep, Death have I sought, eternal sleep", that has lost none of its vitality after a hundred years of operatic development. The second phrase of the aria, sung to the words "Yet ah! sweet death I found it ne'er!" has already been heard in the overture (No. 8). In despair he has driven his ship on to rocks that have been the grave of other vessels, but in vain; he has tempted pirates with his wealth, but the terror of the seas has only crossed himself and fled. His curse he must carry to all eternity.

For a moment he turns again to heaven with the hope in his heart that has been so often mocked — the hope that some day the promised absolution and salvation will come to him:

No. 22

This impressive section of his aria is sung over a succession of tremolando chords in the lower strings, through which pierce from time to time the solemn tones of the trombones.

But this is all delusion, he cries; where upon the earth is eternal faithfulness to be found? And to a broad, sweeping melody:

No. 23

he sings of the one real hope still left to him — that to the earth itself an end must some day come, the "Day of Judgment, last great Day", when the trumpets of God will peal forth and the universe will collapse in ruin, and all the dead will rise again: then will he too know the mercy of annihilation. For that fate he longs: "Ye worlds, end your course! Eternal destruction fall on me!" And as the spectral crew of the ship echo these last words of his in sepulchral tones, the Dutchman, with folded arms, leans gloomily against a cliff in the foreground.

16

At this moment Daland comes up on deck to take the direction of the wind. He sees the strange vessel, which had not been there when he had gone below, and turns to the Steersman for information about it. The Steersman, still half-asleep, makes another attempt at his love song; but Daland takes hold of him and shakes him awake. Then he takes up the speaking-tube and hails the stranger ship. There is no answer — only, after a long pause, an eerie double echo of the "Ahoy!" from the two sides of the bay. Neither another hail from Daland nor one from the Steersman brings any response. At last Daland perceives the Dutch captain on the shore, hails him again, and asks the name of his ship and whence he comes. A gloomy figure in octaves in the violas and 'cellos:

anticipates his reply — "Far have I come: wouldst thou deny me anchorage here while the storm doth rage?" The genial Daland, who has now joined him on the shore, assures him he is welcome. His own ship, he says, has been driven on this rocky coast by the same foul weather, only a few miles from his home. After a laconic statement that he is Dutch and his ship has escaped damage, the stranger tells Daland that for more years than he can measure he has been buffeted about by wind and wave: many lands have harboured him, but the land he longs for he can never find. Will Daland take him into his house for awhile as his guest? He will not repent it, for the Dutchman's vessel is filled with treasures from every zone. He makes a sign to the watch of his ship, and the crew bring on shore a chest which, when opened, is seen by the dazzled Daland to be crammed with pearls and precious stones; and he becomes really interested when the strange captain assures him that all these and more are his in return for shelter for a single night; for the Dutchman, alas, has neither home nor wife nor child (No. 24).

It takes a little time to convince Daland that the Dutch captain is in earnest; but the latter clinches matters by asking him "Have you a daughter?", and, on being told that he has, by saying eagerly "Let her become my wife!" Daland, though he can hardly believe his ears, is overjoyed at the prospect of having this rich mariner for a son-in-law. Remarking in a lengthy sotto voce that he had better close with the offer before it is withdrawn, he decides to accept him. Turning to the Dutchman again, he assures him that he really has a daughter, a good and lovely girl who is his pride, his treasure, his consolation in adversity, his joy in happiness. All this the Dutchman finds very reassuring: so good a daughter, he comments, is bound to prove a faithful wife. Not to be outdone in noble sentiments, Daland tells him that he cannot help pitying the lot of a man who has suffered so much as the Dutchman has, for his large-handedness in the matter of gold and jewels is proof enough for anyone that he has a good heart — not, Daland hastens to add, that he would decline him as son-in-law were his fortune only half as great.

So it is arranged that with the first fair wind they shall make for Daland's home, where the Dutchman shall see the maiden who, he now fervently hopes, will prove to be his long-sought "angel" of redemption. Daland's contribution to the duet that follows is a song of thanks to the storm that has brought him this astonishing piece of good luck, and a promise to himself that he will not let this unexpected fortune slip through his fingers. The episode is excessively long, and the young Wagner is quite incapable of finding music for the situation that will rise above the routine commonplaces of the opera of the epoch. He would have done better, we sometimes feel, to have dispensed almost entirely with Daland; but operatic exigencies, of course, made that difficult.

By this time the weather has cleared, the sea is calm, and the Steersman and the Norwegian crew give a shout of welcome to the south wind that has sprung up. Daland also is rejoiced. He suggests their raising anchor together at once; but the Dutchman begs him to put to sea first, for he wants to give his own crew a rest. (The real reason for postponing his own sailing is of course a matter less of humanitarianism than of practical operatics. Were Daland and the Dutchman to reach land again at the same time Wagner would lose the opportunity for one of the most impressive moments of the opera — the Dutchman's unexpected entry into the spinning scene of the second act).

So Daland goes on board his ship, pipes the crew, and bids them cast loose, which they do to the strain of the Steersman's song (Nos. 19 and 20). The Dutchman returns to his own vessel, and the curtain falls with the orchestra giving out some of the tunes associated with a life on the ocean wave, especially Nos. 3, 15 and 18.

17

The orchestral introduction to the second act begins with a vigorous statement of the second part of the Steersman's song (No. 20), which is followed by suggestions of the sailors' dance (No. 18) and of other motives (Nos. 3, 15) already associated with the seamen and the sea. This repetition was imposed on Wagner by the enforced casting of his drama into three acts. When, at Bayreuth in 1901, the work was played in one continuous act (in accordance with his original intention), a cut was made from bar 26 before the end of the orchestral postlude to the first act to bar 19 of the prelude to the second. These bars are really superfluous, and the work gains in organic unity by their omission.

The curtain rises on a large room in Daland's house — unmistakably a sea captain's room, for on the walls hang sea pictures, charts and so forth. Prominent on the back wall is a portrait of a pale man with a dark beard, wearing a black Spanish costume. Round the fireplace are seated Senta's old nurse, Mary, and a

number of maidens engaged in spinning; while Senta sits a little
apart from the others, leaning back in a long chair with her arms
crossed. She is lost in dreamy contemplation of the portrait.

Motive No. 15, which in the orchestral transition from the first
to the second act was associated with the Norwegian sailors as
they hoisted the sails and pulled at the ropes, now becomes associated in Wagner's mind, in some curious way or other, with
another kind of work, that of the maidens. It becomes an integral
part of the main phrase of their Spinning Chorus:

No. 25   *Allegretto ♩= 66*

The humming of the wheels is suggested in the strings. (The
piece soon became very popular in Germany; Liszt made a brilliant transcription of it for the piano in 1860). The burden of the
girls' song is a prayer to the wind to bring their seafaring lovers
home to them soon. Mary gently reproves Senta for not spinning
with the others: this idleness, she tells her, is not likely to bring
her a gift from her lover. The other girls twit Senta with the fact
that she has no need to spin as they do, for *her* lover does not, like
theirs, sail the seas in quest of treasure; instead of gold he brings
her game, for Erik is a hunter.

Senta apparently does not hear their chatter. She remains immobile: the orchestra gives out a quiet suggestion of a phrase
(No. 6) from the ballad into which she will launch later; and we
are to understand from the stage directions that she is singing
the ballad of the Flying Dutchman softly to herself. Mary asks
her, with motherly solicitude, why she wastes so much of her
young life brooding on the portrait on the wall. Senta's reply is
"Why did you tell me of this hapless man, and fill my soul with
pity for him?" The maidens, unable to comprehend this obsession of hers, mockingly hope that Erik will not become jealous
and do something desperate; and they turn to their spinning
again with more zest and noise than ever, until Senta begs them
to stop. All this humming and buzzing, she says, distracts her;
if they wish to interest her with their singing they must try with
something better than this. We have arrived, it is evident, at

the old-fashioned opera "cue for song", a device which the young Wagner did not as yet know how to dispense with, or at all events how to disguise. Senta suggests that, for distraction's sake, Mary shall sing them the ballad of the Flying Dutchman; but as the older woman recoils in horror from the uncanny idea Senta says she will sing it herself, in the hope of winning their sympathy for the wretched man who is the subject of it. So the others — except Mary, who goes on spinning peevishly by the fire — put their wheels aside and gather round Senta, who begins the ballad still sitting in the armchair.

18

The song tells of a phantom ship, with black masts and blood-red sails:

No. 26

Traft ihr das Schiff im Mee - re an, blut -
Saw ye the ship that rides the storm, Blood-

- rot die Se - gel, Schwarz der Mast?
- red the sails and black the mast?

On her deck stands a pale captain, whose watch is without end. One thing alone can redeem him from the curse that lies on him — the love of a woman faithful unto death (No. 6). But when and where will he find her?

No. 27

Ach! wann wirst du, blei - cher See - man, sie fin - den?
Ah! when poor sea - man, this maid wilt thou find her?

"Pray ye all that heaven will grant him this boon!" As she says this, Senta turns towards the picture on the wall. The maidens listen sympathetically, and even Mary has now ceased to spin.

The second stanza of the ballad tells of the seaman's rash vow to round a certain cape if he had to sail the seas until Judgment Day, and of how Satan took him at his word. The third stanza, which Senta sings with febrile exaltation, describes the Dutch-

man's landing once in every seven years, his vain quest of a faithful woman, and his flight in despair to the sea again. The maidens — this is an effective dramatic touch — are so deeply moved
that almost unconsciously they become first of all co-singers of
the ballad with Senta, and then, when she falls back exhausted into the chair, continue it softly alone. Then, in a sudden access of
enthusiasm, Senta springs up from the chair and vows that if God's
angel will bring the Dutchman to her she will save him by her
loyalty: at this point we hear the melody from which the motive
of Redemption by Love (No. 12) in the overture had stemmed.

The maidens rise to their feet in terror at this fanatical outburst, and just then Erik appears in the doorway: he had heard
Senta's closing words, and gives a startled cry of "Senta! wilt thou
destroy me?" Gloomily he announces that Daland's ship has been
sighted — news that fills the others with joy. The girls, in spite of
Mary's appeal, will do no more work that day: they will be off
to the shore to greet their men-folk and take them food; all which
is made clear to the audience, after the operatic manner of the
1830's, by a great deal of repetition of the same words and musical phrases. It ends in Mary driving the girls out of the room and
following them, for of course the stage must be free now for the
big scene between Senta and Erik.

She would have followed the others out, but Erik restrains her.
He implores her to give him an explanation. Before her father
sails again the old man will keep his promise to give Senta in
wedlock; and Erik speaks passionately of his own unrequited love
for her:

No. 28 ♩ = 66

Mein Herz, voll Treu - e __ bis __ zum
A lov - ing heart a - lone __ I
Ster - ben, mein dürf - tig' Gut, mein Jä - - ger - glück:
bring thee, No goods nor gold, a hunt - er's lot!

Will she not be content to share his humble lot? He knows that
her father's mind runs on wealth alone. Can he rely on Senta to
speak for him, or is her whole affection, as he fears, centred in the

portrait on the wall, and her whole heart in the morbid ballad she has just sung? When he speaks of his own grief she leads him up to the picture, points to it, and asks if he can be blind to the look it turns on her, imploring her pity for the doomed seaman and the redemption of him from the curse.

Exhausted by her conflicting emotions she sinks back into her chair as Erik begins to tell her of a vision he has lately seen. He had been lying dreaming on a high cliff that overhung the sea. He saw a strange ship nearing him, and then two men coming along the shore together. One of them was her father: the other he did not know, but recognised him, by his black garb and gloomy face, as the original of the portrait. From the house Senta had come running to greet her father; but catching sight of the stranger she turned to him and fell on her knees before him. He raised her up; she sank on his breast and kissed him, and then the two sailed away together. It was an excellent dramatic device on Wagner's part thus to introduce first as a figment of the imagination an episode that would become actuality a little later: he afterwards employed the same technique in *Lohengrin*, where Elsa, in a trance, sees her rescuer Lohengrin approaching some time before the swan-drawn boat appears on the river.

While Erik has been speaking, Senta has fallen into a cataleptic state, in which she not only sees incident after incident as her lover describes it but at times, by the force of her imagination, anticipates him. At the climax of his story she comes back suddenly to real life again with an enthusiastic cry of " 'Tis I he seeks! To him must I go! His fate shall be mine!". "My dream was true, then!" ejaculates Erik; and he rushes out in horror and dismay.

19

Senta, her visionary excitement having spent itself, relapses once more into immobility and brooding silence, her eyes riveted on the portrait; then she murmurs softly to herself the refrain of the ballad (No. 27). Just then the door opens, and Daland and the Dutchman appear. Daland pauses on the theshold, as if waiting for Senta to come forward and welcome him as usual; but the Dutchman, with his eyes fixed on Senta, comes slowly towards her, while she, for her part, stands motionless, gazing at him as if spellbound. Wagner creates a feeling of suspense by means of those throbs in the kettledrums and lower strings of which he was to make such good use for a similar purpose in his later operas. There appears, too, in the strings, a tender little figure, the parallel thirds of which are also characteristic of the later Wagner:

as Daland comes forward at last with a gentle reproof to his daughter for her seeming coldness towards him. She takes him by the hand, draws him closer to her, and asks "Who is the stranger?" He smiles affectionately at her, the orchestra launches the bluff motive characteristic of him:

and in a set aria — for in an opera of 1840 the bass, like the soprano, the tenor and the baritone, had to have his aria:

Mögst du, mein Kind, den fremden Mann will-kommen hei-ssen!
Wilt thou, my child, ac-cord this stranger friendly greet-ing?

he urges her to give the newcomer friendly greeting. "A seaman he is, like myself", he says, "long without a home, a constant wanderer over the seas. Great wealth he has won him in foreign lands, and much of it he would give to find a home. Tell me, Senta, wilt thou give him welcome here?" She nods assent. Daland turns joyously to the stranger. "Did I overpraise her?" he asks. "You see her yourself; is she not an ornament to womankind?" The Dutchman, still silent, makes an assenting gesture, and, with No. 28 in the orchestra expressing his tenderness for his daughter, the bluff old captain, whose heart, after all, is in the right place, turns to her again and urges her to consent to marry the stranger on the morrow. Senta makes a convulsive movement:

No 32

but remains silent and soon regains her composure. Interpreting her silence in the wrong way, Daland shews her a quantity of jewellery which, he assures her, is the merest trifle compared with what the stranger owns; and all this will be hers when she becomes his wife.

But the principal pair, wholly absorbed in each other, pay no attention to his chatter. At last it dawns on him that he is not wanted there; so with a parting word of advice and warning to his daughter, and another singing of her praises to the stranger, he departs, observing them narrowly all the while, obviously hard put to it to understand what can be in their minds.

20

When at last they are alone they "remain motionless" for a time, as the stage directions put it, "lost in contemplation of each other"; and Wagner — rather helplessly, for he is unskilled as yet in the art of ringing ever-new psychological changes on his leading motives, — fills in their silence with simple enunciations of the Dutchman motive (No. 1) and that of Redemption (No. 27 etc.) in the orchestra. But he soon finds himself again when the Dutchman begins to speak, which he does at first in a long unaccompanied line of quasi-recitative:

> *Up from forgotten depths of years long vanished*
> *Beams now this maiden's face on me:*
> *Dream-visions seen in days and nights unending*
> *Now turned to substance here I see.*

Then he launches into the first cantilena of the duet:

No. 33 ♩ = 66

	Wohl	hub	auch ich	voll	Sehnsucht mei-ne		Blik - ke,
	Oft	in	the night	my	sighs to heaven as -		cend - ed,
Bass:	B	G♯		E B	G♯	E	A

He speaks of his eternal longing, not so much for love itself as for release through love from his suffering. Senta answers him quietly at first, as if musing within herself rather than speaking to him:

Is all a dream, a vision fair and fleeting?
Can sight and hearing thus betray?
Was all till now illusion born of darkness?
Now dawns at last the glorious day?

No. 34

Then, in more impassioned tones, she takes the lead in a combination of the two voices:

No. 35

Before her, she says, stands at last in the flesh the man of whom she had so often dreamed, pouring his tale of sorrow into her pitying ears. She will bring him salvation and peace, she assures him — an assurance none the less sincere on her part, and accepted with none the less sincerity on his, because it ends weakly with one of those conventional cadenzas which the young Wagner could not help taking over from the opera of the period:

No. 36

The Dutchman takes a few steps nearer to Senta, and earnestly asks her if she is willing to make good her father's word — will she give him the love and faith that alone can redeem him from the curse? She pledges her word, and he kneels before her, imploring heaven's help for her and for himself. Then, rising in great agitation, he asks her if she realises the fate that awaits her if she casts in her lot with his. If she gives him her word it will be beyond recall; does she not shrink from the abyss that opens before her? "Well know I woman's sacred duty", she replies, in the authentic vein of the German romanticism of the epoch. "Take heart, o hapless one: I know full well what is demanded of me: but he to whom I dedicate myself, his am I only, true to death!" And the duet ends in a glow of exaltation on both sides, Senta especially rejoicing in the new spiritual power that has taken possession of her:

No. 37

Daland re-enters to the accompaniment of a festive melody in the orchestra:

to ask, in his blunt way, if they are plighted yet, as the villagers are anxious to begin the junketing that celebrates the ending of each voyage. Senta assures him that her resolution has been taken and she will never rue it; and the act ends with a trio in which Senta and the Dutchman, entirely absorbed in themselves and each other, pay no attention at all to the simple Daland, whose one idea is that they shall come with him and "join the merry maze".

21

When the *Flying Dutchman* was given as a one-act opera in Bayreuth, nothing more in the way of compression and linking-up was necessary at this point than to slice off a dozen bars from the orchestral postlude to act II, for the introduction to the third act is merely a repetition of these. The one-act form is particularly preferable here, for obviously Daland is to be imagined as going straight out of the house to the popular merry-making of which he has spoken.

The joyous atmosphere of the next scene is established in a brief orchestral prelude, which consists mainly of motives and phrases familiar to us by this time — No. 37, No. 12, No. 18, No. 15 and No. 10 (the sailors' song), which last comes to the forefront as the curtain rises, showing a creek on a rocky strand. In the foreground, to the side, is Daland's house, while in the background we see Daland's ship and the Dutchman's, lying fairly close to each other. It is a clear, bright night. The Norwegian vessel is ablaze with light, and on the deck the sailors are singing a merry chorus in praise of the joys of home-coming from the sea (No. 10), and dancing clumsily. The Dutch ship, however, presents a strange and sinister contrast: it is enveloped in an unnatural gloom and a deathlike stillness.

The Norwegian maidens, who have entered carrying baskets of provisions and drinks, are the first to sense this grisly silence and darkness. They draw their own men's attention to it. The Norwegians, concluding that the others are dumb from fatigue

44

after their voyage, decide to take them some of their own food and drink. They go close to the waterside and hail the Dutch crew again and again; but still no sign of life comes from the mysterious vessel:

Finally they come to the conclusion that these strange beings

are old and grey, with hearts of lead,
and all their sweethearts long since dead.

The maidens are terrified and perplexed, and become more so when the men suggest that the other ship must be the notorious Flying Dutchman's, of whom they should beware — for if it is, the crew are not flesh and blood but ghosts. It is evident that the legend of the Dutchman is known to them all, for they jocularly call out to the Dutch crew that if they have any letters to be delivered to friends or grandparents on land they will be delighted to take charge of them. When the Norwegian sailors further suggest that the others might hoist sail and show them how the Flying Dutchman can scud the sea, the girls run away in terror.

At last the seamen philosophically decide that the best thing to do with the dead is to leave them to death; they themselves, being alive, will feast and dance. The girls, after handing their baskets on board, leave the stage: the men fill their glasses and propose to drink their queer neighbours' health. At their cry of "Wake up and join our feast!" a sombre statement of No. 1 is heard in the bassoons and trombones of the orchestra, and a first faint sign of life is observable on the Dutch ship. The Norwegians resume their lively No. 10 in chorus, and the Dutchman's motive rings out more and more assertively in the orchestra.

The water round the Dutch vessel now begins to move, though everywhere else the sea remains calm. A violent wind shrills through the rigging, and on the deck a watch-fire — a blue flame — appears; this seems to call the invisible crew to life, for they are heard hoarsely shouting their "Yo-ho-hoe! Huissa!" (through speaking trumpets). While the wind whistles and the sea roars they sing an ironical song to their captain:

> *Gloomy captain, go on land!*
> *Seven more weary years have flown!*
> *Seek a youthful maiden's hand!*
> *Faithful maid, be his alone!*
> *Merry be, hui!*
> *Bridegroom bold! Hui!*

prophesying cynically the usual end to it all — one more faithless maiden, and yet another voyage for the luckless wooer:

> *Howl then, storm-wind, blow thy worst!*
> *Our good sails thou'lt never burst!*
> *Satan blessed them ages back:*
> *Blow until the heavens crack!*
> *Hohoe! Hoe!*

The Norwegian seamen have listened to all this with growing horror; and now they see the Dutch ship tossed about by the waves, while a furious wind whistles through the rigging, though everywhere else the sea is still calm and the air quiet.

The two choruses now contend with each other for a while. Gradually the Norwegians, frightened by this crazy kind of storm and the shouts of the other sailors, leave the deck and go below, making the sign of the Cross; whereupon the phantom crew burst into shrill, mocking laughter. And then, with startling suddenness, darkness and the silence of death descend upon the vessel once more, the wind dies down, the sea becomes placid. The Dutchman's motive (No. 1) comes out quietly in the horns over a string tremolando, and is answered by the Redemption motive.

22

The momentary calm is broken by an agitated figure in the strings, to the accompaniment of which Senta comes hurriedly out of the house, followed by Erik, who is in a state of wild excitement. Something she has said to him within doors has made him fear the worst. He asks her if it is true, or is he dreaming? She turns away, deeply moved, but unable to answer. Two motives, complementary to each other, each of them expressive of perturbation:

No. 40

and

dominate this episode. Erik reproaches her bitterly for having forsaken him and thrown herself into the mysterious stranger's arms at the bidding of her father. Has she forgotten, he asks her, that she had plighted her eternal troth to him? Senta is aghast. "Eternal troth?" she repeats helplessly. We are not surprised that Erik should stare at her in blank astonishment at this: "O Senta!" he cries; "hast thou forgotten?" But we soon realise that this piece of dubious psychology on Wagner's part is due to the necessity he was under to give the tenor of the opera another aria to sing before he bids not only Senta but the audience farewell for the night: this lame little bit of dialogue, in fact, is merely another "cue for song".

Erik's aria is a mellifluous reminder to Senta of the days when she had given him reason to believe he was not indifferent to her:

No. 42

How often, he asks her, had they stood on the hill together and watched her father's sail disappearing in the distance, after Daland had placed her hand in his and entrusted her to his protection; and then she had twined her arms round his neck and pledged her troth to him anew. "Sure was I then, Senta, that thou would'st faithful be!"

All this has been overheard by the Dutchman, who now rushes forward in great agitation, crying despairingly, "Lost! Lost! All hope of salvation lost!" She places herself in his path, imploring him to stay; but as the storm-wind begins to rise again he pipes on his whistle to his crew, bidding them hoist sail, raise anchor, and take their last farewell of land.

No. 41 becomes the main thematic material for a trio in which Senta protests that she is true to her vow, the Dutchman swears that he has no faith any longer in her or in God, and Erik sees the hand of the Devil in it all and begs Senta to come to her right mind before it is too late. At last the Dutchman tells her, to the accompaniment of a motive that has been gradually asserting itself more and more since the commencement of the trio:

of the awful fate from which he now voluntarily saves her. He is condemned to carry a grievous curse, from which only a woman who will be faithful unto death itself can redeem him. He has had Senta's promise; but it was not sworn before God, and so he will not hold her to it. For the fate of those who swear their troth to him and do not abide by their oath is eternal damnation. "Victims unnumbered I have brought beneath this curse; but thou, Senta, shalt escape it. Farewell! Hope has fled from me for ever!"

He turns to go: Senta holds him back, while Erik, in the grip of a new terror, calls to the house and the Norwegian ship for help. Daland, Mary and the maidens from the house and the seamen from the ship come out in response to his cry. "Well do I know thee!" Senta assures the Dutchman ecstatically. "Well do I know thy doom! Thy face I knew when I beheld thee first. The end of all thy woe is come: my love, true to death, shall bring thee redemption from the curse!" "Thou know'st me not, nor dreamest who I am!" he replies. He points to his ship, the red sails of which are now spread, while the crew, with uncanny movements, are making preparations to depart. "Ask thou the ocean and the tempest; ask thou the seamen of all the seas; they know my ship, of all good men the terror; the Flying Dutchman am I named!"

He rushes on board his ship, which immediately leaves the shore and reaches the open sea, the phantom crew singing their maniacal "Yo-he-hoe!" (No. 1). Senta tries to follow him, but is held back by Daland, Erik and Mary. She manages to tear herself away and reach a rock that overhangs the water. From there she cries with all her strength after the departing Dutchman: "Praise thou thine Angel with thy last breath! Here stand I, faithful unto death!" She leaps into the sea. The Dutch ship at once sinks and disappears with all the crew, engulfed in a wave that becomes a whirlpool. Then, in the glow of the setting sun, the glorified forms of the Dutchman and Senta, clasped in each other's arms, are seen rising above the wreck, soaring heavenwards.

The present orchestral postlude to the opera takes, of necessity, the same course as the revised version of the overture, the older, rather trite ending being replaced by the appearance of the Redemption motive in the transfigured form it had assumed in the overture (No. 13).

Tannhäuser

PRINCIPAL CHARACTERS

HERMANN, LANDGRAVE OF THURINGIA	*Bass*
TANNHÄUSER	*Tenor*
WOLFRAM VON ESCHENBACH	*Baritone*
WALTHER VON DER VOGELWEIDE	*Tenor*
BITEROLF	*Bass*
HEINRICH DER SCHREIBER	*Tenor*
REINMAR VON ZWETER	*Bass*
ELISABETH, NIECE OF THE LANDGRAVE	*Soprano*
VENUS	*Soprano*
A YOUNG SHEPHERD	*Soprano*

1

WAGNER drew up his first plan for an opera on the subject of Tannhäuser in Teplitz in the summer of 1842, and wrote the poem in the following spring. The title originally planned for the work was *Der Venusberg,* but this he abandoned in deference to the wishes of his publisher Meser, who feared that it might provoke ribald comment — as, indeed, the location of the action in the Mountain of Venus did later in the brighter circles of Germany and Paris. According to his own account, it was with the Venusberg scene that he began the composition of the music. The first act was finished in January 1844, the second on the 15th October of that year, and the third on the 29th December: the orchestral score was completed on the 15th April 1845. Wagner's ultimate title for the work was *Tannhäuser and the Contest of Song on the Wartburg.* This fusion of two quite different stories, that of the Wartburg Contest and that of Tannhäuser, aroused the ire of some German scholars of the period, the great Simrock in particular, for reasons which will become clear to the reader when we have surveyed the stages by which the opera poem came into being.

Wagner tells us that when the subject first took hold of him he was not as well versed in mediaeval German poetry as he became later, by which he probably meant that as yet he had not put in much first-hand work upon the ancient texts. He had already, however, a good knowledge of the basic facts. One of his cronies in Paris (1839–1842) had been a philologist of the name of Lehrs, whose brother, a professor in Königsberg, specialised in German mediaeval literature. Lehrs himself was an accomplished Germanic scholar, and to him Wagner owed a great deal of the impulse that drove him during the next few years to make an ardent study of the ancient history and culture of his race. But there were other sources open to him. Like every other German of his day he must have known from childhood E. T. A. Hoffmann's collection of stories entitled *The Serapion Brethren,* out of which the poets and the librettists of the Romantic epoch dug so much of their material.

In one of these stories, *The Singers' Contest,* the tale is told of the Minnesinger Heinrich von Ofterdingen. The teller of the tale, it appears, has been reading Wagenseil's Nuremberg Chronicle, of which we shall hear more when we come to the *Mastersingers.* Fascinated by the old book, he dreams himself out of his lonely chamber into a lovely forest, where, at the pealing of a hunting horn, the animals peep shyly out of their lairs. The music of the horns gives way to that of harps, and as the sounds draw nearer there comes into view a gallant company of knightly hunters, laden with game, with boar-spears in their hands and bright horns slung over their shoulders. At the head of six noble cavaliers rides a man of princely mien, in old German costume, accompanied by a lady of dazzling beauty; at the end of the gay and happy procession comes a train of pages and servitors. We may fairly assume that Wagner remembered this episode when he came to write the fourth scene of his first act, in which the Landgrave and his knights, hunting in the forest, come upon their former comrade Tannhäuser after his flight from the court of Venus.

2

While the student of Wagenseil is musing upon this entrancing vision he is accosted by an old man — none other than Wagenseil himself — who obligingly explains the scene he has just witnessed and tells him the full story of Heinrich von Ofterdingen and the Contest of Song on the Wartburg. In the first decade of the thirteenth century, he says, there were six famous Minnesingers at the court of Thuringia — Heinrich von Ofterdingen, Wolfram von Eschenbach (whom we shall meet again in connection with Wagner's *Parsifal*), Walther von der Vogelweide (who comes into the story of the *Mastersingers*), Reinhart von Zweckstein, Heinrich der Schreiber, and Johannes Biterolf, — all of them of knightly birth except Heinrich von Ofterdingen, who was a burgher of Eisenach. While the others sang songs of purity and gladness, Heinrich's were filled with a pain and longing that made them strange and harsh. In time he separates himself from the noble company and goes back to his native town, where he is sought out by the gentle Wolfram, who, like the others, is distressed by the unhappiness that seems to be eating out his confrère's heart. Heinrich confesses that he has a hopeless passion for the beautiful Countess Matilda, the young widow of Count Kuno von Falkenstein. This was the lady whom the dreamer had seen riding by the Landgrave's side: she was the beloved of Wolfram, who had won her by the sweetness and moral elevation of his songs. Never will he return to the Wartburg, Heinrich assures Wolfram. But one day he finds himself again in the forest near the castle, and, overcome by sad memories, he takes up his lute and pours out his soul in a song in praise of Matilda. He is accosted by a sinister stranger who jeers at his song and at the whole poor craft of the Minnesingers, and offers to teach him the mysteries of a greater art known only to himself, for he is a pupil of the great master Klingsor, who is in bad odour everywhere because he is suspected of trafficking in magic; and the stranger hands Heinrich a little book in which a few of the master's secrets of song are set down.

In the following spring the Minnesingers and their ladies, among them Matilda, are assembled in the great hall of the Wartburg; and just as Wolfram is about to begin a song a young man comes forward whom they joyfully recognise as their long-lost Heinrich. He is given his old place between Wolfram and Walther von der Vogelweide, and permitted by the Landgrave to share in the singing. It is soon evident to all that he is a changed man, proud, confident and scornful; and after Wolfram has sung in praise of the Landgrave and congratulated the company on the return of their old companion, Heinrich seizes his lute and breaks into a song so unprecedented in its manner and so uncanny in its matter that at first the others do not know what to say about it. Then they break into applause, and the fair Matilda crowns him with the victor's garland. When twilight falls Heinrich and Wolfram find themselves alone together. The latter confesses that his friend has proved himself the greatest master of them all, but feels that this mastery has been dearly bought in some way which he does not understand. Heinrich listens in silence, then, covering his face with his mantle, rushes sobbing into the night. In all this, and in part of what follows, we have the basis for Wagner's second act.

As time goes on the other Minnesingers become critical and suspicious of Heinrich's new-found art. Matilda, however, whose praises he is always singing, becomes his advocate. Gradually her character changes as his had done; "she looked down upon the other masters scornfully and arrogantly, and even withdrew her favour from the unfortunate Wolfram von Eschenbach." She herself begins to compose Minnesongs in the new and suspect style of Heinrich. "From that time onward the charm and sweetness of the deluded lady seemed to desert her. Turning her back on everything that is the adornment of noble ladies, on everything, indeed, that is womanly, she became an uncanny something that was neither woman nor man, hated by her own sex and derided by the other." She leaves the court and goes to a castle near Eisenach, whither Heinrich would have followed her had not the Landgrave ordered him to remain and meet the challenge the other masters had thrown out to him. He censures the false brilliance of the young man's art, which Heinrich now confesses he had learned first of all from the little book which the stranger had given him, then from the sinister Klingsor in person.

3

At the Contest of Song he is surpassed by the others, whereupon, mortified and furious, he breaks into a series of lays in which he insults the Landgrave and all the ladies of the court except Matilda, whom he praises in a heathenish style which the others find unbecoming. The knights, as in Wagner's opera, turn upon him with drawn swords, and his life is in danger. He appeals to the Landgrave for protection, and begs for a new contest in which Master Klingsor shall be arbiter. The Landgrave consents, but with the proviso that the executioner shall stand beside Heinrich as he sings, and behead him if he loses. The contest is to take place within a year and a day, and Heinrich is sent out in search of Klingsor.

After a number of episodes that do not concern us here, the contest duly takes place. Wolfram, inspired by the presence of the Lady Matilda, who has returned in all her former grace and innocence, is adjudged victor by all the knights. (Klingsor is present, but he refuses to act as judge, for fear of offending his powerful patron King Andreas of Hungary; he prefers the decision to be left to the Landgrave and the assembly). The executioner advances to mete out justice to the vanquished Heinrich, who, however, suddenly disappears in a cloud of black smoke — a sure sign that he had sold his soul to the powers of evil. Klingsor had imposed on the Landgrave for a while by telling him that a daughter is about to be born to King Andreas whose name will be Elisabeth; she will be of such surpassing piety that the Pope will canonise her, and she will become the wife of the Landgrave's son Ludwig. But now Klingsor is in as bad odour at the Wartburg as Heinrich himself, and he too vanishes. "Some of the warders of the castle said that at the very time when Wolfram von Eschenbach had vanquished the supposed Heinrich von Ofterdingen a figure very like that of Master Klingsor had been seen to dash out of the gateway on a snorting black steed." The story ends with the reunion of Wolfram and Matilda, and a letter from Heinrich in which he confessed that he had been corrupted by the magician, but that his friend's pure song had torn the veil from his eyes and restored him to life and happiness. He sent greetings to the masters, and after a while news reached the Wartburg that he was at the court of Duke Leopold of Austria, singing inspired songs, some of which he sent to the Landgrave. "Thus it was", the story concludes, "that Wolfram von Eschenbach's noble art of song, welling as it did from the purest depths of his soul, won a glorious victory over the enemy and rescued his beloved and his friend from perdition."

In Hoffmann's story, it will be seen, there is no mention of Tannhäuser. The central figures of it are the authentically historical Minnesinger Wolfram von Eschenbach and the dubiously historical Heinrich von Ofterdingen; but the latter is not associated in any way with the court of Venus, and therefore there is no question, at the end, of either his damnation on that account or his repentance and salvation. The nucleus of the story is the Contest of Song. Hoffmann had gone back, under the guidance of Wagenseil, to a long fourteenth century poem which tells of a "Contest of Song at the Wartburg", during the reign of the art-loving Landgrave Hermann of Thuringia (1190–1217), between six Minnesingers, Wolfram von Eschenbach, Walther von der Vogelweide, Heinrich der Schreiber, Reinmar, Biterolf and Heinrich von Ofterdingen; the last-named, who relied on the support of the Hungarian magician Klingsor (who is probably entirely mythical), gave offence to the others by praising Duke Leopold of Austria above all other princely patrons of the Minnesong. Whether such a contest ever took place we cannot be sure. But even if it did, the competitors must be conceived as having expressed their sentiments in verse alone, without the aid of music; this is inferrible from the fact that in an old illuminated manuscript the contestants are depicted without any musical instruments in their hands.

4

From Hoffmann, then, Wagner could have derived, at most, only the basic conception of an opera with a contest of Minnesingers at its core, plus a striking incident here and there. No doubt he read later the old poem of *The Contest of Song at the Wartburg* for himself, for once a subject had taken root within him he never rested until he had learned all there was to be known about it. But here again, of course, as in Hoffmann, he would find himself with Heinrich von Ofterdingen, not Tann-

häuser, as his hero; and it was Tannhäuser to whom, for some reason or other, he found himself being particularly drawn during the
early 1840's. He was well acquainted with the rich treasury of
German legend given to the world by Jacob and Wilhelm Grimm
in their *Deutsche Sagen* (1816–8). There he would have found an
old folk-tale of "the noble Tannhäuser" — a great traveller, who
in the course of his wanderings through the world had spent some
time with Frau Venus in her famous mountain of ill repute. After
a while his conscience had pricked him; wearying of all these
beautiful women and the delights of the flesh he had told Venus
that he must leave her court. As in Wagner's opera, she tried
every blandishment to retain him, but at last he won his freedom
by calling on the name of the Virgin. Filled with repentance he
went to Rome, hoping for absolution and the salvation of his soul.
But the Pope, after hearing his confession that he had spent a
year in the Venusberg, replied harshly, "When the dry staff I hold
in my hand puts forth green leaves shall your sins be forgiven
you, but not before". Tannhäuser, heartbroken at this repulse, left
Rome and returned to the Venusberg, where Frau Venus gave
him a hearty welcome; but on the third day, the staff having miraculously burst into leaf, the Pope sent messengers through every
land in search of him. "But it was too late: he was back in the
mountain again, with his old love, and there he must remain till
the Day of Judgment, when no doubt God will send him elsewhere." And the growing dislike of the mediaeval German world
for the Papacy comes out in the final sentence of the story: "No
priest ought to withhold solace from any sinful creature, but forgive him when he comes to him penitent and desirous of making
atonement."

In Grimm also Wagner must have read the ancient legend of
a contest at the Wartburg in 1208 (or thereabouts) between "six
wise and virtuous men", of whom Heinrich von Ofterdingen was
one. The story as told there is in essentials that of the Wartburg
poem. One feature of it may have struck root in Wagner's imagination, to emerge again, in a slightly different form, in the
second act of the opera — when the other knights turn in anger
upon Heinrich, clamouring for his death, he runs to the Land-
gravine Sophie and takes refuge beneath her cloak; and under
her protection he obtains a year's grace.

Wagner was acquainted also with Ludwig Bechstein's collection of the legends of Thuringia (1835); in this he would find ancient versions of the Tannhäuser story and that of the Wartburg Contest of Song. In the library of his learned Uncle Adolf he had found, when a boy, La Motte Fouqué's pseudo-drama *The Contest on the Wartburg* (1828). But, he assures us, it was not until he read "the homely Tannhäuserlied" and an old German Volksbuch of Tannhäuser that his interest in the theme was really aroused. The Tannhäuserlied is a charming poem of the fifteenth or sixteenth century, excellent English translations of which have been given us by Jethro Bithell [1] and Miss Jessie L. Weston. [2] In this we have the dialogue between Tannhäuser and Venus in the form of dramatic give-and-take. After his repulse by (it was alleged) Pope Urban IV (1261–4) — a dignitary in bad odour in Germany because of his opposition to the Hohenstaufen dynasty — Tannhäuser goes back to the Venusberg, where, after the sprouting of the staff on the third day, the papal messengers lose track of him:

> But he was in the mountain ben
> With his sweet love to be;
> And Urban that fourth Pope is damned
> To all eternity.

This piquant but not unattractive ending did not commend itself to Wagner.

5

So far, then, we can retrace the steps by which he was gradually led to the story of Tannhäuser and Venus and that of the Contest on the Wartburg. But what impelled him to combine the two, for the Tannhäuser of the legends had nothing to do with the Contest, the leading figure of which was Heinrich von Ofterdingen, while the latter was not associated in the popular imagination of a later day with either Venus or the Pope? In *A Communication to My Friends* (1851) Wagner said that after reading Hoffmann and "the homely Tannhäuserlied" he happened to come upon an old Volksbuch in which he "found established, however

[1] In *The Minnesingers* (1909), pp. 144–7.
[2] In *The Legends of the Wagner Drama* (1896), pp. 338–42.

loosely, the connection between Tannhäuser and the Contest of Song at the Wartburg". Thereupon he set himself to study Middle-High-German in order to read the massive old poem of the Contest in the original, a copy of which was in the possession of Lehrs. No Volksbuch combining the two legends, however, is known to German scholars, most of whom doubt whether such a thing ever existed. Wagner's memory seems to have been at fault. The idea of fusing the Tannhäuser and the Contest legends probably came to him from an essay of 1838 by one C. J. L. Lucas, a professor in Königsberg, who had put forward the suggestion that in the same way as the historical Minnesinger Tannhäuser and the legendary Tannhäuser of the old poem had become one in the popular imagination, so the Folk may have effected a further fusion between these two and Heinrich von Ofterdingen. Wagner heard of Lucas's theory through Lehrs, who, as we have seen, had intellectual contacts with Königsberg.

The German scholars in general resented what seemed to them Wagner's high-handed way of dealing with the mediaeval records; perhaps they could hardly be expected to see all at once that what is dubious history may be excellent opera, and in the theatre it is opera, not history, that matters. One learned authority, J. G. Theodor Grasse, the head of the Dresden Library during Wagner's residence in the town, did indeed, for a while, take the side of the composer. In 1846 he published a book in which the Tannhäuser legend and that of the Wandering Jew were "traced and elucidated", as he put it with Teutonic concision, "historically, mythologically and bibliographically". This book he dedicated to "his dear friend the Royal Saxon Chief Kapellmeister Richard Wagner, whose admirable tone-creation, by reason of its lofty poetic text — his own work — will attract afresh the attention of many people to this legend." But Wagner must have done something later to annoy the good gentleman — perhaps by taking so active a part in the Dresden rising of 1849, — for in 1848 another *Tannhäuser* had been produced, with a text by Eduard Duller and music by the now forgotten Karl Mangold; and in the second edition of his book (1861) Grasse not only cut out the earlier dedication to Wagner but said unkindly that "the opera composed by Mangold to a libretto by E. Duller is more sensible than the sanctimonious emendation of the sublime and highly poetic return of Tannhäuser to Frau Venus (as we have it in the German folk-ballad) perpetrated by Wagner in the text of his well-known opera." Duller and Mangold had given their opera a happy ending, with Tannhäuser being married to his Innigis and the naughty Venusberg collapsing in ruins. This charming piece of work was actually revived in Darmstadt in 1892.

6

Wagner had indeed made liberal use of the poet's privilege to deal with history in his own way for his own purposes. He substituted the Tannhäuser who was the lover of Venus for Heinrich von Ofterdingen as the central figure in the Wartburg Contest of Song, though by way of compensation to the latter he gave his Tannhäuser the Christian name of Heinrich. He flouted history by making *his* Tannhäuser one of the singers at the court of Landgrave Hermann in 1207 or thereabouts, when the real Tannhäuser would have been only a tiny boy. According to the poem of the Wartburg Contest, Klingsor had announced the birth of the saintly Elisabeth (daughter of the Hungarian King Andreas II), who would marry the Landgrave's son, the later Ludwig IV of Thuringia. This was the famous St. Elisabeth of history (1207–1231), the heroine of Liszt's oratorio, who went to the Thuringian court at the age of four, was married to Ludwig at fourteen, and was left a widow at twenty. We have seen that in Hoffmann the object of Wolfram von Eschenbach's adoration was the young Matilda, widow of Count Kuno von Falkenstein. We have seen also that in the Wartburg poem Tannhäuser, when the indignant knights are about to wreak vengeance on him, takes sanctuary under the mantle of the Landgrave's wife Sophie. Wagner creates an Elisabeth of his own, the *niece* of Landgrave Hermann, who is as saintly as her historical namesake of Hungary. It is she whom, in the opera, the pure and ardent Wolfram worships from afar; and it is she who saves Tannhäuser from punishment in the second act of the opera by standing between him and the angry knights. And in Wagner the old story of the knight and the Venusberg undergoes a drastic change at the finish. In the legend, the Pope's messengers having arrived too late, Tannhäuser returns to the arms of Venus, where he will remain until the Judgment Day. Had the German scholars, after all, some excuse for jibbing at the rejection of this colourful ending of the story? Could it perhaps be restored in some future opera on the subject, supposing anyone to be bold enough to attempt one after Wagner? He had his own good dramatic and ethical reasons for having Tannhäuser "saved" by the saintliness of Elisabeth, though, as we shall see later, he was not always of the same mind with regard to the handling of the closing scene of his work.

7

Readers of John Livingston Lowes's masterly book *The Road to Xanadu,* in which the magic of Coleridge's *Ancient Mariner* is shown, almost verse by verse, to be the result of the subconscious coalescence of a host of tag-ends, many of them of the most unlikely kind, from the poet's reading, will not be surprised to find that a process of a similar kind contributed to the making of more than one of the Wagner texts, particularly those of *Tannhäuser* and *The Mastersingers.* Many a passage he had lighted upon in his voracious reading must have sunk deep into his subconsciousness, remained dormant there perhaps for years, and then come to the surface in obedience to the urge of a dramatic conception of his own. It has already been pointed out that there is a broad resemblance between the scene in the forest in Hoffmann's story and the meeting of Tannhäuser, the Landgrave and the knights in the first act of the opera. Possibly, too, some fragments had remained in Wagner's subliminal memory from his reading of Tieck's story, told partly in prose, partly in verse, of *The Faithful Eckart and the Tannhäuser,* which had first seen the light in 1799 and was reprinted in 1828. The story as told by Tieck is typical of German romantic fiction at its most absurd.

A certain Friedrich encounters one day a pilgrim on his way to Rome, in whom he recognises his long-lost friend Tannenhäuser, who had mysteriously disappeared some years before. The pilgrim, who is obviously not quite in his right mind, gives Friedrich an account of all that has happened to him. From his childhood, it appears, he had not been as other children were. As a youth he had loved a maiden who preferred another swain. On the eve of the wedding he had killed his rival and then fled to the Venusberg, against entering which he was warned in vain by the Faithful Eckart, who had been posted there centuries earlier in order to save men from giving their souls to the powers of evil. After a while the sensuous pleasures of the Venusberg had palled on Tannenhäuser; he had escaped from the mountain and was now on his way to Rome. Friedrich tries to restore him to reason; *he* is the one-time rival, he assures him, and, far from having been murdered, he had married his Emma and is now living happily with her. But Tannenhäuser is not to be convinced that he has not been doing the Devil's work all these years; to Rome he must go and seek absolution of the Pope. One night some years later he returns to Friedrich, pale, wasted, in rags, and informs him that, the Pope having repulsed him, nothing remains now but for him to return to the Venusberg. He rushes out into the night, after having murdered Emma en route. Nor had Friedrich himself escaped: Tannenhäuser had pressed on his lips a kiss the burn of which will never leave them until the giver of the kiss has been found again. Friedrich runs out wildly in quest of Tannenhäuser, arrives at the Venusberg, enters it, and is seen no more by mortal eyes.

Even this absurd romantic farrago may possibly have left a trace or two in Wagner's imagination. In the scene of the meeting of Tannhäuser and Wolfram in the third act of the opera there may be a faint reminiscence of the corresponding scene between Friedrich and Tannenhäuser. When Wolfram asks to be told about the journey to Rome Tannhäuser replies: "Nun denn, hör' an! Du, Wolfram, *du sollst es erfahren!*" ("Be it so! Listen, Wolfram, and you shall learn what happened"). In Tieck the corresponding passage runs thus: "Nun, so mag dein Wille erfüllt werden, *du sollst alles erfahren;* mache mir aber nachher keine Vorwürfe, wenn dich die Geschichte mit Bekümmernis und Grauen erfüllt." ("Your wish shall be fulfilled: you shall learn all that happened, but reproach me not afterwards if the story fills you with grief and horror"). The words italicised are perhaps a trifle too definite for their occurrence in both episodes to be entirely accidental.

There may have been a faint hark-back of Wagner's memory to Tieck, again, at the point in the opera where Wolfram tries to restrain Tannhäuser from returning to Venus, just as Eckart had tried to warn Tannenhäuser against entering the mountain. Finally, the scene in Wagner's first act where Tannhäuser escapes

from Venus by calling on the Virgin, is suddenly transported back
to earth, and pours out his gratitude to God when he hears the
hymn of the pilgrims on their way to Rome, may be unconsciously
indebted for a word or two to Tieck. "Ich war von dem Glanz
gesättigt und suchte gern die vorige Heimath wieder. Eine unbe-
greifliche *Gnade des Allmächtigen* verschaffte mir die Rückkehr,
ich befand mich plötzlich wieder in der Welt", etc., says Tannenhäuser to Friedrich. ("I was cloyed with all these splendours
and fain would see my old home once more. An inconceivable
grace of the Almighty effected my return; I suddenly found myself in the world again", etc). It may not be pure coincidence that
Tannhäuser in the opera cries out, on his release from his cap-
tivity in the Venusberg,

> Allmächt'ger, *dir sei Preis!*
> *Gross sind die Wunder deiner* Gnade!
>
> (*"Praise to thee, Almighty!*
> *Great are the marvels of Thy grace!"*).

There is no conscious plagiarism in cases of this kind; examples of
similar tricks of the subconscious memory can be culled by the
thousand from the poets from Vergil to Shakespeare and from
Shakespeare to Coleridge.

8

The genuine Tannhäuser legend itself, as we have it now, is a
pastiche gradually constructed by the imagination of the Middle
Ages out of a number of pre-existing and non-correlated elements.
The historical Tannhäuser (Tanhuser, Danhuser, etc.) was a
knightly minnesinger of the thirteenth century, hailing from Salz-
burg and born about 1200; we lose authentic sight of him before
1270. A few of his poems have been preserved: from these we can
learn something, and conjecture a trifle more, about the man himself and his career. More interested in poetry and song than in the
ordinary pursuits of the knight and the small landowner, imprudent in the management of his affairs, he lived for a while under
the patronage of Duke Friedrich of Austria. After the Duke's
death he seems to have been at a loose end. In 1228 he went on a
Crusade to the Holy Land, and then and later saw a good deal of
Italy and Sicily and had many strange adventures by land and

sea. His poems give us the impression of one who lived not wisely but too well, squandering his patrimony, as he penitently says, on "fair women, good wine, dainty meats, and baths twice a week", with the result that he was reduced in the end to dire poverty, having "no roof to his house, no door to his chamber, his cellar fallen in, his kitchen burnt out, his barn empty". He drifted about from one court to another in search of shelter and support, but found that few of his old friends were as glad to see him now as they had been in the days of his prosperity.

We may conjecture that, his name being dimly remembered as that of a poet with a strong bent towards the sensual, he had gradually become, during the later Middle Ages, a semi-mythical character about whom there crystallised one of those legends-with-a-moral of which that epoch was so fond. By the end of the thirteenth century the great period of the Minnesong was virtually over. It had declined with the worldly fortunes of the aristocratic class from which it had mostly flowered. The face of German society was changing: many of the nobles were or were becoming impoverished, as a consequence partly of wars, partly of too lavish expenditure on luxuries, partly of the alienation of the estates of many of them to the Church; and among the greater lords there were few now able and willing to support the smaller ones for their mere songs' sake. And while the aristocracy was thus declining the towns were rising; wealth and power were passing into the hands of the merchants, the burghers, the guilds of craftsmen. Along with all this went a democratisation of ethical standards; the old ideals of the knightly order were not those of the townspeople and the peasant. So it may well have come about that the Minnesinger Tannhäuser began to figure as a symbol of a moral licence upon which the new bourgeois society frowned; it may even be that the new age was scandalised not merely by the references to wine and women in his songs but by his reckless unorthodoxy in the matter of baths. Anyhow he was singled out as the most appropriate figure from the past on which to pin the many old legends then current of a mortal who had forsaken the simpler joys of earth for those of an enchantress reigning over an earthly paradise of her own in the heart of some mysterious mountain or other. So there came into being, in time, the fully-formed story of Tannhäuser and Venus that has been so charmingly told by an unknown fifteenth or sixteenth century poet that Heine, in a passage with which Wagner must have been acquainted, could hail it as worthy to stand by the side of *The Song of Songs*.

9

The legend of the Venusberg had originally no connection with Tannhäuser. Wagner boldly describes his opening scene as representing "the interior of the Venusberg (the Hörselberg, near Eisenach)". The brothers Grimm, in their *Deutsche Sagen,* tell an ancient folk-tale of this Hörselberg, "in which the Devil lives and to which the witches make pilgrimages. Sometimes fearful shrieks and howls come from it, made by the devils and the poor wretched souls. In the year 1398 three great fires broke out in broad daylight near Eisenach, burned for a long time, joined together, then separated again, till at last all three made for this mountain. Country people who were later passing by with a load of wine were enticed into the hill by the evil fiend, and there they were shown several well-known characters who were already sitting among the flames of hell." The place became known as Satansstedt, which name was gradually transformed into Sattelstadt. So much for the Hörselberg as the Middle Ages saw it. The modern identification of this fearsome mountain with the Venusberg, however, was a mere flight of fancy on the part of some nineteenth century German scholars. There is nothing in the Hörselberg legend connecting it with either Venus or Tannhäuser; and it is not an earthly paradise, like the Venusberg, but the haunt of devils.

Classical antiquity had loved to dream of mountains or caves inhabited by beings whose life was one long round of delights, and of favoured mortals who had been permitted to taste of these. Naturally the longer these stories were in circulation the more circumstantial the details of them became. One mediaeval Italian legend, which was possibly the source of that of the German Venusberg, was associated with a Sibyl who reigned over an earthly paradise in what is still known as the Monte della Sibilla, a peak in the Apennines between the modern Norcia and Ascoli. We have a romantic description of the place by an adventurous Frenchman, Antoine de la Sale, who essayed, though he was finally beaten in the attempt, to penetrate to the innermost depths of the mysterious cave of the Sibyl. From the people of the neighbourhood he learned the legends connected with the place, and particularly the story of a German who had actually succeeded in penetrating to the recesses of the mountain, where he found the queen of this paradise seated on a magnificent throne, surrounded by nobles and ladies richly dressed; the felicity of these people, who never lost their beauty and never grew old, would endure, he was told, to the end of the world itself.

The rule of the place was this: a visitor could stay eight days and depart of his own free will on the ninth, but if he did not leave then he would have to remain until the thirtieth, and so on until the three hundred and thirtieth day; if he did not depart then he must stay there for ever. There was only one little blot on this captivating picture: from every Friday at midnight until midnight on Saturday the queen and the other charming ladies transformed themselves into snakes and serpents. Strangely enough, it was only on the three hundred and thirtieth day that the German gentleman discovered this. It made him suspect that he had been guilty of mortal sin in taking up his abode in such a place; so on the three hundred and thirtieth day he bade his charming hostesses adieu and went off to Rome to confess. The Pope was secretly willing to absolve him, but thought it necessary, to discourage others, to pretend to take a very serious view of his case. So he spoke to him harshly and drove him from his presence; and when he changed his mind and sent for him again he found that the poor German, having decided on reflection that if he were going to lose the joys of heaven he might as well make sure of those of earth, had gone back to the paradise of the Sibyl, where, presumably, he still is.[1] This Italian legend was evidently very ancient; and modern French scholars have maintained that it was from Italy that it passed into Germany, there to become, in time, the story of Venus and her magic mountain, and of a repentant Tannhäuser who craved absolution of the Pope and was refused. As Gaston Paris has pointed out, the journey to Rome would have been a natural and easy matter; the German gentleman could have walked there very comfortably from the Monte della Sibilla.

[1] Antoine de la Sale was writing in the early part of the fifteenth century. He had had a predecessor, as regards the Sibyl story, in one Andrea da Barbarino, in 1391.

10

These then are the heterogeneous elements, deriving from many sources, that went to the making of Wagner's *Tannhäuser*. He began his composition, as already mentioned, with the music for the Venusberg scene; a sketch-book of his that happens to have survived contains also jottings made in the summer of 1842 for the Pilgrims' hymn, the end of the first act, the prelude to the third act, etc. In his autobiography he tells us that during that summer holiday in Teplitz he was climbing the Wostrai one day when, "turning the corner of a valley, I was surprised to hear a merry dance-tune whistled by a shepherd reclining on a hillock. I was at once transported to my scene of the chorus of pilgrims filing past the shepherd in the valley. Later, however, try as I would, I could not recall the melody, so I had to make one for myself in the usual way." But in the sketch-book just mentioned there is noted a melody for the shepherd boy in the first act which, we are told, is entirely different from that in the opera. It looks, therefore, as if Wagner's memory was a trifle at fault when he was writing *My Life:* presumably he *had* jotted the tune down at the time, or shortly after, and afterwards decided that it was not suitable for his purpose.

The original poem and score of *Tannhäuser* underwent many changes before they assumed their present form; with some of these, however, we shall deal at the end of our analysis of the work as we now have it. The final page of the score in its first form is dated by Wagner 15th April 1845.

The first performance took place in Dresden, under Wagner himself, on the 19th October 1845, with the following cast for the principal rôles:

TANNHÄUSER	Tichatscheck.
VENUS	Wilhelmine Schröder-Devrient.
ELISABETH	Johanna Wagner (a niece of the composer).
WOLFRAM	Mitterwurzer.
THE LANDGRAVE	Dettmer.
WALTHER	Schloss.
BITEROLF	Wächter.
HEINRICH DER SCHREIBER	Curti.
REINMAR VON ZWETER	Risse.

In the late summer of 1859, having completed the score of *Tristan*, Wagner decided to try his fortunes in Paris, where he arrived in September of that year. His plan for a production of *Tristan* came to nothing; but in March 1860 the Emperor Napoléon, for political rather than artistic reasons, gave orders that *Tannhäuser* was to be produced at the Opéra. Three performances were given, on the 13th, 18th and 24th March 1861; the conductor was the incompetent Dietsch, the statutes of the Opéra not permitting the composer to conduct his own work. The following were the principal singers:

TANNHÄUSER	Albert Niemann
VENUS	Fortunata Tedesco
ELISABETH	Marie Sax
WOLFRAM	Morelli
THE LANDGRAVE	Cazaux

The present analysis is of the Paris version of the opera: some details of the respects in which the later score differs from the earlier one will be given at the end of this chapter.

11

The orchestral introduction proceeds for a while on the lines of the original overture of 1845, which told, in its own way, the story of the opera, by means of a succession of motives drawn from the work itself. The term "motives", however, must not be taken to mean what it does in Wagner's later works. In the *Flying Dutchman, Tannhäuser* and *Lohengrin* the motives are solid blocks of masonry, as it were, which, whenever they appear later in the score, at once recall the character in his entirety; it is very much as if a piece on a chessboard had moved into a new position. Even in *Tristan* a whole section is now and then transported almost *en bloc* to another part of the work, as when a slice from the duet in the second act becomes the material for the Liebestod in the third. It was only by degrees that Wagner mastered the craft of working with motives of only a few notes that are capable of infinite melodic, harmonic and rhythmical mutations, can be employed referentially at any moment, and are capable of contrapuntal combination with each other.

The "solid block" system of motives comes into use at the outset of the *Tannhäuser* overture, in a full-length statement of the song of the Pilgrims:

which, with its second strain:

runs on without a break for thirty-seven bars. No. 1 is then repeated *en bloc* in virtually the full orchestra, accompanied by a febrile figure of broken triplets in the violins;[1] after which No. 2 is similarly treated at corresponding length, but in quieter colours. (In the opera the Pilgrims sing No. 2 to the words "My heart is sad, by sin oppressed", etc.) This exposition of the religious element of the opera extends to eighty bars in all; in its totality it presents us with a picture of the Pilgrims coming gradually into sight, and as gradually disappearing in the distance as night falls.

Next comes a section depicting the seductions of the Venusberg — first of all a feverish phrase in the violas:

then various suggestions of revelry:

---

[1] For Wagner this figure symbolised "the Pulse of Life".

No. 5

No. 6

No. 7

This last culminates in a stanza of Tannhäuser's song in praise of Venus:

No. 8

which covers virtually the space allotted to it in the opera.

Then the bacchanal is resumed, in conjunction now with Venus's cajoling invocation to the lover who desires to leave her:

No. 9

This is followed by a second stanza of Tannhäuser's song, in a higher key than formerly; and after a fortissimo statement of the wild No. 5 we part company with the original overture and plunge into the Paris version of the Venusberg music. The curtain rises, showing the interior of the Venusberg — "the Hörselberg, near Eisenach", as Wagner too confidently assures us. A wide grotto curves round towards the right until it is lost in the background distance; a dim light filters through an opening in the rocks, from which a foaming greenish waterfall plunges down into a basin; it then flows out to the background as a brook, which broadens into a lake in which Naiads are bathing, while Sirens recline on its banks. The cliff walls of the grotto are covered with marvellous coral-like tropical growths. Venus reclines on a couch in the foreground, which is bathed in a soft roseate light; round her are grouped the three Graces, while numerous sleeping Cupids are huddled together in a confused tangle, "like tired children", say the stage directions, "who have fallen asleep after play". Tannhäuser, his harp by his side, is half-reclining before Venus, with his head in her lap. The foreground, with its rosy light through which break the emerald green of the waterfall and the white foam thrown up by its waves, contrasts with a clear blue vapour that fills the background.

Youths with goblets in their hands come down from the heights in response to the signs of the Nymphs, who have begun an alluring dance: there are pursuits, flights and coquetries of all kinds while the dance continues.

To joyous reiterations of No. 4 and No. 5 A, which latter has now an exuberant pendant that was not in the score of 1845:

No. 10
Allegro ♩ = 80

a swarm of Bacchantes comes from the far background and breaks through the ranks of the amorous couples, urging them on to further abandonment "with gestures of exalted intoxication", as Wagner puts it. The dance grows ever wilder, till at last the revellers embrace each other passionately, to a new strain:

No. 11
Molto vivace

Bass: A

that is evidently an offshoot from *Tristan*.

12

Fiery developments of No. 11 are followed by a return to No. 3, with castanets adding a new and exotic touch of colour to it. Satyrs and Fauns, emerging from the clefts in the rocks and intruding their own wild dance into that of the Bacchantes and the pairs of lovers, increase the confusion by pursuing the Nymphs. Wilder and wilder still grows the tumult, until, as it rises to a delirious climax, the three Graces rise to their feet, horror-stricken, and try to restrain the dionysiac rout. Impotent to do so, and fearing that they themselves will be drawn into the whirl, they turn to the sleeping Cupids, awake them, and drive them up the heights, where they scatter for a while, then draw themselves up, as it were, in battle array, and rain down a shower of arrows on the tumult beneath them. A trumpet call rings out; then the music slows down in pace and decreases in volume as the Graces take possession of the wounded and try, with gentle force, to disperse the revellers towards the background. The Bacchantes, Fauns, Satyrs, Nymphs and Youths withdraw, pursued in part by the Cupids from the heights.

The music softens still further as a rosy mist settles upon the scene, growing thicker as it descends. First of all, while No. 5 comes out softly and graciously in the flutes and clarinets, the Cupids disappear; then, as the mist slowly envelops the background, the languorous song of the Sirens:

steals in and is developed in a "symphonic" way that would have been impossible to the Wagner of 1845.

Only Tannhäuser, Venus and the three Graces remain on the stage. The latter, according to Wagner's stage directions, "now

return towards the foreground; gracefully interlocked they draw
near to Venus, and apparently tell her of the victory they have
won over the mad passions of the subjects of her kingdom. Venus
gives them a grateful glance. The mist in the background dissolves, revealing a cloud-picture of the Rape of Europa; she is
being carried across the blue sea on the back of the garlanded
white bull, escorted by Tritons and Nereids." And now we hear
the quiet song of the invisible Sirens — "Come to this strand,
come to this land,[1] where your yearning shall be satisfied in glowing love":

No.14 *Molto moderato*

The orchestra develops the strain in luscious Tristanesque fashion:

No.15 *Dolcissimo*

while "the rosy mist gathers again, obliterating the picture, and
the Graces interpret in a graceful dance the mystic meaning of
the picture as a work of love".

The Sirens' voices (No. 14) are heard again as once more the
mist dissolves, revealing, in the half-light of the moon, Leda reclining on the banks of a woodland lake, with the swan fawningly
laying its head on her bosom. Slowly the voluptuous melodies

[1] The current translations, of the type of "Come to these bowers, fragrant
with flowers", are dictated by the necessity of finding two double-syllabled
rhyming English words for "Strande" and "Lande".

and harmonies sigh themselves out in the orchestra; the picture
fades away and the mist entirely disappears, showing the grotto
lonely and still. The smiling Graces make obeisance to Venus and
retire to the inner Grotto of Love. Venus and Tannhäuser maintain their attitudes unchanged.

13

At last the silence is broken by Tannhäuser, who raises his
head suddenly as if waking from a dream, which he seems to be
trying to recapture as he draws his hand across his eyes. Venus
caressingly asks her beloved to tell her what is troubling him.
He had thought he heard, he replies, a sound that had long been
strange to his ears, that of bells pealing joyously. How long he
has dwelt with her in the Venusberg he cannot say, for days and
months have become all one to him; sun and stars and grass he
sees no longer, nor hears the nightingale singing that spring is
nigh. Will he ever see and hear all this again?

In quietly seductive tones she asks him why he complains thus.
Is he weary of the wonders her love has lavished on him? Does
he long to be a god? Has he forgotten his one-time suffering and
his present transports? Holding out his harp to him she exhorts
him to sing of love as he had done in the days when he had won
her by his singing. His mood changing suddenly, he rises to his
feet, seizes his harp, and sings the first stanza of his song, to the
melody of No. 8. He praises her and all the godlike delights she
has brought him, a mortal. But, he continues, his mood clouding
over once more, such joys as these are for gods alone: he longs to
be a man again and know the sufferings of men: and he implores
her to set him free.

Venus herself now seems to waken from a dream. What has
changed him? she asks anxiously: in what has her love been lacking? how has she deserved this lament? In a second stanza, in a
key a semitone higher, he sings again in praise of her love and
grace; enviable the man who has known the enchantments of her
domain and has tasted joy in her arms! Yet — his mood darkening
again — he longs to fly from her rosy bowers to the green wood-
lands, fresh with dew, and see the blue sky above him, and hear
the song of birds and the chiming of bells; and once more he ends
with an appeal to her to set him free.

Springing from her couch, she reproaches him for his ingratitude and refuses him his liberty; she turns away from him with a cry and buries her face in her hands. Then, after a long pause, she points to a magic grotto that has appeared in response to a sign from her, and turns to him again with a seductive smile, while the orchestra gives out a luscious strain:

No. 16

that might have stepped straight out of the second act of *Tristan*. It is a far cry from the Wagner of 1845 to the Wagner of 1860; and there is no rebutting the charge that here, as in many other places in this opening scene, his new style is incompatible with the old fabric into which it has been woven.

Venus cajolingly invites Tannhäuser to come with her into the grotto, where she will lavish new enchantments of the senses on him. Wagner uses the original material of this episode to some extent, but presents it in more captivating forms, and inlays it with the finer and richer woods of the Paris score. Completely carried away, Tannhäuser seizes his harp once more and sings, again a semitone higher, the third verse of his song. It would have made for greater unity of style, of course, if Wagner had rewritten this song along with so much of the music of the scene. But that was hardly practicable; for one thing it would have meant a total recasting of the overture, while if he had changed the melody of the song the only logical course would have been to rewrite the opening scene from first to last; and if he had done that, logic would have further dictated a re-writing of a good deal of the remainder of the opera. His admirers in 1861 were even more conscious than we of today are that his new style did not cohere with his old, for, it has to be remembered, they listened to all this Tristanesque music without knowing anything of *Tristan* beyond

the prelude,[1] or anything at all of the *Ring*. Wagner himself must
have been fully conscious of all this, but his musical daemon
drove him on inexorably: he had long felt that he could make a
better thing of the Venusberg scene than he had done in his original score, and his experiences of the Paris Opéra in 1859 and
1860 had enlarged enormously his conception of the possibilities
of ballet. So he abandoned himself luxuriously to the joy of writing something more correspondent to his heart's desire than the
meagre capacities of the Dresden stage and his own relative im-
maturity as a musician had made possible for him in 1845, and
cheerfully threw stylistic consistency to the winds.

14

Tannhäuser's third stanza ends, as its predecessors had done,
with an appeal to Venus to set him free. This time she rises in
anger and bids the "madman and traitor" go. In the original score
she had done so to rather conventional vocal and orchestral
phrases; but now, with *Tristan* and much of the *Ring* behind him,
Wagner puts a new fire into it all. A figure symbolical of Venus's
wrath:

dominates her furious harangue, though for a moment she reverts
to the lyrical Wagner idiom of the *Tannhäuser-Lohengrin* period:

[1] This had been given at one of Wagner's Paris concerts in February 1860,
and had provoked Berlioz into a wild denunciation of it in his *Débats* article
of the 9th February.

blö - dem, trü - bem Wahn
fee - ble, troub - led dream,

as she tells him to sate his new desire if he will — to fly from her into the cold and loveless world of men and seek there for grace, though he will seek it in vain.

The episode is greatly extended in the Paris version, Venus becoming a more definite dramatic personality than she had formerly been. She bids Tannhäuser go back to the knightly company whom in his pride of old he had derided and antagonised, reveal his dishonour to them, and bear their scorn. They will curse him and cast him out, and then he will return to her downcast, moaning, "Oh, could I once more find her who once smiled on me! Would she but open again the door that leads to rapture!" For pity, not for love, he will then beg. Let him go from her, then; her kingdom is open only to heroes, not to slaves.

Wagner prolongs the original scene by making Tannhäuser show defiance — out of pride, he now says, he will never return to her — and Venus then breaks down. Her anger having exhausted itself, she loads him with tender reproaches:

No. 19

Wie hätt'___ ich das er - wor ___ ben, wie
How have ___ I brought this on ___ me, where-

träf' mich solch' Ver - schul - den,
- in have I of - fend - ed,

What has she done, she asks, how has she offended, that her beloved will not forgive her? To the Queen of Love alone, then, it

is denied to bring solace to her friend? How often, smiling
through her tears, she had listened to his song! Were she to hear
his sighs and laments again would she not comfort him as of old?
But if her pleas are unavailing, she breaks out again despairingly,
then her curse shall lay the whole world waste; and she be-
seeches him not to leave her but to trust in her love and grace.

But he is unyielding: he who is resolved to leave her "flies from
all grace for aye". He is weary of soft enchantments; he longs for
the world, for combat, even for death. "Then return to me", she
implores him, "when even death shall fly from thee, and the grave
be closed to thy bones." But death, he replies, is already in his
heart; only in penitence and atonement shall he ever find rest.
Once more she assures him that rest and peace will for ever escape him except in her arms: "return to me if thou wouldst be
saved". He gives a great cry of "Goddess of all delights, not with
thee shall my soul find its peace! My salvation lies in Mary!"
Venus disappears, and the scene changes.

Tannhäuser, who has not changed his position, suddenly finds
himself in a beautiful sun-bathed valley, with the old castle of
the Wartburg showing in the background, while the Hörselberg
is visible through an opening in the valley on the left. On the
right a mountain path runs down from the Wartburg to the foreground, where it turns aside; and near the bend, on a slight eminence, is a shrine to the Virgin. From the heights on the left comes
the sound of sheep-bells, while on the high cliffs sits a young
shepherd blowing a pastoral strain on his pipe:

No. 20

(The melody begins in the clarinet and is continued by a cor
anglais behind the scenes). Then the shepherd sings a little song
in praise of Holda, the goddess of spring:

No. 21

Frau Hol - da kam aus dem Berg her - vor, zu
Dame Hol - da fair from the hill drew near, New

zieh'n durch Flu - ren und Au — en,
life to chill earth__ bring - ing,

Between the first two stanzas there comes, in the Paris score, an effective little interlude on the pipe that was not in the original version:

No. 22

The song tells how at Holda's coming the woods were filled with music and the shepherd woke from his dreams to find that May had come; and once more he blows lustily on his pipe, the melody of which continues through the first part of the song of the elder Pilgrims:

No. 23

Zu dir wall' ich mein Je - sus Christ,
To thee I come, my Sa - viour dear,

der du des Pil - gers Hoff - nung bist:
for thou the pil - grim's cry dost hear:

who are making their slow way down the mountain path from the Wartburg. Their song takes a graver turn as they sing of their sense of sin (No. 2) and their hope of pardon, and hearing this the shepherd silences his own joyous melody, waves his cap to them, and cries "God speed to Rome! There for my soul to ask a blessing!"

Tannhäuser, into whom the song of penitence has struck deep, sinks on his knees with a great cry of gratitude to God for mercy.

The pilgrims reach the stage and pass across it in slow procession, continuing their song until it dies away with them in the distance, the shepherd joining in occasionally with his melody before leaving the scene. Tannhäuser, as if sunk in fervent prayer, takes up the pilgrims' strain of No. 2; he too will never rest until his sin has been forgiven. Tears choke his voice: he bows his head and appears to weep bitterly.

15

By an admirable piece of transition the music merges almost imperceptibly into the horn fanfares of a hunting party in the distance:

No. 24

and soon the Landgrave and the minstrels enter one by one from the eminence on the left of the stage. They see what they take at first to be a penitent of noble bearing, whom, however, they soon recognise and greet with joyous cries of "Heinrich!" Has he come back to them in friendliness, they ask, or is he still their foe? The gentle Wolfram reproves them for even suspecting him of hostility; is Tannhäuser's demeanour, he asks them, that of pride? He welcomes his return in phrases wholly characteristic of the melody of the early Wagner:

No. 25

Walther, Heinrich der Schreiber, Reinmar, and even Biterolf, who is from first to last the least friendly towards Tannhäuser, echo Wolfram's welcome. The Landgrave joins in, but asks where the minstrel has tarried so long. Gravely and wearily Tannhäuser turns the question aside; all he will tell them is that he has been wandering in a distant land where he could never find rest or solace. Let them question him no more: he has not returned to contend with them; let them forget his leaving them and permit him to go his way. In a broad ensemble the others implore him to stay with them, but the gloomy man reiterates that it is impossible: his doom is to wander on for ever, not daring to look behind him again.

The knot is cut by Wolfram standing in front of him and exhorting him loudly to "stay for Elisabeth". The name awakens long-slumbering memories in Tannhäuser's bosom: deeply but joyfully agitated, he stands as if spellbound while Wolfram, at the Landgrave's request, tells him how the magic of his song among them in days of old had not only earned the praise of them all but won him the prize of Elisabeth's love:

No. 26

The song is a moving one, in spite of several little evidences in it that as yet Wagner had not shaken himself quite free of the conventional melodic lines of his early days.

Since he had left them in his pride, says Wolfram, Elisabeth had closed her heart against their song; her cheek had grown paler, and she had come no more to the meetings of the minstrels; and he exhorts him to return among them and once more raise his song with theirs. The appeal is built up into a fine ensemble, with a captivating after-strain that lends itself well to imitative interlocking:

No. 27

Tannhäuser, profoundly affected, throws himself into Wolfram's arms, then greets the other minstrels in turn and bows in gratitude to the Landgrave. "Lead me to her!" he cries, and his voice takes the lead:

No. 28

in an animated ensemble that brings the first act to a close. Tannhäuser sees a new life opening out before him:

> 'Tis Spring! 'Tis Spring! a thousand tender voices
> With calls to gladness fill the air.
> My eager heart once more rejoices,
> And cries aloud: "To her! To her!"

During the ensemble the stage gradually fills with the hunting retinue of the Landgrave. The hunters execute an exultant fantasia on their horns. At the end the valley is thronged with people: the Landgrave sounds his horn, and is answered by sonorous horn-blasts (No. 24) and the baying of hounds. The Landgrave and the minstrels mount the horses that have been brought to them from the Wartburg, and the curtain falls on an animated scene, with Tannhäuser's joyous cry (No. 28) ringing out in almost the full power of the orchestra.

16

It is in the orchestral introduction to the second act that we get, already in 1845, a foretaste of the later Wagner. The introduction presents us with a tone-picture of Elisabeth in happy mood after the return of Tannhäuser to the Wartburg. A preliminary mounting figure in the strings:

No. 29

sets the general tone of the piece. It is succeeded by an energetic reminder of Tannhäuser's joyous greeting to the new world that had opened out before his imagination after Wolfram's appeal to him (No. 28). For a moment — and here we get a touch of the real Wagner — the sunny picture is darkened by a harsh reference:

No. 30

to a phrase from Venus's warning to Tannhäuser in the episode the beginning of which is shown in our No. 18: after bidding the ingrate return to "the loveless world of men" the goddess had warned him that there he might seek for grace but would never find it. But when this cloud has passed the music regains its first sunny aspect, and after another reference to the joyous No. 29 Elisabeth herself bursts into song.

The curtain has now risen, showing the hall of song in the Wartburg, with an open background giving a view of the courtyard and the valley beyond. Elisabeth enters with a glad greeting to the beloved hall:

No. 31

She tells of the dreariness that had descended on it and on her when Tannhäuser had forsaken them, and — to the accompaniment of the exuberant No. 29 — of her happiness at his return, never, she hopes, to leave them again; and the aria ends with the orchestra repeating the joyous No. 28 as Tannhäuser, accompanied by Wolfram, enters by way of the staircase in the background. The faithful Wolfram remains at the back of the stage as Tannhäuser advances and throws himself impetuously at Elisabeth's feet. In modest confusion she is about to leave him, but turns graciously to him at his appeal to her to stay, and, to the accompaniment of a typical early-Wagner melody in the clarinet:

No. 32

urges him to rise and take her thanks for returning to the scene of his many triumphs. But where has he been so long? she asks. The music becomes clouded over once more as he replies, in sombre tones, "Far from here, in distant, distant lands, and dark oblivion's cloud between today and yesterday has rolled". His memory of it all is dimmed; he remembers one thing only — that he had lost all hope of ever raising his eyes to her again. A "mighty and mysterious wonder" has brought him back to her:

No. 33

Ein Wun - der war's, ein un - begreiflich ho-hes Wun - der!
A won - der'twas, a migh- ty and mys-te-rious won - der!

She praises this wonder for the happiness it has brought her; and Wagner proceeds to paint, as well as it was possible for him to do at that time, the musical portrait of the imaginative but as yet unawakened girl as he saw her.[1] Quietly and modestly she tells him of the joy the minstrels' songs, and his more than any, had given her in bygone days: his singing had brought her a rapture that was half a mystic pain, stirring in her longings which her childish heart could not comprehend. Then he had left them, and her heart had gone silent, cold and dead; and she ends with

---

[1] The spectator must bear in mind that the matronly Elisabeth one generally sees on the stage is at the furthest remove imaginable from the Elisabeth of Wagner. He visualised her as the St. Elisabeth of history and legend, still in her girlhood, ignorant of the world, with a soul divided between vague promptings of human affection and the call of a latent mysticism.

a poignant cry of "Heinrich! Heinrich! what hast thou done to me?" Tannhäuser answers her with a rapturous assurance:

No. 34

Den Gott der Lie - be sollst du prei - sen!
The God of Love be praised for ev - er!

that it was the god of Love who had then inspired him and who has now brought him back to her; and their voices blend in a glad duet: "Oh blessed hour of meeting, oh blessed power of love":

No. 35

Ge - prie - sen sei_____ die Stun - de,
Oh bless - ed hour_____ of meet - ing,

the technical handling of which seems to have appealed more to Mendelssohn than anything else in the opera. In its latter half it opens out into a new strain:

No. 36

Von Won - ne-glanz um - ge - ben lacht mir der Son - ne Schein,
De - light__ supreme be - stow-ing, Once more the sun doth shine,

as the pair sing of the power of love to recreate the world for lovers. At the climax Tannhäuser leaves Elisabeth and embraces Wolfram passionately: the pair disappear, and Elisabeth, from the balcony, looks fondly after Tannhäuser as the orchestra repeats No. 32 in soft tones.

17

The Landgrave now enters through a side door; Elisabeth runs to him and hides her face on his breast. The dialogue that follows shows Wagner still unable, as he had been in the Daland scenes in the *Flying Dutchman,* to give musical life and blood to an episode or a minor character that had to be there for constructional purposes but did not lend itself easily to musical delineation. The kindly Landgrave reads his niece's secret in her eyes and spares her the telling of it: as for the marvels that the minstrels' songs had once awakened in her, these shall be renewed today. The brief dialogue is obviously there only as a device for introducing the scene that is to follow; and Wagner is very far as yet from full mastery of that art of imperceptible logical transition on which he rightly prided himself in his later works.

"Even now", the Landgrave concludes, "arrive the nobles of my land, whom I have bidden here to solemn festival; larger the concourse will be than of old, for they have heard that thou the victor's brow wilt crown." A trumpet fanfare peals out from the courtyard:

No. 37

succeeded by a quieter strain:

No. 38

as the Landgrave and Elisabeth ascend the balcony to watch the arrival of the guests. Knights and Counts, with their ladies and retinues, gradually fill the hall, being received and formally announced in turn by four noble pages; the ladies and attendants, after doing honour to the Landgrave, remain in the background, while the nobles take the places allotted to them. The ceremonious processional music begins quietly:

No. 39

This is followed by the equally quiet:

No. 40

which, however, soon rises to a climax with:

No. 41

and a repetition of No. 38.

At last brilliant trumpet fanfares introduce the big chorus in praise of the hall of song, "where art and peace alone prevail under the wise rule of Landgrave Hermann, Prince of Thuringia": the chorus is built up out of the material shown in No. 39 (all the voices) [1], No. 40 (the women's voices), No. 41 (the men), and finally the whole company as more and more nobles arrive with their retinues. One needs to have seen the Bayreuth setting and management of this scene to realise the full splendour of it.

18

Some final fanfares ring out at the conclusion of the chorus, by which time the guests have seated themselves in a large semicircle, with the Landgrave and Elisabeth occupying seats of honour under a canopy in the foreground. To the accompaniment of a new and quieter strain:

No. 42

the minstrels now come forward, greet the assembly with dignified bows, and take their seats in a narrower semicircle in the centre of the hall, with Tannhäuser in the middle to the right and Wolfram at the end (left) opposite the guests. The Landgrave rises and addresses the assembly. He reminds them how, after the land had been saved by their swords from the savage hordes that threatened it, they had turned to the cultivation of the arts of peace, the singing of the praises of grace and beauty, faith

---

[1] Wagner had anticipated this melody in a choral "Greeting of his Faithful Subjects to the Beloved Friedrich August" (King of Saxony) in August 1844.

and virtue. Today they celebrate their divine art once more, in a contest of song that will include the minstrel from whom they had been too long parted. Where he has been, how and why he has returned, has not been told them; perhaps the secret may be revealed to them in song. He gives them their theme — the true nature of love: and the singer of the best lay on that theme will be awarded the prize by Elisabeth; whatever his demand may be the Landgrave pledges his word that she will grant it. The fanfares ring out once more, the assembly hails the Landgrave as the protector of the arts, and the contest of song begins.

The choosing of the order of the singers is carried out to the accompaniment of the minstrels' motive (No. 42). Each contestant places a small roll of paper bearing his name in a golden bowl borne by the four noble pages: they present the bowl to Elisabeth, who takes out one of the papers and hands it back to them: they read the name, advance ceremoniously into the centre of the stage, and call out "Wolfram von Eschenbach, begin thou!". Then they seat themselves at the feet of the Landgrave and Elisabeth.

Tannhäuser, leaning upon his harp, seems to be lost in dreams as Wolfram rises to the accompaniment of some solemn chords in the lower strings. He begins quietly with a courtly address to the knights and ladies, whose nobility and virtue, he humbly feels, will dazzle his eyes and make him dumb:

No. 43

But above them all sits throned one pure spirit like a star, before which his soul abases itself in prayer. His vision is of a fountain of stainless joy, from which flows a flood that allays the fever of his spirit: may he never dim that fountain's pure waters with the taint of thought impure:

No. 44

Und nim - mer möcht' ich die - sen Bron - nen trü - ben,
Oh nev - er may I dim that foun - tain's wa - ters,

In humble devotion he kneels before it, glad to give for it his
heart's last blood. That, he concludes quietly, is his song, into
which he has put all he knows of the purest essence of love.

Acclamations break from them all as he resumes his seat —
from all but Tannhäuser, who now seems to waken from his
dream. What that dream has been is told us by the orchestra,
with its reminiscences of the wild Venusberg music (No. 10, No.
3, etc.). (For the Paris version the scene that immediately follows
was changed considerably by Wagner). Gradually his demeanour had assumed the haughty tone that had led to his first separation from the court; now his expression changes to one of ecstasy
as visions of the Venusberg rise before him. Unconsciously his
fingers seek the strings of his harp. An uneasy smile plays for a
while over his features; then, as if possessed by a demon, hardly
knowing where he is, he bursts out into a scornful denunciation
of Wolfram, whose tepid song, he says, shows that he has never
known what love is: "were all men's hearts as chill as thine is,
the world were lifeless as a stone!" Let him praise God and the
stars of heaven if he will; but of life and love as Tannhäuser has
experienced them he knows nothing. He himself will go to the
fountain that alone can rekindle desire as fast as it quenches it;
for of eternal desire he would drink eternally. This, and this
alone, is love as he conceives it.

19

There is general consternation. Elisabeth "is a prey", say the
stage directions, "to conflicting emotions of rapture and anxious
astonishment". Biterolf, in a song that is still early Wagner, rises
angrily, denounces the blasphemous pride of Tannhäuser and defies him to mortal combat. His outburst meets with the approval
of the knights and ladies; and when Tannhäuser, in a gust of anger, calls his critic a poor starveling who, for all his virtuous sentiments, has never known what real love is, the knights rise in

wrath and refuse to hear any more. The tumult is quelled by the Landgrave, who bids Biterolf put back the sword he has drawn, and still more effectively by Wolfram, who rises to implore heaven to send them peace of soul and banish all sinful thoughts from them. His song in praise of the higher love has the regularity of metrical accent which Wagner himself was to note with amusement, in later years, as a characteristic of his early vocal style:

No. 45 ♩=80

Dir, ho - he Lie - be, tö - ne be - gei - stert mein — Ge - sang! —
Oh sa - cred love, my prais - es Flow forth to none — but thee! —

By now Tannhäuser has lost control of himself. Madly he sings his song from the first act in praise of the goddess of earthly love, the fountain of all grace and beauty and joy (No. 8); he ends with a cry to all poor mortals who have never known her love to fly with him to the hill of Venus. At this unblushing revelation of where he had spent the time of his absence from them the assembly breaks up in horror. The ladies leave the hall with gestures of dismay. The Landgrave, knights and minstrels have left their seats and formed into a hostile group. Elisabeth, pale and anxious, trying desperately to preserve her self-control, supports herself against one of the wooden pillars of the canopy. Tannhäuser, throughout the first part of the chorus of denunciation of him that follows, remains isolated at the extreme left of the stage, still intoxicated with the vision he has conjured up in his memory. As the men advance on him with drawn swords he places himself in an attitude of defiance.

The crisis is averted by Elisabeth, who steps forward and shields Tannhäuser with her own body. If he is to die, she says, let her die with him, for no wounds that their swords could give her could match the one that has been dealt her by him. Gradually all the leading threads of the action pass into her hands, and not only psychologically but musically she raises it all to a higher plane. In a long passage commencing thus:

No. 46

Andante ♩=56

Der un - glück - sel'- ge, den ge - fan - gen ein fürcht - bar
This er - ring soul that now is cap - tive To some mys -

mächt'- ger Zau - ber hält,
- ter - ious power of sin,

and culminating in an impassioned plea to them for mercy on the sinner:

No. 47

Adagio ♩=58

Ich fleh' für ihn, ich fle - he für sein Le - ben,
I plead for him, oh spare him I im - plore you:

she tells them that it is she, not they, who has been most grievously hurt by Tannhäuser's impious song, for she had loved him. Now she pleads that he shall be allowed to live and repent, for it was for such as he that the Redeemer died.

Tannhäuser, who has gradually lost his truculence of demeanour as Elisabeth's plea proceeded, at last sinks down, overwhelmed with contrition, as the minstrels, led by Walther, launch a massive choral ensemble in praise of Elisabeth:

No. 48

Ein En - gel stieg aus lich - tem Ä - ther, zu
An an - gel hath from heav'n de - scen - ded, and

kün - den Got - tes heil' - gen Rath.
God's most ho - ly mes - sage brought.

Tannhäuser breaks in with an appeal to heaven to grant him grace for the sake of the angel who has interceded for him, an appeal that reaches its culminating point in a poignant cry for mercy:

No. 49

Er-barm' dich mein, der, ach! so tief in Sün-den,
Have mer-cy, Lord, have mer-cy I im-plore thee,

Finally Elisabeth takes hold of a phrase that had been begun by the knights, and between them they build up with it the climax of a long and impressive ensemble:

No. 50

Ich fleh' für ihn,— ich— fle-he für sein
I plead for him,— oh!— spare him I im-

Le-ben, ich fle-he für sein Le-ben,
plore you, oh spare him, I im-plore you,

We sink to a lower musical plane again when the Landgrave steps forward, reproves Tannhäuser sternly, and pronounces sentence on him of banishment from their midst. One course alone remains open to him to avert God's anger. Some pious pilgrims (here No. 23 is given out in the wood wind) are now making their way to Rome, to lay the burden of their sins, light as it is in comparison with his, at God's feet. The knights and minstrels, to the strain of the motive of Atonement:

No. 51

Mit ih-nen sollst du wal-len zur Stadt der Gna-den-huld;
With them to beg for mer-cy To Rome thou must re-pair;

bid Tannhäuser repair to Rome with them and never return till his sin has been forgiven. For Elisabeth's sake they will restrain

their wrath now, but their swords will take vengeance on him if
he refuses to follow the path of salvation opened out to him. Elisabeth raises her voice above them all in a last plea to him and to
them, Tannhäuser stammers his contrition:

No.52

Più moto

Wie soll ich Gna - de, wie Gna-de fin - den?
How win my par - don, how win my par - don?

Wie soll ich bü - ssen die gros - se Schuld?
How can I ev - er my sin ef - face?

and at the height of the turmoil the song of the younger pilgrims
strikes in from the depths of the valley — "To God's high feast of
grace I go, My burden at his feet to throw". All involuntarily
moderate their gestures; Elisabeth, who has made a movement as
if to protect Tannhäuser from the knights, calls his attention to the
promise of comfort held out by the song; Tannhäuser, suddenly
calmed, listens intently to the song as it soars to its climax and
then dies away. A ray of hope lights up his face: he throws himself convulsively at Elisabeth's feet, kisses the hem of her garment,
and rushes out with a cry of "To Rome! To Rome!" The others
echo the cry, and the curtain falls to the strain of No. 51 in the
orchestra.

20

The orchestral introduction to the third act is an expressive
tone-painting of Tannhäuser's pilgrimage. First we hear (now in
the key of E flat) the pilgrims' solemn song (No. 23), upon which
breaks, in the soft tones of oboe and clarinet, the melody of Elisabeth's pleading for Tannhäuser (No. 47), as it were a thought, at
once sad and consoling, passing through the penitent's mind as he
trudges along with the others. Then a second phrase of the pilgrims' song is followed by a motive of Tannhäuser's wretchedness
that will play a considerable part in his own later story of his pilgrimage:

No. 53

Further elaborations of these contrasting motives lead into a return of the motive of the Pulse of Life from the overture: this is twice broken in upon by the motive of the Feast of Grace in Rome of which Tannhäuser will tell Wolfram later; it takes first of all this form:

No. 54

then thunders out in greater majesty still:

No. 55

Then, after another brief reference to Tannhäuser's despair, the music slowly settles down into another statement of No. 47 and dies away in a soft E flat chord in the high wood wind.

At this point the curtain rises, showing the valley in front of the Wartburg, as at the end of the first act, but now in sad autumnal colours. Evening is falling. On the slight eminence to the right we see Elisabeth prostrate before the shrine of the Virgin, deep in prayer. Wolfram comes down slowly from the wooded heights on the left, catches sight of her, and pauses. Gravely he sings to himself of her constant praying day and night for Tannhäuser: now she is awaiting the home-coming of the pilgrims, whose return surely cannot long be delayed now that the sere leaves are falling. Will *he* be among them, pardoned and redeemed? For that mercy he prays for Elisabeth's sake, or for some solace for her if her heart's desire should not be granted.

As he is about to descend further into the valley he is arrested by the song of the returned pilgrims (No. 1) welling up from the valley, greeting gladly the home they are soon to see again. Elisabeth too has heard the song, and a tremor passes through her as she murmurs " 'Tis they! They have returned! Show me, ye saints, my task, that I may worthily fulfil it!". Gradually the chanting pilgrims reach the stage and go slowly past the rocky eminence down the valley to the background, their song festooned with the broken triplet figure of the Pulse of Life. The song rises to a great "Hallelujah!"; then, to the strain of No. 1 again, the procession passes out of sight in the now setting sun. Tannhäuser is not among them.

As her last hope has died within her Elisabeth has poured out her grief in one of the great phrases of the opera, in which the throbbing strings add an extra poignancy to the simple words and as simple melodic line:

No. 56

When she is left alone she falls on her knees in an ecstasy of grief and resignation: for the first time the mysticism of her young being finds full expression in a prayer to the Virgin to take her from this world of care:

No. 57

All-mächt - ge Jung-frau, hör' mein Fle - hen! Zu
Oh bless - ed Vir - gin, hear my plead-ing! Thou

dir, Ge - pries - ne, ru - fe ich!
queen of glo - ry, grant my prayer!

Through the quiet plaint a figure in the bass clarinet — a typically later Wagner touch, this — keeps winding its melancholy way:

No. 58

Lento

She ends with a quiet prayer to the Virgin to give ear to her pleading and pardon the sinner his great sin:

No. 59

Mach, dass ich rein und en - gel-gleich
Oh let my spi - rit, pure and white,

ein - ge - he in dein se - lig Reich,
En - ter in - to thy king - dom bright,

after which an orchestral postlude in the pure tones of the higher wood wind seems to carry her supplication aloft.

As she rises slowly to her feet she perceives Wolfram approaching her. May he not lead her homeward? he asks. With a silent gesture of refusal she conveys to him an expression of her gratitude and affection and a request that he will leave her to traverse alone the path she has marked out for herself for the short remainder of her days. She ascends the height and gradually disappears in the direction of the Wartburg, the faithful Wolfram following her with his eyes, and the orchestra dwelling sweetly and sadly on phrases from his song in the second act in praise of spiritual love (No. 45) and

No. 60

21

The stage has by now grown darker, and with the disappearance of Elisabeth the orchestra, with a chord or two in the quiet tones of trombone and tuba, tunes us in, as it were, to the gloom that will envelop the remainder of the dramatic action. Wolfram seats himself at the foot of the rising ground to the left and begins to improvise on his harp. Evening, he muses, is falling on the valley like a foreshadowing of death, terrifying and beating back the soul that would fain ascend to the heights:

No. 61

But one fair star there is whose friendly beams beckon a way through the vale; and he begins that song to the evening star that may seem old-fashioned to us now, but in its own day was rich in new harmonic suggestions:

No. 62

His song ended, the orchestra continues to muse upon the theme of it while Wolfram raises his rapt eyes to heaven.

The stage is now quite dark. Suddenly a troubled figure in horns and bassoons:

No. 63

cuts harshly into the serene atmosphere as Tannhäuser appears in
the tattered garb of a pilgrim: his face is pale and tortured: he
walks falteringly, leaning heavily on his staff. He is at first not recognised by Wolfram, but Tannhäuser knows the latter at once and
describes him scornfully as "the practised minstrel". The gentle
Wolfram runs to him eagerly, but cannot refrain from wondering
that he should venture again, unabsolved, into the domain of the
Landgrave. Tannhäuser acidly bids him calm his fears: he seeks
the company of none of them — his one consuming desire, he adds
feverishly, is to find again the path that leads to the Hill of Venus;
and the orchestra entwines the dialogue with the wild strains of
No. 3 and No. 10. The trembling Wolfram tries to hold the madman back. Has he not been, then, to Rome? he asks; did he not
sue for pardon? Yes, replies Tannhäuser bitterly; he has been to
Rome. Wolfram pours out his heart's compassion for him, while
the wood wind breathe softly the phrase (No. 47) of Elisabeth's
intercession. Wolfram's sympathy surprises and touches Tannhäuser; he had thought the minstrel his foe like the others. Exhausted, he seats himself at the foot of the rock: Wolfram is about
to join him there, but Tannhäuser motions him back; "Away from
me! Wherever I rest me is accursed!", and the grievous No. 63
wells up in the orchestra once more.

Wolfram shall hear his story, he says; and he breaks into that
long recital of his pilgrimage that placed Wagner, in 1845, on a
musical height to which none of the Marschners of the epoch could
ever hope to rise. To the accompaniment of the tortured No. 53
Tannhäuser tells how he had gone to Rome with an ardour in
his soul such as no pilgrim had ever known, his old arrogant pride
chastened, his heart set on justifying Elisabeth's appeal for grace
for him. To that end he had pitilessly multiplied the mortifica-
tions of his flesh, always taking the rough road rather than the

smooth, refusing to quench his thirst in the burning heat, shunning the friendly hospice and sleeping in ice and snow, his eyes blind to the beauty of everything around him, — all that Elisabeth's grief might find an end. At last he had reached the holy city, where the bells were pealing from every steeple and every soul was filled with joy (No. 54). With the others he had knelt before him who holds the keys of heaven, and thousands were shriven, thousands went on their homeward way rejoicing. No. 53 reappears as Tannhäuser goes on to tell how he in his turn approached with head bent to earth, confessed his sin, and begged for deliverance from the fetters of earthly longings. The Pope's harsh reply — that if he has felt these vile desires, warmed himself at the fires of hell, dwelt in the Venusberg, he is eternally accursed:

> As on this dead staff in my hand
> never a leaf again shall grow,
> so from hell's all-consuming brand
> salvation canst thou never know!

— is punctuated by orchestral ejaculations of the tortured No. 63. Tannhäuser had fallen to the ground, crushed and confounded. When he awoke night had fallen and he was alone, but from afar he could still hear the happy song of the other pilgrims (No. 54). With horror in his heart he had fled, possessed now by only one desire, to feel again the transports he had known in the Venusberg, the themes of which now leap into flame in the orchestra as he sings, to the melody of No. 9, a frenzied appeal to Venus to take him to her bosom once more. The Venusberg music takes full possession of the orchestra as the frenzy of Tannhäuser and the horror of Wolfram increase.

22

A thin vapour spreads over the stage and soon begins to glow with a rosy light, and as the infernal rout grows madder in the orchestra first a confused whirl of dancing figures becomes visible, then Venus herself is seen reclining on her couch. To the melody of No. 14 she welcomes Tannhäuser again, reminding him of her warning that the cruel world of men would reject him and he would be glad to take refuge in her arms once more. The three voices unite for a while, Venus renewing her seductions. Tann-

häuser straining towards her for a sign of pity, Wolfram vainly en-
deavouring to hold him back. He reminds the madman of one
who is now an angel pleading for him in heaven and giving him
her blessing; and the knot is cut, as it had been in the first act, by
Wolfram crying "Elisabeth!". At the sound of that name Tannhäuser, who had struggled free of Wolfram, stands as if rooted to
the spot; and at the same time there comes from behind the
scenes a choral song of the minstrels and other mourners com-
mending to God the soul of the pure Elisabeth. "Her prayer is
heard! Heinrich, thou art redeemed!" cries Wolfram. Venus disappears with a cry of "Woe! he is lost to me!" The vapours dis-
solve, morning dawns, and from the Wartburg a funeral procession, with torches, comes down into the valley, singing a hymn of
the blessing of Elisabeth:

No. 64

Hei——lig die Rei——ne, die nun ver‑eint
Blessed be the pure one, who now ap‑pears,

gött——li‑cher Schar vor dem E——wi‑gen steht!
One——with the saints round the throne——of the Lord!

Tannhäuser has been led by Wolfram to Elisabeth's bier; he
bends over it in a quiet prayer, "Sainted Elisabeth, pray for me!",
and falls dead to the ground. All invert their torches and so ex-
tinguish them, the only light now coming from the red glow of
the dawn. A band of younger pilgrims enters from the rocky
eminence in the foreground, bearing in their midst a staff covered
with fresh green leaves, and singing a chorus of praise for the
miracle:

> *The barren staff the priest did bear*
> *with tender green is clothed again:*
> *the sinner need no more despair,*
> *for God shall cleanse him of his stain.*
> *High over all the Lord doth reign,*
> *no man doth call on Him in vain.*

The whole assembly unites with the orchestra in a sonorous statement of the pilgrims' song (No. 1), which is once more accompanied by the triplet figure we had heard festooning it in the
overture.

23

A good deal of confusion seems to exist as to the date of origin
of what is known in the concert room as "the *Tannhäuser* Overture and the New Venusberg Music". We read, for example, that
"in the original form of the overture, which is the one usually
played at concerts, the Salvation motive re-enters and gradually
overcomes the [old] Venusberg music, coming to a triumphant
full close in the usual manner. When, however, Wagner made his
preparations for the ill-starred production at Paris in March 1861
he omitted the last part of the overture and made the Venusberg
music run straight on, without a break, into the first scene." This
is quite wrong. It was not the present coalesced form of the old
matter and the new that was given in Paris: the original overture
was played intact, and followed, after the usual brief interval, by
the new Venusberg scene in place of the old one. Both Wagner
and Malwida von Meysenbug say definitely that the house broke
into applause "after the overture". There is other contemporary
evidence to the same effect — that of Marschner, for instance, who
was present on that occasion. It is clear, again, from passages in
Bülow's contemporary letters from Paris, in which he sets forth
the alterations Wagner was making in the opera, that no change
was contemplated as regards the overture.

For brevity's sake let us refer to the original overture of 1845 as
A, the Venusberg ballet scene that followed it as B, and the re-
cast Paris version of this last as C. In the 1845 version of the
opera, after the usual interval for applause after A, act one began
with a scene described in the score as "the Venusberg". The stage
showed the interior of the hill of Venus: the enchantress reclined
on a couch, with Tannhäuser half-kneeling by her side; nymphs
and bacchantes indulged in a bacchanal during the course of
which a chorus of sirens was heard in the background. When the
music finally died away the vocal portion of the opera began with
Tannhäuser's words "Beloved, say, where stray thy thoughts?"

Both Wagner's musical and his dramatic sense told him later

that this procedure was faulty, for two reasons — it involved a certain amount of repetition of the same musical matter in A and B, and B was insufficiently orgiastic. As early as March 1852 he told Uhlig that he now saw that the "proper place" for the 1845 overture was "in the concert room, not the theatre". If the decision rested with him he would now play, in the theatre, only "the first tempo of the overture" — i. e., as far as the end of the pilgrims' chorus; the remainder is "too much to be given in front of the drama".

Later he became dissatisfied with B. It was plainly the weak spot in the opera, he wrote to Frau Wesendonk from Paris in April 1860. What was needed was something much wilder, more voluptuous, to serve as background to the spiritual tragedy of Tannhäuser. He had long been aware of this, he said, but only after he had completed *Tristan* did he feel that he was musically equal to such a task. He accordingly intended to write a new B in a style that would "astonish" the Parisians. He gives no hint, however, of any intention to modify the overture. That, in a sense, had by now passed out of the hands of its creator; it had become immensely popular both in the theatre and in the concert room, and opera directors, conductors and audiences alike would have been horrified at the suggestion that it should be curtailed. All that Wagner had in his mind now, in Paris, was a new and better version of B, the expanded scenario for which he sketched for Frau Wesendonk.

The further question now arises, when was the dovetailing of A and C effected?

In the summer of 1867 the opera was given in Munich, under Bülow, for the gratification of King Ludwig. This was simply the Paris version of 1861 again, with C following A, and, of course, with all the changes in, and additions to, the vocal parts made in 1861. The coalescence of C with a curtailed A was probably effected about 1871/2, for on the 12th May 1872, at a concert given by Wagner in Vienna in aid of his Bayreuth plan, he conducted the first performance of what we know now as "the *Tannhäuser* overture and the New Venusberg Music". The new arrangement was first heard under *operatic* conditions in Vienna on the 22nd November 1875, at a performance of the work under Wagner. But after he had left the town the Vienna Opera reverted to the original version — A followed by B: the overture — the most popular work of the period — was a *bonne bouche* of which the public objected to being deprived, while the new bacchanal (C) was frowned upon by many pundits, among them Hanslick, as a glorification of sensuality in music. Another Vienna critic, Ludwig Speidel, informed his readers that the New Venusberg Music was made up of "howls and shrieks, an endless succession of piercing dissonances. We hear the Spanish flies [cantharides] buzzing, and the draught served up by the satyrs is simply gin laced with cayenne pepper. Even in Wagner it would be difficult to find so horrible, so foul a musical daub."

24

Apart from the re-modelling of the overture and the bacchanal scene Wagner made several changes in *Tannhäuser* in the course of the years. The work had become so popular in Germany, and was always so badly performed — as, indeed, it still is — that in the summer of 1852 he was driven to write a brochure *On the Performing of Tannhäuser*, in which he tried to set the theatre directors and producers and singers on the right path with regard to it. Owing to the imperfections of some of the singers and of the stage management in Dresden in 1845 he had been compelled to make various cuts for the first few performances; the other theatres, to suit their own convenience, chose to regard these cuts as "authorised by the composer", and they faithfully reproduced them, to his great annoyance, in their own productions; and Wagner's brochure was partly intended to correct misconceptions of this kind. But in addition there were several variants between the earliest published scores in use in the theatres and the later ones, the result of second thoughts on his part; and he wanted to impress it on the German theatres in general that it was the second version which they were to follow.

This was particularly the case in connection with the long orchestral introduction to the third act. A comparison of this as it stands in the earliest and in the present scores reveals several changes and curtailments. The final version runs only to 92 bars; the original ran to 155, and told the story of Tannhäuser's pilgrimage at rather greater length than was necessary, as Wagner himself recognised later. "The long instrumental introduction to the third act", he says in the brochure, "I wish to be performed in the re-modelled and abridged form in which it appears in the scores now supplied to the theatres. When first writing this piece I allowed the subject matter which I was describing to betray me into recitative-like phrases for the orchestra; but when we came to perform it I felt that while it made its meaning clear enough to me, because I could follow in my imagination the episodes with which it dealt, it could not be equally intelligible to others" — a point to which the composers of symphonic poems who are coy of revealing their "programme" to us might take note. "Nevertheless", continues Wagner, "I must insist on the *complete* performance of this introduction in its new form, as I deem it indispensable for establishing the mood necessary for the reception of what follows."

The most drastic change of all was made in the ending of the opera, which seems to have given Wagner some trouble from the beginning. In the original version of the final scene Venus did not appear in person; she was to be conceived by the spectator merely as a figment of the frenzied imagination of Tannhäuser, with the Hörselberg showing in a red light in the distance, and bells tolling from the Wartburg announcing the death of Elisabeth there. Evidently the spectators of 1845 did not grasp the full meaning of all this; yet, perversely enough, when Wagner improved it for them they resented being deprived of the dénouement to which they had grown accustomed. When originally writing this final scene, Wagner said in the brochure, his conception of it was just as clear to him inwardly as it became in the later version, but he had not been able to express it in terms of the theatre. "I had banked too completely on certain scenic effects, which, however, proved inadequate when put into actual practice: the mere glow from the Venusberg in the back distance could not produce the disquieting impression that was to lead up to the dénouement; still less could the far-away dirge and the lighting up of the windows of the Wartburg bring home instantly to the uninformed spectator the sense of the catastrophic stroke which Elisabeth's death brings into the action." The only way to make it all clear to the audience beyond any possibility of misunderstanding was by bringing Venus in person upon the stage to make a last effort to draw Tannhäuser into her coils again, while instead of Elisabeth's death being only suggested by the sights and sounds from the distant Wartburg, Tannhäuser was now to sink dead upon her actual bier. It seems probable, from certain fragments of indirect evidence, that Wagner made a tentative change of this kind as early as 1846. The work was played with its original ending, however, as far as the thirteenth performance, on the 7th February 1847, and with the new ending, for the first time, on the 1st August following.

It is unnecessary to set forth here all the details of the Paris recasting of the opera. The most important of the changes appear in the first act. Not only was the bacchanal extended and intensified but the colloquy between Venus and Tannhäuser was worked out on a larger scale. This landed Wagner in some difficulties later. He wrote the new music for this episode to a French version of his new German lines; consequently when he came later to prepare a definitive German edition of the score he had to translate the French text back again into German. This of necessity compelled him sometimes to replace the regular metrical scheme of his German text by a sort of free verse in order to make the words fit the melodic line. A single example will suffice to give the reader an idea of what happened. At one point he had written the following lines for Venus:

> *Da liegt er vor der Schwelle,*
> *wo einst ihm Freude floss:*
> *um Mitleid, nicht um Liebe,*
> *fleht bettelnd der Genoss.*

In the process of fitting German words to the melody that had been composed to the French text these lines lost their metre and their rhyme and became these:

> *Auf der Schwelle, sieh' da!*
> *ausgestreckt liegt er nun,*
> *dort wo Freude einst ihm geflossen!*
> *Um Mitleid fleht er bettelnd,*
> *nicht um Liebe.*

It is not to be wondered at that occasionally the new words fall awkwardly from the tongue.

Other changes from the text of 1845 to that of 1861 have been indicated in the foregoing analysis of the opera.

Lohengrin

PRINCIPAL CHARACTERS

LOHENGRIN	*Tenor*
ELSA OF BRABANT	*Soprano*
FRIEDRICH VON TELRAMUND,	
A COUNT OF BRABANT	*Baritone*
ORTRUD, HIS WIFE	*Soprano*
HENRY THE FOWLER, GERMAN KING	*Bass*
THE KING'S HERALD	*Bass*

Time and place of the action: Antwerp, first half of the 10th century.

1

WAGNER has told us how, during a holiday and "cure" in Marienbad in the summer of 1845, the subjects of *Lohengrin* and *The Mastersingers* engrossed him almost simultaneously. He had been sadly over-worked in Dresden, and his doctor had ordered him a complete rest. To this end he had taken with him, by way of light reading, the poems of Wolfram von Eschenbach and the old anonymous German epic of *Lohengrin*. But as he pored over these in the neighbouring woods, he says, "an ever-increasing excitement" took possession of him. Memories revived in him of the Paris days when he had read an article by the Königsberg Professor Lucas on the Lohengrin epic. "Thus", he said in his account of that Paris period, "a whole new world opened out before me, and though I could not find then and there the form in which to cast this *Lohengrin*, yet the image of it persisted undimmed within me." In Marienbad, as a result of his making acquaintance with the epic at first-hand, "there suddenly sprang up before my eyes a

Lohengrin complete in every detail of dramatic form: in particular the saga of the swan, which forms so significant a feature of the whole complex of myths with which my studies had familiarised me, exercised an enormous fascination on my imagination."

Remembering his doctor's injunction not to do any writing during his "cure" he fought hard at first against this fascination, and tried to drive Lohengrin out of his mind by thinking of Hans Sachs and the Mastersingers of Nuremberg, about whom he had been reading in Gervinus's *History of German National Poetry*. The result was that the whole ground-plan of an opera on the subject of the Mastersingers at once took shape within him. As it was a comedy theme, he says, and therefore not likely to tear his exhausted nerves to tatters, he thought he could commit the plan to paper without really disobeying the doctor's orders; he hoped, indeed, that it would drive out the desire to set to work at *Lohengrin*. But in this he was mistaken: no sooner had his mind got into full working order again under the influence of the Nuremberg subject than that of Lohengrin clamoured more and more insistently for realisation. A similar thing was to happen to him more than once in later life; when the mighty dynamo of his imagination got really to work on one theme the sheer energy of it would force to the forefront some other subject which until then had been only hovering about in the hinterland of his consciousness. Getting into his bath at Marienbad at noon one day, he tells us, "I was suddenly overcome by so powerful a longing to commit *Lohengrin* to paper that, unable to stay in the bath the regulation hour, I jumped out impatiently after the first few minutes, and, hardly giving myself time to dress, ran back like a madman to my lodging to write out what was pressing so heavily on my mind. This went on for several days, until I had set down the detailed stage plan for a *Lohengrin*." It is not to be wondered at that his doctor gave him up as hopeless, the sort of man on whom a water-cure was wasted: Wagner was now so excited that he sometimes spent the night wandering about instead of sleeping.

Back in Dresden again in August, his time during the next few months was fully taken up with his duties at the theatre and the rehearsing of *Tannhäuser*, the first performance of which took place on the 19th October 1845. With that off his hands he could settle down in good earnest to turning his Marienbad Prose

Sketch for *Lohengrin* into verse. This first form of the poem, the existence of which was unknown to the world in general until 1912, when the original manuscript came into a Berlin auction sale, he at once read to some of his Dresden friends. It met with their general approval, though Schumann was unable to see how the plan could be carried out musically, there being no provision for the usual operatic "numbers"; and Wagner found an impish delight in reading detached portions of it to him as if they were arias and cavatinas, whereupon Schumann smilingly declared himself satisfied.

2

The preliminary Prose Sketch, which bears the end-date "Marienbad, 3 August 1845", runs to nearly thirty pages of print.[1] In most essentials it corresponds to the present poem. When Wagner came to cast it into verse he of course kept a more observant eye on the stage picture as it would work out in an actual production; consequently we find him here and there expanding a detail or making some little change or other to throw it into higher relief. The musician in him also took a larger part in the planning now, providing opportunities at this point or that not only for emotional elaboration or intensification but for a deeper psychological probing of character.

For instance, in the Prose Sketch Telramund, after his account of Elsa's alleged murder of her brother Gottfried, tells the assembly that she is a "haughty visionary" who had behaved high-handedly towards him, her rightful wooer, as soon as she had disposed of Gottfried; she now saw the way clear to making herself the mistress of Brabant and marrying some secret lover. When Elsa is called upon by the King to meet the charges against her she merely replies that she is innocent and looks to some one whom she does not know and cannot name to come forward as her defender. The trumpets are sounded, and soon there comes into sight a swan-drawn boat with a knight in silver armour in it, leaning on his sword, helm on head, shield on arm, a horn hanging at his side. Both the dramatist and the musician in Wagner saw later how all this could be made more effective in the theatre

---

[1] It was published in full, for the first time, in the Bayreuth *Festspielführer* for 1936.

107

than it had been in the Prose Sketch. So in the poem we are not merely *told* by Telramund that "traumselig ist die eitle Magd, die meine Hand voll Hochmuth von sich stiess" ("Given over to ecstatic dreaming is the vain maid who so arrogantly rejected my hand"); we now actually *see* her, at her first appearance on the stage, in one of her semi-trances. "Speak, Elsa", says the King; "what have you to confide to me?", whereupon Elsa, "gazing fixedly and tranquilly before her, as if transfigured", describes, more to herself than to the others, how once, during her dark and lonely days of prayer, she had fallen into a trance in which she saw a knight approaching her who seemed the very symbol of purity, a golden horn at his belt, leaning upon his sword. This new handling of the situation served a triple purpose: it allowed for the insertion, in what before and after is only sober narrative, of the lovely monologue of Elsa ("Einsam in trüben Tagen"), it *shows* her, before them all, as a visionary, instead of her merely being *described* as one by Telramund, and, best of all, it added tenfold to the dramatic force of the later appearance of Lohengrin at the bend of the river — the King and the nobles can have no doubt now of her innocence and her supernatural protection, for here, in the flesh, is the very knight she had seen in her trance, the deliverer sent to her from heaven, garbed and accoutred exactly as she had described him.

3

In the Prose Sketch the first act ends thus, after Lohengrin has spared the life of the defeated Telramund: "Outburst of jubilation on all sides. Lohengrin is enthusiastically praised; Elsa falls on his breast in ecstasy; the King[1] blesses her. Despair of Friedrich and Ortrude." That Wagner already had his doubts about the effectiveness of this ending is shown by two interrogative jottings in the margin of the Sketch: "??Friedrich and Ortrude pronounced to have forfeited honour and banished: the King wants to invest Lohengrin with the kingdom of Brabant; he declines it,

[1] In the Sketch he figures as "the Emperor". No doubt some one in Dresden pointed out to Wagner that this was historically inaccurate, Henry the Fowler never having formally assumed that title; so in the poem he is given his proper rank of "German King". Elsa, by the way, appears in the Sketch as Elsam, Ortrud as Ortrude, and Telramund as Count Friedrich von Telramunt.

declaring that he wishes to be called merely Brabant's protector??". Wagner must soon have realised that all this would have lowered the emotional tension to the verge of anti-climax: the right ending was the one adopted later in the poem — a great ensemble of jubilation, flecked here and there by the despair of Telramund and the fury of the indomitable Ortrud.

We see the same keen sense of the stage at work in some portions of the second act, the same unerring perception of the best moment at which to bring in a particular stroke. The scene, for example, in which Ortrud tries to instil the poison of doubt into Elsa's mind is handled far more subtly in the poem than in the Sketch. In the latter we are shown the processes of Ortrud's plot-spinning in too great detail. Professing gratitude for Elsa's kindly treatment of her after her downfall, she throws out a hint of how she may be able to repay her; " 'she has been endowed with a peculiar gift of seeing more than ordinary mortals do; perhaps she may warn Elsam to be on her guard and not trust too blindly to her good fortune'. *Elsam:* 'What mean you by that?' Ortrude tries, by means of vague suggestions, to arouse doubts in her regarding the stranger: may she never regret having given him her trust, etc. Elsam counters with the expression of unconditioned confidence in him whom God has sent to her; his prohibition [with regard to her asking who he is and whence he came] is dear to her; never will she disobey it. *Ortrude:* 'O fortunate one, so will you never experience what may seem to you evil; may he reward you with the same trust, and never leave you in the same incomprehensible fashion in which he came'. Elsam, after a momentary shudder, quickly repeats her assurance of rapturous confidence. Ortrude checks herself and now takes the line of flattery, praise of her goodness, etc. Elsam invites her in; she will give her splendid garments, and they will go to Mass together, where Elsam will await the bridegroom to whom she is to be joined for ever. *Ortrude:* [to herself] 'Perhaps I can work upon her better through her pride' ". Whereupon the two go into the kemenate.[1]

All this, as Wagner must have seen when he came closer down to the problem of the actual staging, is not only too elaborate in itself but anticipates too much the dramatic later scene at the minster, in which Telramund tries to stir up general suspicion

---

[1] The women's quarters in the palace.

against Lohengrin. So in the poem he cuts the scene between Ortrud and Elsa down to its barest essentials. Ortrud now merely throws out a vague suggestion that she may be able, by her gift of second sight, to preserve Elsa from some future evil — may not this Lohengrin leave her by the operation of the same magic as had brought him to her? That is all. Elsa answers her in kindly wise, hoping that Ortrud too will one day find such happiness as hers; and the further workings of Ortrud's mind are sufficiently revealed in an aside of hers that accompanies the quiet raptures of Elsa:

> *Ha! dieser Stolz, er soll mich lehren,*
> *wie ich bekämpfe ihre Treu':*
> *gen ihn will ich die Waffen kehren,*
> *durch ihren Hochmut werd' ihr Reu'!*

("Ha! From this pride of hers will I learn how to break down her faith: against it I will turn my weapons, and her own arrogance will be her undoing").

4

In the third scene of the second act Wagner's riper judgment dictated the elision of an episode which, in the Prose Sketch, smacks too much of conventional opera. There the Herald, after having announced (as in the present opera) the degradation and outlawry of Telramund and the wedding of Lohengrin and Elsa, had launched out into a description of the coming festivities and an enumeration of the benefits that will come to Brabant through its new ruler — "Blessings and peace will come upon the land. Every home shall know security; the fields will bear richly, so that all the poor can dedicate themselves to the King for resistance to the Huns; on the morrow, the day of the wedding, all shall be armed for the march. The people express their delight, and praise Lohengrin's coming and the blessings to be expected from his rule: this hope for happiness under the saviour who has come to them from afar assumes an exalted form; they see in him the wonder-worker, sent to them to create a heaven on earth for Brabant. The infirm and the blind are brought in, begging to be healed by him on his way to the church." All this, which would have been well enough in a Meyerbeer opera or in *Rienzi*, would have been out of place in *Lohengrin*, coming as it would at the point when the psychological tragedy inherent in the situation was just about to develop to its climax. By 1845 Wagner had travelled too far as a dramatist to revert to machine-made operatic conventions of this sort. So when he came to write his poem he dealt ruthlessly with this section of the Sketch, compressing it all into a few lines for the Herald and an answering cry of jubilation from the male chorus; and the action moves straight on to the meeting of Telramund and the four Brabantine knights who are not ill-disposed towards him in his disgrace.

Towards the end of the second act, at the point where Lohengrin, turning with an expression of confidence to Elsa, is dismayed to read in her face that Telramund and Ortrud have instilled something of their poison into her, Wagner has written in the margin of his Sketch "adagio" — a clear sign that even when he was engaged on the first draft of the scenario he saw it all in terms not only of stage action but of music. (Actually, in the opera, the tempo becomes andante moderato, after two or three pages of presto, at the point in question). And at the very end of the act we see once more how his imagination must have been constantly playing upon his material, moulding it, improving it, making every detail co-operate to the one great dramatic end. The final lines of the second act run thus in the Sketch: *"Lohengrin:* 'Hail, Elsam! Now let us go before God's altar!' All doubt is suddenly dissipated; with renewed enthusiasm they all cry, 'He is a knight of God!' The procession moves towards the church." But in the poem we have the touch which the reader will remember is so effective on the stage. The directions now run: "To the solemn sound of bells the King ascends the steps of the minster, Lohengrin on his left hand, Elsa on his right. As she reaches the top step her gaze falls on Ortrud below, who stretches out her hand to her threateningly; horrified, Elsa turns away and anxiously presses close to Lohengrin. He leads her into the minster as the curtain falls." [1]

[1] In the score of the opera the sense is the same as in the separate editions of the poem, but the wording is different: "Here the King and the bridal pair have reached the highest step of the minster; Elsa, deeply moved, turns to Lohengrin, who takes her in his arms. Still in his embrace, she looks timidly and anxiously down the steps to the right and perceives Ortrud, who raises her arm against her as if in triumph. Elsa averts her face in terror."

As regards both the text and the stage directions Wagner's scores often

5

In the third act Wagner made several changes with a view to tightening up the action. The more important of these are in the final scene. The reader will be acquainted with what is known in the concert room as "Lohengrin's Narration", in which the hero tells the King and the others of Monsalvat and his father Parzival and the brotherhood of the Grail. In the Prose Sketch he had made Lohengrin continue with a long account of how news had come to the brotherhood that a maiden was in distress; how they saw a swan approaching down the stream, drawing a boat by a golden chain; how, after Parzival had consulted the Grail for guidance, they learned that the swan was a human being, the victim of an enchantment, who would remain with them for a year; and how Lohengrin was sent out in the boat, with the Grail's blessing, to champion distressed innocence. Here Wagner was following closely the old epic of *Lohengrin*. But drama cannot indulge itself in the leisurely descriptions of epic; and so not a word of all this appears in the poem of the opera. But Wagner had not only worked it out in detail in the original version of the poem but actually set it all to music. On the 2nd July 1850, however, we find him writing to Liszt, who was making preparations for the first performance of the work in Weimar, "Give my opera as it is, without cuts! Just one cut I myself prescribe: I want you to take

---

differ considerably from the poem as he printed it later in his Collected Works. The discrepancies, especially in the case of *The Mastersingers*, run into hundreds; and the question has frequently been debated which of the two versions should be taken as the definitive one. Do the variants in the scores represent the composer's second thoughts which override the first ones? If so, why, when he published the poems later in the Collected Edition, did he print these in their earlier form? The subject has been discussed at great length during the last forty years or so, with a copious quotation of instances and a vast amount of insistence on the superior claims of this reading or that. Ever and anon there goes up the cry for a " definitive edition " of the poems and the scores, to be achieved by the co-operation of a committee of experts. But the experts are in irreconcilable disagreement with each other on almost every point. The problem bristles with difficulties of all kinds, and, it is safe to say, will for ever remain insoluble. As it is, the text and the stage directions as they stand in the scores need to be constantly studied in connection with those of the poem in its "literary" form.

out the second part of Lohengrin's Narration in the big final scene of the third act. After Lohengrin's words, 'Sein Ritter ich, bin Lohengrin genannt' ['Its knight am I, and Lohengrin my name'] fifty-six bars are to be omitted, down to 'Wo ihr mit Gott mich alle landen saht' ['Where all of you saw me land in God's name']. I have many times performed the whole work to myself, and I am now convinced that this second section of the Narration can have only a chilling effect. The passage must also be omitted from the text-books."

He had already effected a similar piece of compression, to the decided benefit of the work, at the point immediately after the solo in the last act in which Lohengrin hands his sword, horn and ring to Elsa, bidding her give them to her brother if he returns. In the Sketch this had been followed by a long monologue for Ortrud, in which she vaunts her triumph over Elsa, for now that her rescuer is returning to Monsalvat her brother, transformed into a swan, can never shake off the enchantment Ortrud has laid on him. In the poem all this is compressed into a few lines. Then comes an episode that aptly illustrates a fact that has often to be borne in mind when we are listening to a performance of a Wagner opera; in the final process of alteration or compression he has omitted, or touched upon too lightly, some little point or other that only becomes fully clear to us after we have read his first Sketch. In the final version, after Ortrud's last jubilant cry of "Erfahrt, wie sich die Götter rächen, von deren Huld ihr euch gewandt!" ["Learn from this how the gods from whose protection ye have turned avenge themselves"], we have the stage direction, "Lohengrin, who has reached the bank, has heard what Ortrud says. He now sinks on his knees in silent prayer. The eyes of all are riveted on him in tense expectation. Suddenly he perceives a white dove hovering over the boat; with a look of gratitude he springs up and loosens the Swan's chain, whereupon it immediately sinks; in its place appears a beautiful youth garbed in gleaming silver — Gottfried — whom Lohengrin lifts to the bank." [1] To understand what was the nature of this silent prayer of Lohen-

[1] There are a few trifling differences between the stage direction in the poem and that in the score. For greater clearness sake I have combined the two.

grin we have to turn to the Sketch, where we read: "Lohengrin kneels on the shore. 'Give me a sign, eternal God, that shameless evil shall not mock at Thee! A sign of propitiation let me have from Thee that I may lay as balsam upon the wound dealt to the purest of beings by the sin of doubt. O Lord my God, hear me in my humility' . . . Here his voice sinks to so soft a whisper that it is hardly audible. Again he prays silently. Intense concentration [on the part of the beholders]." It is out of love for Elsa, then, to spare her the bitterest consequences of her sin of doubt, that, in the opera, he "silently" prays for a sign from heaven; and the spectator should bear this in mind as he watches the action.

Then comes a very curious feature of the Sketch. In the opera, after his prayer Lohengrin calls out, "Behold the Duke of Brabant, who shall be your leader", and then leaps into the boat, which is led away by the Swan. But in the Sketch we find this: "A soft melody is heard, coming from the Swan:

> *Leb wohl, du wilde Wasserfluth,*
> *die mich so weit getragen hat;*
> *leb wohl, du Welle blank und rein,*
> *durch die mein weiss Gefieder glitt:*
> *am Ufer harrt mein Schwesterlein,*
> *das soll von mir getrostet sein.*

['Farewell, wild flood that has carried me so far. Farewell, pure bright waves over which my white feathers have glided. On the shore my sister awaits me; by me she shall be consoled']. A white dove suddenly hovers over the boat", etc.

Wagner not only cast this episode into verse at the very time when he was writing the Prose Sketch but set it to music later. But in the Composition Sketch the page in question bears the following note in his handwriting: "For reasons of dramatic economy I could not make use of this song of the Swan in my *Lohengrin* . . ." This jotting was evidently the draft of an inscription to his friend Frau Lydia Steche, into whose album he copied the discarded words and music of the song in August 1853. There can be no question that he was right in deleting this episode from his score; it could only have relaxed the dramatic tension just as it was mounting to its climax.

6

Though few of those connected with an ordinary performance of *Lohengrin* — spectators, conductor, singers, producer and so on — appear to be aware of it, the opera is rather more than the story of a virtuous first soprano, a noble tenor, a wicked second soprano, and a baritone of good intentions but easily led astray by his wife. To the average performer and opera-goer the King, the nobles and all the rest of the ensemble are merely lay figures, theatrical devices for padding out the drama in the moments when the principal characters are not in action, pretexts for a little solo or two and a big chorus now and then, especially at the end of an act — all in the accredited style of opera construction. Wagner's background to the Lohengrin-Elsa story, however, is not simply so much operatic machinery. It is historical, and the interest of the action is increased if this is realised by the producer and borne in mind by the audience.

Henry I of Saxony (Henry the Fowler) reigned from 919 to 936. He was an energetic upholder of German rights and a fighter for German unity, features that commend him to the affections of the Germans of our own epoch. He set his face against the pretensions of the Roman Church to interfere in German politics, refused to accept his crown from the hands of the Archbishop of Mainz, and reserved to himself the right of appointing bishops. Saxony at that time was the most considerable of the German states. By wise rule and power of arms he made his own duchy internally strong, while externally he fought to save Germany from being overrun by alien hordes, in particular the Hungarians, who at that time were a formidable military power. Saxony was a relatively new state, based largely on the village community. Henry persuaded his people to aggregate into towns, and then to fortify them; and to win time for the realisation of these and other plans, such as the building of a number of strongholds, he concluded a nine years' truce with the Hungarians in 924, at the cost of an annual tribute. Then he brought in a new system of conscription for national defence and trained his men in the latest developments of the art of war; so that when the truce expired in 933 he was able to face the dreaded Hungarians on equal terms and defeat them, thus saving the German lands from the eastern menace of that period. Secure on this frontier, Henry now turned his attention to the west, extending his rule over the territories round and beyond the mouth of the Elbe. He was, in fact, not a king of opera but a very important historical person; though Wagner was incorrect in describing him, in his Prose Sketch, as the Kaiser, he was given the unofficial title of "Pater Patriae et Imperator Romanorum", and in point of fact he was "German Emperor" in everything but name.

In the opening scene of the opera we see him in Brabant; the pact with the Hungarians is nearing its end, war is imminent, and Henry has come to Antwerp to try to persuade the Brabant nobles and people, in their own interest, to take up arms with him against the eastern peril. They receive him cautiously; it is only after Lohengrin has appeared miraculously among them and been accepted as their protector that they range themselves enthusiastically on the side of the Saxon king. Wagner gives us in the third scene of his second act a hint of this holding back, a hint which always passes unnoticed by the spectator who is not thoroughly familiar with the text. After the Herald's proclamation of the ban upon Telramund and the appointment of the Knight of the Swan as Protector of Brabant, four nobles detach themselves from the jubilant crowd and discuss the new régime furtively and without enthusiasm. "You hear?" says one of them; "he [the King] means to take us outside our own borders." "To march against an enemy", says the second, "who has never yet threatened us!" "So bold a venture may not turn out well for him", says the third; and the fourth, "But who can hold out against him if he orders us to march?" Telramund overhears them and succeeds in working upon them; these, indeed, are the four disaffected nobles who make the attempt upon Lohengrin's life in the third act. This little episode, which occupies only some eleven bars, is often omitted in performance. This is typical of the measure of understanding the average modern producer has of the drama of the Wagnerian work he is supposed to be producing.

7

The antithesis of the Saxon and the Brabantine worlds, then, is a dramatic point that should be made as clear as possible to the spectator. Apparently this was never properly done, or perhaps even attempted, until the Bayreuth performances of 1894, which set the model, in many ways, for the impressive production of 1936. In the first and the final scene of the opera there should be the clearest distinction to the eye between the costumes and the weapons of the Saxons and those of the Brabantines. One need not press the point too far; perhaps some of the historical niceties of the 1894 production would have escaped the notice of all but specialists in the manners and costumes of the tenth century. But that a visible differentiation shall be made, and perceived by the spectator throughout the opera, is essential to a real understanding of the milieu of the drama. The importance which Wagner himself attached to this matter is shown in various little ways.

In the final scene the King, the nobles and the people are assembled once more in the same setting as that of the opening of the first act. Among the stage directions for the final scene we find this: "Gradually, from various quarters, the Brabantine Heerbann [1] pours upon the stage. Each section is headed by a Count, whose banner-bearer plants his standard in the ground, about which the others gather; children carry the shield and spear of the Count; servitors lead the chargers aside. When the Brabantines have all entered, King Henry comes in from the left with his Heerbann; all are in full war-equipment." These are the directions in the poem. In the score they read thus: "A Count enters with his adherents, dismounts, and gives his horse to a servitor; two noble youths carry his shield and spear. He plants his standard, round which his adherents take up their positions." This procedure is repeated several times while the martial music goes on, until finally the King enters with his Saxon troops. These earlier arrivals are in fact the Brabantines who, after the triumphal advent of Lohengrin, have responded to the King's call to arms: one significant sentence in the stage directions as given in the score runs thus: "The Counts and nobles greet each other, examine and praise their weapons, and so forth". The intention of it all is to make it clear to the spectator that the Brabantines have at last come in on the Saxon side. But Wagner's fidelity to history does not end here. The horses which the Brabantines bring with them are not merely there for stage effect: they are meant to give a touch of real history to the action. The Hungarians had been

---

[1] The "arrière-ban", or levy.

formidable by virtue of their light cavalry; Henry had defeated them, in the last trial of strength between them, by the heavy cavalry he had trained during the nine years' truce.

Should there be any doubt in the reader's mind whether Wagner attached so much importance as this to the historical point, he has only to look at a letter from the composer to Hans von Bülow of June 1867. On the 16th of that month there had been a grand new production of *Lohengrin* in Munich, under Bülow, by command of King Ludwig. The work was to be given exactly as Wagner had planned it. On the 27th we find him writing to Bülow: "I hear, incidentally, that his Majesty has given orders that horses are not to appear in the third act. You are acquainted with my reasons for insisting on these in a gathering entirely of mounted men. I should have desired these horses to be caparisoned in conformity with the manner of the period. Since not only has there been no royal command to that effect but the horses are to be cut out altogether, I now request you to omit also the whole of the music that accompanies this gathering, for now it ceases to have any meaning; and as the royal command was that the score should be given complete, this omission must in duty bound be notified to his Majesty." He was prepared, then, to face the risk of offending the King by omitting the long orchestral introduction to the final episode of the opera if the scene of the Heerbann were not staged as he had originally planned it — with horses, or at least with a suggestion of them as part and parcel of the Brabantine contribution to Henry's army. So important did it appear to him that the spectator should grasp the significance of the contemporary political background of the story he was telling!

8

The legend of Lohengrin and the Swan has a long and interesting history, but as most of it has no bearing on Wagner's opera we need not trace the evolution of it in detail here. The essential points are these. From time immemorial there had existed stories of heroes who came to the aid of virtuous maidens in distress, stories of mysterious swans coming from afar, stories of children who had been transformed by magic into swans, stories of knights whose device was a swan, stories of children or heroes or gods who drift to some land or other in a boat (sometimes, but not necessarily, drawn by a swan), and so on. Episodes from all these stories gradually coalesced, and, as the final stage in the process, some time in the twelfth century the figure of a Swan-Knight was worked into the legend of the Grail. We first find this done in the concluding pages of Wolfram von Eschenbach's epic *Parzival*, which dates from about the beginning of the thirteenth century; [1] but there are grounds for conjecturing that this particular coalescence may have been effected in the lost poem on the Parzival subject which Wolfram alleges to have been the source of his own.

In the final section of Wolfram's poem we see Parzival, now the custodian of the Grail, appointing his son Kardeiss to rule over his territory of Brobarz, while he himself retires with his other son, Loherangrin, to Monsalvat.[2] Loherangrin "is chosen to serve the Grail", Parzival tells the boy's mother Kondwiramuir; "to it he shall be dedicated". One day there comes to Monsalvat news of a princess of Brabant, pure and unworldly, who had many kingly and knightly wooers, and was blamed by her people for not choosing one of them for consort and ruler of the land. At last she called them together and declared that she would give her hand only to one sent to her by God. Such a one, the brave, handsome, spotless young Loherangrin, comes to her from Monsalvat; a swan bears him across the waters to Antwerp in a boat. At his first meeting with the princess he had told her, before them all, that he would have to leave her if ever she sought to learn who he is and whence he came, a condition which she accepted. They had many fair children, and for years he ruled the land wisely and defended it against its enemies. But one day the princess asked the fatal question, whereupon the swan appeared again, and Loherangrin, in great distress, departed as he had come, leaving with her a horn, a ring and a sword. The whole story occupies no more than a few score lines of the *Parzival* epic; and Wolfram neither gives the Brabant princess a name nor associates her in any way with a brother who had been laid under an enchantment. Loherangrin goes to her aid simply in accordance with the Grail's

[1] The epic will be discussed in the chapter on *Parsifal*.
[2] The name Loherangrin (elsewhere Lorangrime, Lohengârin, etc.) seems to have been taken from a French epic: "Loherens Garin" signifies Garin of Lorraine (Lothringen).

rule of service, and when she sins against the divine nature of the Grail by bringing its chosen representative down to common earth through her question, his mission is at an end and he must leave her.

The later adventures of Loherangrin are set forth in another poem, *Der jüngere Titurel,* which was formerly attributed to Wolfram von Eschenbach, but is now credited to one Albert von Schaffenburg. In this poem, Loherangrin goes to Lyzaborie (Luxemburg?) and marries one Belaye, who loves him so much that she cannot endure separation from him. One of her maids tells her that she can secure his constancy by cutting off a morsel of his flesh and eating it. This the horrified Belaye cannot bring herself to do, so her parents, to whom the maidservant has slandered Loherangrin, plot to mutilate him for the purpose. One night he dreams of a thousand swords being brandished over him. He awakes and slays more than a hundred of his assailants. But they are too many for him; he is wounded in the left arm and dies; and Belaye too dies of grief for his loss.

9

Wagner must have been familiar with most of the twelfth and thirteenth century variants of the Lohengrin legend, for his poem is a skilful amalgam of incidents and motives from various quarters. We need consider here only two of the main sources, the Walloon-French epic of *Le Chevalier au Cygne,* belonging to the second half of the thirteenth century, and the German epic *Lohengrin,* which dates from about 1260 and the author of which is unknown. In the former, Oriant, king of the island of Lillefort, marries the beautiful Beatrix, who, during his absence, gives birth to a daughter and six sons: these the King's mother, the sorceress Matabrune, who hates Beatrix, sends by a servant into the forest to be murdered; and on the King's return she accuses Beatrix of having been unfaithful to him. The children, however, have not been killed but only abandoned. They are cared for by a hermit, who gives the eldest boy his own name, Helyas. The King, out hunting one day, finds these seven children, and on his return speaks of them to Matabrune, who, realising who they are, sends another of her men to make away with them. When he arrives, the young Helyas is absent with the hermit; pitying the others, the emissary merely takes away with him the silver chains they wear upon their necks, whereupon they change into swans and fly away. Matabrune now makes fresh charges against Beatrix, who is condemned to death by the King unless some champion comes forward to vouch for her innocence. In response to her prayers God sends the young Helyas to Lillefort, where he vanquishes the accuser put forward by Matabrune. (Before he leaves the forest the hermit predicts that from the line of Helyas shall spring Godfrey of Bouillon). Six swans alight on the water near the castle, and when Helyas puts round their necks the chains the servant had taken, five of them are transformed into King Oriant's children again; the sixth, however, Esmeré, whose chain had been melted down by the King's goldsmith and made into a cup, remains a swan.

One day Helyas sees a swan — his brother Esmeré — approaching the palace, drawing a boat; and he knows that this is a summons to him from heaven to depart with the swan in search of adventures. This he does after his father has given him a magic golden horn. Drawn by the swan he makes his way to Nimwegen, where, at the court of the Emperor Otto, the Count of Blancquebourc (Blankenbourg) is claiming the heritage of the Duchy of Bouillon, alleging that his brother, the previous Duke, has been poisoned by his Duchess, Clarisse. As usual, the issue is to be decided by combat. The swan and the boat appear in the river: Helyas champions the innocent Duchess's cause, weds her daughter Ydain, and becomes the ruler of Brabant; their daughter Ydain, we are solemnly assured, was the mother of the famous crusader Godfrey of Bouillon. It is not until seven years after the wedding of Helyas and Ydain that the latter asks the forbidden question about her husband's name and lineage; then the sorrowing Helyas gives her into the care of the Emperor and departs to Lillefort with the swan Esmeré, who is restored to human form again and baptized. After various strange adventures Helyas becomes a monk, is discovered by some of his vassals from Bouillon, and dies in his wife's arms. (It is conjectured that this association of the house of Bouillon with the Chevalier of the Swan was invented to fill up an awkward gap, due to a misalliance, in the pedigree of the Counts of Bouillon)

10

Comparatively little of this naive story, of course, could be of any use to Wagner: it will be observed, too, that in *Le Chevalier au Cygne* it is not the injured Duchess but her daughter whom the hero marries, there is no association of Helyas with Monsalvat, and the union of the pair lasts seven years. Wagner found material more to his purpose in the German epic *Lohengrin,* where the long story is supposed to be told by Wolfram von Eschenbach as his contribution to the routing of Klingsor at the Contest on the Wartburg. It was here that Wagner found the names of Elsa and Count Friedrich von Telramund, and the association of Lohengrin with King Henry the Fowler. In the German poem the dying Duke of Brabant has entrusted the guardianship of his kingdom and of his daughter Elsa to the brave and respected Telramund; but when she refuses his hand he claims the kingdom and appeals to the Emperor for judgment in his favour. Attached to Elsa's rosary is a little golden bell which she had taken from the leg of a lamed falcon that had alighted near the castle; and whenever she wept for grief this bell would ring. One day the sound of it came to the court of King Arthur at Monsalvat, and it rang without ceasing until the knights learned from a writing on the Grail that in Brabant there was a pure maiden in great distress, to whose aid the young and spotless Lohengrin must be sent. As he is about to mount his horse a wild swan appears, drawing a boat; and in this Lohengrin embarks, taking with him neither horse nor food. After some days he arrives at Antwerp, where the swan departs.

Lohengrin is received with great honour by Elsa and the people of Brabant, and after many festivities they go to Mainz, where, before the Emperor, Lohengrin vanquishes Telramund — who is condemned to execution — and marries Elsa, having first exacted from her a promise that she will never seek to know who he is and whence he came. They lived happily together for many years, during which Lohengrin fights with the Emperor against first the Hungarians, then the Saracens. The catastrophe comes at a great jousting at Cologne after the Emperor's return, in which Lohengrin defeats the Duke of Cleves and breaks his arm. Thirsting for revenge, the Duchess stirs up the people's suspicions with regard to this mysterious hero from afar: who is he?

whence comes he? is he of noble origin? The poison works in Elsa, who at last, disregarding Lohengrin's warnings, asks him the fatal question. Thereupon, before the Emperor and the court at Antwerp, he declares that he comes from Monsalvat, that his father Parzival is the custodian of the Grail, that his own name is Lohengrin, that he had been sent to Brabant by the Grail's command, taking with him a sword and horn given him by his father, and a ring, the gift of his mother, that Elsa has broken her promise not to question him about these things, and that now he must leave her for ever. The swan appears in the river: Lohengrin commends his wife and children and kingdom to the Emperor's care, steps into the boat, and is seen by them no more.

11

Here also, it will be seen, Wagner's mediaeval source supplied him with nothing more than the general outline and the raw material for a possible dramatic subject. He had to do a great deal in the way of selection, condensation and adaptation before the shapeless mass could take operatic form. In particular he had to create entirely the striking figure of Ortrud out of the faint hint afforded him by the character of the Duchess of Cleves in the German epic. Ortrud becomes the *fons et origo* of the ultimate disaster. Wagner makes her the antithesis of all that Elsa stands for — the woman incapable of love set over against the woman who is all love, the old Germanic paganism in implacable opposition to the new Christianity. Telramund, weak but not in himself evil, is only a pawn in the great game the masterful Ortrud is playing.

And there is one point that is not made entirely clear in the Wagnerian poem but should never be lost sight of by the spectator. Humourists have made delighted play with the notion of a woman simple enough to marry a man without knowing his name or antecedents and being coldly abandoned by him because in the end her curiosity gets the better of her discretion. But to look at the matter in that simple unimaginative way is to betray one's ignorance of the nature and the reason of the prohibition laid by Lohengrin upon Elsa. In Wolfram von Eschenbach's epic grief immeasurable had come upon the young Parzival and upon the land because the untutored boy, on his first entry into the castle of the Grail, had failed to ask a simple question of the suffering Amfortas.[1] From that event has come a double reason for Lohengrin's silence about himself. In the first place, since that prime failure of Parzival the Grail brooks no questioning of those consecrated to its service. (Wagner has to pass that point by in silence because to have made it clear would have meant a great deal of explanation — the telling, indeed, of the whole previous story of Parzival and the Grail). In the second place, it is a condition of the Grail's service to the unhappy world of men that while its emissaries may descend to it for noble ends they shall not become part of it. They represent a spiritual order whose service and whose motives must be accepted with unquestioning faith.

The motive of trouble ensuing from the indiscreet asking for a name occurs frequently in ancient myths; for primitive humanity the name was part of the man or the thing, and to learn the one was to acquire a certain power over the other. But Wagner is not using the motive with any such primitive connotation as this. He himself has told us, in *A Communication to My Friends*, that he saw in the Lohengrin prohibition the counterpart of that in the story of Zeus and Semele. The god, for love of the mortal woman, had assumed human shape. But when, having realised that for all his love and hers she does not know him in his true being, Semele asks the god to reveal himself to her as he really is, Zeus knows, as Wagner puts it, that on the revelation of his true substance he must leave her; "he himself suffers from this knowledge, from the compulsion to destroy her the moment he complies with her desire", and when he shows himself to her in all the splendour of his godhead he signs not only his own death-warrant but hers. We need not follow Wagner in all his ingenious elucidations of the meaning of the myth and his psycho-analysis of love and woman as he conceived them to be: it is sufficient for us to have a better understanding of what Lohengrin's prohibition really means than those do who regard it as only a rather childish relic of a fairy tale.

12

As we have seen, Wagner completed the Prose Sketch for the opera in Marienbad on the 3rd August 1845, and set to work at

[1] For the meaning of this see the introduction to the chapter on *Parsifal*.

the poem in Dresden towards the end of October. The first draft of this (dated 27th November 1845), which is now in some private collection or other, has not yet been published in its entirety; but extracts from it, showing some of the variants between it and the final poem, were given in an article by Julius Kapp in *Die Musik* in 1912, at the time when the manuscript was offered for sale by auction in Berlin. It is clear that the poem in its first form followed precisely the scenario of the Prose Sketch, which was printed for the first time in 1936; and the main differences between Wagner's first conception of the subject and his final handling of it have been set forth in the preceding pages of the present chapter.

The manuscript of the Sketch supplies one more proof of the fact, vital to our understanding of Wagner, that even while drafting the first prose outline of an opera he was already seeing the situations and the characters in terms of music. On the margin of one of the pages of the manuscript we find the following musical jotting:

for an episode in the duet between Lohengrin and Elsa in the third act, which in the opera takes the shape shown in our example No. 46. It is a mistake to assume, as is generally done, that the sometimes crude form in which certain Wagnerian themes make their first appearance in some sketch or other indicates that this was a form that seemed to him adequate at the time, and that he gradually hammered it into a better shape later. The truth is that the first jotting was intended merely as a shorthand memorandum of the line and the harmony in general to be followed by the music in its final elaboration. In the present instance the A sharp in the first bar is clearly to fix a modulatory point; the theme was to begin in bar two as a return to the main key of E major after a hint of a modulation away from it. At the time the musical jotting was made not a line of the poem had been written; all that Wagner had before him in the Prose Sketch was an outline of Elsa's response to Lohengrin: "Elsam schildert ihm in entzückter Rührung das unaussprechliche Glück, das ihr durch ihn zu Theil geworden; wie sie vor Dank, vor gränzenloser Liebe vergehen möchte". ("Elsa, deeply moved, describes in ecstatic terms the happiness that has come to her through him, how she could die of gratitude, of the sense of boundless love"). In the poem this became:

> *Fühl' ich zu dir so süss mein Herz entbrennen,*
> *Athme ich Wonnen, die nur Gott verleiht.*

The musical idea, then, was in Wagner's mind, complete in rhythm and harmony, before the words — which we erroneously assume to have generated the music — were in being.

Wagner began his composition with the third act, the music of which was finished on the 5th March 1847. The first act was then taken in hand and finished on the 8th June; the second was completed on the 2nd August, the prelude to the opera being written on the 28th of that month. The orchestral score occupied him until the end of March 1848. The work was first produced in Weimar, under Liszt, on the 28th August 1850, with the following casting of the principal parts:

LOHENGRIN	Beck
ELSA	Aghte
ORTRUD	Fasztlinger
TELRAMUND	Feodor von Milde
KING HEINRICH	Höfer

Wagner, who had had to fly from Dresden in May 1849 because of his complicity in the insurrection in the Saxon capital, did not hear his work until the 15th May 1861, in Vienna.

13

The prelude to *Lohengrin* was the early Wagner's finest achievement of the kind both in expression and in form. While it is thematically related to some extent to the drama it is neither a mere string of melodies from the score nor an attempt, as in the

Flying Dutchman and *Tannhäuser* overtures, to tell the story of
the opera by the succession and interplay of leading motives. In
the *Lohengrin* prelude he works for the first time not on exterior
but interior lines, as it were. The sole subject of it is the mystic
Grail, the nature and being of it, its descent to the mundane
sphere, its gradual revelation of its spiritual glory, then its gradual
return to whence it had come. Wagner's own programmatic eluci-
dation of it cannot be bettered:

"Out of the clear blue ether of the sky there seems to condense
a wonderful yet at first hardly perceptible vision; and out of this
there gradually emerges, ever more and more clearly, an angel
host bearing in its midst the sacred Grail. As it approaches earth
it pours out exquisite odours, like streams of gold, ravishing the
senses of the beholder. The glory of the vision grows and grows
until it seems as if the rapture must be shattered and dispersed by
the very vehemence of its own expansion. The vision draws nearer,
and the climax is reached when at last the Grail is revealed in all
its glorious reality, radiating fiery beams and shaking the soul
with emotion. The beholder sinks on his knees in adoring self-
annihilation. The Grail pours out its light on him like a benedic-
tion and consecrates him to its service; then the flames gradually
die away, and the angel host soars up again to the ethereal heights
in tender joy, having made pure once more the hearts of men by
the sacred blessing of the Grail."

Some quiet reiterations of the chord of A major in upper strings,
flutes and oboes having raised us at the outset into the rarefied
upper air, the divided violins give out the theme of the Grail:

No. 1

the falling second shewn in bar two being more specifically related in the opera to the swan that is the material symbol of the
Grail's commission to Lohengrin to go to the aid of Elsa. The
Grail motive is continued for a further four or five bars along the
same lines:

As it gradually draws nearer to the world of men it repeats itself on another plane (this time in the key of E major) in the middle wood wind, with delicate violin embroideries. After a long slow descent it begins to ascend again in a variant of itself:

the stressed notes in the second and third bars of the quotation being of particular importance in the texture. Slowly the theme develops itself in solider harmonic masses and richer colours, always festooned with the same decorative figures, until, having touched the lowest point of its windings, it gathers itself up again for another great ascent, this time approaching the basic A major by way of D major, with the melody standing out in all the majesty of trumpets, trombones and tuba:

The actual climax comes at the opening of the fourth full bar of our quotation, where the kettledrums and cymbals strike in with arresting effect. This is the point at which we may visualise the Grail as revealing itself for a moment to the eyes of mortals in the blinding fulness of its spiritual splendour. Once more, as will be seen in the latter part of No. 4, it soars aloft into its own rarefied atmosphere; then, after a long downward sweep of the melody:

it fades away in the distance in the tenuous violin harmonies of the commencement.

The prelude is perfect in its fusion of musical theme and dramatic meaning, its harmonious design, and its choice of the moment for releasing its maximum of energy. The thunderous chord in No. 4 to which reference has been made above sets free all the forces that have been slowly accumulating inside the music from the first note of the prelude, and what follows is the natural ebb of the preceding flow. There is a law in certain species of musical design — not a law, of course, to which composers consciously conform but a procedure which they follow intuitively — that might be called the law of two-thirds, the time-period that follows the climax being to the time-period of the ascent to the climax numerically as one to two. The peak-point, of course, may be a trifle more or a trifle less on this side or that of the mathematical 2:1; a bar or two one way or the other makes no perceptible difference over a total time-stretch of several minutes.[1] In the *Lohengrin* prelude the pivotal point comes with almost mathematical exactitude. The total length of the prelude is 75 bars; the cli-

[1] More will be said on this subject of ascent-climax-descent in our analysis of the prelude to *Tristan*.

mactic chord comes in bar 54; at the slow pace of the music the time-relation of the two sections is as near as makes no matter 2:1.

14

With the rising of the curtain we necessarily sink for a time to a lower musical plane: Wagner now has to explain to us the events precedent to the opera that have brought the action to the point at which the drama opens, and this can only be done, working as he still is with the conventional opera apparatus of the period, by means of a pedestrian exposition in quasi-recitative.

The scene is a meadow on the banks of the Scheldt, near Antwerp. Under a judgment oak sits King Heinrich, flanked by Counts and nobles of the Saxon armed levy. Opposite these are Counts and nobles of Brabant, headed by Friedrich von Telramund, by whose side is his wife Ortrud. At a sign from the King's Herald four trumpeters blow a summons, after which the Herald explains to the Brabantines that the German King has come to parley with them on affairs of state. Heinrich tells them that his land and theirs are once more threatened by the Hungarian hordes. By force of arms he had been able to impose on them a nine years' truce, which he has used to strengthen the Saxon defences, building castles, fortifying towns, training men. The truce has expired, and once more the eastern hordes are clamouring for tribute. Now is the time to decide for good the age-old question — which is to rule, East or West? If each Germanic land does its duty now the menace can be met — a sentiment which is greeted by the Saxon group with a clashing of their weapons and a cry of "Arise for the honour of the German land!"

The King goes on to say that he had come to Antwerp to invite the Brabantines to a military concentration at Mainz, but to his sorrow he finds them disorganised and leaderless, one faction at feud with another. So now he calls on Friedrich von Telramund, whom he knows to be a brave and honourable knight, to explain the cause of this disunion. Telramund does so. It appears that when the late Duke of Brabant was dying he had appointed Telramund guardian of his daughter Elsa and his son Gottfried, and Friedrich had tended them with loyal care. But one day he learned that Elsa had gone into the forest with the boy and returned alone, feigning anxiety for news of him, the child, she had said, having strayed from her side and not been seen again. Search for him had been fruitless; and when Telramund questioned Elsa more closely her pallor and trembling betrayed the secret of her crime. Filled with loathing, he had renounced the right given him by her father to claim her hand and had chosen for wife Ortrud, daughter of the prince of Friesland. Advancing a few steps, to the accompaniment of a figure in striding octaves of a type which Wagner will handle much better when he comes to portray his Wotan:

No. 6

Telramund solemnly accuses Elsa of the murder of her brother and claims for himself the kingdom of Brabant, he being nearest of kin to the late Duke, and Ortrud a descendant of the one-time rulers of Friesland.

15

The bystanders comment on the story in awestruck tones. The King asks how Elsa could have brought herself to the commission of such a crime; and Telramund explains that she is a moonstruck visionary, always lost in dreams, and moreover possessed by a guilty passion for some man or other whom she hopes to take openly for lover once the kingdom has passed into her hands. The King, with a prayer to heaven for guidance, orders her to be brought before him for trial: he constitutes the place a court of justice by hanging his shield on the oak-tree, not to be removed thence until he has pronounced judgment at once stern and merciful. The warriors all draw their swords, the Saxons thrusting theirs into the ground, the Brabantines laying theirs flat on the earth in front of them. Then the Herald summons Elsa to appear.

For a little time after her entry on the scene she remains with her attendant ladies in the background; then she advances slowly and timidly, accompanied by a plaintive phrase in oboe and cor anglais:

No. 7

which is completed in this fashion:

No. 8

as the bystanders comment sympathetically on the innocence of her demeanour. The King asks her if she is Elsa of Brabant, and she silently bows her head, still to the strains of No. 7 and No. 8, which continue to accompany her as she signifies, without speaking, in reply to the King's further questions, that she is aware of the accusation brought against her but will make no answer to it. When at last she breaks her long silence it is simply to murmur to herself, as if her thoughts were far away, "My hapless brother!" Gently the King exhorts her to trust him with her story; and she tells them all:

No. 9

how one day, lost in sorrowful dreams, she had poured out her soul to God in a lament that floated high in the air:

No. 10

then it had drifted away and she had sunk into a sweet sleep.

The King tries gently to recall her to a sense of her present position, but she does not hear him. Her expression changes from one of dreamy ecstasy to the fanatical exaltation of the visionary, the Grail theme vibrates softly in the upper air, and she tells the further story of her dream that day. She had seen a knight in splendid armour, who seemed purity incarnate, leaning on his sword, a golden horn at his side:

No. 11

He had come towards her and in courtly wise consoled her; he it is who shall be her defender now. This she sings ecstatically to the theme of the opening of No. 8, which now, however, takes a confident close in place of its former one of melancholy and frustration as she says, "This is the knight I choose: he shall fight for me":

No. 12

and once more she appears to lose herself in a blissful dream.

The King has been impressed by her mystical self-confidence, but Telramund passionately declares that he is not her dupe: has she not herself proved the truth of his accusation by this admission of a paramour? But he scorns to have his cause decided by any judgment but that of arms. He reminds the King of the gallant service he had rendered him in the war with the Danes: let him now grant him permission to vindicate his honour with his sword. God shall decide, says the King. Drawing his sword and thrusting it into the earth in front of him, to the accompaniment of an imperious figure in the heavy brass:

No. 13

he puts the formal questions to accuser and accused: "Wilt thou, Friedrich Count von Telramund, have thy cause tried in mortal combat before the throne of God? . . . Art thou, Elsa of Brabant, willing that thy cause shall be decided in combat?" Each returns a "Yes!", Telramund vehemently, Elsa quietly, without raising her eyes.

16

Telramund demands the name of her champion. The music of her vision is heard once more in the orchestra as she repeats firmly her assurance (No. 11) that the shining knight who had appeared to her then will fight for her now; and on this champion sent her from heaven she will bestow her hand and her kingdom.

At the command of the King the Herald advances with four trumpeters, who take up their stand at the four points of the compass of the central space and sound a summons; after which the Herald calls on whoever chooses to accept the challenge to fight on behalf of Elsa of Brabant to come forward. There is no answer. Elsa's air of tranquil confidence now changes to one of uneasy expectation, and we get a foretaste of the later Wagner of the *Ring* in a phrase that projects itself in the dark colour of the bass clarinet:

No. 14

Telramund taunts Elsa with her inability to produce her champion, whereupon she approaches the King timidly with a request that he shall be summoned again: "perhaps", says the dreamer innocently, "he dwells so far away that he has not heard."

The summons is repeated by the trumpeters and the Herald,

but again with no response — only a repetition of the uneasy No. 14 in the clarinet. Elsa falls on her knees and prays fervently to heaven to send her the rescuer it had promised her in her dream. The prayer is answered. As the tempo increases, No. 11, the motive of Lohengrin, is heard in the trumpets, softly, as if coming from afar. The bystanders nearest the river bank catch sight of a figure in a boat, drawn by a swan, in the further reaches of the stream. They draw the attention of the others to this wonder; and the excitement increases as the knight gradually becomes visible to them all and they comment eagerly on his beauty and the splendour of his armour. For a little while Lohengrin has been visible to the audience also; then we lose sight of him at a bend in the river, his slow approach being suggested to us only by the greater and greater excitement of the comments of the chorus, men and women, who have all rushed to the back of the scene for a better view of the unheard-of marvel. In the foreground only the King, Elsa, Friedrich and Ortrud remain: the King, from his raised place, looks down the river: Friedrich and Ortrud are rooted to the spot in amazement: Elsa stands motionless, thrilled by the cries of the bystanders, but not daring to look around. As the excitement piles up to a great climax in the orchestra Elsa's women fall on their knees with a cry of gratitude to heaven for its intervention on behalf of the innocent.

With No. 11 ringing out in the orchestra more commandingly than ever and the chorus hailing the hero sent by God, the boat reaches the river bank in the centre background. In it stands Lohengrin, in gleaming silver armour, helmet on head, shield on his back, a small golden horn hanging by his side, leaning on his sword. Elsa, who had turned round as the chorus sent up a great cry of thankfulness:

No. 15

gives a startled cry at this coming to reality of her vision. Telramund is too astonished to move; and even Ortrud, whose proud demeanour had shown that her courage had so far not deserted her, is perplexed and dismayed at the sight of the swan. The others all uncover their heads in awe.

As Lohengrin makes the first movement to leave the boat a tense silence falls on them all. Softly the violins, in their upper register, give out the theme of the Grail, and in an unaccompanied monologue he addresses the swan:

No. 16

thanking it for having brought him to his goal, and bidding it return, its task accomplished, to the serene sphere from which he and it had come. The tiny figure shown at A in our musical example No. 1 now takes the definite shape of a Swan motive in oboe and clarinet:

No. 17

as Lohengrin murmurs his farewell to his companion, on which his gaze lingers sadly and tenderly for a while as the swan turns the boat round and slowly swims away up the stream. The chorus, led by Elsa's women and some of the tenors, murmur admiration of this visitant from an unknown land:

No. 18

Wagner's marking for the ensemble is "as delicately as possible".

17

Meanwhile Lohengrin has left the bank and advanced slowly
and solemnly towards the King, to whom he makes his obeisance,
and to whose German cause he wishes success and eternal glory.
"It must be heaven that has sent thee here", replies King Heinrich. To the solemn strains of No. 1 and No. 3 the knight announces that he has come to do battle for a maiden accused of a
crime: then, turning to Elsa, he asks her if she will accept him as
her defender. His voice wakens her from the trance into which
she had fallen again; now she throws herself ecstatically at his
feet, hailing him as her rescuer and offering him herself and all
she has to bestow. The Grail music throbs in the air once more as he
asks if she will be his wife. She humbly consents. Then comes the
crucial motive of the drama: his next question is, if she and her
lands are to become his and he is never to leave her, will she make
him a solemn promise — never to ask him whence he came, or
what his name and race:

No. 19

Nie sollst du mich be-fra-gen, noch Wissens Sor-ge tra-gen, wo-

-her ich kam der Fahrt, noch wie mein Nam' und Art!

(This motive had been foreshadowed in an oath-taking chorus in
a work sketched by Wagner in 1837).

Softly, half unconsciously, she gives her word. He repeats the
all-important question with still greater urgency, and again, this
time with rapturous fervour, she assures him that the trust he is
placing in her will never be betrayed. He takes her to his breast
with a cry of "Elsa, I love thee!", and the chorus repeat the heart-
felt No. 18.

Lohengrin leads Elsa forward and gives her into the care of the
King; then, turning to the others, he declares that the prince of
Brabant is free of all guilt, and that Friedrich von Telramund has

sworn falsely. The nobles try to avert a conflict, but Telramund will not yield; whatever sorcery may have brought this stranger here, he says boldly, he does not fear his threats, for he himself has sworn truly. So the ring is set for the combat. Three Saxon nobles advance for Lohengrin, three Brabantines for Friedrich; they mark out a circle and define it by thrusting their spears in the ground. The Herald warns everyone against interference in the fight: the freeman who offends will pay for it with the loss of a hand, the serf with his head. Then, advancing to the centre with great solemnity, the King prays to heaven to look down and see that justice is done; and the concluding strain of his prayer:

No. 20

Des Rei - nen Arm gieb Hel - den - kraft, des Fal - schen Stär - ke sei er - schlafft:—

is taken up by the assembly and developed into an impressive ensemble. Elsa and Lohengrin commend their cause to God, to whom Telramund also appeals that his name may not be disgraced: the imperious Ortrud places her trust in her husband's strong arm.

18

The long chorus over, the six nobles take up their positions by the side of their spears, the other fighting men massing themselves around them. Elsa and her ladies are with the King under the oak-tree. The trumpets blow the battle summons; the King draws his sword from the earth and strikes three blows with it on his suspended shield; Lohengrin and Friedrich enter the lists; and the combat begins. The twenty bars that accompany it in the orchestra have for present-day ears all the naïveté of their epoch. The more practised Wagner of the later years would have somehow or other caught up this little episode in dumb show into the main stream of his music; in 1847 he could do nothing better than put No. 13 through some obvious repetitions and imitations. At

the seventeenth bar the Lohengrin theme (No. 11) rises in triumph as the knight of the Grail fells his adversary, and in the
twenty-first a downward plunge of the lower strings depicts Telramund's vain attempt to rise and his final collapse with Lohengrin's sword at his throat. The hero grants his enemy his life, however, bidding him devote it to repentance for his crime.

The King takes down his shield from the oak-tree and sheathes
his sword; the six orderers of the combat withdraw their spears
from the earth, and all press eagerly and joyously forward. Elsa
runs to Lohengrin, and with a great cry of gratitude:

No. 21

launches the jubilant finale; Wagner the musician is back in his
true element once more. Elsa surrenders her whole being to her
deliverer in the last soaring phrase of her glad cry to him:

No. 22

Out of these two melodies, and a third of similar contour but in
a contrasting key:

No. 23

plus the Lohengrin motive proper (No. 11), Wagner builds up an
ensemble that reaches its climax in a line thrown out in the highest relief by Elsa against a sequence of ascending chromatic harmonies:

No. 24

This was a favourite technique of Wagner's throughout his life for creating emotional tension by a prolonged conduct of a falling upper and a rising lower line, converging in closer and closer chromatics. (Our quotation, of course, shows only the skeleton structure of the passage).

Throughout the general jubilation Ortrud and Friedrich, could we hear them through the enveloping thunder of tone, would be found to be expressing their own sentiments about the situation. Telramund, still prostrate on the ground, laments his defeat and the shame on his honour, in which he sees the hand of God. Ortrud, whose gods are those of heathen mythology, asks herself and the universe wonderingly who this hero can be that has vanquished her husband and brought her plans crashing to the ground: but, now as always indomitable, she cannot bring herself to believe that the last blow has been struck and all her hopes destroyed.

At the end of the ensemble the proud No. 11 rings out once more as the younger warriors raise Lohengrin upon his shield and Elsa upon the King's, over which they have spread their mantles, and carry the pair off amid general rejoicing.

19

The second act, as we have seen, was the last of the three to be composed; and it has many touches that show Wagner to have been developing in musical-dramatic power all the while he was engaged on the opera. In the character of Ortrud in particular he has achieved a new kind of characterisation, in a vein that was to be opened out more fully later in the *Ring*. The second act, indeed, may be said to be mainly Ortrud's. She now comes into the forefront of the action: the determining dramatic threads pass into her masterful hands, and we see her shaping, half with purpose, half unwittingly, the ending of the drama she had set in motion before the opera began.

There is a foretaste of the *Ring* — of Alberich and Hagen as instruments of evil — in the orchestral prelude to the second act, which first of all projects across the scene the sinister personality of Ortrud in a long 'cello melody the rises and falls and syncopations of which combine to produce an impression of something evil uncoiling itself in the darkness:

No. 25

The slow development of this is twice interrupted by the motive of Lohengrin's warning (No. 19) in the cor anglais. Ortrud's mind is festering with Telramund's and her own defeat and hatred primarily of Elsa, secondarily of Lohengrin. The latter, she knows instinctively, she cannot harm directly. But he may be driven away, and Elsa brought to ruin, by sowing the seeds of doubt in her mind: somehow she must be brought to ask her deliverer the question she had promised not to ask on pain of losing him. How to accomplish this end is the subject of her scheming when the curtain rises for the second act.

It is now night. The scene is the citadel of Antwerp: at the back is the Pallas (the knights' quarters), on the right the minster, on the left the kemenate. Ortrud and Telramund, both meanly clad, are sitting on the minster steps, Friedrich sunk in gloomy thought,

Ortrud never taking her eyes off the windows of the Pallas, which are brightly lit. From inside there comes for a moment the sound of festal music, with which is linked a reminder of Elsa (No. 8); and a return of No. 25 in the orchestra shows the mind of Ortrud still at work on her evil plan.

At last Friedrich rises suddenly with a cry of "Bestir thyself, companion of my shame! The dawn of day must not find us here." Ortrud does not move. "I cannot go", she says; "I am bound here by a spell. From the sight and sound of our enemies' feasting I would distil a deadly poison that would put an end alike to their exultation and our shame." Then, in an outburst of grief and rage, Telramund reproaches her bitterly for having brought him to the present pass. "Unholy woman! what keeps me bound to thee? Why do I not leave thee and fly somewhere where my conscience may find rest again?" Through her he has lost honour and reputation; his sword is shattered, his escutcheon soiled, his ancient house disgraced. Shame is henceforth his sole portion, wherever he may go; would he had died in the fight! In a paroxysm of despair he flings himself on the ground.

There is another wave of festal music from the Pallas: then Ortrud speaks, still without moving. Why, she asks Friedrich with quiet scorn, has he lost faith in her? At this he breaks out afresh. Was it not she who, with her false witness, had induced him to make the charge against the innocent Elsa? Had she not assured him that from a window of their castle she had seen with her own eyes the maiden drown her brother in the pond? Had she not assured him that Radbod's ancient princely house would rule again in Brabant? Pouring these lies into his ears, had she not persuaded him to renounce Elsa's hand and take *her* to wife? And for his belief in her lies God has smitten him into the dust. Scornfully the pagan woman replies that his "God" is only his name for his own faintheartedness; and when he moves threateningly towards her she tells him that had he confronted the stranger as boldly as he does her, victory would have been his: for in face of anyone who knew how to meet him the knight would have been as feeble as a child. To Friedrich it appears that the more vulnerable his antagonist the more apparent it is that he had been aided by God. Give her the power, she rejoins, and she will prove to him how weak is this God that fought for his enemy.

Filled now with a strange fear of the sinister creature, Telramund would fain learn more. She points to the Pallas, the windows
of which are now quite dark, and, with No. 25 A stealing in in the
cor anglais, she bids him seat himself by her, and she will tell him
what her second sight reveals. More and more helpless in her
hands, he listens while she unfolds her plan for vengeance. The
stranger knight's strength is given him by magic; but it will desert
him if he is compelled to disclose who he is and whence he came.
"So that", ejaculates Friedrich, "was why he laid that ban on her!"
No one, continues Ortrud, can wrest his secret from him but Elsa,
so it is through her that they must work. Telramund is not to flee
the land but stay, and waken suspicion in Elsa by accusing the
knight of having obtained judgment in his favour by magic. If
this plan should fail, Ortrud has another. She is versed in black
arts; she knows that if one protected by magic loses only the
smallest limb the charm fails and his strength is at an end; had
Telramund so much as wounded a finger of him in the fight he
would have had him at his mercy.

Pride and rage combine to make him credulous: he had been
tricked and degraded by fraud, he cries. He will live now to
avenge his shame, retrieve his honour, and drag his rival down.
But if Ortrud should be again deceiving him let her beware! The
opening bars of No. 25 are heard again, this time threateningly in
trumpet and trombone, as she assures him that he shall yet taste
the sweets of vengeance; and together they call on the powers of
darkness to aid them:

No. 26

The duet, in which the voices are in octaves throughout, ends with
a warning to those lying in happy sleep in the citadel that calam-
ity awaits them:

No. 27

When the voices have ceased, two reiterations of a sinister phrase in the bass clarinet, followed by a quiet trombone chord, complete the dark picture. But instantly a new mood is established by a placid melody in the wood wind that looks forward to the wedding music at the end of this act. (See No. 38). Elsa, robed in white, appears on the balcony of the kemenate: Telramund and Ortrud, on the opposite side of the stage, maintain their positions on the minster steps. Elsa pours out her happiness in lyrical strains to the breezes of the night:

No. 28

those soft caressing breezes to which she had so often confided her pain, that had brought her rescuing hero to her, and that now cool her glowing cheek. Between the phrases of her song we hear the muttering of Ortrud and Friedrich: "she will live to rue the day", says the former venomously, "when her eyes again encounter mine!" Hastily she bids Friedrich withdraw for a while and leave the dreaming maid to her: the stranger knight shall be his concern later. So Telramund disappears in the shadows.

The calm atmosphere that has enveloped Elsa's monologue is suddenly disturbed by a minor harmony in oboe and stopped horns and a cry of "Elsa!" from Ortrud; and we have an unmistakeable touch of the later Wagner in the instantaneous suggestion, with this minimum of means, of Lohengrin's warning (No. 19):

No. 29

With a shudder at something eerie which she senses in the air Elsa asks who it is that is calling her name. Has she forgotten the voice, Ortrud asks her, of the hapless woman whom she has consigned to utmost misery? In hypocritical, insinuating tones she paints the quiet happiness of her life in days gone by:

No. 30

How had she ever injured Elsa? Her life had been one of mourning for the vanished glory of her ancient line: how could Elsa envy her the good fortune of having become the wife of the man whom *she* had rejected in scorn? Misled by powers of evil she had brought a false accusation against Elsa; now she is condemned to fearful punishment and racked with remorse. Elsa is happy; after a brief moment of undeserved suffering life smiles on her again: let her turn now from Ortrud and leave her to her fate. From time to time Elsa has interrupted her with a pitying word or two: now she gives a cry of gratitude to God for this chance to bestow blessing on a poor creature kneeling in the dust before her; and she hurries back into the kemenate to open the door to her enemy.

21

Ortrud springs up in a frenzy of exaltation. She cries loudly to her dishonoured gods to avenge themselves and her:

Ent - weih - te Göt - ter!   Helft jetzt mei-ner Ra-che!

"strengthen me in my fight for you; make an end of the vile pride of this apostate!" She calls on Wodan the strong, on Freia the gracious, to bless her and make her revenge sure.

The fury of the orchestra dies down as Elsa, accompanied by two maids carrying lights, enters by way of the lower door of the kemenate. Abruptly changing her tone, Ortrud throws herself humbly at her feet. Elsa is grieved by the change in her since last she saw her in her pride and pomp. With kindly words and gestures she exhorts her to rise and believe that there is no enmity in her own heart towards her. On the morrow she is to be wedded to her rescuer; she will entreat him to pardon Friedrich for her sake. Let Ortrud, then, reappear on the morrow in fine raiment and go to the minster with her and see her become the honoured bride of her hero. Ortrud thanks her humbly; she will live henceforth as a beggar in the sunlight of Elsa's charity and grace.

Then she begins to lay her snare. In her abasement, she continues, she has lost all her former powers but one, but in virtue of that she may be able to protect Elsa's life and ward misfortune from her.[1] She warns her against believing too blindly in her present happiness; and to ward evil from her, let Ortrud read the future for her. This suggestion is accompanied by the motive of

---

[1] This is the text as it appears in the scores and in Wagner's own imprint of the poem, but an error seems to have crept in somehow. In the manuscript of the full score the second and fourth lines end not with "gegeben" and "Leben" ("only one power is *given* to me. . . . Perchance with it I may guard thy *life*") but with "geblieben" and "Lieben" ("only one power *remains* to me . . . perchance with it I may guard thy *love*"). As the eminent Wagnerian scholar Wolfgang Golther has pointed out, this latter reading makes the better sense: "it is not Elsa's life that is threatened", he says, "but her love". He would not take it on himself, however, to change the current wording, though he tells us that the great Wagnerian singer Anna von Mildenburg used always to sing "Lieben", not "Leben", at Bayreuth, and that Hans Richter had assured him that Wagner himself had ordered "Lieben" to be inserted in the score for the Vienna production of 1875. On the general difficulty of arriving at a definitive text of the Wagner operas see *supra*, p. 111.

Ortrud's machinations (No. 25 A) in the bassoon, which is followed by the motive of Lohengrin's warning as she continues to distil her poison into Elsa's ear. Has she reflected, she asks, that he who had come to her by magic art may some day by magic leave her? Elsa turns on her for a moment indignantly; then, filled with sorrow and compassion, she says, "Thou, poor one, canst never know love so trustful as mine, the love born of perfect faith":

No. 32

To a phrase that will become important later, in the colloquy of Lohengrin and Elsa in the third act:

No. 33

she exhorts Ortrud to come with her and learn the happiness that love and faith alone can bestow. As she repeats these last words Ortrud mutters to herself, "Ah! this very pride of hers shall teach me how to destroy her faith; I will turn her own weapon against her!"; but the orchestra envelops the brief duet in a tranquil melody of its own:

No. 34

on which it dwells ardently while Ortrud, with hypocritical reluctance, accompanies Elsa into the kemenate, the two serving-maids lighting their way and closing the door after them. When all have disappeared, Friedrich comes out of the shadows with a masterful cry: "Thus enters evil into yonder house! Carry to the end, my wife, the craft thou hast begun; no power have I to hinder thee. With my abasement began this fateful mischief; now let those who cast me down into the dust fall with me. One thing only see I in the mists around me — the destroyer of my honour shall himself be destroyed!"

22

The stage directions at this point are "First gleam of dawn". We have now to imagine, in defiance of the laws of solar time, even of stage time, that several hours have elapsed between the chord that accompanies Telramund's final words and the one that immediately follows it. For in a trice a new day is here, the wedding morn of Lohengrin and Elsa. "Day gradually dawns", we read a little later, and soon, evidently, the whole population is awake. We would have been less conscious of the anachronism had Wagner removed Friedrich from the scene after his monologue and brought him back later. But he does not: he makes Friedrich seek, before our eyes, a "place of concealment from the concourse of people", which he finds behind a buttress of the minster. In a few minutes Elsa will reappear on the stage; she can manifestly have had very little time for her talk inside the kemenate with Ortrud, and none at all for sleep before the wedding; for very soon we shall see both her and Ortrud in festal raiment. There is no way of making sense of the situation. The stage directions at the opening of the second act had been "It is night"; and later Ortrud and Friedrich had described the occupants of the citadel as "sunk in soft sleep". Later still, when Ortrud calls out Elsa's name, the latter says, "How fearfully and mournfully my name resounds in the night". Later, again, she speaks of her wedding as "tomorrow". Wagner's confusion is further shown by his giving contradictory stage directions in the poem and the score: in the latter "Day gradually dawns" at the commencement of the scene that immediately follows the exit of Elsa and Ortrud into the kemenate, while in the poem we are told "It is full daylight" — which has come up, seemingly, between one bar and the next. Wagner must have been fully aware of the illogicality of the situation, but presumably was indifferent to it. The difficulty probably arose with Telramund: he had to be on the stage when the Herald appears and reads his sentence of banishment, and a plausible reason for sending him off and bringing him on again later could not be found; so Wagner keeps him there, lurking behind a buttress, and blandly telescopes several hours into a stage minute or two.

The time, then, is now morning. Two trumpeters on the turret of the citadel blow a reveille:

No. 35

which is answered in softer tones from a distant tower. The same procedure is followed with the next phrase:

No. 36

and its successors; and gradually the orchestra takes up the fanfares and builds them up in great masses while the watchmen descend and open the citadel gates. Servants enter from various quarters, greet each other, and then go quietly about their routine duties, some drawing water from a fountain, others going into the Pallas. Eventually the four royal trumpeters emerge from the Pallas doors; and an arresting effect is made by a sudden unexpected switch for a time from the key of D major to that of C major. The trumpeters blow a stirring summons, in response to which the Brabantine nobles and the personnel of the citadel pour in from various quarters and greet each other excitedly — in an extended double chorus, as the operatic conventions of the 1840's demanded. They speculate as to what new wonders the day may bring forth to cap those of yesterday.

The King's Herald advances from the Pallas, and after a fresh fanfare from the four trumpeters he proclaims the royal decree: for his impious acceptance of the ordeal of trial by battle before God, Friedrich von Telramund is disgraced and banished, and

with him all who side with him and harbour him.[1] The chorus
break into wild curses of Telramund; but a fanfare calls them to
order again, and the Herald resumes his proclamation — Lohengrin will be Protector of Brabant: today he will celebrate with
them his wedding feast, but on the morrow he will lead them
against the eastern enemy.

23

While the chorus are enthusiastically acclaiming all this and
clamouring to be led into the field, four nobles, formerly liegemen of Friedrich, detach themselves from the crowd, advance to
the front, and express their discontent with the new turn of
events: so Brabant is to have a new ruler, who is to lead them
against a foe who has not threatened them? But who is there to
gainsay him? "I!" says Friedrich, who has approached them un-
observed and now reveals himself by uncovering his face. They
are astonished at his braving danger and death by still being in
Antwerp. He dares do more, he tells them — he will convict the
intruder of sorcery. Horrified, they take the raging man aside and
conceal him among them by the minster; he is lost, they tell him,
if he is recognised by the crowd.

Just then four noble pages appear on the terrace of the Pallas
and announce the coming of the princess, Elsa von Brabant: they
clear a way through the willing crowd to the minster steps, where
they take their stand. On the balcony of the kemenate appear four
more pages, the advance guard of the procession of Elsa's ladies,
who come out richly robed and make their slow way to the minster, on the steps of which the first comers group themselves. In
time Elsa herself appears, the nobles greeting her with bared
heads. The magnificent final scene of the act is now launched. The
orchestra gives out a solemn strain:

No. 37

which has a pendant equally majestic:

[1] It had been Wagner's original intention to have the ban — on both Friedrich and Ortrud — proclaimed in the first act.

150

No. 38

these are gradually built up into an imposing choral and orchestral ensemble in praise of Elsa. Among the ladies accompanying her is Ortrud, now richly dressed. Apparently it occurred to Wagner at some time or other that her presence there after the ban on Telramund might arouse some wonder in the spectator, for in the Prose Sketch he has a marginal note running thus: "the ladies keep aloof from Ortrud in the procession, which seems to offend her greatly", and in the poem this is expanded into "among the ladies who follow Elsa and close the procession is Ortrud, also richly dressed. The ladies nearest her keep at some distance from her, hardly concealing their displeasure, so that she appears markedly isolated: her expression is one of sullen anger".

As the chorus of greeting reaches its climax of power and Elsa places her foot on the second step of the minster, Ortrud breaks from the ranks, hastens to the front, and faces her truculently. "Stand back, Elsa!" she cries. "No longer will I endure it that I must follow thee humbly as a serving-maid! Precedence is mine, here and everywhere; before me thou shouldst bow thyself in due humility!" What is hers she claims of right, she tells the astounded onlookers; for what she has suffered she will have revenge. Elsa is as amazed as the others at this change from the suppliant of last night to the termagant of the present moment; how, she asks, can the wife of one whom God himself has condemned now flaunt her arrogance before her? Ortrud, assuming an air of outraged dignity, replies in a melodic vein that anticipates to some extent the Fricka of the *Valkyrie*:

No. 39

"Though my husband has been condemned by a false judgment, his name is honoured in this land, his virtues praised, his sword feared. But *yours* — who here can know him, since his bride herself cannot call him by name?" Despite the angry protests of the bystanders she goes steadily on: can Elsa assure them that her hero is of noble race, tell her whence the river had brought him to her, when and whither he will go from her again? She does not know; and to keep her from knowing, the stranger has craftily persuaded her that to ask these questions would bring disaster on them both.

Elsa replies exaltedly that her lover is so noble that only the basest of beings could doubt his lofty mission; and she appeals to the assembly to choose between him and his traducers. Ortrud plays mockingly upon the weakness of Elsa's case — she will not ask by what magic the stranger has triumphed because she dares not, because she is racked by doubt of him. As Elsa's ladies come forward to support her the door of the Pallas opens and the King appears, heralded by the fanfares of the trumpeters, and accompanied by Lohengrin and the Saxon Counts and nobles.[1] Elsa falls on Lohengrin's breast with a cry of "My lord! My rescuer!", and tells him how she had taken Ortrud in out of compassion, and now the woman taunts her with excess of faith in him. Lohengrin cows Ortrud with a look and bids her go; then he bends tenderly over Elsa and exhorts her, if she must weep, to shed tears of joy.

24

He is leading the way with her to the minster when Friedrich appears suddenly on the steps. All recoil from him in horror and loathing. Wildly he tells the King and all of them that they have been deluded by an enchanter's craft, and demands a hearing. At the King's command they seize him, and as he struggles frenziedly with them he accuses the shining knight of having imposed on King, nobles and people by magic arts. They should have asked him, before they allowed him to enter the lists, the questions Telramund asks him now — what is the name, what the station of this stranger brought to them down the river by a wild swan? Has an honourable knight need of such an escort? "Now let him stand and

---

[1] Thus in the score. In the poem it is "Saxon and Brabantine Counts and nobles".

answer. If he can, then was I justly cast down: if not, let it fare with this pretended pure one as evilly as he deserves."

All, including the King, are impressed by Friedrich's vehemence and his evident conviction, and they look expectantly towards Lohengrin. Proudly he tells Friedrich that he refuses to answer the charges and satisfy the doubts of one so degraded. Not even to the demand of the King and of all the princes of earth for his name and origin would he accede. What doubt can they have of him? They saw his deed, which is its own witness of its worth. To one alone he owes an answer — Elsa. He turns towards her confidently; but as the baleful Ortrud motive (No. 25 A) steals out in the orchestra, followed by No. 19 (his warning to Elsa), he pauses in dismay when he sees that she is gazing fixedly before her, pale and trembling, a prey to the wildest agitation. What his secret can be baffles them all, they murmur, but — to the accompaniment of No. 25 in the orchestra — in Elsa's face they can read the doubt taking shape in her heart despite her effort to fight it down. In a trance, oblivious of the others, she murmurs, "What he hides would doubtless work him evil were he to reveal it before them all. I, whom he rescued, would be traitor to him were I to ask for it. Did I know his destiny I would faithfully keep the secret; yet in the depth of my heart doubt raises its head." "Let him keep his secret", say the King and the others. "His deed is witness enough to his nobility. We stand by the hero's side with full belief in him, even if his name he will not tell". Lohengrin thanks them warmly, pressing the hands stretched out to him.

While he is thus occupied, standing a little in the background, Friedrich goes up to Elsa, who remains a little apart from the others, lost in thought, not daring to look at Lohengrin. With the sinister No. 25 A again uncoiling itself in the bass clarinet he addresses her softly with feigned sympathy: "Give me your trust: I can show you a means by which you may learn the truth. Let me but wound even his fingertip, and, I swear to you, all will be clear that he is now concealing. So will he be faithful and bound to you for ever. Tonight I shall be nigh; call me, and it will be done in a trice."

Elsa repulses him with horror, and Lohengrin, stepping forward, commandingly bids Ortrud and Friedrich depart and never be seen by him again. Friedrich makes a gesture of rage and despair. Lohengrin raises Elsa, who had sunk at his feet, bewildered and exhausted. "In thy hands, in thy faith", he says, "lies all our happiness. Does doubt still torture thee? Wouldst thou ask me the question?" Torn between shame and exaltation she replies, "My preserver, my saviour, my hero in whom alone I live, my love shall soar above all clouds of doubt!" Taking her by the hand he leads her to the King, the nobles and ladies dividing respectfully to let them pass, and No. 37 is once more built up into a massive choral and orchestral ensemble, with bells ringing and the organ pealing from inside the minster, and trumpet fanfares piercing through it all from the turret of the Pallas and from the balcony. Taking Elsa by the right hand and Lohengrin by the left, the King conducts them to the top of the minster steps, where Lohengrin takes Elsa in his arms. But at the supreme moment she looks back apprehensively and sees Ortrud raising her arm as if in triumph, while trumpets and trombones thunder out the motive of warning, which, however, is swept aside by a final fanfare as the bridal pair enter the minster and the curtain falls.

It is not to be wondered at that Wagner left the composition of the second act to the last, for psychologically and musically it confronted him with the most difficulties. He was quite at home in choral and lyrical episodes, and his Ortrud of the second act was a dramatic creation of a kind new to opera. But he was still ill at ease in what we may call the passages of lower emotional temperature, essential to the carrying on of the action but not always of the stuff that music can take to its heart. He had not yet reached the stage at which he could see his own solution of the age-old operatic problem of making the whole tissue musical — in the first place by so constructing his drama that pedestrian explanation could be reduced to the minimum, in the second place by a continuous symphonic weaving of significant motives in the orchestra. It was no doubt the intuition that this problem would somehow have to be solved in the *Ring* that made him delay the composition of the *Rhinegold* for six years after the completion of *Lohengrin*.

25

In the third act, the first of the three to be set to music, we get a hint of the line along which his development as a musician might have proceeded had not that deep inner change taken place in him that was to result in an entirely new synthesis of the factors of opera. The third act is predominantly lyrical, and the ease and power with which Wagner creates in this field suggest that had he been allowed to remain content with the old formulae he could have endowed them with a new life. This third act shows him at that stage in the development of a great artist when not only does each component of his genius seem to have attained its fullest individual development but all are in smooth equilibrium. It is the stage represented, for example, by Beethoven in his fifth symphony and Goethe in the First Part of his *Faust*. But artists of this type, by the very nature of their complex genius, cannot rest on their oars when this kind of consolidation of their various faculties has been accomplished. Their daemon drives them on to create difficulties of all kinds for themselves, difficulties of conception, of architecture, of craftsmanship; and by the very process of overcoming these difficulties they become masters of a new way of thinking and a new way of working. So it was with Wagner after *Lohengrin*. To have stood still would have been, for him, to go back; but going forwards meant the slow conquest of entirely new territory. Of such conquests, however, only the most powerful minds, with infinite capacity for growth, are capable. *Lohengrin* was finished in January 1848. By 1858 Wagner had written the *Rhinegold,* the *Valkyrie,* two-thirds of *Siegfried,* and the major part of *Tristan.* In no ten years of the life of any other great creator is the distance so enormous between the first peak scaled and the second.

In the third act of *Lohengrin* Wagner abandons himself to the luxury of lyricism. It opens with an animated orchestral introduction descriptive of the wedding festivities. In some respects Wagner was at this time more at his ease technically in what we may call free music than in music that had to go in harness with words. Attention has already been drawn to that four-square regularity of beat in much of his earlier vocal writing at which he himself could smile in later years. It was the inevitable result of his casting his libretti in the ordinary poetic moulds — long lines in regular metre with click-clack end-rhymes; the uniform line-lengths and the goose-step of the verbal accents imposed on him a certain monotony of melodic stress, from which he only emancipated

himself later by a drastic shortening of the lines and, in general,
an avoidance of the fetters of rhyme. But already in the *Flying
Dutchman-Tannhäuser-Lohengrin* period he was feeling his way
towards a more flexible rhythm in the orchestra, of which we have
a foretaste in the varied accentual footfalls of the brilliant introduction to the third act:

No. 40

This is followed by an energetic theme in horns, bassoons and
'cellos:

No. 41

which appears later strengthened by trombones and tuba (in
which presentment it is generally vulgarised by conductor and
players alike). There is a contrasting section in a quieter vein in
wood wind and horns:

No. 42

after which Nos. 40 and 41 are resumed.

The curtain rises on the bridal chamber. In the middle background stands a richly furnished bed, and on the right a low
couch by an open oriel casement. Through two doors in the back
come two processions, one of ladies escorting Elsa, the other of
the King and the nobles with Lohengrin. During the few bars of
transition from the close of the introduction to the stage scene
we are to imagine the bridal music drawing nearer and nearer.

When the two cortèges reach the centre of the room the King presents Elsa to Lohengrin, and the pair embrace while the chorus sing a simple little song of congratulation:

No. 43

Noble pages divest Lohengrin of his rich outer vestment and lay it, with his sword, on the couch. Eight ladies similarly disrobe Elsa. The King embraces the pair, the pages give the signal for departure, and, to the strains of No. 43, the two processions reform and go out slowly, their song dying away gradually in the distance.

26

By a sudden enharmonic shift of key, from B flat major to E major, the atmosphere changes to one of tender intimacy as Lohengrin, seating himself on the couch, draws Elsa to him, and, accompanied by the muted strings, begins the long duet. First he sings of his happiness at being alone with her for the first time since they had met, and at her loving confidence in him:

No. 44

A tender little phrase in the clarinet:

No. 45

soon becomes the subject of a fresh development:

No. 46

Fühl' ich zu dir so süss mein Herz ent-bren-nen.

as Elsa assures him of her own happiness. Little more than this broad outline of the colloquy of the pair is necessary to the listener, for what they have to say in words is said more directly and more ardently in the music, in which theme succeeds theme in spendthrift profusion, the total effect being of a symphony of solo song and duet. Lohengrin launches a new melody as he speaks of their having been destined for each other from the beginning, he to be her rescuer, she to be drawn to him by love:

No. 47

Wie hehr er - kenn' ich uns - rer Lie - be

We-sen! Die nie sich sah'n, wir hat-ten uns ge - ahnt;

She had already beheld him in her dreams, she replies, so that his appearance on the river — here No. 11 is breathed softly by flute and clarinet — had been only her dream made reality.

But soon we have a hint of the impending tragedy, the seeds of which had been sown in Elsa's heart by Ortrud. Her name sounds sweet in his mouth, she says: perhaps some day she will be able to murmur his, some day when they are alone together and the world cannot overhear. Lohengrin, however, only draws her to the open window, points to the garden, and tells her that as the flowers give forth their scent unasked, so her beauty and innocence had stolen irresistibly on his senses at the first sight of her:

No. 48

Andante animato

Ath-mest du nicht mit mir die sü - ssen Düf - te?

She replies that she longs to be worthy of his love, to serve him even at the cost of suffering. The motive of warning (No. 19) in-

trudes itself softly into the orchestral tissue as she goes on to surmise that perchance his secret contains in it a threat of evil to
him should the world discover it: but if she were allowed to share
it no power on earth would tear it from her. In growing excitement she begs for his confidence, for the thought of his mistrust
weighs heavily on her: "reveal to me thy noble being; tell me
whence thou comest; of my silence be assured."

Gravely he reminds her that when he came to her he had put
his whole trust in her, accepting her word that she was innocent
of the charge against her; then he turns lovingly to her again, and
the orchestra, with a new theme:

No. 49

launches him once more on a flood of protestations; he had given
up more than she knows to come to her in her need, and in return he asks for nothing but love and faith. The warning No. 19
is heard again as he entreats her to put doubt away from her: one
thing alone he can tell her — "I come not from night and woe, but
from a home of light and bliss".

The Ortrud motive threads its way through the texture again
as Elsa recoils from him. He had thought to reassure her, but his
words have only stirred more anxious doubts in her:

No. 50

Das Loos, dem du ent - ron - nen, es war dein höch-stes Glück;

He has come, then, for her sake from a land where all was joy.
Will he not be always longing to return? What power has one so
poor as she to hold him? The day will come when he will regret
his sacrifice: wasting away, must she count the days until the one
dawns when she must lose him? In vain he assures her that so
long as she is free from doubt he will not change towards her: to
another insistent reiteration of the Ortrud motive she wails that
as by magic he had come to her, so by magic he may be taken

from her: that fear will ever haunt her. She becomes again the visionary she was in the first act, but now with a touch of madness in her. In imagination she hears and sees the swan (No. 17 in flute and oboe) approaching down the river, and Lohengrin summoning it to take him away. That vision will ever be before her eyes: Lohengrin alone can rid her of it: she must know his name, what his race, whence he came; and the orchestra points the climax of her delirium with an ominous upsurge of No. 19.

Lohengrin has tried in vain to check her. Suddenly she is recalled to reality by the sight of Friedrich and his four partisans, with drawn swords, breaking in through one of the doors at the back. With a wild cry to Lohengrin to save himself she hands him the scabbard that is resting against the couch. Swiftly drawing the sword he strikes Telramund dead; the others let fall their weapons in terror and kneel before him. To the tumult succeeds a fateful silence — which Wagner intensifies, as he was so often to do in his later works, by a throbbing pulse in the kettledrums — and a last melancholy suggestion of the motive of Ortrud's machinations:

No. 51

Lohengrin makes one brief, poignant comment on it all — "Alas, now is our happiness for ever at an end!":

No. 52

To a sad reminiscence of No. 46 in clarinet (then oboe) and strings he bends down over Elsa, raises her gently, and places her on the couch. "Oh God in heaven, have pity on me!" she moans. At a sign from Lohengrin the four prostrate nobles rise; "Bear this body to the King's judgment seat", he commands them. When they have gone he strikes a bell: two of Elsa's women enter, whom he bids take their mistress away and prepare her for her appearance before the King, to whom he will disclose who and what he is. Then, slowly and sadly, he himself leaves the stage, the orchestra giving out first the motive (the latter half of No. 19) that had accompanied his warning to Elsa at their first meeting, then the warning itself (the first part of No. 19), and finally the solemn Grail theme (No. 1).

27

The curtain having fallen, trumpet calls, sounding from the courtyard, prepare the way for the orchestral introduction to the final scene. When the curtain rises again we see once more the meadow on the banks of the Scheldt, as in the first act; it is dawn, broadening into full daylight as the action proceeds. To the accompaniment of martial music, with recurrent trumpet fanfares, the Brabantine nobles and men-at-arms come on the scene from various directions and take up their positions by their respective banners.[1] When all are assembled the King enters with the Saxon levy, and after a fanfare he thanks them all for their welcome. He is about to lead them against the foreign foe; but where is he whom God had sent to be the guardian and the glory of Brabant? The assembly is startled by the entry of the four Brabantine nobles carrying a bier with a covered body on it. All look round fearfully and questioningly; the men, they say to each other, are Telramund's liegemen, but whose is the corpse they bring? "We come", say the four, "by order of the Protector of Brabant: who he is he himself will make known." Then all eyes turn wonderingly to Elsa, who comes in slowly and falteringly with her ladies, the orchestra giving out the motive of warning and its afterstrain (No. 19), followed by the motive of Ortrud's evil. The King goes to meet her and conducts her to a seat opposite the oak. Why is she so pale and sad? he asks her: is it for grief at parting? She cannot speak; she tries to raise her eyes to him but cannot.

From the background come shouts of "Make way for the hero

[1] See *supra*, p. 117.

of Brabant"; and soon Lohengrin enters, fully accoutred as in the first act. The King and the others greet him warmly as their leader in the coming campaign; but to their dismay he declares that he cannot take the field with the heroes who have rallied to the banner at his summons. He comes among them now only as an accuser demanding justice. Uncovering Telramund's body he says, "This man fell upon me in the night; say now, did I right in slaying him?" All absolve him. Then he accuses Elsa, "the woman God gave to me", of having allowed herself to be betrayed by evil counsel into falsity to him. They all had heard her sacred promise never to ask his name: that promise she has broken. Now she shall learn what she desired to know, and that before them all. "Learn then", he says, drawing himself up proudly, "whether I am as noble as any here."

To the accompaniment of the Grail music of the prelude to the opera he tells his story. Far away from here, in a land which they will never see, stands a castle, Monsalvat by name:

No. 53

Within it is a shining temple, the like of which for splendour the earth cannot show; and within the temple is the holiest of treasures, a cup divinely blessed, brought down from heaven to earth by an angel host and given into the keeping of stainless men. Once in each year a dove descends from heaven to renew the mystic virtue residing in the cup. It is called the Grail; it preserves unsullied the knights who are dedicated to its service. Whomever it summons to that service it endows with supernatural might; evil is powerless before him. Some are called by it to go into distant lands to champion the cause of innocence in distress. Nought can prevail against a knight of the Grail so long as the secret of his origin remains unrevealed; but if it is disclosed to the profane world he must return whence he had come. He himself had been sent among them as an emissary of the Grail: the King of the

Grail is his father Parzival: "his knight am I, and Lohengrin my name"; at which last words the proud No. 11 rings out in the full orchestra.

28

The King, the women and the men muse upon the mystic story to the strain of the concluding portion of the prelude (No. 5). Elsa gives a cry of despair: Lohengrin takes her in his arms and tenderly, but in profoundest sorrow, reproaches her for having wrung his secret from him by her betrayal of his trust. She pleads desperately to be allowed to make reparation, but he assures her that it is in vain; he has no choice; he must leave her. The King and the others add their supplications to hers, imploring him at least to lead them into battle. But this also he has to refuse; if he, the servant of the Grail, should disobey the Grail, he would only bring disaster on them. He prophesies, however, success for the German cause: "no eastern hordes, now or in times to come, shall lord it over German lands".

Amid the excitement comes a cry from the men at the back — "The swan! the swan! see, it draws nigh again!" Elsa, waking from her swoon, stands up and sees, like the others, the swan at the bend of the river, drawing the empty boat. She gives a wild cry that agitates Lohengrin: too long, he says, as No. 17 hovers in the air, has he lingered: the Grail has sent for him. Watched in suspense by the others he goes up to the bank and bends mournfully over the swan. "My beloved swan", he murmurs, "now for our last sad journey":

No. 54

"How gladly would I have spared it thee! Within a year, thy term of service o'er, the Grail would have freed thee, and I would see thee in another guise." Then he turns with a cry of bitter regret to Elsa: had he spent but one year with her in happiness the Grail would have restored to her her brother Gottfried, whom she believed to be dead. "Should he return, though I shall then be far away:

No. 55

Kommt er dann heim, wenn ich ihm fern im Le - ben,

give him this horn, this sword, this ring. The horn will bring him
help in time of need, the sword victory in battle; as for the ring,
let it remind him of one who saved thee from shame and woe." He
bids the fainting Elsa farewell: "wroth is the Grail with me that I
have tarried so long"; and he goes quickly to the river bank, accompanied by the lamentations of them all.

Suddenly Ortrud emerges from the crowd and comes to the
front with a cry of triumph: "Go home in all thy pride; and to thy
foolish one I will tell who it is that draws thy boat. Well do I
know the chain about his neck, the chain by which I had made
him not child but swan: he is the heir of Brabant." Then, turning
exultantly to Elsa, "My thanks that you drove your hero hence.
Now the swan takes him home again: had the knight bided here a
little longer he would have freed your brother!" The men press
round her with curses and threats, but she faces them undis-
mayed: "See now how the gods avenge themselves on you for having turned away from them!"

Lohengrin, who has heard all this, sinks on his knees in silent
prayer while the Grail music pulsates in the air above him once
more. The white dove of the Grail descends and hovers over the
boat: perceiving it, Lohengrin springs up with a look of gratitude
and loosens the chain, whereupon the swan sinks beneath the
waves and in its place stands a beautiful youth — Gottfried —
whom he lifts to the bank, crying, "Behold the Duke of Brabant;
he shall be your leader!" To the accompaniment of the chivalrous
No. 11 he springs into the boat, and the dove, seizing the chain,
draws it down the river. Ortrud, at the sight of Gottfried, has
fallen to the ground with a shriek. Gottfried, after making obeisance to the King and receiving the acclamations and homage of
the men of Brabant, runs joyously to Elsa. She looks despairingly
at Lohengrin, who is now visible in a further part of the river,
standing upright in the boat with drooping head, leaning on his
shield; and with a cry of "My husband!" she sinks lifeless into
Gottfried's arms. As Lohengrin slowly disappears in the distance

the curtain falls, the last word of the opera being given, as the first had been, to the music of the mystic Grail.

29

Strange as it may seem to us today, Wagner was urged by several people to change the ending of his opera. Among the friends to whom he read his poem in 1845 was one Hermann Franck, who could not stomach the cruelty, as he thought it, of Elsa's abandonment by Lohengrin. "Serious reflection", Wagner tells us in *My Life*, "aroused in me later grave doubts — which had been expressed to me in thoughtful and tactful fashion by Franck — with regard to the tragic element of the subject. Franck found the punishment of Elsa by Lohengrin's departure rather offensive; he recognised that this highly poetic feature was a characteristic of the legend, but at the same time he doubted whether it met adequately the demands of tragic feeling in relation to dramatic actuality. He would have preferred to see Lohengrin die before our eyes because of Elsa's treachery-through-love. As this did not seem feasible, however, he would have liked to see him spellbound by some powerful motive or other and so prevented from leaving her. Although of course I could not agree to all this, I went so far as to ask myself whether I could not avoid the cruel separation and yet retain the essential element of his departure. So I sought for a means by which Elsa could go away with Lohengrin, paying some sort of penance that would mean her withdrawal also from the world." Franck approved of this. Wagner, however, in his perplexity, spoke of his difficulty to Frau von Lüttichau, the wife of the Intendant of the Dresden Opera, who told him bluntly that Franck must be devoid of any sense of poetry if he could not see that Wagner's dénouement was the only right one for the work.

Wagner had a somewhat similar experience five years later in connection with the journalist Adolf Stahr, who, after seeing a performance of the opera under Liszt in Weimar, raised much the same objection to the tragic ending. Wagner was for the moment quite shaken by this apparently widespread view of the matter; and as by that time he had rather lost touch with the characters and the milieu of *Lohengrin* he was weak enough to write to Stahr that in the main he agreed with him. But after some days of mental misery his artistic sense steadied him again, and he sent a laconic message to Liszt, who had been incensed by Stahr's article: "You have the right understanding of *Lohengrin,* Stahr hasn't. I withdraw my agreement with his judgment; I wrote in too much of a hurry."

His own considered view of the moral and dramatic problem of the ending was set forth in a long letter of May 1846 to Franck. Elsa's peculiar offence, he points out, can be atoned for only by separation, not by chastisement of any kind or by death. "Elsa has forfeited *Lohengrin:* their remaining together is impossible, because the pair have already been severed by her asking him the question." Wagner had given a great deal of thought to the matter from the moment of his first acquaintance with the legend, he tells Franck; and he had rejected every other dénouement as illogical and impossible. To alter it now would mean a total re-casting of the drama, leaving only the mere externalities of the story, the spiritual nucleus of it having gone. He sees it as a fundamental point that although a supernatural being and an earthly one may come into contact with each other it is impossible that their association shall endure; for the lower nature is bound to act according to the law of its own being.

30

But though he cannot adopt Franck's suggestion that the ending shall be changed he has decided, he says, to make Lohengrin's share in the tragic outcome clearer to the spectator. How the knight originally becomes involved in the action he has already shown sufficiently in the first act, more especially in the music, which can convey so much that it is beyond the power of words to express — Lohengrin has come only to carry out the command of the Grail, but at the first sight of Elsa he is filled with love for her. Wagner can change nothing in the passage in the duet in the earlier part of the third act in which Lohengrin assures Elsa that her love will be for him compensation more than enough for the surrender of his heritage of the Grail; and once more he insists that his *music* at this point makes the import of the words doubly clear. But he is prepared to make an alteration later in the act, after Lohengrin has told the assembly the story of his home and origin and the mission entrusted to him by the Grail. In his poem Wagner had made the knight turn to Elsa, after the "Narration", in sad reproach: "O Elsa, what hast thou done to me? When first I saw thee my heart was filled with love for thee and with a sense of a new happiness. The noble power inherent in my origin I was prepared to surrender for love's sake. Why didst thou force my secret from me? Now, alas, I must part from thee." He will now alter this, he says, after the first two or three lines, and will continue thus: "At once I loved thee warmly, and felt my heart turning away from the chaste service of the Grail. Now must I endure endless remorse and pay eternal penance for having longed for thee more than for God. For alas! I see now my transgression — that I thought a woman's love could be of heavenly purity!"

After that, Lohengrin is to tell Elsa, as in the poem, that there can be no changing of her punishment: they must separate, even though his grief is as profound as hers. Then the dialogue is to continue with some new lines: "*Elsa:* Woe is me! could punishment be harder? Parted from thee, nothing remains for me but death! *Lohengrin:* The knight of the Grail must live far removed from here; but thy husband, alas, succumbs to the necessity of parting."

In the end, however, Wagner decided that his original handling of the final scene was the only logical one, and virtually none of the alterations he had outlined in his letter to Franck were carried over into the poem, which agrees with the Prose Sketch in all essentials.

But we have only to study the Sketch to realise how the necessity for compression for stage purposes forced him to omit or condense several features that are vital to our full understanding of the drama. As has been pointed out on an earlier page, he cut out in 1850 a large section, which he had actually set to music, from Lohengrin's "Narration" in the third act, in which the knight had told in detail how the mission to go to the rescue of Elsa came to be laid on him by the Grail. From the stage point of view he was right in sacrificing all this: it would have made the "Narration" inconveniently long. But psychologically the excision was a mistake, for the passage throws a needed light on Lohengrin, his origin, his super-earthly nature and his mission, that is lacking in the opera as we now have it.

The same comment has to be made on the deletion of a passage in an earlier part of the "Narration" which begins thus in the Prose Sketch, after the point at which Lohengrin has told the assembly of the powers of the Grail: "Whoever is dedicated to its service must forswear the love of woman: to the King of the Templars alone is it permitted to take a pure wife, to the end that his exalted line shall be perpetuated unsullied." An emissary of the Grail may descend to the common world of men to relieve oppression or rescue the innocent, but he must never disclose to profane eyes either his origin or the mystery of his supernatural powers. If these secrets should be wrung from him he must return at once to Monsalvat. Lohengrin's dwelling among the Brabantines would have brought untold blessings upon the land — on the sole condition that the Grail's secret remained inviolate; and this fair prospect had been blasted by the feminine indiscretion of Elsa, who had brought about a fatal clash between the higher and the lower elements of the world. Reconciliation of the two is impossible: so for all his love for Elsa he must abandon her and return to the spiritual world from which he had come.

The character of Lohengrin, we see, is a far more complex problem than any singer of the part ever realises. It is not enough for him to be just a tenor; he must be a psychologist and a student of mediaeval poetry as well. And for the complete key to the character he and we must sometimes go, as so often happens to be the case, to Wagner's first extensive prose draft of the drama, which contains a number of vital pointers which stage exigencies compelled him to omit from his poem.

Tristan and Isolde

CHARACTERS

TRISTAN	*Tenor*
KING MARKE	*Bass*
ISOLDE	*Soprano*
KURVENAL	*Baritone*
MELOT	*Tenor*
BRANGAENE	*Soprano*
A SHEPHERD	*Tenor*
A STEERSMAN	*Baritone*
A YOUNG SAILOR [1]	*Tenor*

1

A
s is the case with many another great legend, the origins of that of Tristan and Isolde are lost in the mists of antiquity. This or that element in it may possibly have its roots in remote historical fact; others are no doubt connected with some primitive form of hero-worship or god-worship; others again are importations, at the first or the fifty-first remove, from romances of the Graeco-Roman past. The moving final motive of the black sail and the white, for instance, is met with in Plutarch's life of the legendary Theseus, and elsewhere in classical literature; it appears that when the ship carrying the annual tribute of youths and maidens for the Cretan Minotaur set out from Attica "no one had any hope for safety", says Plutarch, "so they used to send out the ship with a black sail, as if it were going to a certain doom. But now Theseus so far encouraged [his father] Aegeus, and boasted that he would overcome the Minotaur, that

[1] The Young Sailor sings, but does not appear in person.

169

he gave a second sail, a white one, to the steersman, and charged him on his return, if Theseus were safe, to hoist the white one, if not, the black one as a sign of mourning." On the return of the victorious Theseus, however, "both he and the steersman in their delight forgot to hoist the sail which was to be the signal of their safety to Aegeus; and he in his despair flung himself down the cliffs and perished."

When we first meet with the Tristan story in literary form in the twelfth century it is already ancient; the poets and prose writers who gave it shape at that time were working on the basis of a number of episodes that had long been popular in oral form. The perambulating jongleurs would find everywhere, in the relatively cultured baronial court and among the unsophisticated people, eager listeners to the ever-fascinating tale. Each of them would embroider it according to his fancy, inventing, on occasion, new adventures to kindle fresh interest in those who had heard it already more than once; and the quality of these inventions would vary with the intellectual and moral constitution of the narrator and the level of culture and taste in his audience of the place and the moment. Even in the final literary forms in which the legend has come down to us the noble central motives are profusely encrusted with adventures of a rather crude kind.

2

Scholars today mostly agree that the story originated in the Celtic regions of Wales or south-west England, whence it passed in time to Brittany.[1] The French poets Crestien de Troyes, — whom we shall meet again in connection with the Parsifal legend — and La Chèvre reduced it to writing, but no trace of their work has survived. The oldest extant French or Anglo-Norman versions of the tragic story of Tristan and Isolde are the poems of Béroul and Thomas; both belong to the twelfth century, the former being slightly the older. Neither of them has come down to us complete. Towards the end of that century one Eilhart d'Oberge, a Saxon vassal of Henry the Lion, Duke of Brunswick, made a German version that agrees more with that of Béroul than with that of Thomas; the inference is that he and Béroul based themselves

[1] A Persian origin has been claimed for it, but a consideration of this theory would take us too far afield.

on some common source. Early in the following century the German minnesinger Gottfried von Strassburg combined a little of the Eilhart with the main Thomas form; and it is from his version that Wagner mostly drew his material. Gottfried died before completing his work, which was continued by two of his compatriots, Ulrich von Türheim (about 1240) and Heinrich von Freiberg (about 1300). By an odd coincidence, Gottfried's unfinished narrative breaks off at virtually the exact spot at which the surviving fragments of Thomas's poem begin.

This latter was imitated in prose, in 1226, by a Norwegian writer, a monk of the name of Robert, at the behest of a king of Denmark, Haakon V, who was an ardent admirer of the French romances of chivalry. This manuscript, which figures in the treatment of the subject by modern scholars as "the Saga", has fortunately survived intact and is accessible in print. Another valuable source for the reconstruction of the legend is a poem entitled *Sir Tristrem,* apparently dating from the early years of the fourteenth century, which was discovered in the library of the Faculty of Advocates in Edinburgh and published by Sir Walter Scott in 1804. The only other source that need be mentioned here is a manuscript in the Bodleian Library, dating probably from the end of the twelfth century, of a poem dealing with *The Mad Tristan* — a series of episodes that play a large part in the story, but for which, of course, Wagner had no use.

3

A critical scrutiny and comparison of all the manuscript versions now accessible to us led the great French scholar Joseph Bédier to the conclusion that at the root of all of them lay a lost poem by some man of genius who wrote in the early part of the twelfth century. Bédier's argument is that the Tristan story, in the literary form it took about that time, is not, like certain other epic narratives, the result simply of the more or less fortuitous accretion of a number of independent "lays" treating of the adventures of a hero. Whereas in the case of legends that have grown to great size by the mere aggregation of particles it makes no great difference in which order the episodes are taken, the Tristan story follows a definite and coherent plan. The end is kept in view from the beginning; the nature and the order of the episodes are designed for cumulative effect; the characters and their motives are throughout consistent with themselves and psychologically related to each other; in all the versions which we possess the incidents are largely the same and occur in the same order; and always there is the same over-riding sense of the lovers being in the grip of a fatality to which they were born and against which they and others strive in vain. Bédier draws the conclusion, therefore, that the many ancient versions now accessible to us, English, French, Italian, Russian or Northern, are sub-products of three main works — that of Thomas (about 1160–1170), that of Eilhart (about 1190–1200), and a French prose romance (about 1230). The Saga, the English *Sir Tristrem* and certain other forms derive from Thomas, and Gottfried from Thomas and Eilhart; while the only forms not stemming directly from the main three are that of Béroul (about 1180) and *The Mad Tristan* (about 1170). And the ultimate source of them all is presumed to be the lost poem of the unknown poet.

Bédier conjecturally sets forth the main genealogical table thus:

x representing the archetypal work of the unknown prime-poet, and y some source or other, ultimately deriving, like the others, from x, which was used by Béroul and Eilhart. Manifestly all the episodic Tristan legends current in the early twelfth century were known to the prime-poet, who was perhaps an Anglo-Norman: presumably it was he who welded them into an organic whole some time before the middle of that century. But for him, Bédier opines, we should have no real "story of Tristan and Isolde" but only a number of loosely connected episodes.

There is no necessity for the ordinary reader who is interested in the Tristan saga only as a background to Wagner's opera to embark on the labour of working his painful way through all the mediaeval versions of it. His task has been simplified for him by Joseph Bédier, who, in his book *Le Roman de Tristan et Iseut,* has fused the essentials of all the versions into a single coherent story, told in a charming style that had become second nature to the great scholar through his long absorption in the literature of the Middle Ages. From this one volume the reader can get all the material he needs as a preliminary to the study of Wagner's handling of the legend. The ancient story will be told here mostly along Bédier's synthetic lines,[1] but the reader must bear in mind that the episodes and the names and places differ from each other in an infinity of small points in the various originals.[2]

4

Marc, "King of Cornwall and of England", being hard pressed by his enemies, is aided by Rivalen, King of Loonnois; and in recompense for his services Marc bestows on him the hand of his sister Blanchefleur.[3] The time comes when Rivalen has to return to his own kingdom to defend it against the attacks of his enemy

---

[1] It is upon Bédier's book that the Swiss composer Frank Martin has based his very attractive "oratorio profane" *Le Vin Herbé.*

[2] There is an excellent English prose version of Gottfried's poem by Miss Jessie L. Weston — *The Story of Tristan and Iseult,* 3rd edn. 2 vols., 1907. Miss Weston omits a few passages of minor importance, and completes Gottfried's unfinished story from Heinrich von Freiberg and Ulrich von Türheim.

[3] At the outset we have a typical example of how the versions differ from each other in minor details. In some of them Rivalen is lord of Ermenie or Parmenie. He comes to Marc's court in the first place in pursuit of glory. He and Blanchefleur love each other in secret, and when she finds herself with child the fact has to be concealed from the King for fear of his resentment; "she conceived in distress the child whose story you are about to hear, who was fated to bring suffering and distress to all, man or woman, who should love him." Rivalen returns to his own land to fight Duke Morgan, and Blanchefleur, unable to bear her grief alone and dreading shame, follows him there. Through all this multiplicity of variants in the sources, however, the main features and psychological motives remain the same; as regards the present matter, for example, Tristan, as his name imports, is in every version a child born to suffering and sorrow beyond those of other mortals. The Fates have marked him down as their victim from the beginning; even his parents ·have loved under a fateful compulsion, with death as their inevitable portion.

Duke Morgan. He takes Blanchefleur, who is now with child, back with him to his castle of Kanoel, and going forth to the war leaves her in charge of his faithful marshal Rohalt. The news comes to Kanoel that Rivalen has been slain; after three days of grieving Blanchefleur gives birth to a son, on whom, because he has come into the world *par tristesse,* she confers the name of Tristan. To save the boy's life after the capture of the castle Rohalt passes the infant off as his own, and after seven years commits him to the charge of a trusty squire named Gorvenal, under whose care he grows up to be a model of manly strength and grace and beauty, skilled not only in arms and hunting but in the seven arts and all other noble accomplishments.

One day the boy is trapped by some Norwegian merchants on their ship and carried off over the seas; but a storm that arises they read as a sign of the displeasure of the gods, whom they placate by setting their captive adrift in a small boat, which carries him to Cornwall. He is taken to the court of King Marc, to whom he soon becomes dear for his comeliness and courtesy — though his cautious account of himself is that he is the son of a merchant in a land beyond the seas. (Some of the old romancers make it clear to us that Marc's great love for him comes from obscure stirrings in the King's heart towards the memory of his sister Blanchefleur). But the time comes when Rohalt arrives in Cornwall, tells Marc that Tristan is his own nephew, and summons the youth back to Loonnois to rid his land of the usurper. This he does; and then, out of the nobility of his heart and the love he bears his uncle, he delegates his lands to Rohalt and returns to Cornwall.

He finds the kingdom in great grief, for a formidable Irish knight has come to claim the tribute due to the King of Ireland, — three hundred noble Cornish youths and three hundred maidens to be taken back with him to serfdom. The emissary is Morholt, whose sister, Queen Iseut, is the wife of the Irish King: he is a man of gigantic stature, invincible in battle. None of the Cornish noblemen dares a trial at arms with him; the young Tristan alone accepts his challenge to single combat. In spite of the entreaties of Marc and the nobles he accompanies Morholt to a nearby island: there he slays the giant, whose body, with a fragment from Tristan's sword embedded in the head, is taken back in mourning by the men of Ireland; "and from that day Iseut the Fair" — the daughter of the Queen — "learned to hate the name of Tristan of Loonnois."

But Morholt's sword had been dipped in poison, and a wound he had dealt Tristan was beyond the skill of healing of anyone in Cornwall. So dreadful was the odour that came from it that none could bear to be at his bedside but those who loved him most, King Marc, Gorvenal, and the faithful knight Dinas de Lidan. He longs for death, yet life and the light of the sun are still dear to his brave young heart; so at his urging they place him in a small boat, without oars or sail, and commit him to the hazard of the sea. After seven days and nights he is cast up on the shore of Ireland. (In Gottfried, Morholt, before the last stage of the combat, tells Tristan that his wound is poisoned, and that no one can heal it but his sister Queen Iseut, who knows the virtue of every herb and the remedy for every ill. Morholt proposes peace between them: Cornwall shall pay the tribute, and he himself will conduct Tristan to Ireland, where the Queen will heal him. Tristan rejects the offer, the fight continues, and Morholt is slain). Those who have rescued him take him to Iseut the Fair: "she alone, skilled in philtres, can save him, but she, alone among women, desired the death of Tristan." When, thanks to her magic arts, he recovers and realises the danger he is in if he is recognised, he saves himself by a ruse: he is a minstrel, he tells her, who had been sailing for Spain, there to learn the lore of the stars; but pirates had boarded the ship, he had been wounded in the fight and had escaped in the tiny boat in which he had been found. All believed him, for not even the Irish warriors who had seen him in Cornwall could recognise him, so cruelly had the venom in his veins changed his appearance. After forty days, being almost wholly cured and restored to his former strength and comeliness, he flies in secret from Ireland, and after escaping many dangers at sea finds himself once more at the court of King Marc.[1]

---

[1] In Gottfried's poem Tristan goes of his own accord to Ireland to seek healing of Iseut. He arrives at the port of Develin (Dublin), whence he is taken to the court. Knowing that, as the slayer of Morholt, he is taking his life in his hands, he tells Iseut that his name is Tantris. This was a touch that would delight the imagination of the Middle Ages, which always admired cunning in the outwitting of an enemy. To us, of course, it is charmingly naïve; it is

5

There his enemies, in particular four "felon barons" who hate
him for his favour with the King and do not desire to see him
their ruler when Marc shall die, begin to plot his ruin. How has
he been able to work wonders beyond the power of ordinary
men? they ask. Only by enchantment could he have made his way
to Ireland without sail or oars; and now he is once more casting
his magic spell upon the King. So they urge Marc to marry some
king's daughter who will bear him an heir to his kingdom. Of
himself he would never have yielded to them, so great was the
love he had for his nephew. But the noble Tristan himself, scornful of the suspicion that he had wormed his way into the heart of
the King only for his own profit, swears to him that if he does not
do as the barons desire he will leave Cornwall and never return.
Wagner makes good psychological use of this motive in his second act.

Thereupon the King, in deep distress of soul, looks about him
for a way by which he may appear to yield to the importunities
of the barons and yet find a way of escape. One day, as he is musing sadly in his chamber, two swallows who are building their
nest fly past, and from the beak of one of them there floats
through the open window a long thread of golden hair, finer than
any silk, that glistens in the sun. Marc bids the barons assemble,
Tristan among them: he will do as they desire and marry, he tells
them, but only the woman from whose head the golden hair has
come. The barons are baffled: how to find this woman? who can
say from what distant land the swallows may have flown? They
suspect some crafty ruse on Tristan's part to frustrate them. But
he, having examined the golden thread, and knowing whence it
could alone have come, turns to Marc with a smile: he himself, he
says, will find the head from which it grew, even though it should

---

very much as if a modern novelist were to ask us to believe that Mr. Winston
Churchill managed to maintain himself for some weeks in the Cabinet coun-
cils of the Nazi party by calling himself Chinston Wurchill. Still, there it is
in the legend, and an important feature of it; and we have to accept it in
the spirit in which it is offered. Wagner himself has to take over the Tristan-
Tantris motive in order to account for certain episodes and their psychological results.

be more difficult to return alive from the lady's land than it had been from the island whither he had gone to fight Morholt.[1]

To Ireland, then, he goes, in the guise of a merchant, taking with him a hundred Cornish men of high degree, their rich apparel being concealed under the bridge of the vessel. Apparently he has not thought out any plan for the vicarious wooing of Iseut; but accident puts him in the right way. The ship anchors on the Irish coast, and for a while he and his companions pose as traders. Then, one morning, Tristan hears that a fearsome dragon is terrorising the countryside. He returns to his ship, arms himself, brings out his horse, and attacks the dragon, which he slays; its tongue he cuts out and places in his tunic. But the beast has poisoned him with its noisome belchings, and, faint after the combat, he makes his way to a pool in the distance, where he falls unconscious.

6

Now the King had promised the hand of his daughter Iseut to whoever should rid him of the dragon; and his seneschal, though an arrant coward, has gone out that day as usual to see if fortune will somehow favour him, for he desires Iseut. Finding the body of the dragon, and near it a dead horse and a shattered shield, he concludes that the slayer of the monster has himself been slain; so he cuts off the dragon's head, bears it to the King, and claims the promised guerdon. The King summons his vassals to meet him in

[1] In Gottfried and *Sir Tristrem* it is the nobles who choose the Irish Iseut as bride for Marc, whereupon Tristan, who alone knows her and the King her father, and has already sung her praises to Marc, volunteers to fetch her. Both Gottfried and the author of *Sir Tristrem* mention the story of the swallow, but Gottfried gravely argues that it is improbable that any swallow would have taken the trouble to go all the way from Cornwall to Ireland for material for its nest and return with a single hair. How could it know, asks the implacably logical German poet, that it would find this hair in Ireland, and, if so, on whose head? Why should it make that long journey over the sea when there would be no lack of building material in its own neighbourhood? Gottfried comes to the stern conclusion that those who tell this tale of the golden hair are romancing. Bédier and others think it likely that Thomas, in the lost portion of his poem, had similarly argued against the truth of the episode. To us, however, it is too charming to be rejected on strictly ornithological grounds. That mediaeval swallow evidently had an eye for romance.

three days, when the seneschal will be required to make good his claim before them all. Iseut, learning that she is to be given to the despised dastard, laments her evil fate; but suspecting some imposture on his part she goes in secret with her maid Brangaene and her squire Perinis to the dragon's haunt, where they find the headless body and a horse; the latter, Iseut observes, is not harnessed or shod in the Irish fashion. They light upon the unconscious Tristan, whom they carry back and conceal in the women's quarters of the castle.

As Iseut is removing his armour she discovers the dragon's tongue. She revives him by virtue of a herb, tells him of the treachery of the seneschal, and asks if he will expose the deceit two days later in combat. He consents. The next day she prepares a bath for him and anoints his body with a potent balm of which her mother alone knows the secret. She finds him comely, and hopes his prowess will match his beauty. Recovering his strength, Tristan opens his eyes, looks at her, and smiles. The reason for this she does not understand. Has she somehow failed in duty to her guest? Has she omitted to cleanse his armour, tarnished by the venom of the dragon? She goes to where his sword and halbert are being kept, and finds them goodly. But when she draws the sword from its sheath she sees a gap in it that reminds her of the splinter taken from Morholt's head. A doubt assails her. She examines the fragment and lays it on the sword: the two fit perfectly. Then she returns in fury to Tristan: "You are the murderer of Morholt", she cries; "now die in your turn"; and she raises the sword to strike him. Tristan knows he is helpless; only his wits can save him now. She has not only the power but the right to take his life, he tells her, for twice he has owed it to her. He was the "minstrel" she had healed in days gone by, after he had slain Morholt in fair fight. It was for her that he had fought the dragon. Let her kill him, then, if that will bring her praise and glory, and in the arms of the seneschal she can think of the wounded guest who had twice risked his life for the conquest of her, and whom she had killed defenceless in his bath. Then he tells her of the swallows and the golden hair left at Tintagel. It was for her he had come a second time to Ireland; and he shows her the hair interwoven with the gold embroidery of his tunic, and still lustrous while that had faded. She looks at the sword and the tunic, and for a long time she is silent: then she kisses him on the lips in token of peace between them.

When the vassals assemble, Tristan appears with his hundred men in their richest apparel. Iseut addresses her father. The seneschal had sworn falsely, she tells him; here is a knight ready to prove in combat that it was he who delivered the land from the scourge: will the King promise to forgive him any ancient wrong he may have done them and grant him mercy and peace? Her father pledges his word. She brings Tristan forward, and at once the Irish knights recognise the slayer of Morholt and clamour for his death. But Iseut reminds her father of his promise; and he kisses Tristan on the mouth in pledge that there is peace between them. Tristan produces the dragon's tongue and defies the seneschal to combat, who dares not accept the challenge. Then Tristan tells the King that twice he has conquered Iseut, once through Morholt, and now through the dragon, and so has the right to take her with him over the sea. But in order that the Irish and the Cornish lands may henceforth live not in hatred but in amity she will be given as wife to King Marc. The hundred Cornish squires vow to serve her in all fealty as their queen. But Iseut is overwhelmed with shame and anguish. This splendid Tristan, having conquered her, now disdains her; perhaps his story of the golden hair was only a falsehood; and now he is delivering her over to another man. But the King, faithful to his oath, places her right hand in that of Tristan, who grasps it as pledge that he takes possession of her in the name of the King his uncle.

7

When Iseut leaves Ireland the Queen her mother gives the maid Brangaene a potent philtre she has brewed by her magic art. None but Brangaene is to know of it, she tells her; on the nuptial night she is to pour it secretly into the cup that will be drained by Marc and his bride. Its virtue is that those who have drunk it will love each other henceforth with all their soul and all their senses, in life and in death.

On the ship Iseut never ceases to brood upon her cruel destiny; and when Tristan approaches her with courteous and respectful speech she repulses him angrily, her heart being full of resentment against him. She hates him for that he had killed Morholt, that he had torn her from home and kindred by stratagem, and above all because he had not claimed her for himself but is carrying her to a strange country to be given to another. Then one day, when the ship lies becalmed in the torturing heat, the pair call for something to slake their thirst. A little serving-maid finds the flask which the Queen had given to Brangaene, and they drink the philtre in the belief that it is wine. "But it is not wine; it is passion, it is bitter joy, and anguish without end, and death for the twain." A strange new emotion courses through their veins. Tristan reproaches himself for unwilled treason to the good King his uncle: he had been free of the taint of desiring his kingdom, yet now he loves the King's bride. Iseut, for her part, had willed hatred to Tristan but can only love him now. They sail on in torment of soul, trying to avoid each other, wretched when apart, more wretched still when they meet, trembling at the sight of the abyss of suffering and danger that has opened before their eyes. And all the while Brangaene, who alone knows what and how the Fates have wrought, watches them in terror. They try to understand and justify themselves and each other; till at last, on the third day, their lips meet. Not until then does Brangaene disclose that they have drunk the draught of love and death. "Then let death come!" cries Tristan; and the lovers become one in soul and in flesh to the end of time.

Our central concern being not the legend in itself but the use made of it by Wagner, we need not set forth in detail the long story of the devices to which the lovers, after their arrival in Cornwall, are compelled to resort to gratify their passion in secret. Many of these devices are very naïve, in the mediaeval fashion; others are crude, and some, to modern taste, rather repellent. We can pass on to the tragic end of the story.

The day comes when Tristan, surrounded by spies and enemies and in danger of his life, has to fly to Brittany. For two years he has no news of Iseut: he believes she has forgotten him, and his weary heart fails him. He aids Duke Hoël and his son Kaherdin in their wars, and Hoël, in gratitude, offers him his beautiful daughter Iseut of the White Hands in marriage. "Sire, I will take her", he says; "and for that word he was to die". He weds her; but as his servants are disrobing him there falls from the sleeve of his tunic a ring of green jasper that had been the other Iseut's gift to him;

and he sees that once more, unwittingly, he has been for a while false to troth. Iseut of the White Hands remains his wife only in name. In time, tormented by his memories, he goes back once more to the court of King Marc, where, to be near his only love, he disguises and degrades himself and passes himself off as a fool (in the double mediaeval sense of the word).[1] In the end Iseut recognises him; and when dangers accumulate and he has to return to France she swears that she will follow him when he shall call to her.

The legend now repeats itself to some extent, suggesting that two primitive versions of it had at some time or other become fused into one. Yet again Tristan is dealt an incurable wound by a poisoned weapon. Knowing that he is dying, and unable to go to Iseut, he sends Kaherdin to Cornwall to beg her to come to him. Iseut of the White Hands, concealed behind a partition, overhears their talk; hatred of a rival springs up in her soul, and she plans revenge on the lovers. Iseut the Fair obeys Tristan's call. It has been arranged between him and Kaherdin that if he is bringing her back he shall hoist a white sail, if not, a black one. The sick man, unable to stir from his couch, sends Iseut of the White Hands to keep watch for the coming of the ship. At last, she tells him, it is in sight of the shore, making for land — under a black sail. Then Tristan turns his face to the wall; he murmurs three times the name of Iseut, and dies. When Iseut the Fair at last finds her way to him she kisses his lips and takes him in her arms, and mouth to mouth, body to body, soul to soul, she joins him in death.

When Marc hears of the pitiful end of the lovers he sails to Brittany, has the tombs opened, and carries the two dear bodies back with him to Tintagel. There he buries them, Tristan on this side of the chapel, Iseut on that. But when night fell there sprang from the grave of Tristan a briar that flung its branches across the roof of the chapel and sank them into the tomb of Iseut.[2] Three times

[1] This phase of the legend, for which, of course, Wagner had no use, has been treated in dramatic form by Ernst Hardt in his *Tristan der Narr*. (3rd edition 1903).

[2] There are several mediaeval variants of this miracle. The story as told above is the one found in a printed edition of the French prose romance (1514), though not in the surviving manuscripts.

the men of the country cut it down, and three times it grew afresh; then Marc forbade that a hand should ever be laid on it again.

8

Certain modern writers, afflicted by Providence with more prim piety than poetic imagination, have turned a coldly censorious eye on the legend of Tristan and Isolde, especially on some of the episodes in the middle part of it. "It will not be worth our while", says one of them, "to follow the details of the rest of the story, which is made up of a series of shameless tricks played by the lovers upon King Marke, whereby they are enabled to enjoy their love together in secret . . . From the time when Isot and her intriguing mother enter on the scene the story is as dull as it is immoral. What sane-minded person can possibly take an interest in a succession of childish tricks played by two lovesick boobies upon a half-witted old man?"[1] This is the type of mind that would ask, after reading *Othello*, what sane-minded person could possibly take an interest in a coloured soldier of violent temper who is such a booby as to conceive a murderous hatred of his wife because she had lost a handkerchief that had belonged to his mother, or in a story like the mediaeval one of Parsifal, where an infinity of suffering comes upon many people because an untutored boy refrains from asking the simple question, "Uncle, what ails thee?"[2]

This sort of moral indignation misses the target badly in a matter of art. It is quite true that we of today do not react to some of the incidents in the Tristan legend as the Middle Ages did. That epoch had its own standards of human excellence, and, living as it did surrounded by dangers, it dwelt with gusto on the ruses by

[1] Whatever modern re-telling of the legend the reader may elect to read, it should not be that of Tennyson in the *Idylls of the King* ("The Last Tournament"). The poet went to the worst sources for his material; and Miss Weston is right in saying "it is incomparably the worst version of the story ever given to the world — a gross libel alike on the lovers and on King Mark. For Tennyson's own sake it should be excluded from any future edition of his works: it is little to his credit, either as man or as poet, that in the most famous love-tale of all time he could see nothing but the lowest and most sordid of intrigues."

[2] On this point see the chapter on *Parsifal*.

which a favourite hero outwitted his enemies. As Ernest Muret, the editor of the Béroul fragment, has put it, the story is "one of 'adventure', glorifying the two qualities most prized in the Celtic world in which it originated — physical prowess and agility of mind." A society so largely given over to violence and treachery found a healthy human delight in dwelling on the satisfaction of revenge, and a sort of professional admiration of ingenuity in the art of saving one's life by trickery. Every face in the audience must have been wreathed in approving smiles as the jongleur told how cunningly the hunted lovers defeated justice when Iseut was summoned to prove her innocence by undergoing the ordeal of the red-hot iron. Without considerable craft she could hardly have come through that test successfully. But her woman's wit was equal to the occasion. She sends secret word to Tristan, who is in hiding near by, telling him to disguise himself as a poor pilgrim and wait on the further bank of the river beside which the trial is to take place. When the boat has crossed the stream she protests that she cannot land without soiling her robe in the mud. Thereupon the knights call on the shabby pilgrim, who, unlike them, has nothing on him to spoil, to carry the Queen over to the dry land in his arms. He does so. Then Iseut goes with great dignity to the brazier to make her declaration of innocence, raises her right arm towards the relics of the saints, and swears by all that is sacred that never has any man born of woman taken her in his arms except the King and this poor pilgrim. She plunges her bare arm into the brazier, takes hold of the iron bar, walks nine steps with it, throws it down, and crosses her arms on her breast with the palms upward. All see that her lovely flesh is unscathed. Therefore she has spoken nothing but the truth; and there goes up from them all a great cry of praise and thankfulness to God.

The modern reader may wonder why offended Heaven did not expose and punish the fraud. Even Gottfried was well aware of this little moral difficulty, and he indulges in some ironical reflections about Providence allowing itself to be outwitted sometimes by the wicked. But the people who originally inserted the story of the ordeal into the Tristan story — it appears, by the way, in various forms in various settings in more than one country — evidently had no qualms about the matter. They and their listeners, as Miss Weston and other scholars have pointed out, "really regarded

Tristan and Iseult as irresponsible victims of Fate, and evidently saw no incongruity in their appeals to heaven to demonstrate their innocence."

9

The portrait of Tristan would not have been complete according to mediaeval notions had it not shown him as the superior of his enemies not only in valour but in cunning. Thus Gottfried describes with evident satisfaction the hero's reception by the admiring court when he returns to Cornwall, sound again and safe, after his first audacious visit to Ireland: all laughed heartily when he told how he had gone alone and unarmed into the enemy's country and been healed by the Queen and the daughter of the King: "all agreed that never in their lives had they heard anything so wonderful".

But in the first place the majority of these episodes, in which cunning matches itself against cunning, guile against guile, and the hero and heroine of the tale are of course the most prolific in resource of them all, are merely patches upon the essentially grave and noble fabric of the Tristan story: they probably date from an earlier and half-barbaric period, and had to be retained by the literary romancers of a later day because many of their readers or listeners already knew them and expected them. In the second place, some of the episodes have, for all their naïveté, a curious pathos and beauty of their own. An outstanding example is the tale of how Tristan and Iseut, compelled to flee from the court and live a hunted life in a forest, are discovered by a spy who betrays them to the King. Marc, with vengeance in his heart, comes by night and finds them sleeping in a grotto. He sends the spy away and draws his sword; they are at his mercy. But he see that while their lips are touching, between their bodies lies a naked sword. A great pity and love for them both, for his beautiful adored Queen and for the nephew who is the dearest of all men to him, take possession of his heart. He will spare them, but he will let them know that he had tracked them down and their lives had been in his hand. He leaves his glove where it will shield the lovely face of Iseut from the unkind light. He takes from her hand an emerald ring he had given her: once it had needed forcing upon her finger to make it fit; now it slips from it, so wasted is she with privation and suffering. In its place he leaves his own royal ring, and with it his sword; that of Tristan he takes away with him. When the lovers awake they realise how near they had been to death, and the greatness of soul and profundity of love of the man who had spared them. There are few incidents in the whole of mediaeval romance more beautiful.

It stands to reason that the legend would never have captured the imagination of the later Middle Ages as it did had it been the mere tale of a couple of lovesick boobies imposing on a half-witted old man. No story was so widely diffused over cultured Europe or evoked so great an imaginative response in the finest minds of the day. Dante, though the stern moralist in him would hardly have approved of the pair, as poet could not resist their appeal. In the fifth canto of the *Inferno* they figure among other great lovers of the fabled past pointed out to him by his guide Vergil:

> "*L'altra è colei che s'ancise amorosa,*
> *e ruppe fede al cener di Sicheo;*
> *poi è Cleopatràs lussuriosa.*
> *Elena vedi, per cui tanto reo*
> *tempo si volse, e vedi il grande Achille,*
> *che con amore al fine combattèo.*
> *Vedi Parìs, Tristano": e più di mille*
> *ombre mostrommi e nominommi a dito,*
> *ch'amor di nostra vita dipartille.*

(" 'The next is she [Dido] who slew herself for love and broke faith with the ashes of Sychaeus; then wanton Cleopatra. See Helen, for whose sake so many cruel years revolved; and see the great Achilles, who fought at last with love; see Paris, Tristan': and he showed me more than a thousand shades, naming them as he pointed to them, who were parted from our life by love.") The mind of the epoch spent itself affectionately in one medium after another upon this or that episode of the Tristan and Isolde legend, in detached poems, in tapestries, in illuminated manuscripts, in ivories. The mediaeval musicians put some of their best songs into the mouths of the hapless lovers, for Tristan, according to tradition, was a great minstrel, and Iseut too poured out her heart in song. Gottfried speaks of "many lovely melodies" concerning them "that were known far and wide" in his time. He speaks with particular feeling of one noble lay composed by Tristan which, he says, is loved in every land and will not be forgotten as long as the world endures. This song, unfortunately, has been lost; but others have survived, and the words and music of one of them — the "lai de plor" (the song of tears) which, according to the legend, was sung by the wounded Tristan in the little boat that carried him the first time to Ireland — may be found in some of the modern books on the subject.

10

Some of the nineteenth century opponents of Wagner foamed at the mouth over the "glorification of adultery" in this opera of his. Had they read his poem with any understanding they would have realised that the Tristan story, as he tells it, is the most tragically ascetic of tales. But even for the Middle Ages the essential things were not the episodes, the ruses by which the lovers were enabled to gratify their secret passion, but the beauty and pitifulness of their love. The legend became as popular as it did not because of the piquancy of some of its details but because, in its fundamentals, it had all the qualities that go to make one of those great sagas into which each following age can read itself afresh. There have not been many of them in modern times; they can be counted on the fingers of one hand — the Nibelungenlied, Tristan and Isolde, Faust, the Cid, Don Juan. In all these the characters and events have the quality of rising from the particular into the universal. They are at once personal and symbolic. Faust is not merely a scholar who strives after knowledge and power: he is the symbol of all striving after those illusions. Don Juan is not merely a licentious young Spanish nobleman: he is the life force for ever condemned to the vain quest of seeking to accomplish itself in the satisfaction of the senses. And Tristan and Isolde were already in mediaeval times not simply a chance pair of lovers but the symbol and the essence of a love so overpowering that it is impossible for the human victims of it to achieve their heart's desire except in death.

From the very beginning the threads of Tristan's life are spun for him with slow inexorable intent by the Fates. He is born of sorrow and for sorrow, as the musician Wagner so finely conveys

to us in his third act, where the fevered man's memory runs back
to the last time he had heard the mournful strain now piped by
the Herdsman — it had filled Kareol with its lament when his
father, and again his mother, had perished in the flower of their
youth and beauty. It is Fate that in devious ways draws Tristan
twice to Ireland and Isolde, Fate that weaves the threads that
gradually intertwine Isolde's life with Marke's. And even for the
Middle Ages the love-philtre that is the explosive core of the
story, the point towards which everything that has happened before inevitably tends and from which everything that happens
later inevitably flows, was not solely and simply a magic brew,
working by physical means, but a symbol, the instrument through
which Love has its imperious way with men and women. Gottfried
achieves a finer touch than his French predecessors by not speaking of love in the abstract but incarnating it in Frau Minne, the
old Teutonic goddess of Love: it is always Frau Minne who is
working her irresistible will upon these two fated human vessels.

The sympathies of the old romancers are all with Tristan and
Isolde even as against the good King Marke. Tristan, for them, is
in his inmost self always the flower of truth and loyalty and
honour; it is precisely because of these great qualities in him that
he unwittingly forges the first link in the chain of his own destruction — his altrustic bringing of Isolde to Cornwall to be the bride
of King Marke, so that he may free himself of the suspicion of any
taint of self-interest in his love for and gratitude to the King his
uncle. (Wagner makes great use of this psychological motive in
his second act). And the final testimony of the Middle Ages to its
belief in the essential innocence of Tristan and Isolde is the ending of the story, with that exquisite symbolic figure of a tree
springing from the grave of each of them and twining its branches
with those of the other. This, as Wolfgang Golther points out, was
the poetic mediaeval way of indicating that physical love had
been purified into the spiritual by death. The "flower-symbol", he
says, "in the sense it carries in the legend, means that before
God's throne Tristan and Isolde are absolved of all guilt . . . An
earnest, pessimistic spirit breathes through the story from first to
last; whoever turns away from it on moral grounds has simply
misconceived its profoundest being and its true worth, which consist in this — that behind all the glitter of the incidents there lies

a conception of the utmost gravity . . . Not every one of the poets was conscious of it, of course; but the really great masters, and Gottfried most of all, has at least an intuition of it."

Wagner penetrated as no other modern poet or dramatist has done to this spiritual core of the saga, and thanks largely to the unique expressive power of music he has been able to raise the lovers from the plane of the individual to the higher sphere of the symbolic. His poem is not a mere re-telling of the ancient story of Tristan and Isolde but in several respects a radical re-creation of it.

11

He had made the acquaintance of the legend in the course of his study of mediaeval literature in his Dresden period, and we may be sure that it had often been in his mind since then. He had read Gottfried in the modern German rendering of Kurtz, a second edition of which was published in 1847. Kurtz had made an ending of his own for the unfinished original, and, in a passage that no doubt struck light and fire into Wagner's imagination, had said that the story contained all the materials for a tremendous tragic drama. Wagner was also acquainted with certain by-products of the legend that had been discussed by F. H. von der Hagen in the fourth volume of his *Minnesinger,* a mine of information about the German poems of the 12th, 13th and 14th centuries (1838). We first hear of the story taking definite shape within him as an opera in a letter of his of December 1854 to Liszt, at the time when he was engaged on the music of the second act of the *Valkyrie.* He hopes, he says, to finish the *Ring* by 1856 and produce it in 1858. But, he continues, "since never in my whole life have I tasted the real happiness of love I mean to raise a monument to that most beautiful of dreams, in which, from beginning to end, this love shall really sate itself to the full for once. I have in my mind a plan for a *Tristan and Isolde,* the simplest but most full-blooded musical conception; in the 'black flag' that waves at the finish I shall then enshroud myself — to die." From this it would appear that his intention at that time was to introduce the second Iseut — Iseut of the White Hands — and the dramatic culminating motive of the white flag and the black. As the reader knows, he dispenses with these addenda in his poem, though, it is true, he makes his Tristan, during his delirium in the third act, see in imagination Isolde's ship approaching with "the flag at the mast" — as it stands a somewhat irrelevant touch, the significance of which comes home only to the listener who is acquainted with the episode of the second Iseut and the two flags from other sources than the libretto. But it was not only in this respect that the final conception of *Tristan and Isolde* was to differ from that outlined in the letter to Liszt.[1]

The lovers of romantic biographic fiction will have it that Wagner wrote *Tristan and Isolde* because he was in love with Frau Wesendonk. That he loved the fair Mathilde during those Zürich years is beyond question, also that there was a close emotional association in his mind between her and the opera all the time he was writing it. But to suppose that Mathilde "inspired" *Tristan* is to take a very unsophisticated view of the nature and the workings of the artistic imagination. The mind of a great creator is a much more complex piece of machinery than this would suggest; and in Wagner's case there were other and even more potent forces at work within him than the golden hair of the pretty young lady in the luxurious house on the Green Hill at Enge. He was in a highly febrile state all through those years. The fact that he was intensely unhappy cannot be regarded as a prime determining factor in the conception and execution of *Tristan*, for the side of the artist that has daily commerce with the outer world and the side that is concentrated inwards have often the minimum of connection with each other. Wagner was equally unhappy, if not, indeed, more so, during most of the time when he was writing *The Mastersingers*, which is the sunniest of all his works. To suppose that a great artist is optimistic or pessimistic in his creative work according to whether things are going well or ill with him in actual life at the moment is to assume, to borrow a phrase of John Stuart Mill's, that because there is pepper in the soup there is pepper in the cook.

What was really happening in the depths of Wagner during the middle 1850's was that an enormous volume of music, of a type which the world had not yet known, was pressing imperiously for another outlet than the heroic *Ring*, upon the composition of

[1] He had originally intended to bring in Parsifal in the third act. On this point see *infra*, pages 662/3.

which he was engaged at that time. It was a common experience with him to find that the very intensity of his concentration on one subject called up from the deeps another that had long been slumbering in his subconscious. In the present instance the whirling nebula of incandescent dust from which the *Ring* music was being generated spontaneously threw off, at a given place and time, without much conscious volition on his part, a mental and musical world entirely different from the other. He himself saw clearly enough, in later years, what had happened within him about 1854. He would have smiled then at the theory that *Tristan* had been "inspired" by Frau Wesendonk, whom, it is instructive to note, he no longer saw through quite the same eyes of idealising romance when the score of the work was off his hands and the volcano that had been raging within him had died down. When he came to write his memoirs he was able to see more clearly the hidden inner processes that had brought forth *Tristan*. As usually happened with him when his musical faculty was working at high pressure, he says, there had come over him in 1854 an urge to express himself in poetry. It is a fundamental misconception of him to suppose that his practice was that of the ordinary opera composer — first of all to decide upon a "subject", make a three-act "libretto" of it, and then sit down and invent music to fit the words and follow the action. The process with him was, in some essentials, the reverse of this; a more or less indefinite and mainly musical complex within him kept calling on him to give it poetic and dramatic actuality, for which words and a stage action would be necessary.[1] His melancholy broodings in the 1850's upon the innate tragedy of the cosmos had been both clarified and intensified by his reading of Schopenhauer at that time. The result of it all, as he himself tells us, was that the attempt to find "an ecstatic expression of the profoundest elements" in this philosophy "generated in me the conception of a *Tristan and Isolde*."

---

[1] "I can conceive a subject", he once wrote to a friend, "only when it comes to me in such a form that I myself cannot distinguish between the contribution of the poet and that of the musician in me; and its completion in word and tone is simply the ultimate realisation of something that had originally presented itself to me only in vague outlines. This is the foundation of all my productive, and more particularly my musical-productive, power."

12

He talked the matter over with his young Zürich companion Karl Ritter, who, it appeared, had also become interested in the Tristan theme. Ritter showed him his own plan for a drama on the subject. The experienced eye of the musical dramatist saw at a glance that the young man had gone entirely the wrong way about it. Evidently he had lost himself in the picturesque details and the conventional "love interest" of the tale, whereas what was needed was a concentration on the eternal and tragic core of it, with the employment of no more incident than would be necessary to show this core in conflict with the world of material reality. So after thinking it all out on one of his walks Wagner drew up a scenario of his own in three acts.

Whether that sketch has survived among his papers we do not know; it is possible that he destroyed it when, in 1857, he took up the operatic plan again in good earnest. During those three years a great deal had happened to him, internally and externally. Continual brooding upon philosophical problems and eager readings of Schopenhauer and of Buddhist literature had deepened his feeling that the outer world is a tragic illusion. He had last appeared before the public as a composer with *Tannhäuser* in 1845 and *Lohengrin* in 1850. Since then he had written the *Rhinegold*, the *Valkyrie*, and the greater part of *Siegfried*, works in which he had developed opera to a point hitherto undreamed of. Of all this astounding creative work the public as yet knew nothing. The completion of the colossal *Ring* seemed at the moment to lie in a distant future; and when the scores of the tetralogy were finished there would still be before him the terrifying task of staging the huge work. Meanwhile the problem of merely existing was becoming more and more difficult. So on the mundane side of him he came round to the view of his friends that he ought to write something more practicable, under existing conditions, than the *Ring*, something for which he could hope for immediate payment from the German theatres. He deluded himself with the belief that his *Tristan* would be such a work, for it would call for only five principal singers and a couple of subsidiary characters, virtually no chorus, and the minimum of staging. Little did he dream at that time that his *Tristan* was to turn out to be the most difficult work in any dramatic genre which the world had yet seen.

But perhaps more potent than any of these influences was the fact that although his mind was alive with music, a large part of it was unconsciously seeking an outlet which the *Ring* could not supply. He had been continuously engaged on the poems and the music of the latter since 1848, and no doubt he was beginning to feel a little weary of the company of his more-than-life-size Germanic gods and heroes. In the summer of 1856 we find him telling Liszt that at the moment he would rather write poetry than music, and that he had "two marvellous subjects" which he *must* work out. One of them was the *Tristan* of which he had already spoken; the other was an Indian theme. This latter work, the title of which was to be *The Victors*, haunted his imagination for another twenty years or so but never came to fruition, partly because much of the emotional and metaphysical impulse that would have gone to the making of it had been expended on *Tristan*, partly because, in the late 1870's, he found that a good deal of what he would have to say in connection with it was finding its natural expression in *Parsifal*.

In the primitive Teutonic world of the *Ring* he was probably becoming, from sheer repletion, less interested each month. A crisis was reached in June 1857. On the 28th of that month he wrote to Liszt that he had "torn *Siegfried* from his heart and buried it alive under lock and key": "there will I keep it; no one shall see anything of it, for it will be sealed up even from myself." "I have led my young Siegfried into the beautiful forest solitude again; there I have left him under a linden tree, and, with tears from the depth of my heart, said farewell to him: he is better there than anywhere else." (The point in the score to which he was referring is the second scene of the second act: after the hero's words "Dass der mein Vater nicht ist" he had written in his Composition Sketch, "27th June 57. R. W. When shall we see each other again?"). So long as his letter of the 28th June to Liszt was the sole source of our knowledge of this matter it was naturally assumed by the biographers that it was at that point that work upon *Siegfried* was suspended for several years. We know now, however, that he took it up again a fortnight later and completed the second act on the 30th July. No doubt he foresaw that the composition of *Tristan* would mean a long separation from the *Ring*, and he thought it as well to finish the second act of *Siegfried* while the "feel" of the *Ring* milieu was still lively within him.

13

Letters of his to other friends confirm and amplify the evidence of his letter of June 1857 to Liszt. As early as the 19th December 1856, while he was engaged on the *first* act of *Siegfried*, he told the young Princess Marie Wittgenstein (the daughter of Liszt's unofficial wife Princess Carolyne von Sayn-Wittgenstein) that while trying to work "today" at the music of *Siegfried* he had "unawares fallen into the Tristan" subject. "For the moment", he continues, "music without words: several things I would rather treat in music than in verse" — one of the many indications we have that the prime impulse to the writing of his dramas was generally not so much a literary as a musical one. "Today, as I have told you", he goes on to say, "Tristan has come between [myself and Siegfried] in the shape of a melodic thread which, though I fain would have quitted it, kept on spinning itself, so that I could have spent the whole day developing it."

The precise meaning of this will appear in a moment. Meanwhile we must draw attention to a salient characteristic of his artistic psychology. As a rule he was occupied simultaneously with more than one work; even if he were not actually putting B upon paper it was gestating in his subconsciousness while he was formally engaged upon A. His dramatic characters and situations had a life of their own within him that was independent of his surface consciousness and even of his volition, so that while at work on the score of one opera a theme would suddenly spring up within him which had nothing to do with the subject in hand but, as he would soon realise, belonged of right to some other work that had not been consciously occupying his thoughts at the time. One day in 1876 when he was writing the American Centennial March the idea flashed across him for the ensemble of the Flower Maidens in *Parsifal;* and in 1859, while engaged on the third act of *Tristan*, the joyous melody of the Herdsman took, without his willing it, a turn which, as he soon saw, was more appropriate to his forgotten young hero Siegfried: it became later

the "Love's Resolution" motive of the Ring.[1] And after telling
Marie Wittgenstein, in December 1856, that he could not get on
with *Siegfried* because the Tristan subject kept throwing out its
own musical roots within him, he informed her in the following
August that the reverse had latterly been the case. He had carried,
he said, the composition of the second act of *Siegfried* as far as
the words "Das der mein Vater nicht ist", and then closed the
score with the intention of saying a long farewell to his hero. A
few days later, he continues, he had sat down at his desk to make
a sketch for the poem of *Tristan*, "when suddenly I was overmas-
tered by so pitiful a longing for *Siegfried* that I took the score out
again and decided to complete at any rate the second act. This
has now been done: Fafner is dead, Mime is dead, and Siegfried
has followed the flying Forest Bird; and this, my dear child, has
turned out very nicely, so that now I know my hero is all right.
Yet all this has been a great strain on me, for while I was once
more working at *Siegfried* I could get no peace from *Tristan*. I
actually worked simultaneously at them both, the *Tristan* taking
more and more definite shape, and I being so passionately occupied with it that in the end the double labour was a perfect torment to me."

The truth is that a tremendous psychic upheaval had begun in
him as early as 1856, which put him rather out of tune for the
time being with the joy-in-life of which his youthful hero Siegfried had been the ardent optimistic expression. He had become
introspective, pessimistic, mystical. Three days after his letter of
the 19th December 1856 to Marie Wittgenstein he wrote thus to
Otto Wesendonk, who was at that time in Paris: "I can no longer
get into the mood for my *Siegfried;* my musical sensibility is now
reaching out far beyond that, into a realm more consonant with
my mood — the realm of melancholy. It is all coming to me,
though as yet quite flatly and superficially." He was beginning, in
fact, to *feel* the Tristan subject very definitely as music, before it
had taken a definite shape within him dramatically.

14

Let us now turn back to the passage in the letter to Marie Wittgenstein in which he says that while working at the music of the

[1] See *infra*, musical example No. 153 in the analysis of *Siegfried*.

first act of *Siegfried* he had "unawares fallen into the Tristan subject" . . . "for the moment, music without words", in the form of
a "melodic thread" which kept on "spinning itself" almost against
his will. We are fortunate in being able to identify that "thread"
now.

There has survived in the Wahnfried archives a scrap of music
which was evidently intended to accompany an (unpublished)
letter of his to Frau Wesendonk of the early part of 1857. It consists of eighteen bars beginning thus:

The reader will recognise this as the foreshadowing of one of the
most important themes of the second act of *Tristan*. (See musical
example No. 41). In the opera it appears in 3/4 time, but in this
primitive form it is in 4/4: the harmony on the third beat of the
first bar is less chromatic and therefore less poignant than it afterwards became, while after the third bar the strain develops in a
manner rather different from the one we know so well in the
opera.[1]

Wagner was only copying, however, for Frau Wesendonk's benefit, from a still earlier sketch, which also happens to have been
preserved. This is dated by Wagner himself "19 Dec. 56" — i.e.,
the very day on which he was telling Marie Wittgenstein that a
"melodic thread" had been "spinning itself" of its own volition
within him. There can be no doubt, then, that this is the "thread"
to which he was referring.[2] And, again fortunately for us, this

[1] A facsimile of the manuscript page will be found in the Bayreuth *Festspielführer* for 1938, p. 160.
[2] The word "thread" (*Faden*) was one often used by Wagner to describe
the material from which he did his musical "spinning". It does not mean
simply a "theme" in the sense in which other composers employ that word,
but, as it were, the musical incarnation of a situation, a character, or a mood,
from which all conceivable tonal and psychological mutations would follow
later as a matter of course. Thus he told Cosima in 1871 that his heart was
not really in such a work as the *Kaisermarsch,* and he was writing it with
some difficulty. It "meant" nothing to him: "I must have my big threads",
he told her.

earlier sheet contains not only the above-mentioned eighteen bars with a few variants, but the first draft of what was afterwards to become world-famous as the motive of "Longing" or "Desire" in the opera (see No. 1 B); and the sheet is headed "Love Scene; Tristan and Isolde". Now it was not until August 1857 that Wagner began the Prose Sketch for his drama — some ten days after he had finished the composition of the second act of *Siegfried*. It is clear, then, that even in December 1856 — that is to say, while he was still working at the *first* act of that opera, — the *music* of *Tristan* was already imposing its will upon him before he had drawn up so much as a formal scenario of the action. There could be no more convincing demonstration of the truth of the statement that if ever there was an opera born of the spirit of music itself it is *Tristan and Isolde*.

Towards the end of April 1857 he drafted a scenario for *Tristan* that served as foundation both for a later detailed Prose Sketch (finished on the 20th August and now available in print), and then for the poem. The latter was completed on the 18th September of that year. The Prose Sketch and the poem do not differ greatly from each other; where they do, the Sketch is useful as showing more clearly what was at the back of Wagner's mind here and there, for the hyper-laconic style in which the poem is written makes it a little difficult sometimes to grasp his full meaning.

15

As usual with him, his first concern had been to rid the immense mass of mediaeval material of everything merely accessory and condense the sprawling action into its essentials. He dispenses, for example, with the four "felon barons", enemies of Tristan, who in the legend play a considerable part in laying traps for him and denouncing him to the King. All he needed in this respect was the single character of the false friend Melot, and even of him we learn more through the mouths of others than in person, for he makes only two very brief appearances in the drama — at the end of the second act, where he brings in King Marke to surprise the lovers, and in the final stage of the third act, where he sings a couple of lines "off" and then enters only to be slain by Kurvenal.

To the whole opera Melot contributes no more than twenty bars of music. The King, again, appears only twice, and as a commentator on events rather than a participant in them; his share in the long chain of episodes stretching from Tristan's combat with Morold to the final catastrophe we mostly learn from others. Of ordinary stage incident there is exceedingly little in the opera; it is virtually unnecessary, for the veritable drama is not in what "happens" to Tristan and Isolde in the world of reality but in what evolves within themselves, and this is revealed to us principally by the music.

Wagner's most difficult problem was in connection with the love philtre. It was impossible for him to employ this in its more materialistic mediaeval sense – to make the inextinguishable "passion" of the lovers for each other the crude physical result of a magic brew; though unfortunately it is still in that naïve sense that the majority of listeners to the opera still conceive it. Even the more refined of the old romancers, as has already been pointed out, seem to have had a poetic intuition of it as a symbol rather than a material agency; that is to say, the lovers were pre-destined to each other in life and in death, and the draught brewed by Isolde's mother for a purpose of her own was merely the Fates' way of accomplishing their far-seen purpose. But Wagner would have to refine this central motive of *his* drama far beyond this. Manifestly the problem was the most crucial of the many he had to face; and the only valid solution of it was the one finally adopted by him – Tristan and Isolde were to be shown drawn together from the beginning by some compulsion which they themselves did not comprehend; the near approach to the shore of Cornwall, where Isolde would be handed over to the King and Tristan would depart from her sight and Marke's for ever, had strained both of them to breaking-point, so that each of them saw that the only way out of a lifelong torment was through the gates of death; to that end they were to drink gladly of what they imagined to be a poisoned cup; and then, in the belief that death was at hand, the barriers raised between them by Tristan's sense of honour and loyalty to King Marke would go down, and they could confess their love without restraint and without self-reproach. In this reading, the love draught is really a subsidiary rather than a cardinal motive; it does indeed fill their veins with a fire that can never be extinguished, but only because the materials for the fire were there before.

16

The point was, how could Wagner introduce this new psychological motive, which transformed the saga so radically as to make his own version of it virtually a new creation on his part? Obviously it would have to become operative during the first (and only) sojourn of his wounded "Tantris" in Ireland. The moment chosen by Wagner to constitute this nodal point of his drama was that in which Isolde stays her avenging hand just as she is about to slay the man whom she recognises as the hated vanquisher of her affianced Morold; and the medium through which this was to be brought home to the audience was Isolde's Narration to Brangaene in the first act. That Wagner was at first not entirely clear how this was to be done is manifest in the Prose Sketch.

The old poets had told how Tristan, at Isolde's mercy in his bath when she discovered that the splinter taken from Morholt's head fitted exactly into the notch in the sword, had saved his life in the first instance by denying that he was Tristan, and then by a crafty appeal *ad misericordiam*. In the end it is the "sweet womanliness" in her, as Gottfried puts it, that gets the upper hand of her fury; she throws away the sword and weeps bitterly. The Queen, Isolde and Brangaene go out and take counsel together. Brangaene's advice to them is to spare the alien knight, in the first place because they will need him to dispose of the troublesome seneschal who is claiming Isolde's hand, in the second place because this Tristan has evidently been sent to Ireland on some important mission, and it behoves them to find out what it is. When they return he once more begs for grace, and promises them that if his life is spared the young Irish princess shall go back with him to be the proud wife of his uncle the noble and powerful King Marc, and the two countries will henceforth be bound together in friendship. The three women kiss him on the lips in token of amity, Isolde, however, with reluctance, for to her he is still Ireland's enemy and hers. Then he confesses that he had ventured to Ireland the second time for the very purpose of taking back with him Iseut, whose beauty he had praised to Marc. The Irish King is summoned and let into the secret, and he too makes peace with Tristan and with Cornwall.

17

Obviously this very earthly web of mediaeval intrigue and ruse could not be utilised for Wagner's drama, the central psychological point of which was to be that the pair already loved each other before the stage action opens, that Tristan had fought down his love out of loyalty to King Marke, that Isolde was torn between love for the hero Tristan and hatred of him as Ireland's conqueror, and that the pair feel themselves liberated from all worldly constraints only at the moment when, as they believe, they are about to end their souls' intolerable torment by a voluntary death. Wagner could safely follow the old story, as indeed he does in Isolde's Narration, as far as the moment when she refrains from killing Ireland's enemy and hers with his own sword. But why does his Isolde so refrain? "Recognising him as the slayer of the Irish hero", so runs the Prose Sketch in its outline of the Narration, "and recalling her vow of vengeance, she had seized the sword and rushed at Tristan to kill him; then she had felt pity for the wretched sick man". The reader will recall that whereas in the legend this episode occurs during Tristan's *second* visit to Ireland, when he is helpless not through sickness but because, like the doomed Agamemnon, he is in his bath and unarmed, Wagner transfers it to the first visit, the motive of which, in the legend, had been to win healing from the magic medical art of Isolde's mother. This enables him to employ with all the more force the motive of "sweet womanliness", as Gottfried calls it, the sudden surge of pity in Isolde for the grievously sick and helpless man. But of itself that psychological motive, moving as it is, is still insufficient for Wagner's full purpose; it does not explain how, from that moment onward, each had read *love* in the eyes of the other.

The problem of how to bring this new and vital factor home to the listener must have cost Wagner much anxious thought. This is clear from an insert he has made in the Sketch — manifestly an afterthought — after the sentence quoted above, "she had felt pity for the wretched sick man"; before passing on to the next stage of the Narration, in which, very much as in the legend, Isolde communicates to Brangaene her discovery of the identity of Tristan and Tantris, he now inserts in a parenthesis, "Here she makes it clear that it was an awakened passionate inclination towards him that had stayed her hand". But in the Sketch he still does not go on to show just how this is to be "made clear" to the audience, perhaps because he himself did not know precisely how at that time. But when he came to write his poem, a few weeks after the completion of the Sketch, he saw a satisfactory solution of his problem, though in terms more of music than of verbal exposition. He makes the wounded man turn upon Isolde a look that melted her heart, for she read in it the secret of an unspoken love:

> *Then from his sick-bed*
> *up he gazed —*
> *not on the sword,*
> *not on my hand —*
> *his eyes in mine were looking;*
> *and his woefulness*
> *pierced to my heart;*
> *the sword — fell from my hand.*
> *The wound that Morold dealt him,*
> *with my own hand I healed it,*
> *that home he might betake him*
> *and rid me of the load of that look!*

But even this does not make the psychological point absolutely clear to us when we read the poem alone for the first time; illumination comes rather from the music, from the so-called "Look" motive that wells up in the moving tones of a solo viola:

a motive that has already played a most significant part in the prelude, and is later to be charged with an infinity of meanings in the opera itself. Wagner never tired of assuring his correspondents that something that was not quite clear to them in a text of his would be made perfectly clear by the music. This is a case in point.

The poem of *Tristan and Isolde* was completed and the manuscript presented to Frau Wesendonk on the 18th September 1857. (A few changes in the text were made by Wagner in later years). The dates of composition of the music are as follows:

Composition Sketch.[1]

Act   I.   1 October — 31 December 1857.
Act II.   4 May — 1 July 1858.
Act III.   9 April — 16 July 1859.

Orchestral Sketch.

Act   I.   5 November 1857 — 13 January 1858.
Act II.   5 July 1858 — 9 March 1859.
Act III.   1 May — 19 July 1859.

The full orchestral score was finished on the 8th or 9th August 1859.

The first performance of the opera was given in Munich, under Hans von Bülow, on the 10th June 1865, with the following cast:

TRISTAN	Ludwig Schnorr von Carolsfeld
ISOLDE	Malvina Schnorr von Carolsfeld
BRANGAENE	Anna Deinet
MARKE	Zottmayer
KURVENAL	Mitterwurzer
MELOT	Heinrich

18

Wagner was a *musical* dramatist, a fact which permitted him a technique of exposition entirely different from that of the prose or poetical dramatist. The normal way of the latter is to start at A and go step by regular step to Z. Wagner, relying at least as much on music as on words to tell us who and what his characters are and what they feel at a given moment, and being more concerned,

[1] The "Composition Sketch" of a Wagnerian work was, in general, the first swift outline of the music. The "Orchestral Sketch" was a rather more developed lay-out, with a summary indication of his orchestral intentions. The final stage was the Orchestral Score.

in the main, with mental states than with incidents,[1] could plan his stage action in ways that would give the freest imaginable play to music. This was especially the case with *Tristan and Isolde*, which is *musical* from centre to periphery — so much so that the bulk of the opera would make an organic musical whole if played through by the orchestra without the voices. If ever there was an opera "born out of the spirit of music", to adapt the title of one of Nietzsche's books, it is this. The words are not so much the generators of the music as the crystallisation of musical moods into the accepted symbols of speech. Wagner himself pointed out how different his procedure had been from that of the ordinary dramatist or poet. The latter would have had to explain, for example, at the outset, at some length, who Tristan was, how he came into the world, what adventures he had already gone through, and so on; and out of all this statement of fact there would emerge, bit by bit, our emotional reaction to the characters, their milieu, and the things that happen to them. But the musician, says Wagner, can strike at once to that emotional core which it takes the poet or the prose romancer so long to reach by the slow way of description; we are given the whole complex of longing and suffering that is the essence of the souls of the two chief characters in the opening bars of the prelude. The music in and by itself shapes their total stage life into a kind of ring, a circle in which there is no apposition of starting-point and finish; the strain of longing is the first that greets our ears in the prelude, and it is the last to resound in them in the opera; and, as with a ring, it is equally appropriate to say that the work begins where it ends as that it ends where it began.

19

The musical texture of *Tristan* is different from that of any other of Wagner's works in that it is almost purely "symphonic"; often he abandons himself to the sheer intoxication of "developing" the mood symbolised by a particular motive for pages at a time, the stage situation meanwhile remaining stabilised. Not

---

[1] In the *Mastersingers*, of course, incident follows incident in quick succession and in the order of actual life; but that is because here the drama comes nearer to the world of ordinary people than in any other work of his maturity.

only is there hardly any action, but action of any kind would mostly be out of place: the movement of the drama is not realistic but psychological, not external but internal, the music passing through all kinds of metamorphoses to which the words serve only to give us the objective clue. For the greater portion of the time the actors hardly need to change their positions on the stage; the consequence is that when something does "happen", in the ordinary theatrical sense of the word, it strikes with tremendous force; it does precisely what Wagner intended it should do — the brief intrusion of reality gives us a blinding sense of how entirely Tristan and Isolde had lived, in the only sense that they would have called living, in a world of non-reality of their own. In the first act, apart from the episode of the coming of Tristan into the presence of Isolde, very little "happens" until the end, when the ship arrives in Cornwall and the King and his courtiers and people come to the shore to meet it; and the stir and excitement of this are suggested in the music rather than shown on the stage. In the second act there are only two disruptions of the inner drama by external reality — the entry of Tristan, and, later in the act, that of Marke and Melot, with the wounding of Tristan. In the third act there is virtually no action until the very end — the arrival first of Isolde, then of Marke and the others.

The real drama, as has been already pointed out, is not external but internal, a state of affairs made possible to the musical dramatist only in virtue of the vast superiority of music to speech and to the pictorial arts in range and subtlety and intensity of emotional expression. Taking advantage of this, Wagner exploits a favourite technique of his; instead of burdening his stage with a multiplicity of characters and "effective" episodes he concentrates the very essence of these into a reference to them by one of the few main actors at some vital point or other. There is no need, for instance, for him to begin by telling us in words that Tristan was foredoomed to sorrow from the moment of his birth: he conveys this to us not at the commencement of his story but near the end, and that by the simplest and most affecting of means, by a few bars in which, moved by the Shepherd's mournful melody, the hero's thoughts go back to the tragic death of his father and mother. Again, Wagner shows us nothing of the Breton and Cornish milieu in which the young Tristan had lived, nothing of the events that had led up to the fateful journey to Ireland, nothing of what happened there. All that is necessary for us to know about these and other things he communicates to us through the mouths of the lovers in the first and second acts, where the story is told not for its own picturesque sake — as it would be by a poet — but because it furnishes the explanation of the situation and the state of mind in which the lovers now find themselves: it is not the incidents themselves that he gives us but the incidents remembered in, and blindingly illuminated by, emotion.

It has to be admitted that the rigour with which he follows this system in *Tristan and Isolde* sometimes makes it difficult for the casual listener in the theatre to follow all the windings of his poetic imagination. It is impossible, indeed, to see the work precisely as the creator of it conceived it without a close study not only of the poem but of the Prose Sketch — which accounts for the fact that even today ninety-nine people out of a hundred in the theatre come away with a totally wrong idea of much of it. If they had the smallest understanding of it they would not speak of the second act, as they do, as "the love duet", for all the world as if "love" meant here what it does in the case of Romeo and Juliet, or Faust and Marguerite, or Pinkerton and Madam Butterfly, or a hundred other operatic lovers. Throughout the poem Wagner restricts himself to the barest minimum of words — sometimes no more than two or three to a line of verse, — having no need of speech beyond what is necessary to concretise the emotion that is being poured out by the prime expressive instrument of the work, the music. Occasionally his condensation has been so drastic that, as we shall see when we come to the analysis of the second act, it is only after reading his more detailed exposition of events and motives in the Prose Sketch that the almost too laconic poem conveys its full meaning to us.

20

The selection from *Tristan* known in the concert room as the Prelude and Liebestod — the latter being the closing scene of the opera — makes an admirably rounded whole, musically and psychologically. It is worth noting, by the way, that when Wagner first linked up the Prelude with the finale for concert purposes it was to the former that he gave the explanatory title of "Liebes-

tod"; the finale he described as "Verklärung" (Transfiguration).
In a programme note of his own on the concert arrangement he
explained the Prelude (in his nomenclature at that time the Liebestod) as a progression from "the first timidest lament of inap-
peasable longing, the tenderest shudder, to the most terrible out-
pouring of an avowal of hopeless love", the music "traversing all
phases of the vain struggle against the inner ardour, until this,
sinking back powerless upon itself, seems to be extinguished in
death." The Verklärung he elucidated thus: "Yet what Fate divided in life now springs into transfigured life in death: the gates
of union are thrown open. Over Tristan's body the dying Isolde
receives the blessed fulfilment of ardent longing, eternal union in
measureless space, without barriers, without fetters, inseparable."

Until the final scene of the opera was written, the Prelude, of
course, would have to stand on its own feet if given in the concert
room; and as it has no formal ending, one would have to be provided. A passage in a letter of Wagner's to Bülow of the 12th
March 1859 has misled many people into imagining that the ending now in use was Bülow's work. As a matter of fact what Wagner
had said to him was, in effect, this: "If you want to give the Prelude at your concert in Prague, well and good. But you will have
to supply an ending of your own; don't ask me to make one." No
doubt Bülow did the best he could; but the few bars he quotes
from his effort in one of his letters to Wagner do not suggest that
included in the talents with which Providence had so richly endowed him was the capacity to write Wagner's music for him.
Wagner explained later to Frau Wesendonk that his reason for
refusing Bülow's request had been that he himself had not seen at
that time precisely how the thing was to be done, that perception
having come to him only after he had written the last page of the
opera, in July 1859. In the following December he sent Mathilde
a sheet of music containing his own ending to the Prelude in
piano score.[1] He had made it for performance at the concerts he
gave in Paris on the 25th January and 1st and 8th February 1860.

His own exposition of the thus re-modelled Prelude in a pro-

---

[1] A facsimile of it will be found in both the German and the English edition
of the Wesendonk correspondence. A separate edition of the Prelude, with
the new concert ending, was at once published in full score by Breitkopf
and Härtel.

gramme note written for these concerts is interesting. The tale of
Tristan and Isolde, he says, is one of "endless yearning, longing,
the bliss and the wretchedness of love; world, power, fame, honour, chivalry, loyalty and friendship all blown away like an in-
substantial dream; one thing alone left living — longing, longing
unquenchable, a yearning, a hunger, a languishing forever renewing itself; one sole redemption — death, surcease, a sleep without awakening." For the composer whose aim it was to express
this in music, he continues, there was but one over-riding care,
"how to impose restraint on himself, since exhaustion of the subject is impossible." So "in one long succession of linked phases" he
"let that insatiable longing swell forth from the first timidest
avowal to sweetest protraction, through anxious sighs, through
hopes and fears, laments and desires, bliss and torment, to the
mightiest forward-pressing, the most powerful effort to find the
breach that will open out to the infinitely craving heart the path
into the sea of love's endless delight. In vain! The exhausted heart
sinks back, to pine away in a longing that can never attain its end,
since each attainment brings in its wake only renewed desire, till
in final exhaustion the breaking eye catches a glimpse of the attainment of the highest bliss — the bliss of dying, of ceasing to be,
of final redemption into that wondrous realm from which we only
stray the further the more we struggle to enter it by force. Shall
we call it Death? Or is it not the wonder-world of Night, whence,
as the story tells, an ivy and a vine sprang of old in inseparable
embrace over the graves of Tristan and Isolde?"

This may not be ideally lucid, but Wagner can be forgiven for
that; he was engaged on the impossible task of finding equivalents
in the crude medium of words for the infinite intimacies and
trackless subtleties of music. But what was in his mind is clear
enough for all that: the Prelude, as he had conceived it, traces
the vicissitudes of inextinguishable longing, yearning ever renewed after each illusive satisfaction of it and finding real consummation only in death. We shall see in a moment just how he
rounded off this mystical conception, so far as the Prelude is concerned, by the concert close he wrote for it in December 1859;
meanwhile let us look at the Prelude as it appears in the opera.

21

There is here no attempt, as in the Prelude to the *Mastersingers,* to epitomise the stage action and the characters of the opera. Wagner concentrates on the inmost essentials; the Prelude is the slow musical elaboration of a single bitter-sweet mood. For convenience' sake we have to attach labels to the "motives" upon which it is constructed, but the reader must be warned against interpreting these too literally. As a rule the commentators have decided upon a label from a hint given by the words or the situation with which a motive is associated on its first appearance in the opera. But we shall go hopelessly wrong if we allow that particular association to occupy our minds each time we hear the motive; it may undergo all kinds of metamorphoses and take on all shades of meaning as the drama goes on.

It is easy for the casual listener to get a false notion of the opening bars of the Prelude:

No.1

The melodic line seems to be a continuous one, running from the opening A in the lower clef to the final B in the higher. But in reality there are two motives here: the first (No. 1 A), extending from the opening note to the D sharp of the second full bar, is given out by the 'cellos in the upper register of the instrument, where the tone has a peculiar poignancy; the other (No. 1 B) comes out in the penetrating timbre of the oboes, over a wood wind harmony of bassoons, cor anglais, and (in the second bar) clarinets. We shall call No. 1 A the Grief or Sorrow motive, though it must be understood at the outset that its expression in the course of the opera is too multiple and too complex for it to be always tied down to the connotation of a single word: it has in it at various times something of longing, of pain, of hopelessness, of resignation, and many things more. No. 1 B is called by some analysts the motive of Desire, by others the motive of Magic, for no better reason than the fact that when it is first heard in the opera Isolde is speaking of her mother's craft in the brewing of magic potions. Our own rough-and-ready label for it will be Desire, with which the magic art of Isolde's mother necessarily has a certain external connection. But it must always be borne in mind that, as has been pointed out in the foregoing pages, Wagner never intends to imply that the love of Tristan and Isolde is the *physical consequence* of the philtre, but only that the pair, having drunk what they imagine to be the draught of Death and believing that they have looked upon earth and sea and sky for the last time, feel themselves free to confess, when the potion begins its work within them, the love they have so long felt but have concealed from each other and almost from themselves. Nor will the reader need to be reminded that this motive No. 1 B was committed to paper in December 1856, before a word of the scenario of the opera had been written. Consequently there is no warrant whatever for identifying it literally, as we were taught to do at one time, with the "magic" of Isolde and her mother: for Wagner it stood primarily for the predestined yearning of the lovers towards each other.

He himself, in a letter of March 1860 to Frau Wesendonk, has given us a clue to the complex of emotions the motive symbolised for him. He is in Paris, unhappy and sick to the depths of him with a sense of loneliness and alienation from his environment, and looking forward wistfully "towards the land of Nirvana". But Nirvana, it appears, becomes identical in his mind with Tristan, and Tristan and himself with the Buddhist theory of the origin of the world — the troubling of the primal cloudless heavens by a breath that swells and swells and finally condenses into our visible world in all its "inscrutable and impenetrable variety"; and he gives us the key to his meaning by quoting the music of our No. 1 B, in a way that shows that he identified it just then with the "breath" out of which the cosmos has condensed. In a word, it is Desire, for ever expanding and retracting, for ever seeking to realise itself and for ever being frustrated.

22

Repetitions of No. 1 at various pitches and in various colours lead to a sforzando which introduces two new motives:

No. 2

The first of these (A) relates particularly to the Anguish of Tristan; the second (B) is generally described as the Look (or Glance) motive, from the fact that it first appears in the opera at the point in the first act where Isolde tells Brangaene how her resolve to avenge herself on the slayer of Morold melted away under the glance that the sick Tristan had turned on her. No. 2 merges insensibly into a third motive of a similar cast, which the commentators associate with the love philtre:

No. 3

A half-passionate, half-mournful development of this is broken **at** one point by the reiteration of figures of this type:

which answer each other in different registers and colours. In his letter of December 1859 concerning the concert close to the Prelude, Wagner tells Frau Wesendonk that she will "recognise ivy and vine in the music, especially when you hear it in the orchestra, where strings and wind alternate with each other". He was referring to the antiphonal figures shown in No. 4. But it would be the height of folly on our part to take all this too literally. The ivy-and-vine legend plays no part whatever in Wagner's drama. It may have pleased him and Frau Wesendonk to associate privately No. 4 (and themselves) with ivy and vine, but nowhere in the opera has the motive any such connotation; and here in the Prelude it depicts simply one more phase of the yearning of the lovers.

A point that should not be overlooked is the bass line (B, C, D sharp) in the fourth and fifth bars of No. 3. It wells up and subsides ominously in the double basses, bassoons and bass clarinet, and symbolises Death (or Fate). It is curious that Bülow, who made the first piano arrangement of the score, should have failed to see that these three notes constitute a definite motive; otherwise he would not have altered Wagner's slurring of them in the arbitrary way he does here and elsewhere.

Wagner now works up to his climax by way of a new motive:

which incorporates in itself more and more insistent reminiscences of No. 1 B. The culmination is heralded by a fortissimo enunciation of No. 2 B in increasingly complex harmonic forms, and with a terrific fortissimo in the full orchestra the climax is reached and passed. The fortissimo quickly subsides to a piano; the orchestra dwells sadly upon echoes of No. 1, No. 2 B and No. 4, and the music gradually ebbs away into a heaving figure in the 'cellos and basses:

No. 6

that prepares us for the sea setting in which the opera will open.

23

The Prelude is a perfect specimen of musical form at its most consummate, not a schematic mould imposed upon the "thematic material" from the outside but a form that has come into being simply as the outcome of the ideas. Once more, as in the Prelude to *Lohengrin*, Wagner unconsciously obeys that natural law of structure that brings in the climax at a point about two-thirds of the time-distance between the beginning and the end. This is not only good art but ordinary experience; while it takes a long time to scale a mountain, the descent may be accomplished in half or a third of the time. Some conductors ruin Wagner's perfect design by pumping an accelerando into the music during the long crescendo that leads up to the climax. Wagner, who, though some conductors will receive the news with incredulity, knew infinitely better what his music was about than they will ever do, has not specified a single change of tempo during the prolonged ascent to the peak-point. He prescribes a slight holding-back after the peak has been reached, which is entirely in keeping with the general law of descent after a toilsome climb. The Prelude — and the same is even more true of the Liebestod — is far more tremendous in its tension when the ascent is not hurried in order to get a conductor's effect of "increasing passion", a cheap showman's trick upon which Wagner used always to pour out his scorn. The last thing he wanted was that his music should reach the hearer not as he had conceived it but as it appears after it has passed through the distorting and sometimes vulgarising medium of a conductor's mind.

As early as 1852 he had written to a friend, "I don't care in the least whether my works are given or not: all I am concerned with is that they shall be performed as I conceived them. Whoever can't and won't do that may leave them alone." Upon tempo he always laid the utmost emphasis: it was his constant complaint during his last years that he did not know a single conductor who could be trusted to find unaided the correct tempi for any of his works.

Let us now glance for a moment at the ending he himself devised for use when the Prelude is to be played in the concert room without the Liebestod. His instinct for form told him that in the first place the terrific climax would have to be dispensed with, since the goal was now different and the descent from the peak-point was going to be accomplished in a new way. With the closing scene of the opera in his mind the ebb of the psychological tide of the Prelude would necessarily have to be brought about in terms of that "Verklärung". So Wagner cuts out the original climax, which had come in the Prelude in bars 83 and 84. In bar 82 the trumpets and trombones had given out No. 2 B. He begins his new close at this point: he swiftly dissolves the fortissimo into a diminuendo, cuts out bars 83 and 84, and continues quietly, as in the original, with bars 85 to the first half of 94. Here begins the short "Verklärung". A change in the latter part of bar 94 serves to introduce a motive of ecstasy that had appeared in the opera for the first time in the opening scene of the second act:

(See also No. 31 below). The remainder of the new matter consists almost entirely of wistful broodings upon this theme, until at last it assumes the form in which it plays a dominant part in the closing stages of the Liebestod, with the poignant No. 1 B piercing through the texture at the finish, as it does at the end of the opera. (See No. 60). Wagner ends his arrangement, however, not in B major, as in the final bars of the opera, but in A major, thus rounding off the A minor in which the Prelude had begun.

24

A final word on the Prelude may not be out of place: it may help to clarify for the reader the whole problem of Wagner's use of "motives". We are compelled to attach labels to these, for otherwise we could not refer to them in our discussion of a work; but some of these labels have done considerable harm by bringing up in the listener's mind the same too literal connotation each time the motive appears. There are Wagnerian motives, of course, the meaning of which is virtually unchanging; they are definitely associated with a particular character (such as the Beckmesser or the Gutrune motive), or with an object that is at once physical and symbolic, and therefore static (such as the Spear motive in the *Ring*). But Wagner's conception and employment of motives varied with the nature of the work he had in hand; and when, as in *Tristan*, stage action and external reality count for very little and psychological states for virtually everything, the import of a motive can rarely be pinned down throughout to any particular person, object or episode. The motives are sensitive, plastic musical materials, on a par with those of the symphonist, with which the composer weaves a fabric of thought and emotion of a kind that can exist only in music.

Now the Prelude to *Tristan* was not written, as most introductions to operas are, after the completion of the work, when the composer has the whole of his thematic material before him and can select from it just what seems to him best suited to epitomise the contents of the whole work. The *Tristan* Prelude contains no motive specifically correlated with the second and third acts, for the simple reason, among others, that Wagner had not even begun formal work upon these when the Prelude was written. He commenced the music of the first act on the 1st October 1857; and apparently he began with the Prelude. As his own programme note shows, it is in no way dramatic or pictorial: it expresses the incessant projection and recoil upon itself of a single emotion — that of longing without satisfaction and without end. Even if the opera had never been written the Prelude would still be a perfectly organised piece of mood-music that requires no "explanation" outside itself, a symphonic epitome, as it might be, of an unwritten drama. When Wagner was composing it the separate themes of it had probably no such precise meanings for him as the labels we attach to them are apt to suggest. When the time came for him to embody them in the opera, each of them would necessarily be associated on its first appearance with this, that or the other psychological point of the moment. But it is an error to assume, as the commentators have been inclined to do, that because at this point or that a motive is first heard in connection with certain words or a certain situation it relates specifically to that sentiment or that situation whenever it occurs later in the opera, or, before that, in the Prelude.

25

Our Nos. 2 B, 1 B and 4 are cases in point. Because No. 2 B first appears in the opera when Isolde tells Brangaene how the sick man looked up at her from his couch and the sword fell from her hand, the analysts have agreed to call it the Look motive, with the result that people innocently read that too definite meaning into it each time it occurs in the Prelude and in the opera. The truth is that it is a musical theme of generalised import, the expression of the love that Tristan and Isolde were fated from their birth to feel for each other; it is only the dramatic exigencies of the text that lead to its first putting in an appearance when Isolde recalls the outer circumstances of their realisation of this fatality. So with No. 1 B: there is no necessity, and indeed it is misleading, to tie the meaning of this down to the "Magic" of Isolde's mother merely because it is first given out by the orchestra when Isolde says bitterly, "O futile art of the sorceress, that only balsams can brew!", and is heard again later when Brangaene says to Isolde, "Hast thou thy mother's arts forgot? Think'st thou that she who knows all secrets would have sent me with thee into a strange land without counsel?" — by which she means the philtre that is to ensure Isolde the love of King Marke. The true psychological significance of the potion has already been dwelt upon in the foregoing pages: it is not the prime cause of passion but the symbol of it. To think of the philtre in its material sense on each of the many occasions when the motive recurs later in the opera — for instance, in the prelude to the second act, or in the subtle transformation it undergoes in the introduction to the third act (No. 47) — is to fall into the rankest absurdity.

Again, although Wagner, in his letter to Frau Wesendonk, lets his fancy play upon the ivy and the vine in connection with our No. 4, we must not suppose for a moment that he originally shaped the theme with the intention of setting up any such permanent connection in the listener's mind. For him it was simply another aspect of the predestined passion of the pair. He uses it, for example, when, after drinking the philtre, they fall at last into each other's arms:

No. 8

Here any association of it with ivy and vine would manifestly be out of place.

26

The Prelude ends, as we have seen, with a suggestion in the 'cellos and basses of the heaving sea — a figure fraught with foreboding.

When the curtain rises, say the stage directions, we see Isolde's "tent-like apartment on the fore-deck of a ship; it is richly hung with tapestries, which at first are quite closed in at the back; on one side a narrow companion ladder leads below. Isolde is on a couch, her face buried in the cushions. Brangaene, holding open a curtain, is looking over the side of the ship." From the masthead we hear the voice of an invisible young sailor, singing, as sailors will, a farewell to the girl he has left behind him: "Westward turn my eyes; eastward the ship flies. A homeward wind is with us now: my Irish child, where waitest thou? Is it thy sighs, my maiden, wherewith my sails are laden? [1] Waft us, o wind! But

[1] Sind's deiner Seufzer Wehen,
  die mir die Segel blähen?

Wagner's sketches show that these lines were originally preceded by two which he rejected later:

dem englischen Gast
auf ödem Mast,

("for the English guest on the dreary mast"). The two discarded lines were also excluded from his imprint of the poem.

alas for thee, my child, my Irish maid, thou wild, winsomest maid!":

No. 9

West-wärts schweift der Blick, ost-wärts streicht das

Schiff.   Frisch weht der Wind der Hei - mat zu.

etc.

The curious little unaccompanied song is invariably taken too slowly. It is some minor tenor or other's only chance during the entire evening to show what he can do; naturally he wants to make the most of it, and the conductor, instead of keeping him on a tight rein, too indulgently gives him his head. Wagner's tempo marking is "moderately slow", i.e., faster than the decidedly slow of the Prelude. The tenor, left to his own devices, is fairly sure to turn it into a spineless, rhythmless adagio.

Isolde hears the song and reads into the "Irish maid" a Cornish jibe at herself, the captive of Tristan, the trophy destined for King Marke. A surge of No. 2 B in the orchestra shows that the subject of all her brooding during the voyage — the wrong that has been done her by Tristan — has now come uppermost in her mind; and her anger at the Sailor's words are expressed in a turbulent motive in octaves in the lower strings that will be drawn upon more than once in the course of the act:

No. 10 *Animato*

Dragged back violently to the world of reality she asks Brangaene distractedly where they are. A phrase from the Sailor's song (No. 9 A) now becomes a kind of Sea motive, the symbol of the transit from her home to an alien land. Above this foundation in the orchestra Brangaene, unconscious of the storm that is raging in Isolde's bosom, tells her with a certain satisfaction that the sea is smooth, the ship is sailing swiftly, and by evening they will touch land,[1] where, as the unsuspecting maid believes, a brilliant future awaits her adored mistress. "What land?" asks Isolde absently. "Cornwall's verdant strand", Brangaene replies. "Never!" cries Isolde passionately, revealing for the first time what had been festering in her heart all through the voyage: "not today nor tomorrow!"

Brangaene, alarmed at this outburst, lets the curtain fall and runs anxiously to her side. Isolde breaks out into a violent denunciation of her own "degenerate race, unworthy of its fathers". Where, she asks, is the famed power of her mother over sea and storm, that her child should be delivered up helpless to Ireland's hated Cornish conquerors? As No. 1 B sounds in the orchestra she reproaches her mother for brewing nothing now but draughts of healing; she calls on the slumbering winds to obey her will — to whip up the dreaming sea to a fury of greed and make it devour the rich human prey the ship offers it: "Destroy this arrogant ship, engulf its shattered fragments! Take all that lives and breathes on it, ye winds, for your prize!"

At last Brangaene senses that her mistress has been hiding some secret grief from her all this time. She loads her with endearments and begs her to tell her all:

> *Without a tear*
> *from father and mother didst part thee,*
> *and scant farewell*
> *to friends and kindred gav'st.*

[1] "Blue stripes [of land] have appeared in the west", says Brangaene. It has often been pointed out that the Cornish land towards which she is looking lies not west but east of the ship. The slip of the pen probably came about through Wagner having changed the layout of the Prose Sketch at this point when he came to write the poem. In the former the song of the sailor at the mast-head had run thus: "Towards the west longs the heart; towards the east we sail. Fair the wind, smooth the voyage, calm the sea; blue stripes announce the distant but ever-nearing coast of Cornwall." Here Wagner's geography is correct. A few lines later Brangaene tells Isolde, in the Sketch, that "in the distance blue stripes are coming into view" — probably the Cornish coast", which again is correct. There was no necessity, however, for both the seaman and the maid to talk, within a minute or two of each other, of the appearance of the blue stripes. So in the poem Wagner reserved this announcement for Brangaene; but in a careless moment he carried over into her speech the "westward" from the sailor's "westward turn my eyes".

From thy home thou wentest
mute and cold,
pale and speechless;
eat thou would'st not,
neither sleep;
numb and wretched,
wild, o'erwrought:
o what sorrow
thus to see thee, —
thine no more to be,
strangers thou and I!

and she implores her "sweetest and dearest" to take her to her heart and into her trust. For the accompaniment to all this Wagner plays in various forms with an urgent new figure with which No. 1 B is incorporated:

No. II

Brangaene's appeal ends in a long-drawn cadence of melting sweetness and tenderness.

Isolde's only reply is a despairing cry of "Air, air, or my heart will burst! Open there! Open wide!"; and Brangaene quickly draws asunder the curtains in the middle of the ship, just at the moment when the young Sailor breaks once more into a fragment of his song.

27

Through the opening now made in the curtains we see to the stern of the ship,[1] with the sea stretching out beyond it to the

---

[1] There has been a good deal of unnecessary controversy about the proper setting of the first act of the opera. The stage directions say that "we see right down the ship to the *Steuerbord*." This has been taken in some quarters to mean that we see "to starboard", and it has consequently been argued that the vessel should be shown not end-on to the spectator but slantwise.

horizon. Round the centre mast sailors are reclining, busied with ropes; further back, on the stern-deck, are recumbent groups of knights and squires; a little apart from them stands Tristan with folded arms, sunk in thought, looking out to sea; Kurvenal, his rough, fanatically faithful retainer, lies in a careless attitude at his feet. Isolde's eyes at once settle on Tristan. In an aside, as if communing darkly with herself, she sings softly, to the strain of No. 1 B, some words the mystical meaning of which is as yet known only to her — "Chosen [destined] to be mine, lost to me; peerless, proud; brave and craven! Death-devoted head! Death-devoted heart!"

No. 12

The melody and harmony of the phrases are those of No. 1 B, but they are given a new and extraordinary significance by the orchestration and the dynamics — a shuddering *tremolando* in the

---

The Prose Sketch, however, makes it abundantly clear that "Steuerbord" has not its modern nautical meaning here, but simply that of the place where the steering gear is. When Brangaene goes at Isolde's command "along the deck to the *Steuerbord*" it does not mean that she takes a list to starboard but simply that she goes to the spot where Tristan is standing by the helm. So again when Isolde, during the dialogue between the maid and Tristan, "keeps her gaze immovably fixed *nach dem Steuerbord*", it means not that she keeps her eyes glued to starboard but that she looks steadily at the spot — the steering place — where Tristan is. "Steuer" is the German for "helm", "rudder". The verb "steuern" means "to steer".

muted violins and violas, with a crescendo surge in each phrase. Winding its way through this texture we hear No. 1 A in the poignant quiet tones of a cor anglais. The passage culminates in a harsh fortissimo chord in the wood wind at "Todgeweihtes Haupt" ("Death-devoted head"), ending in a sudden hush and a solemn harmony in the brass at "Haupt", while at the end of "Todgeweihtes Herz" ("Death-devoted heart") the orchestra subsides again into the original fateful shudder in the muted strings:

Then Isolde becomes conscious of her surroundings again. Partially recovering her proud poise, she asks Brangaene, with a nervous, uncanny laugh, what she thinks of the menial[1] there, "the hero who averts in shame and fear his eyes from mine". The simple, unsuspecting maid sings the praises of Tristan as the flower of knighthood. "Yet", replies Isolde, "in craven fear he shuns my presence while he carries home the corpse of a bride he has won for his lord." Does Brangaene doubt this? Let her then ask this "free man" if he dares at last approach his lady with the

---

[1] The usual convenient English translation of the line, "Was hältst du von dem Knechte?" is "What think'st thou of the knight there?" But "Knecht" carries the meaning not of "knight" but of "menial": "knight" misses the scorn of Isolde's reference to the man who, instead of boldly declaring himself her lover, behaves only as the respectful servant of his King and the foreign Princess.

homage due to her — a duty and a courtesy he has neglected all through the voyage, so full of fear is he, this peerless hero. "Oh, well he knows why! To the proud one go: take him his lady's word — let him, as my servitor, at once approach me." "Shall I ask him?" says Brangaene timidly. "No, command him!" is the proud reply: "I, Isolde, bid the stubborn one do my will!"

Obeying her imperious gesture, Brangaene goes humbly past the sailors to where Tristan is standing: Isolde strides back to her couch, where she remains throughout the episode that follows, her eyes never leaving the little group in the stern of the ship. In the orchestra we hear the Sea motive as Brangaene slowly approaches Tristan, who is still motionless, lost in his thoughts. Kurvenal, without rising, plucks at his master's cloak with an ironic "Beware, Tristan! A message from Isolde!". Tristan, torn from his dream, makes a convulsive movement, but at once recovers himself and inclines his head courteously as the messenger nears him.

In what immediately follows there is no interplay of musical motives, for it has no psychological bearing on anything that has gone before or anything that will come after; it is just a conversation, conducted quietly to the accompaniment of simple harmonies. Tristan throughout is fencing with Brangaene; he is the soul of courtesy to her and to her mistress, but he has no intention of letting himself be diverted from his prudent resolve not to hold converse with Isolde while the voyage lasts. What, he asks the maid, is his lady's will? He is at her service; whatever she may command he will obey. If the voyage has irked her, it will soon be over, for before night falls they will reach the land. There, in the green meadows beyond the blue haze of the sea, the King awaits his bride; and to conduct her to him will be Tristan's high privilege and his alone. The more importunate Brangaene becomes the more evasive are his replies, the calmer and more distant his courtesy. The noble and lovely princess can dispose of him in every way but one — for how, if he leaves the helm, can he steer the ship in safety to King Marke's land?

No.14

Wie lenkt' ich si-cher   den Kiel   zu Kö-nig Marke's Land?

The maid, in desperation, repeats Isolde's imperious summons; but before Tristan can speak Kurvenal leaps to his feet with a pugnacious "May I make answer?". "What answer would you give?" asks Tristan quietly. "This!" replies Kurvenal. "Let her speak thus to Dame Isolde; it is not for him who won for the Irish maid the crown of Cornwall and the realm of England to do more than conduct her to his royal uncle, for whom she is intended. Tristan the hero is famed throughout the world. Thus speak I; go thou [Brangaene] and repeat it, let a thousand Isoldes rage at it if they will!"

The whole character of Kurvenal as he appears later in the opera — the brave, rough watch-dog, living only in and for his beloved master — is limned in this song of his, the intervals and harmonies of which are as rugged and forthright as himself:

No. 15

As he goes on to sing before all the crew the story, so hateful in Isolde's ears, of Ireland's abasement and hers, Brangaene turns sadly on her heel. Tristan tries to restrain Kurvenal by a gesture, but he continues at the top of his voice with the savoury tale of how Morold came across the sea to take tribute from Cornwall, how Tristan slew him in single combat on an island, and how the dead man's head was sent back to Ireland as the sole payment that Cornwall would deign to make to the Irish king. "Hail to our Tristan", he concludes, "who pays tribute in a fashion of his own!"; and the knights and sailors repeat with glee the final wounding words of the song:

No. 16

At last Tristan, with a gesture of annoyance, sends his gruff old henchman below.

28

Brangaene, confused and distressed, has returned to Isolde. She closes the curtains behind her in the vain hope of shutting out from her mistress the sight and sound of the men. Isolde rises with a gesture of rage and despair, while the maid throws herself at her feet with a cry of "Woe, ah, woe is me, that I should have to suffer this!" For a moment Isolde does not speak, but the storm within her is expressed by some furious bars in the orchestra. Mastering herself, she insists on Brangaene telling her all that had passed between her and Tristan. When the maid gives the latter's smooth excuse, "Did I for a moment leave the helm, how could I steer the ship in safety to Cornwall and King Marke?" Isolde repeats the words and the music of the answer (No. 14) with bitter irony: "Yes", she says harshly, "to lay at the King's feet the tribute [herself] he had wrung from Ireland!" — sung to the strain of the corresponding passage in Kurvenal's song. But when Brangaene would repeat the rest of Kurvenal's insulting words Isolde cuts her short. "That have I heard", she says; "not a word of it escaped me. You heard my shame; hear now, then, how it was wrought." Her final words are accompanied by a furious upward rush in the orchestra:

No. 17

which, it will be seen, is an expansion of No. 1 B; and it is one more proof that we must not read into that motive anything so narrow in its application .as the notion of the "magic art" of Isolde's mother: the theme has many a significance beyond that.

Isolde now begins the long monologue that is sometimes sung in the concert room under the title of "Isolde's Narration to Brangaene". It serves a treble purpose: it carries the drama on to its next vital phase, it explains and justifies Isolde's anger over the scene that has just been enacted, and it places the spectator in possession of most of the essential facts anterior to the opera.

The Narration is based mostly on subtle modifications of the opening phrase (No 1 A) of the Prelude, the motive more particularly associated with Tristan and his sorrows. It now assumes the following form:

and is generally referred to as the motive of the Sick Tristan. It weaves for some time a symphonic web of its own in the orchestra as Isolde tells Brangaene how once a frail boat had drifted to the Irish coast, with a man in it calling himself Tantris, sick nigh to death, who had come to consult the far-famed healing art of the Irish princess (here No. 1 B is heard in the wood wind); how, after healing his wounds, she had learned, from the splinter and the notch in his sword, that he was no Tantris but the Tristan who had slain Morold. No. 18 goes through some moving metamorphoses — beginning each time in a gust of fury but always dying away at the end of the phrase — as Isolde describes how a voice within her had called to her to kill this man, who was Ireland's deadliest enemy, and she had stood over him with the sword raised to take vengeance for Morold, when of a sudden he looked up, not at the sword, not at her hand, but into her eyes, and his wretchedness melted her heart and the sword fell from her grasp. As she begins this part of her story the tempest in the orchestra dies down, and we hear No. 18 in a peculiarly poignant form:

The scoring is noteworthy, but one rarely finds the full expressiveness of it realised in performance. The melody is sung by the violas, with the violins beneath them; the tenor part of our quotation is entrusted to the 'cellos, where the curious sob of the dotted note and the following slur, if properly brought out, is extraordinarily moving. At the words "He looked into my eyes" we hear No. 2 B in the expressive tones of a solo viola.

Still to the accompaniment of No. 18 Isolde tells how she tended the sick man again, that he might go home healed and rid her of the anguish of that look. And so the conquering Tristan (No. 16) had left her and Ireland, after having sworn a thousand oaths of gratitude and fidelity. "Hear now", she says bitterly, "how a knight keeps his oath!" He whom she had protected as Tantris and allowed to go away unscathed, unrecognised by her kindred, had returned in pomp and pride as Tristan, to solicit the hand of the Irish princess for Cornwall's old and weary King, his uncle King Marke. Had Morold lived, who would have dared to put that insult on Ireland and on her? And it was herself who had wrought her own shame; "the avenging sword! instead of striking with it I let it fall from my feeble hand; and now I am thrall to him who was my vassal!" Through all this we hear frequently the motive of Isolde's anger (No. 10).

29

After an astonished interjection from Brangaene she renews her complaint. They had all of them been weak and blind, she says. Tristan had been a traitor; while she had hidden from her own kindred all she knew and felt in the troubled silence of her heart, he had returned to Cornwall and sung her praises to the court as a splendid morsel for the King, and had himself offered to go to Ireland and bring her back with him. In this part of the Narrative two motives are dominant, that of Tristan as conqueror of Ireland (No. 16), and a triplet figure of this type:

No. 20

which had been heard in an earlier part of the Narration but now assumes greater prominence; Wagner makes it express now rage, now tenderness, now deep suffering. Isolde's outburst ends with a wild curse on the traitor and a call for vengeance on his head.

Brangaene runs to her mistress in an access of tenderness, draws her gently to the couch, and pours out words of comfort, to a new and tender figure in the orchestra:

No. 21

But she still cannot unravel the complex of emotion in Isolde's heart. Her simple mind finds what Tristan has done quite natural; how better could he show his loyalty to his King than by bringing him so fair a bride, and how better prove his gratitude to the princess who had saved his life than by conducting her to a splendid throne? But when Isolde finds speech again it is clear that she has hardly been listening to Brangaene. Looking fixedly before her, as if staring into a future visible only to herself, she says in a low, brooding tone, "I, unloved, to have ever before my eyes the noblest man of all! How could I endure that torture?"

Once more the maid misunderstands her; she takes these words to refer to the noble King Marke. The orchestral tissue seems one long caress:

No. 22

as she asks where in all the world there lives a man who could see Isolde and not love her and gladly die for her? But in the worst case, were the King cold, or turned against her by magic, Brangaene is the custodian of the secret of a stronger magic that will bind him to Isolde by a spell. Lowering her voice confidentially she asks, to the accompaniment of No. 1 B in the orchestra, "Know'st thou not thy mother's arts? Thinkst thou that she who knows and weighs all things would have sent me with thee into a strange land without counsel for thee in the hour of need?"

30

Well is Isolde aware of the love philtre her mother has brewed to ensure her the love of the old King. But she ignores the obvious meaning of Brangaene's words and gives them one of her own. "Truly I know", she says darkly, "my mother's counsel, and her arts I prize. They can accomplish vengeance for betrayal and bring rest to the heart in anguish" — this to the significant motive of "Death-devoted head! Death-devoted heart!" (No. 13). "That casket there — bring it hither to me!" Still misunderstanding her, Brangaene does so: "it holds", she says soothingly as she points to the phials it contains, "what will bring the balm thou need'st to thy soul"; but the orchestra, with the motives No. 4 and No. 5, gives another significance to her words than the one her simple mind intends. "Here they lie as thy mother laid them out, the mighty magical potions — balsam for woe and wounds, for grievous poisons antidotes, and" — as she draws one of the phials from the casket — "here the noblest draught of all."

"Thou err'st", replies Isolde; "I know better the one I need." She seizes another of the phials and holds it up: "*This* draught it is that serves my end! I graved a secret sign upon it"; and beneath the outline of No. 1 B in wood wind, horns and tremolandi strings we hear, in the dark colours of the bassoons, trombones and bass tuba, the sinister motive of Death (No. 3, bar 4), beginning softly but quickly swelling to a fortissimo. "The draught of Death!" cries Brangaene, recoiling in horror. Isolde starts from the couch in panic as the sailors are heard shouting roughly to each other to go aloft and take in sail: the moment so long dreaded by her has arrived — the ship is nearing the Cornish land.

The rhythmical cry of the crew:

No. 23

and a brisk handling of the Sea motive in the orchestra fill the scene with excitement; and the intrusion of the real world upon Isolde's broodings is carried a step further by Kurvenal, who comes boisterously through the curtain roaring a message from his master that the two women are to make themselves ready for the landing. For a moment Isolde recoils aghast; then, recovering her regal self-mastery, she quietly but firmly bids Kurvenal take Tristan her greetings and a message: she will not stand by his side to be conducted to King Marke until, as ancient custom prescribes, he has made atonement to her for a wrong as yet unexpiated. To this the rough old warrior replies merely with a defiant and insolent gesture. Isolde repeats her words, still calmly, but with an added emphasis: she will not prepare herself, she will not stand at Tristan's side, until her forgetfulness and forgiveness have been granted for a dire wrong unatoned; let the knight then come and ask her grace. The quiet resolution of her words is underlined by a steady beat in the orchestral accompaniment.

31

Kurvenal is quelled into obedience, but is still defiant: he will take her message, he blusters, but let her wait and see what kind of answer his master gives! When he has left, Isolde turns quickly to her maid and takes her into a feverish embrace. "Now farewell, Brangaene!" she cries; "greet for me the world; greet for me father and mother!" Brangaene does not understand. "What is it?

Would'st thou flee? Whither am I to follow thee?" Once more the sinister motive of Death surges up from the depths of the orchestra as Isolde makes her purpose clear to her. She is not fleeing; she will await Tristan here; Brangaene is to obey her in everything to the letter, and first of all prepare the drink of atonement and peace. All this time the Death motive — our clue to what is really in her mind — has become more and more insistent; at last it finds its culmination in the motive of Desire (No. 1 B) as Isolde takes the fateful phial from the casket and hands it to the maid. Wagner's use of the motive at this point is one more proof that for him it does not signify merely a product of the magic art of the Irish Queen, designed to fill the veins of Isolde and King Marke with passion. For Wagner, as for Isolde, Desire is the gateway to Death, and Death the sublimation of Desire.

At long last everything becomes clear to Brangaene. She takes the deadly phial in her hand and throws herself in terror and horror at her mistress's feet. The imperious Isolde subdues her as she had subdued Kurvenal. With bitter irony she flings in Brangaene's face the maid's own words in an earlier scene, giving them now a new application: "Know'st thou not my mother's arts? Think'st thou that she who knows and weighs all things would have sent me with thee into a strange land without counsel for me in the hour of need? Balsam for woe and wounds has the Queen given; for deadly poisons antidotes; and for the deepest woe and greatest grief of all — the draught of Death; let Death now give her thanks!", which the orchestra points with a statement of the "Death-devoted head! Death-devoted heart!" motive.

Hardly knowing what she is saying, Brangaene echoes in stricken tones Isolde's "O deepest woe! O greatest grief!", while the oboe wails over a string tremolo and the basses project the sombre outline of the motive of Death:

No. 24

Oboe

Lento

Cellos & Basses (*8ᵛᵉ lower*)

She raises herself, frightened and bewildered, as Kurvenal enters with a brusque announcement of "Sir Tristan!". For a moment Isolde's old anger flames out again; then she says calmly and proudly, "Sir Tristan may approach!" Kurvenal withdraws, and the trembling Brangaene retires to the back of the scene. Isolde, mastering herself with a mighty effort, walks slowly and with royal dignity across to the couch, on the head of which she leans, her eyes fixed on the opening in the curtain.

32

In the few moments that elapse before Tristan appears and the characters find speech again the orchestra conveys the tremendous inner tension of the situation in an impressive passage of thirty bars commencing thus:

No. 25

The new motive shown in the opening bars of this quotation has been given different labels by different commentators. Because it is associated later with Tristan's words when he takes the fateful cup from Isolde:

Tristan's honour —
highest troth!

*Tristan's anguish —
proudest scorn!*

it is called by some the motive of Tristan's honour. Others have
dubbed it the Morold motive, because it recurs when Isolde
speaks of Morold. If one prefers to call it the motive of Isolde's
anger one does so purely as a matter of convenient shorthand. As
with so many of Wagner's motives, it is simple in itself but complex in its range of psychological reference. On the broad view, it
is the expression of Isolde's anger and her thirst for revenge for
the slaying of Morold; but as this anger and this thirst trail other
ideas and emotions along with them from moment to moment,
and as there is always something at the back of her mind that
does not reveal itself in her words — which, indeed, are sometimes designed less to express her thoughts than to conceal them
— the precise nuance of its meaning is to be sought elsewhere
than in the words — in the music.

This is a point that has to be constantly borne in mind in connection with the dramas of Wagner's maturity. As the musician
in him grew to greater power it aimed more and more at making
the drama music's own concern. His aim was to reduce words to a
minimum; and in trying to do this his poems, in and by themselves, sometimes veil his meaning rather than disclose it. This is
particularly the case in *Tristan;* there are many passages which
we have to read again and again, not merely by their own light
but by that thrown on them by some perhaps distant part of the
drama, before we can pierce to the real meaning of them, or all
the meanings they can convey. Wagner was perfectly aware of this
difficulty, and his answer to friends who, after reading his text,
drew his attention to it was always the same — "Wait until you
hear the work with the music; that will make everything plain to
you, in terms, however, not of words, which are a clumsy tool created by human reflection, but of feeling; for music, which comes
from the foundations, not the surface, of man and things, is capable of a thousand shades of suggestion that are beyond the
capacity of words." [1] If we apply his advice to "wait for the music"
to the present case our difficulty with regard to finding a label for

---

[1] I am of course condensing and paraphrasing a number of his remarks on
this subject at different times.

example No. 25 vanishes: it symbolises not just Morold *qua* Morold, or Tristan, or anyone or anything else with a fixed material outline, but the obsession of fury that has been taking more and more complete control of Isolde's soul from the moment when Tristan had claimed her, in Ireland, as King Marke's bride, to the present moment when, hardly knowing herself whether she loves or hates Tristan more, she is bent on making an end of herself and of him. Within that broad framework of complex passion there is room for an infinitude of nuance of thought and emotion from moment to moment; and that is where music comes into its own. For music can not only express, where feeling is concerned, far more than words; it can, if need be, subtly give the lie to the words that accompany it — as Gluck pointed out to his critics long ago in connection with a famous episode in his *Iphigenia in Tauris.*

33

To resume our survey of the opera.

As yet, while Isolde has told us a good deal about herself, and about others as they appear in her eyes, we have learned next to nothing about Tristan from his own mouth; and even during the remainder of the first act he scarcely lifts a corner of the veil that hides his secret self from us. Yet he is not, as the casual spectator is apt to think, a merely negative character all this while. One critic has told us that in the scene with Isolde that now follows he is "as helpless as a bird in the claws of a cat". It is true that Isolde does most of the talking, in tirade after tirade, Tristan making no attempt to match her in either fluency or vehemence or even to counter her in argument. But if his rôle is largely one of silence, or of an economy of speech that is hardly more than a nuance of silence, that is by no means because he is merely the helpless negative to Isolde's vehement positive. He is silent not because he has nothing to say but because he has far more within him than he can find words for at present.

The key to his reticence will not be given us until the second act. Here, in the first, we hear Isolde's case against him stated in full: his defence we do not hear, because if he were to allow himself the luxury of stating it he would be false to what it is in him that makes him most truly Tristan. Superficially Isolde is justified in her charge of treachery again.t him: out of pity she had spared his life when it would have been so easy for her to slay the Cornish enemy who had vanquished Morold and humbled her country, and he had repaid her, on his return home, by singing the praises of her beauty to King Marke, and then coming once more to Ireland to carry her back with him as a sort of rich tribute to the royal house of Cornwall. But Tristan had acted as he had done in the name of the loftiest of knightly principles, that of honour. To give Cornwall internal peace he had put away from himself the succession to Marke's crown; he had brought his noble benefactor the fairest jewel among princesses to be his Queen and to bear him an heir, he himself, his mission accomplished, intending to leave Cornwall afterwards for ever.

But to make a parade of his honour now would be to lapse from his own lofty standard of honour; so he says nothing in reply to Isolde's furious upbraidings. He himself, indeed, is as yet not fully aware of the true meaning, the mystical meaning, of the dilemma in which he now finds himself, how it is that in willing the highest good he has wrought the direst harm. The full consciousness of all this only comes to him, and to us, in the second act: the world of Day in which he had been living until now has cheated him into acceptance of its own false values. Worldly fame and even worldly honour, he realises at last, are only the glittering simulacra of things really beautiful and worthy and desirable; the ultimate and only value is Love — not earthly love but a mystical consummation that can be found only in Death. Three times in the course of the drama we shall find him deliberately seeking death as the gateway to a purer happiness than the shows and gauds of earth can ever bring him after having learned to know Isolde — first when he accepts what he believes to be death in the cup she proffers him, then when he lowers his own sword before the thrust of Melot's. At his third attempt, at the end of the drama, he succeeds; when, to the worldly eye, he has attained the summit of his desire in the reunion with Isolde, he tears the bandages from his wounds and dies in her arms. Lovers such as they can never, in their own language in the second act, be wholly one in the garish Light of Day, but only in the ecstatic Night of Death.

34

The motive of Isolde's anger (No. 25) may be said to dominate the scene now to be enacted, though of course a number of other motives with which we are already familiar, and especially the "Death-devoted head" motive and that of the Sick Tristan, play their psychological parts in the orchestral texture. Tristan enters halfway through the orchestral interlude that commences as in No. 25. For a moment he stands respectfully at the entrance to Isolde's apartment. Her agitation increases as he comes slowly towards her, and an upsurge of the Death motive in the orchestra tells us what is the purpose at the back of her mind.

Tristan asks quietly why she has sent for him. Her reply is that he must know that full well, even though the fear of having to obey her will has kept him discourteously aloof from her throughout the voyage. He pleads, in excuse, his respect for her: in his country, he says, knightly custom dictates that he who brings the bride home must remain apart from her. She reminds him of a custom no less binding — that atonement must be made to foes if they are to be turned into friends. He professes not to understand: "Who then is my foe?" he says. "Ask of thy fear!" she retorts; "between us lies blood-guilt." "No", Tristan rejoins; "that feud was ended by the solemn oath of us all, taken in the open field." "Not by me!" replies Isolde; "for I had learned silence." She has had to do with two Tristans, she continues. The earlier one was the sick Tantris whom she had spared when he was in her power, though she knew him to be the slayer of Morold: yet even when checking the sword in its descent she had sworn within herself to have vengeance. "Betrothed he was to me, the noble Irish hero. His weapons had I blessed. For me he fared forth to fight. When he fell, shamed too was I. In my soul's dire anguish I swore an oath — he should be avenged, if not by a man's hand then by mine." At this point we hear a new figure in the violas that plays a prominent part in the texture for a while:

No. 26

Bass: F♯

It is impossible to label it definitely; to call it, as some analysts have done, the "motive of psychical excitement" is to say no more than that it gives an extra orchestral emphasis to Isolde's exasperated words, now and later.

Then she begins to be a trifle self-contradictory. Hardly have the words "if not by a man's hand then by mine, a maid's" left her lips than she veers round to another line of attack. "You were in my power, sick and faint", she says; "why did I not strike thee then?" The answer she gives to her own question is a curious one: it reads thus in Mr. Frederick Jameson's translation, which, though not strictly true to the original, we may adopt for convenience' sake: "Thy wound I tended that, when hale and strong, then vengeance might strike thee down, by a hand that Isolde should choose." [1] But, she continues, since all men join in paying homage to Tristan, who is there to strike him down?

Tristan, pale and gloomy, replies: "If Morold was so dear to thee, take my sword" — which he draws from its sheath and offers to her, — "grasp it firmly and wield it better than that other time". Isolde answers that King Marke would have small cause to thank her were she to slay the best of his knights, who had won him his crown and his land and is now bringing him his Irish bride. Her tone is bitter and ironic; but, as is Wagner's way, the orchestra, in a curiously softened transformation of No. 25:

[1] "She states the reason why she did not slay him when he was in her power", says Mr. G. Ainslie Hight, "in language so strange that I can only give a literal translation: 'I nursed the wounded man that, when restored to health, the man who won him from Isolde should smite him in vengeance'. Such is the German; what it means I must confess myself unable to explain, and can only suspect some corruption in the text."

The German runs thus:

> Ich pflag des Wunden,
> dass den Heilgesunden
> rächend schlüge der Mann,
> der Isolden ihn abgewann.

My own conjecture is that the accusative "ihn" should be the ablative "ihm", in spite of the fact that "ihn" appears not only in the poem but in the scores, including the manuscript of the orchestral score. I take it that what Isolde means is this: "I tended your wounds in order that when you were sound again you should be struck down in vengeance by a man [some future lover] who had won Isolde from you."

No. 27

tells us that her anger with him is not so great as her words would suggest. "Put up thy sword", she continues; "once I raised it against thee, when thy measuring gaze was turned on me to judge if I were a fitting wife for the King. But I let the sword fall from my hand: now let us twain drink atonement."

35

The dramatic action is mounting to its climax. The orchestra gives out a solemn statement of the Death motive (No. 3, bars 4 and 5) in conjunction with No. 26, as Isolde makes a sign to Brangaene to prepare the draught. The horror-stricken maid can hardly bring herself to obey, but Isolde urges her on with nervous gestures. The psychological tension of the scene is broken in upon for a moment by a loud cry from the seamen, "Ho-he-ha-he! All hands aloft! Take in sail!", to the strain of No. 23; and Brangaene's anguish is painted in the oboe figure (see No. 24) to the accompaniment of which, in an earlier scene, she had wailed "O deepest woe! O greatest grief!" when Isolde had commanded her to prepare not the love elixir but the potion of death.

The shouts of the sailors rouse Tristan from his sombre brooding. "Where are we?" he ejaculates convulsively. "Near the goal!" replies Isolde; and the subtle double meaning of the word "goal" — the outer one of reaching the Cornish land and the inner, veiled one of nearing their own last hour — is brought out by the orchestra with an enunciation of the "Death-devoted head! Death-devoted heart!" motive in dark wood wind colours. "Tristan", she continues, "shall I be given atonement? What word hast thou for me now?" His reply is an antithetical play upon words:

> *Des Schweigens Herrin*
> *heisst mich schweigen: —*
> *fass' ich, was sie verschwieg,*
> *verschweig' ich, was sie nicht fasst.*

("The mistress of silence commands me silence. What she concealed I can grasp; but what I concealed she cannot grasp.") That is to say, he had long ago divined the love for him that she had endeavoured to conceal under a mask of enmity; but the sense of honour that forbade him to confess his own love for the King's bride she does not understand, nor can he speak of it.[1]

But Isolde reads, or professes to read, a meaning of her own into his words. "Thy silence I grasp", she says; "thou wouldst fain evade the issue between thee and me. Wilt thou not make atonement?" The cries of the sailors break in harshly once more. Brangaene, in response to an impatient gesture from her mistress, brings the cup — not of death but of love — to Isolde, who takes it from her and strides towards Tristan. "We are nigh our goal", she says again; "in a moment we shall be standing before King Marke"; and to these last words she gives an ironic inflection. Then she plays her last card: "Were it not well that thou couldst say to him: 'My lord and uncle, look upon her! A gentler wife thou couldst not find. I slew her lover and sent her his head. My wound she healed in kindness. My life was in her power, but the gentle maid gave it to me. Her country's dishonour and shame — these too she gave that she might become thy bride. And these gracious thanks for worthy gifts I earned by a sweet draught of atonement, graciously offered me by her in expiation of all my guilt'".

She says all this quietly, for the time for storming is past; and the deceptive surface-placidity of her words is reflected in the or-

---

[1] The passage was evidently a stumbling-block to some of Wagner's contemporaries, for we find him patiently explaining it in 1876 to a correspondent.

chestra, which plays in one honeyed modulation after another upon a variant of No. 26:

No. 28

It is only the muttering of the Death motive towards the end of her appeal, as she speaks of the "sweet draught of atonement", that lets us see what is really in her mind.

36

Again there comes from the ship's crew a shout of "Stand by the cable! Let go the anchor!" For a moment the seaman in Tristan is recalled by habit to the real world: "Drop the anchor!" he cries wildly; "put the helm round to the tide! Furl the sails to the wind!" Then he turns to Isolde, takes the cup from her hands, and for the first time in the whole scene finds words for what had been locked in his breast: "Well do I know Ireland's Queen and the magic might of her arts. Once, of old, I took for my weal the balsam she gave me; now I accept from her the cup that will bring me full and final healing this very day.[1] Here is my atonement-oath: I give it thee with thanks; mark thou it well. 'To Tristan's honour — supremest troth! To Tristan's distress — boldest defiance!' [2]

---

[1] The Prose Sketch makes it clearer than the poem does that Tristan is fully aware that there is death in the cup. The Sketch runs thus at this point: "Healing potions she brewed for me, balsam to heal all wounds, even the most mortal", — that is to say, not the physical wound that Morold had once dealt him but the unendurable suffering which his hopeless love for Isolde had brought him. And to the words "blessed be this draught thou proffer'st me" Wagner added later in parentheses, "whatever marvel it may work in me, whether it takes me to hell or to heaven".

[2] Wagner's economy of words has obscured his meaning for most readers of the passage. The German runs thus:

Tristans Ehre —
höchster Treu'!

Heart's delusion; dream of presage! Sole balsam for endless grief! Kindly cup of oblivion, I drain thee without flinching"; and as he raises the "cup of oblivion" to his lips the orchestra gives out again the significant motive of "Death-devoted head! Death-devoted heart!" He drinks what he imagines to be the fatal draught. Isolde wrests the cup from him with a cry of "Betrayed here too? Mine the half! Traitor, I drink to thee!" The orchestra gives out a passionate statement of the "Look" motive; in what the pair believe to be their last hour their thoughts go back to the moment that had been the decisive point in their lives — when Isolde stayed her hand because of what she read in the helpless man's eyes.

Then follows the episode — generally an awkward one on the stage — that makes heavier demands on the singers as actors than any other situation in Wagner's works, demands which not one Tristan or Isolde in a hundred can meet. The slow operation of the philtre, the clearing away of the mists from their tortured brains, the gradual recognition that the barriers are down at last and the love of each for the other cannot and need not be any longer concealed, are depicted in reminiscences in the orchestra of the opening bars of the prelude to the opera, the characters remaining silent. The stage directions run thus: "Seized with shuddering, excited but motionless, they look fixedly into each other's eyes, in which the expression of defiance of death soon gives way to the glow of love. Trembling seizes them; they clutch convulsively at their breasts and pass their hands over their foreheads. Then their eyes again seek each the other's; for a moment they sink in confusion, then fix themselves again on each other with increasing longing."

At last, to the strains of No. 2 and No. 4, they ejaculate "Tristan!" "Isolde!" "Faithless dear one!" "Most blessed of women!" They fall into each other's arms. The orchestra lashes itself into a

---

Tristans Elend —
kühnster Trotz!

"Ehre" (honour) and "Elend" (distress) may be either nominatives or datives. It is in the latter sense that we must take them: Tristan's meaning, in more expanded terms, is this: "In taking this oath and drinking this draught I am supremely faithful to my honour, and I hurl defiance in the face of my misery".

passion which, it now seems, it has been holding in leash ever since the first bars of the prelude: No. 4 is marked no longer "slow and with yearning" but "animato, with a crescendo of passion". The ship's crew strike in with an excitement of their own as a trumpet fanfare, ringing out from the land, announces that the ship bearing the King and his retinue has come in sight.[1] Brangaene, who has been standing at the side of the ship, her face averted in confusion and horror, turns round at the brazen clang of the trumpets and the sailors' jubilant shouts of "Hail, King Marke, hail!" She sees the world-forgetting lovers locked in an embrace, and rushes forward, wringing her hands in despair; for she foresees all the tragic consequences of her substitution of the love potion for the draught of death. "Woe! Woe!" she cries; "not death but inescapable, endless woe! This well-meant deceit of mine, the work of my foolish fidelity, now wails to high heaven!"

37

But Tristan and Isolde neither see nor hear Brangaene and the others; they are lost in their brooding upon their self-delusion in the past and the dazzling illumination that has suddenly come to them. Tristan's honour, Isolde's shame, what meaning has all this now? they ask themselves and each other. How could they have been so blind? There is no room in their hearts at this moment for anything but supreme joy; and the orchestra envelops their ecstatic cries in a rich texture derived from the prelude, with the old yearning, however, now changed into rapture.

But once more the world of crude reality breaks in upon them. The curtains across the centre of the stage are flung wide apart, showing the whole ship thronged with knights and sailors, shouting and making jubilant gestures towards the land, where we now see a cliff crowned with a majestic castle.

Brangaene forces herself between the lovers, who are still blind and deaf to everyone and everything but themselves, and throws the royal mantle round the tranced and passive Isolde. The shouts of the men on the ship, "Hail, King Marke!", are borne upon an

---

[1] Bülow, in his piano score of the opera, has shirked the problem of incorporating the fanfare in the complex harmonic texture. He merely inserts the stage direction "Trumpets on the stage".

exuberant version of the Sea motive (No. 9 A) and more fanfares in trumpets and trombones. Kurvenal enters, in high spirits, to tell Tristan that the King is nearing them in a boat, rejoiced at the arrival of his bride. The dazed Tristan can only ejaculate *"Who is* coming? *What* King?" His clouded eyes mechanically follow Kurvenal's pointing finger, while Isolde turns to Brangaene with a bewildered cry of "What call is that? Where am I? Do I live? What was the draught you gave us?" "The draught of love!" is the maid's despairing answer. Then at last the full horror of her earthly destiny dawns on Isolde. She falls on Tristan's breast with a despairing cry of "Tristan! Must I still live, then?", while a great tragic cry is wrung from the knight, "O rapture rich in spite! O bliss dedicated to guile!" By now a bridge has been lowered, people have swarmed on board from the land, and as the curtain falls a tumult of joy on the part of the seafolk, with fanfares ringing out in the brass, indicates that the King and his retinue have arrived. Perhaps the most shattering feature of the whole first act is this stark antithesis of physical joy present and spiritual suffering to come with which the act ends.

38

The second act opens with a long orchestral prelude which originally began at what is now the ninth bar of the score, where we meet with a new motive expressive of Isolde's Impatient Expectation. In the course of this act Wagner had made great use of an important motive known as that of Day, the mystical significance of which word will become clear later: this motive he prefixed later to the original opening of the prelude, which thereby assumed its present form:

No. 29

A being the motive of Day, B that of Isolde's Impatience as she awaits the coming of Tristan. Soon a fresh motive, that of Love's Longing, appears in the upper strings:

No. 30

in combination with a modification of No. 29 B in the 'cellos. Then comes a reminiscence of the motive of Desire (No. 1 B), which leads into yet another new motive, that of Love's Bliss (derived from No. 1 B):

No. 31

which will be chosen later by Wagner to be the last strain to linger in our ears when the final curtain falls.

At the end of a rich symphonic development of this feverish material the curtain rises, showing us a garden with high trees in front of Isolde's chamber in the castle, with steps leading up to this on one side of the stage. It is a clear, balmy summer night. The door to the castle is open, and at the side of it is fixed a burning torch. From the adjacent forest comes the distant and slowly receding sound of the hunting horns of King Marke and his knights:

No. 32

Bass: F

Brangaene is looking anxiously back into the chamber, from which Isolde is shortly seen approaching.

For a long time the orchestral texture is made up of a free play upon motives by now familiar to us, in particular combinations of No. 30, No. 31 and No. 1 B, with the distant horn fanfares piercing through the complex of sound from time to time. Isolde is fretting for the moment to arrive when she can give Tristan the signal to leave the hunt and come to her; that signal, at once material and symbolic, is to be the extinguishing of the light of the torch.[1] Brangaene warns her mistress again and again that the horns of the hunters are not so far away as Isolde, in her impatience, is too inclined to imagine, for all *she* can hear is the rustling of the leaves and the gentle laughter of the wind. Brangaene tells her that she is deceived by her desire, hearing only what she would fain hear. The orchestral tissue softens to an exquisite sweetness as Isolde sings of the loveliness of the night and the lover who is straining towards her far away in the velvet silence of it.

39

Brangaene becomes more urgent: he for whom Isolde is looking so eagerly is being spied upon, she says. "Because thou art self-blinded, deem'st thou that the eye the world turns upon thee is blind? On the ship, when Tristan's trembling hand delivered the pallid bride to Marke, and all gazed in wonder on her, and the good King spoke kindly of the hardships of the voyage, one there

---

[1] Wagner remarked one day to Frau Eliza Wille, after playing to her the music of the second act to which the lovers sing their rhapsody upon Night and Death, that "the ancients used to depict Eros as the genius of Death, with a torch turned downwards in his hand".

was — I heeded him well! — whose crafty, evil eyes never left Tristan, seeking some sign in him that would serve his own ends. Oft have I seen him, since then, lurking and spying and laying subtle snares for thee. Beware, I say, of Melot!" But the love-blinded Isolde will not believe her. "Is not Melot Tristan's trustiest friend? When my dear one must shun me, it is with Melot alone that he bides." Brangaene repeats that she distrusts the man: "Melot's way to King Marke lies through Tristan, and he is sowing evil seed. Those who hastily planned this hunt by night were bent on a nobler quarry than thou, in thy illusion, dost imagine."

No! Isolde insists. Was it not Melot, the trusty friend, who, out of pity for her and Tristan, had devised the stratagem of this hunt to serve them? "Better than thou he cares for me; ways he opens that thou wouldst close. Oh end this my misery of waiting! The signal, Brangaene! Give the signal! Quench the last of the torch's light! Give Night the sign that she may descend upon us and enfold us. For now she has spread her silence over castle and grove, filling the heart with shuddering bliss. Put out the light! Make an end of its frightening glare! Let my loved one come to me!"

In vain does Brangaene continue to plead with her. The distracted maid curses the moment when, out of excess of love and mistaken fidelity to her mistress, she had substituted the potion of Love for that of Death. The deed of woe has been hers, and the guilt of it will be hers for ever. "No", replies Isolde, "not thy work but Frau Minne's, the mistress of magic, the queen who subdues the boldest spirit, the shaper of the whole world's destinies. Life and death are thralls to her, out of joy and sorrow and hate and envy she weaves love. Presumptuously I took the work of death into my hands; Frau Minne snatched it from my grasp: me, the Death-devoted one, she took in pledge, made the work her own." The orchestra gives out a gracious new motive of Frau Minne as the source and symbol of Love:

No. 33

upon which Wagner proceeds to execute a symphonic fantasia, as he does with the other themes of this scene.

Isolde continues with her rhapsody: "Whatever the turn she gives it, whatever the end she has appointed for it, whatsoever she may have in store for me, whithersoever she may choose to lead me, hers was I, hers alone; now let me show obedience to her." In vain does Brangaene repeat the warning and implore her to have a care, this day of all days: "Let the bright beacon, the token of peril, burn on today, at least today! Extinquish not the torch!" Isolde only repeats that what she is about to do is simply to fulfil Frau Minne's will; "Let Night descend, that she may shed her light." This fixed resolve of Isolde's is the turning point of the action; and Wagner throws it into the highest relief by a sudden great broadening-out of the time-values of his melodic and harmonic line, which until now has been one of unceasingly shifting and intertwining smaller notes:

(The harmonic texture is here shown in skeletonised form). This broadening-out is a simple stroke, but a most effective one: the action seems to pause and take a great breath after the haste and fever that have characterised it until now, and to be gathering strength for its next passionate flight.

40

Isolde snatches the torch from its socket and with a glad laugh throws it to earth, where the flame gradually dies out; and Brangaene, at her bidding, ascends the outside steps leading to the battlements, slowly disappearing from our sight.

The orchestra now takes possession of the field once more for a while as Isolde looks nervously down the avenue, listens intently, and then beckons again and again with a veil, at first at intervals, then more and more continuously as her impatience increases. A sudden gesture of delight indicates that she has seen the beloved in the distance. She hastens to the top of the steps, whence she beckons to him. The orchestra works itself up into a tornado of passion by way of No. 29 B and, in combination with this, an excited new figure that is repeated incessantly in one form and another:

No. 35

Tristan enters, and Isolde rushes to greet him. For a while the ecstasy of the pair can find voice only in breathless ejaculations — "Tristan!" "Isolde!" . . . "Art thou mine?" "Once more I hold thee?" . . . "Can I believe it?" and so on.[1] At first they cannot believe in the reality of their happiness. "Tristan mine!", "Isolde mine!", "For ever one!", they cry, to cumulative repetitions of the passionate motive of Love's Bliss (No. 33) in the orchestra. Then the "action" — in the ordinary theatrical sense of that term — of the opera becomes suspended for a considerable time; that is to say, it ceases to be in any degree physical and becomes entirely psychological. The lovers launch into a long mystical meditation and communion upon their past and present and future, which they see in terms of an antithesis of the real world — symbolised as Day — with its deceits, its illusions, its false values, and a mystical other-world symbolised as Night, in which all that is superficial and transitory in the human mind and heart is merged in the eternal, the only true. The extinguishing of the torch has been symbolic rather than realistic; it marks the severance of the last bond that had held the supra-mundane love of Tristan and Isolde in servitude to the cruder world of Day.

What follows now in the opera, until the irruption of realistic

[1] There has been much talk about the "deceit" of King Marke, and commentators, with the mediaeval legend too much in their minds, have assumed previous clandestine meetings of the lovers. There is not the smallest authority in Wagner's text for that assumption. We are nowhere told how long or how short an interval of time has elapsed between act I and act II, nor is there a single line in the poem to indicate even that the wedding has yet taken place. Wagner's mystical drama was not concerned with realistic irrelevancies of that sort. It is inferrible, from one passage and another in the text, that this is the first time the lovers have been thus alone with each other since they arrived in Cornwall.

Day once more into their ecstatic dream-world when Melot brings King Marke and the others upon the scene, is the most difficult section of the whole work for both the listener in the theatre and the reader of the poem. Not one spectator in a hundred grasps the inner meaning of the lovers' long poetic fantasia upon Night and Day,[1] or, if he happens to have read the text, perceives even the meaning of many of Wagner's lines, for his imagery becomes more and more recondite, his words fewer, and his syntax more and more condensed and elliptical as he indulges himself in the luxury of exploring this mystical world that lies deep below and high above the material one. Yet without a complete understanding of all that the characters are saying it is a pure impossibility to know what the whole opera *Tristan and Isolde* is really "about".

Only an integral reproduction of the text of the remaining hundred pages of the second act could reveal all the psychological subtleties of Wagner's handling of his poetic thesis. That being impossible — and in any case a great many of the lines are almost inconvertible into English or any other language, — the next best thing is for the student of the opera to read a translation of the outline of the scene given by Wagner himself in his Prose Sketch. He will then see that, for the first time, Wagner here discloses one or two psychological "motives" antecedent to the opera which were passed over in silence in the first act, but which are vital to our comprehension of the drama. We now realise, for example, what Tristan meant when he spoke to Isolde, in the first act, of his "honour" having barred him from an admission, even to himself, of his love for Isolde: before his fateful second visit to Ireland he had vowed within himself, in order to save Cornwall from internal strife and not to have it believed that he had played upon his uncle's love for him for his own ambitious ends, to leave the country for ever after having persuaded the King to marry and beget an heir to the throne. Honour, in the world's sense of that word, had forbidden him later either to break that vow or reveal it to Isolde.

[1] Matters in this respect are not improved by the cuts made in the second act in the ordinary theatre performance. Cuts are unavoidable except when the opera is given under "festival" conditions; but they make a sad mess of both Wagner's musical design and his poetic idea.

Here, then, is a translation of the relevant pages of text and stage directions from Wagner's Prose Sketch.

41

(Tristan rushes in. A long and passionate embrace. Overflow of long-suppressed emotion. Exultant rapture. Praise of Night, which has brought them joy after the agonies of Day . . . Impeachment of Day as the bringer of all sorrows for lovers: they outbid each other as to who has suffered most from Day. Tender reproaches).

Is. Day it was when you wooed me for Marke.

Tr. Day it was that blinded me, persuading me that honour was the world's highest treasure, dazzling me with its false beams and making me strive after vanity and emptiness. [In an insert Wagner elucidates this as "Fame".]

Is. What lie did Day tell you to make you betray me?

Tr. The image of you in the pure Night of my heart it seduced me into disclosing in its shameless glitter: loudly I sang your praises before them all,[1] awaking desire and envy. All would have you for their Queen, to the end that they might avenge themselves on me for my fame and good fortune. The noble Marke, who had chosen the orphan to be his son, had promised him the inheritance of his kingdom, vowing that he himself would never marry. For that, and because fortune had been bountiful to me, all envied me. The courtiers urged the King to wed — Isolde were a fitting bride for him, and Tristan should woo her for him, for the ancient blood-feud between the two kingdoms made them all dread the perilous quest for themselves. All believed I would refuse, and then they could make it appear that I was a self-seeker bent on my own advantage alone. So I was goaded into claiming the task as mine and renouncing my heritage in favour of the offspring that would be born to the King. Thus I paid homage to my Day-sun — to honour and fame.

Is. And so you surrendered me to increase your honour and fame?

Tr. Accuse the Day, that blinded me into revelling in arrogance!

---

[1] I.e., in Cornwall, after his first stay in Ireland.

Is. How can *I* accuse the Day, I who let it urge me on to death and revenge? It showed you to me only as an evil-doer, my coldest, most treacherous foe. When I would fain see you in another light , as you were in the depth of Night in my heart, always there lingered in me that harsh picture of you as my deadly enemy alone.

Tr. When you proffered me the Draught of Death, then dawned within me sublime Night. My senses swooned; I would fain plunge into Death, there to belong to you for ever.

Is. Yet alas! it was the Draught of Love that bore you away from Night, and bringing you Love brought you also the falsity of Day?

Tr. O rapture! Hail to that Draught! Through the gates of Death it opened out to me the blissful realm of Night, in which till then I had only been groping blindly: now there fell away from me everything that had been deluding me so long.

Is. Yet Day took its revenge. For your trespass we had to pay atonement to him: you had to deliver me over to the King: to the stars of Day you had to yield, leaving me solitary in empty splendour. How did I ever bear that?

Tr. But then we were consecrated to Night: Day could divide but no more blind us. We laugh at its vain glitter: Fame and Honour — mere fleeting motes in the sun — were scattered: their falsehood became manifest in face of the profound secret that Night confided to us, a secret that disclosed to us the deception even of troth and friendship themselves. Day may still hold us fast in his toils, but he deludes us no more: to eyes that have Night-sight he is but desolate darkness. One longing only have I in the Day, the longing for holy Night! Descend upon me, Love's own Night! Take me up into thy bosom! Let me forget that I live, blot out the world from my eyes! When I find myself, how poor am I! When I lost myself wholly, how rich I became! Then my gaze is blinded with rapture. When the world I see no more, then am I myself the world, life uplifted to holiest Love! When the sun no longer lights me, its warmth lies hidden in my heart; then to light me I have the stars of bliss! Heart to heart with you! Mouth to mouth! When sight is shattered I am ruler of the world! — (Mutual heightening of the utmost transport, release from the world, intoxicating presage of death. Never to wake again! Longing for death! Speech fails. Brangaene's watching-song — deepest woe! Dismay at the thought of awaking! Warning. It sinks into Isolde. Anxiety!).

Tr. Let me die. (Sorrowfully tender reproaches from Isolde).

Tr. How could we die? What is there in us that could be slain that were not Love itself? Are we not wholly and solely Love? Can our love ever find an end? Could the day come when the love of Love could die in me? [Then, in a footnote: My body is Death's property: stood he before me, would my love quail? Were I to die, would my love die too? What does not die with me, how could that ever cease to be? And I myself, am I aught but Love, Love without end?] Did I will to die now, would Love also die, seeing that we are naught but Love?

Is. Yet it is we who love, Tristan and Isolde, you and I? Were Tristan to die?

Tr. Then would not merely that pass away that bars me from loving you for ever?

Is. Of Tristan's dying I can think only along with Isolde's death!

Tr. Thus would we have died only to love. Then could no Day divide us any more: wakened no more by its dismaying gleam, for ever would we be hidden in the Night of Love: what rapture were higher than this, which is freedom from all torment? (A still more anxious summons from Brangaene. Tristan becomes aware of it). Who calls to me there to awaken?

Is. Death! Tristan, let me die!

Tr. He summons us to waken: not yet does Day dawn for us, still is eternity ours. (Isolde's growing anxiety for Tristan, allayed by him in a renewed ecstasy).

Tr. Should we flee from the fate that leads us to an eternity in which there will be no awakening? Death joined us together: at his gates we drank Love: dedicated to Death, ever-loving, ever-living, let us clasp each the other, to be separated no more! (Redoubled rapture. New and highest intoxication: an ardent embrace. Day dawns. A cry from Brangaene. Marke, Melot and courtiers enter hurriedly. Before this, a short combat — in the foreground Kurvenal falling back before the assailants). Isolde sinks in terror on to a flowery bank. Tristan, holding his cloak before her with one arm, as though to conceal her, stands immobile, as if turned to stone, his eyes fixed on the newcomers. A long silence.

Tr. (in a choked voice) The dreary Day has dawned! [1]

42

With this epitome of the poem firmly fixed in our minds we can devote our attention mainly to the musical working-out of the scene.

The lovers begin with a lament over their enforced separation: "How long so far apart! How far apart so long! [2] So far when near! So near when afar!" — to the strains of No. 33 and No. 30. This latter motive (Love's Longing) is given a darker and wilder significance as Tristan speaks of the warning light that seemed to have been burning for so intolerable a time:

No. 36

(In the centre voice of this quotation No. 35 is seen weaving its way in and out in the second violins).

It is impossible to set forth in detail the infinitely subtle recurrences and metamorphoses of the motives in this great sym-

[1] The antithesis of the passing falsity of Day and the eternal truth of Night had been a favourite one with the German romantics, and it had found its most elaborate expression in Novalis's *Hymns to Night* (1800). The reader with a knowledge of German who wishes to follow up the subject will find a number of parallels between the *Hymns* and the *Tristan* text set forth in an article by Arthur Prüfer on *Novalis Hymnen an die Nacht in ihren Beziehungen zu Wagners Tristan und Isolde*, in the Wagner-Jahrbuch for 1906, pp. 290–304.

[2] These "longs" are not to be taken literally, as signifying that a considerable time has elapsed between the first act and the second. The separation has been "long" in the sense in which lovers invariably speak of separations, even the shortest.

phonic structure. When first Isolde, then Tristan, speaks of the lovers' defiance of the hateful, envious Day we hear the first statement of the Day motive (No. 29 A) which, as we have seen, was afterwards used by Wagner to introduce the prelude to the second act. As the light of the torch had kept the lovers apart that night, so the lying light of Day, the false standards of the Day in which the outer world lives and moves and has its being, have been the source of all their miseries from the first moment they looked into each other's eyes. It was through craven subservience to these false standards that Tristan had allowed his impulse of honour towards Marke and Cornwall to prompt him to undertake the mission to Ireland, a mission that had ended in self-denial of his love and treachery towards Isolde. She too had been Day's dupe, hating Tristan as Ireland's enemy and hers; until, on the ship, the moment had come when she would have made an end of it all in death:

> *The light of Day*
> *I fain would flee;*
> *away into Night*
> *fare forth with thee,*
> *where an end to falsehood*
> *my heart foretold;*
> *where the dreaded might*
> *of the lie would vanish;*
> *there would I drink*
> *our love for ever,*
> *us twain, thou one with me,*
> *would I in death entwine!*

It was death, rejoins Tristan, that he had gladly accepted at her hands. Yet the false draught, she reminds him, had practised a deceit on him; instead of the hoped-for Night, Day had dawned for him once more. But Tristan now sings the praises of the draught, of which, on the ship, he had been conscious only of the horror of its deceit of him: the gates of death had been flung open before him, and through them he had passed from Day to "the wonder-world of Night".

Once more Isolde extends the poetic antithesis: the affrighted Day had taken its revenge on him, for Tristan had been compelled to take up his life in the real world again. But he sweeps her reproaches and regrets aside: Day might indeed still hold them in his toils, but no longer had he power to delude them:

> *O now were we*
> *to Night enhallowed!*
> *The envious Day,*
> *with hate o'erbrimming,*
> *could but hold us apart,*
> *but no more blind us with lies!*
> *Its empty pride,*
> *the vaunt of its glare,*
> *derides he whom Night*
> *her own has made!*
> *All its fugitive lightning's*
> *flickering flashes*
> *blind us twain no more.*
> *Who at death's dark Night,*
> *love-led, has gazed,*
> *who at her heart*
> *her secrets has learned,*
> *the lies of daylight,*
> *honour, fame,*
> *profit and power,*
> *how dazzling soe'er,*
> *no more to him are all these*
> *than dust before him driven.*[1]
> *In the daylight's foolish fancies*

[1] In the poem, at this point, are eight lines which will not be found in the score:

> Selbst um der Treu'
> und Freundschaft Wahn
> dem treu'sten Freunde
> ist's getan
> der in der Liebe
> Nacht geschaut,
> dem sie ihr tief
> Geheimniss vertraut.

Wagner had set them to music in his Composition Sketch, but he rejected them later.

holds him one single yearning —
the yearning hence
to holy Night,
where unending,
only true,
laughs to him Love's delight.

The orchestral texture in this section of the score is made up of an endless series of metamorphoses of the relevant motives: Wagner, having no stage traffic to distract him, can abandon himself to the luxury of weaving his musical material into ever new patterns.

43

Gradually a change comes over the music. No. 31 (the motive of Love's Happiness) is spun into a thread of long-drawn sweetness:

as Tristan, according to the stage directions, "draws Isolde gently down on to a flowery bank, sinks on his knee before her, and lays his head on her arm." The Day motive, now shorn of its hard urgency, steals out softly in cor anglais and horn, and the scene settles into a kind of rapturous nocturne as the pair call upon Love's Night to descend upon them and bestow on them oblivion of the world. The new theme that dominates the scene had been foreshadowed harmonically a little earlier, at Tristan's words, "Da erdämmerte mild erhab'ner Macht im Busen mir die Nacht" ("Then Night descended on my bosom in mild majestic might"); now it comes out in its full form, with the harmonies in throbbing irregular pulses: [1]

---

[1] Wagner drew upon this music for his setting of the song *Träume*, the words of which were by Frau Wesendonk. He called it a "Study for *Tristan and Isolde*". Two sketches in one of Wagner's pocket-books reveals the curious fact that at one time he associated the words "O sink' hernieder, Nacht

No. 38

The motive of Day (No. 29 A) recurs in a softened and subtle form, and later No. 38 generates a new theme:

No. 39

der Liebe" not (as in the present score) with the melody of No. 38 but with that of Love's Peace (No. 39). The first sketch begins thus:

Sink' her-nie-der, Nacht der Lie-be, nimm mich auf in dei-nen Schoss

This is generally referred to as the motive of Love's Peace, but there is no need to attach any definite label to it. It becomes of special importance at a crucial point in the third act.

"Heart to heart", Tristan and Isolde sing,

> *and lip to lip;*
> *thou and I*
> *one soul, one breath;*
> *faint with bliss*
> *my eyes are failing,*
> *the world with all*
> *its shows is paling —*
> *world that the Day*
> *lit with its lies;*
> *from blinding illusion*
> *now set free,*
> *I now,*
> *I am the world,*
> *life in rapture stirring,*
> *life of holiest loving —*
> *no more waken, —*
> *swooning,*
> *thus and now to die!*

As their world-forgetting ecstasy reaches its climax:

No. 40

and dissolves in soft harmonies, Wagner introduces one of his most telling strokes — one that is at once musically serviceable and dramatically effective. The lovers have still much to say to each other, but a relief from the intensity of their emotion is as

and the second thus:

necessary, at some point or other, to them as it is to us. Wagner takes advantage of this momentary muting of their passionate song to introduce a warning voice from that outer world which they had forgotten; and he brings in that voice in felicitous accord with the mediaeval milieu of the story.

Some of the most deeply felt of the Minnesinger poems are what are known as "Warder's Songs".[1] In that age of loveless aristocratic *mariages de convenance* the sympathy of the poets and romancers was all with lovers who defied the bonds of the law; and this sympathy found expression in the song of a watching friend in a tower, who, at the approach of dawn, gave the lovers warning that the night was past and they must tear themselves from each other's arms. It was an artistic convention of the period, but one into which the Minnesingers and Troubadours threw themselves with passionate sincerity: sometimes the Watchman's song alone floats down from the tower, sometimes the Lady dialogues with him, reproaching him for his cruelty and bewailing the harshness of separation from her beloved.[2]

This convention is now put to admirable use by Wagner. As Tristan and Isolde sink back upon the bank of flowers the warning voice of the unseen Brangaene peals out from a turret:

> *Lone I watch here*
> *in the night;*
> *ye there, lost*
> *in love's delight,*
> *to my warning*
> *give good heed:*
> *o'er the sleepers*
> *evil broods;*
> *wake, I warn you,*

[1] Or "Watchman's Song", "Dawn Song", "Alba", "Aubade", "Day Song", "Morning Song", etc.

[2] Some charming English versions of mediaeval "Watchman's Songs" will be found in Jethro Bithell's *The Minnesingers*. The reader will hardly need to be reminded of Swinburne's glowing poem based on an old Provençal alba commencing

> En un vergier sotz folha d'albespi
> tenc la dompna son amic costa si.

Each of the stanzas ends with the lady's cry of "Oi Deus, oi Deus, de l'alba! Tan vost vel".

waken now!
Have a care!
Have a care!
Soon the night will pass.

44

The orchestra plays subtly round Brangaene's words with suggestions of the lovers' own music, particularly Nos. 37, 38 and 39. As her song dies away, No. 39 reappears in its fuller and true form in the quiet tones of the strings:

No. 41

and Tristan and Isolde resume their fond dialogue upon Love and Life and the impotence of Death to part lovers such as they. Of what, Isolde asks, could Death make an end but the bar to their eternal union? And they sing in antiphony, "Then should we together die, one for ever, never waking, never fearing, the very names of us forgotten, thou and I, with no life but in our love":

No. 42

Isolde sinks her head on Tristan's breast. Once more the warning voice of Brangaene breaks in upon them: "Have a care! Now Night gives way to Day!" And once more they turn smilingly to each other, defying Day and his menace and avowing their faith in Night; [1] and their last words before the disaster of the world's Day falls on them are an ecstatic hymn to sweet Night, eternal Night, in which their individual beings shall be lost: "Thou Tristan, I Isolde!" Tristan cries; and she answers antithesis with antithesis — "Thou Isolde, Tristan I!". "How to grasp it?", they cry, to a rapturous expansion of the melody of No. 40:

No. 43

As they speak of their "tender yearning" and "sweet longing", first the clarinet, then the flute gives out a tender little figure:

No. 44

that is destined to play an important part later in the final Liebestod. The climax of their ecstasy is reached with No. 31 piling up in wave on wave in the orchestra.

But their final long cry of "Highest joy of love!" ends in a rending dissonance in the orchestra, accompanied by a piercing shriek from Brangaene, who from the turret has seen the coming of the catastrophe she has dreaded. Kurvenal rushes in with drawn sword, shouting "Save thyself, Tristan!" as he looks with horror behind him into the forest, from which Marke, Melot and the

---

[1] In the poem, between Isolde's "Lass' den Tag dem Tode weichen" and Tristan's "Des Tages Dräuen nun trotzten wir so?", there are fourteen lines which Wagner set to music in his Composition Sketch but omitted from his final score.

courtiers, in hunting attire, now come upon the scene. They are accompanied by a curiously harsh re-statement by the orchestra of the motive of the hunting horns (No. 32) that had figured so largely in the prelude to this second act. At that time Isolde, in her infatuation, had refused to listen to them, to believe they were what they really were; now they have become the most tragic of realities to her.

Brangaene comes down from the tower and hurries anxiously to her mistress. Isolde, "seized with involuntary shame", as the stage directions have it, "leans on the flowery bank with averted face. Tristan, with a movement that is also involuntary, stretches out his mantle with one arm so as to hide Isolde from them all. In this position he remains for some time motionless, staring blindly at the men, who keep there eyes fixed on him with a variety of expressions. The day begins to dawn." The orchestra gives out mournful variants of No. 43 and No. 44; and, to the accompaniment of the Day motive (No. 29 A), Tristan at last breaks the long silence with the despairing words, "The dreary Day for the last time dawns!".

45

The treacherous Melot [1] points in triumph to Tristan and asks King Marke if he has not been as good as his word: "Plain is his guilt; have I saved thy name and honour from shame?" A mournful figure in the bass clarinet:

anticipates the old King's sorrowful reply. "Hast thou, in sooth?" he asks Melot; and he points to Tristan:

> *See him there,*
> *of all true men the truest;*
> *look on him,*
> *most faithful he in friendship:*

[1] In the old legends Melot is a cunning dwarf.

'tis his loyal
deed of old
now my heart
with base betrayal wounds!
Tristan traitor,
why dost mock me
with the hope
that my lost honour
by a Melot's word
now can be restored?

Tristan ejaculates convulsively:

Daylight phantoms!
Morning visions!
Lying and vain,
away, begone!

The King, deeply moved, reproaches him with his deception: if his Tristan can be false, where in all the world is honour left? Tristan's eyes sink slowly to the ground as Marke continues, with increasing grief, to paint the situation as it appears to his uncomprehending eyes. A new motive in the bass clarinet:

No. 46 *Andante moderato*

p dolce espress.

threads its melancholy way through his long lament, the burden of which is the futility now of all the loyal service Tristan has done him in the past. They two had loved each other greatly; Marke had destined him to succeed to his kingdom, and Tristan had unselfishly sacrificed himself to confer the loveliest of Queens on Cornwall. And now his peerless knight has dealt him this deadly wound where his heart lay most open; and the greatest grief of all to him is not to know where to look for honour now that his Tristan has been false. How has it all come about?

Why this shame immense
for which no grief atones?
The secret and unfathomed
cause of all my woe
who will e'er reveal?

Tristan turns a look of profound compassion on him: "That", he says, "I cannot tell thee: the meaning even of thy question is beyond thy grasping"; but the motives of Grief and Desire (Nos. 1 A and 1 B) in the poignant timbres of cor anglais and oboe give us the answer to the riddle.

Tristan turns to Isolde, who looks up tenderly at him; and with the orchestra musing softly and sadly on the theme of their dreamed-of escape from the world (No. 39 etc.) he asks her a mystical question which only she among them all can understand: "Where I am going now wilt thou, Isolde, follow? It is to a land unlit by the sun, the dark land from which I took my being, in which my dying mother bore me. The wondrous realm of Night it is that Tristan offers thee now; will Isolde follow him there, loyal and true?" For the second time, then, of his own accord he is about to choose death; and for the second time she is willing to die with him. Once, she reminds him, she had followed him unwillingly into a strange land — when he, untrue to love, had torn her from home and kindred to take her to Cornwall as King Marke's bride. Now he is summoning her to go with him to a "land" of his own, a "land" that spans the whole world:

To Tristan's house and home
glad will Isolde go:
the road that, fair and true,
she now must follow,
prithee show!

He bends over her and kisses her gently on the forehead, while the orchestra turns, as it were, a last wistful glance back on their world-forgetting happiness of an hour ago (No. 37, No. 44).

Melot steps forward furiously with drawn sword. Tristan draws his own sword and faces him. "This was my friend", he says sorrowfully and scornfully. "Once he loved me truly, cared more than any for my fame and honour. 'Twas he who led those on who urged me on to win more fame, more honour, by bringing thee, Isolde, to be the King's bride. But thy glance blinded him too; and from passion he betrayed me to my King, whom I betrayed." He hurls himself on Melot; but as the latter strikes at him Tristan lets his own sword fall, and sinks, wounded, into Kurvenal's arms. Isolde throws herself on his breast. The King holds Melot back; and the curtain falls to some mournful mutations of the main motive of the grief-stricken Marke (No. 45).

46

The orchestral prelude to the third act begins with a melancholy transformation of No. 1 B in the strings (in six parts), which spirals out into the upper air, as it were, in a slowly ascending passage in the violins:

The music gives an extraordinary impression of the loneliness, physical and spiritual, of the wounded Tristan as he lies on the rock on the Breton coast to which the faithful Kurvenal has borne him, where he awaits in longing and suffering the coming of Isolde. She alone had been able to heal him that earlier time, when, as the sick Tantris, he had been cast up on the Irish shore: she alone, old Kurvenal has divined, can heal him now, and he has sent a ship across the sea to bring her.

After an extended development of No. 47 and of a new motive, which is afterwards associated with the Distress of Tristan:

the curtain rises, showing a castle garden on a rocky height, with the sea visible here and there as far as the horizon: "the whole place suggests", say the stage directions, "the absence of a master; it is ill-tended, in places overgrown, and in ruinous decay." On one side of the garden is a suggestion of a lofty castle, on the other side a long fortification-wall broken by a watch-tower. In the foreground Tristan, seemingly lifeless, lies on a couch in the shade of a great lime-tree: at his head sits Kurvenal, bending over him in grief, listening intently, anxiously, to his breathing. From without comes the sound of a shepherd's pipe:

No. 49

This long unaccompanied cor anglais melody is one of the strangest and most poignant ever imagined by man. It accelerates towards the end in a series of triplet turns:

No. 50

and at last dies out mournfully in the lowest register of the instrument.

His tune ended, the shepherd shows himself above the parapet. He hails Kurvenal, asking solicitously if the master is yet awake. The old retainer shakes his head sadly: were Tristan to awake, he says, it would only be to leave them for ever, unless there comes first the only leech who can heal him. Has the shepherd yet caught sight of a sail on the sea? he asks. No, replies the shepherd; when he does, the tune he will pipe will be merrier than the one he has just played! But what is it ails his lord? Kurvenal evades the question: "That thou could'st not understand: only watch thou, and if thou seest a ship, pipe lustily and merrily." The shepherd turns and looks over the sea, shading his eyes with his hand; and seeing nothing he goes slowly out, playing his sad melody once more.

But the tune had awakened Tristan. To Kurvenal's astonishment and joy he opens his eyes, turns his head a little, and asks feebly, "What ancient tune is that that wakens me? Where am I?" "Safe here in Kareol", the old man answers, to the accompaniment of a characteristically bluff motive in the orchestra:

No. 51

"Here in thy father's castle. It was thy own shepherd that woke thee, piping as he tends thine own flocks on thine own hill. Thou art among thy faithful people, who served thee before thou turned'st thy back on all that was thine to go and dwell in Cornwall." "Am I then in Cornwall?" Tristan asks faintly. "No, here in Kareol. I bore thee on my broad shoulders to a ship, and from the ship here to the castle. Thou art at home, in the land of thy fathers, with the old sun shining on fields and herds; here wilt thou be healed of thy sickness"; and the old man lays his grizzled head on his master's breast.

47

Consciousness comes back to Tristan very slowly. He remembers little of what has happened to him — only that he had been in a strange land:

> *The sun I could not see,*
> *nor land, nor people:*
> *but what I saw,*
> *of that I nought can tell thee.*
> *I was*
> *where once I drew my being,*
> *where once again I go:*
> *the vasty realm*

of dateless Night.
But one thing
is there our knowing:
godlike, endless
all-forgetting!
How faded then the presage?
Longing and foreboding,
these it was
that once again
to light of day did urge me?
What still is left within me,
life's fever madly raging,
from rapturous dread of death
towards the light now drives me,
that dazzling, false and golden,
round thee, Isolde, shines!

Tristan says all this like a man only half-emerged from sleep, trying to recapture the elusive threads of a dream: but things that are as yet not quite clear to him are made clear enough to us by the orchestral commentary — the motive of Longing, for instance (No. 1 B), and the phrase to which he had sung, in the second act, "Life of holiest loving" (No. 40). The motive of Day (No. 29 A) is added as Tristan goes on to speak, with growing excitement, of Isolde being still in the realm of garish sunlight, and of his longing to see her again: "I heard the crash of Death's door closing behind me. But now once more it stands ajar, forced open by the sun's beams; and I, with eyes open and clear, must now break forth out of Night, and go to find her with whom alone united Tristan may find surcease of being." This to the accompaniment of a passionate reminiscence of No. 42.

The gloomy transformation of No. 1 B with which the third act had opened (No. 47) comes to the forefront again as Tristan speaks of the horrors which he knows await him on his return to the outer world of Day and its attendant deceits. "Cursed be the Day and its lying appearances!" he cries frenziedly. "Must thou ever wake and re-wake my anguish? Must the light for ever burn that even in the night kept me far from her? O Isolde! Sweet one! Fair one! When at last shall be quenched the beacon that keeps me from thee? The torch — when dies it out?" He sinks back exhausted as the muted violins give out the softest and sweetest reminiscence of No. 31:

No. 52

Kurvenal, stirred to pity by his master's grief, makes a mighty effort to shake off his own dejection. "Once, from fidelity to thee", he says in self-reproach, "I scorned and defied her; but now my hunger for her is as great as thine. Trust thou my word; thou shalt see her again, here, today, if only she yet be living." But Tristan's mind is still in the borderland between sleep and waking, where past and present run confusedly into one. "The torch still burns", he says faintly; "not dark is it yet in the house; Isolde lives and watches; she called me out of the night." If she is living, Kurvenal assures him again, then let him take heart and hope. For he, the rough untutored one, had been wise enough, he says, to see that the wound the traitor Melot had dealt Tristan could be healed only by the physician who had once closed the wound inflicted by Morold. To Cornwall he has sent a trusty messenger for her, and soon Isolde will be here.

48

Beside himself with excitement, Tristan draws Kurvenal to him, embraces him, and sings the most moving paean to friendship ever penned. Always this old Kurvenal of his has been the faithfullest of friends, his master's shield and guard in battle, one with him in sorrow and in joy: "whom I hated, him hated'st thou too; whom I loved, him too thou loved'st; to good King Marke thou wast true when I was true, false when I was false; never thine own but always mine, when I am suffering thou sufferest with me — but the depth of my suffering, that canst thou not fathom! This terrible yearning that sears my soul, this fever of longing that eats out my heart — could I name it, could'st thou but know it, no longer here would'st thou stay; thou would'st be there at the watch-tower, straining for a sight of the sail that will bring me Isolde and her love!"

> *It nears! it nears,*
> *so blithe and fast!*
> *It waves, it waves,*
> *the flag at the mast!*
> *The ship! the ship!*
> *it glides by the reef!*
> *seest thou it not?*
> *Kurvenal, seest thou it not?*

The musical texture of these few passionate pages is a remarkable weaving of motives, sometimes so metamorphosed harmonically and dynamically, however, as to strike the ear at first as new. The motive of Longing, for instance (No. 1 B) now takes this form:

No. 53

and, later, still more subtle shapes. Nos. 40 and 48 (the latter the motive of Tristan's Distress, from the prelude to the third act) appear in new forms, with new psychological nuances. The scoring, too, takes on new colours; the orchestra lashes itself into a tempest as Tristan, in growing excitement, tries to make Kurvenal see the ship that is only a figment of his own disordered imagination. The episode ends with a piercing reiteration of a B flat in octaves high up in the violins and violas as Tristan cries in a final frenzy, "Kurvenal, seest thou not?"

He looks up in expectant silence at the old man, who hesitates whether to leave his master or not. But there is no need for him to go to the tower to see if Tristan's vision of the ship is fact or fancy: the poignant wordless answer to the cry is given by the shepherd's pipe, which once more strikes in, from afar, with its mournful melody (No. 50). Kurvenal understands: "Yet is no ship in sight!" he says in deep dejection. Tristan, his fever now dying down, begins also to perceive the bearing on his own life and lot of that old tune, familiar to him from childhood, immemorially associated with his tragic house:

> *This was the meaning, then,*
> *thou song so old, so mournful,*
> *of all thy long lament!*
>> *On breeze of evening*
>> *wailed it once*
>> *when I, a child,*
> *my father's death did grieve for:*
>> *through mists of morn*
>> *it rang yet sadder*
>> *when the son*
> *his mother's fate was told.*
> *When he begat me and died,*
> *When dying she gave me birth,*
>> *the tune so olden*
>> *wept and wailed,*
>> *upon their souls*
>> *its pain it poured.*
>> *It asked me then,*
>> *and asks me now,*
> *what fate it was before me*
> *to which my mother bore me?*
>> *o what the fate? —*
>> *Again the strain*
>> *tells me truly: —*
> *for yearning — and dying!*

Throughout Tristan's long monologue the mournful melody of the shepherd keeps weaving its way in and out in one orchestral voice and another.

Yearning and dying — between these two poles his life has been one long oscillation: "in death for ever yearning, yet of yearning never able to die!" And now this ancient tune rings out in appeal to the distant healer, bidding her come and bring her lover the peace of death. His mind, now calm and clear again for a brief spell, runs over the episodes of his life in which Isolde has figured. When, long ago, he lay in the boat, mortally wounded as he thought, that ancient strain had sounded in his ears. The wind had carried him to Ireland; there Isolde had healed him, but only to deal his heart a worse wound. Later she had given him a poisoned draught to drink — a draught intended to be of death, but one that had turned to unquenchable fire within him. And at the thought of that fire his fever returns. With growing excitement he speaks of the endless torment of longing to which he is now condemned, a torment from which death itself cannot free him. Brain and heart are on fire in the terrible heat of the Day; where will they ever find a cooling shade? All this has been the work of the potion, "and I myself it was who brewed it":

> *from father's grief*
> *and mother's woe,*
> *from all earth's endless*
> *tears of love,*
> *from laughter and weeping,*
> *sweetness and sorrow,*
> *did I distil*
> *the potion's poison!*
> *Thee that I brewed,*
> *thee I created,*
> *on whose delight*
> *I ever feasted —*
> *I curse thee, terrible draught!,*
> *and him who brewed thee first!*

49

He sinks back exhausted. Kurvenal, who has vainly been trying to calm him, gives a terrified cry of "My master! Tristan!", and breaks out into a bitter reproach of Love, its illusions and deceptions, for it is that that has brought his Tristan to this sorry pass, Tristan, the flower of knighthood, loving as no man had ever done, loved as no man had ever been; and for the first and only time in the work the old warrior reveals the wealth of tenderness that lies at the heart of his rough nature.

He turns to his master again with a sob, listens to his breathing, and is rejoiced to find he is still alive. The orchestra, with its soft, honeyed reminiscences of themes previously associated with the longing and the rapture of the lovers, tells us where Tristan's thoughts are. He asks Kurvenal faintly if the ship is yet in sight, and the old man assures him fondly that it will come that very day. Thereupon Tristan loses himself in beatific contemplation of an Isolde smiling on the deck, bringing him atonement and the final peace. No. 41 now becomes the basis of a rich four-part harmony in the horns:

No. 54

over which Tristan dreams his dream of the coming of the gentle, smiling Isolde:

No. 55

ending with a long-drawn sigh, that is half pain, half ecstasy, on the words, "Ah, Isolde! How fair art thou!"

Then his fever begins to master him again. He bids Kurvenal go to the watch-tower and look for the ship. He struggles to rise from his couch, and while Kurvenal is trying to restrain him the shepherd's pipe is heard preludising in a new way:

No. 56

and then breaking out unrestrainedly into the joyous melody for which Kurvenal has so long been waiting: [1]

[1] Like its predecessor, the shepherd's new melody is allotted in the score to the cor anglais. But at the foot of the page (307) on which it appears in Wagner's manuscript of the full score the following note has been added —

No. 57

The old man runs to the watch-tower, looks out over the sea, and excitedly announces the coming of the ship. "The flag? The flag?", asks Tristan breathlessly. "The flag of joy!" Kurvenal assures him. Excitement is piled on excitement as he describes to the anxious Tristan how the ship is making its way safely through the dangerous reefs, for the steersman is a chosen man, skilled and trusty. The shepherd too has been watching the course of the ship; and when at last he sees she is safe he pipes his merry tune more exultantly than ever before, while Kurvenal, from the tower, and Tristan, on his couch, shout for joy. The ship is safe in port, the old man tells his master; Isolde is springing to shore. At Tristan's imperious command he goes down to bring her to him.

When Tristan is alone the fever mounts in his blood and brain once more. How, he asks, can he stay fettered to his couch on this best of all days? He must rise and be with the others. He manages to stagger to his feet. Against a reiterated G in the violins, the horns, wood wind and lower strings thunder out a variant of No. 39. This motive, which in the second act had expressed the emotion of the lovers at its peak-point of mystical ecstasy, now has a touch of madness in it. It is in 5/4 time, and much of the music that follows is a combination of triple, quadruple and

---

apparently at some later date, for the script is slightly different from that in the score itself, as if another pen and another ink were being used: "The cor anglais should produce the effect here of a very powerful natural instrument such as the Alpine horn: it is therefore advisable to have it reinforced (according to the particular acoustic circumstances) by oboes and clarinets: unless, which would be the best plan, a wooden instrument of the type of the Swiss Alpine horn could be specially made. This, by reason of its simplicity — it would need only to be capable of producing the notes of the natural scale — would be neither difficult nor costly." This note was printed at the foot of the page in the published score. When the Vienna Opera was engaged on its abortive rehearsals of the work in 1861–2 Wagner told the conductor, Esser, that the proposed horn should be "of wood, at least three feet long, almost trumpet-like, but with a rather crooked curve at the end, so that the bell faces sideways"; its tone was to be "that of a medium-sized Alpine horn, fairly powerful, even rough, but in any case of a natural naïveté."

quintuple metres: simple as the device is, it is sufficient, by sheer contrast with all the other rhythms of the work, to convey to us that something has broken in Tristan.[1] "Tristan the hero", he cries, "exulting in his strength, has snatched himself from death":

No. 58

Tris - tan, der Held, in ju - - bein-der— Kraft,—

"Once with a bleeding wound I fought with Morold; now, bleeding from another wound, will I today make Isolde my own!" They are mystical words, the inner sense of which is apt to be missed by the casual listener in the theatre: for the third time Tristan is bent on seeking union with Isolde not in life but in death. "Heia, my blood!" he raves as he tears the bandage from his wound; "joyfully flow now!" He springs from his couch and staggers forward. "She who shall close my wound for ever draws near to save! Let the world perish; jubilantly I hasten to her!"

50

As he stumbles towards the centre of the stage a wild cry of "Tristan! Beloved!" is heard from Isolde (without), and, by one of those psychological strokes of which music alone among the arts is capable, the orchestra, by a harmonic mutation of No. 30, brings us a bitterly ironic reminder of that earlier scene, in the second act, in which it had been Isolde who was so impatiently awaiting the coming of Tristan. His mind, too, goes back to that night, but in its delirium it runs sensations of sound and of light into one; by a bold use of poetic imagery Wagner makes him, when Isolde's cry rings out, imagine he is *hearing* the light of the signal torch. "It dies out!" he cries; "to her! to her!" Isolde enters breathlessly. Tristan, in wild excitement, but near the end of his

[1] The device had previously been employed by Handel in the second act of his opera *Orlando* (1733). "The whole last scene of this act", says Burney, "which paints the madness of Orlando, in accompanied recitatives and airs in various measures, is admirable. Handel has endeavoured to describe the hero's perturbation of intellect by fragments of symphony in 5/8, a division of time which can only be borne in such a situation." The formal-minded eighteenth century evidently found it a little difficult to reconcile itself to so "irregular" a metre, even as a token of "perturbation of intellect".

strength, makes his halting way towards her. They meet in the centre of the stage; she clasps him in her arms, and he sinks slowly to the ground, locked in her embrace. The orchestra, playing reminiscently upon motives with which the prelude had opened (No. 1 A, 1 B, etc.), and the lovers, with their last cries to each other of "Tristan!" "Isolde!", take us back in imagination for a moment to the scene in the first act that had followed immediately upon the draining of the love potion.

Tristan, with a last look up at Isolde, dies in her arms. In vain does she call on him to speak to her. She had come there to die with him; and he has cheated her of that last satisfaction, for which she had waited through so many weary days. Her wretchedness had been equal to his, as the orchestra tells us by accompanying her with the motive of Tristan's Distress (No. 48). Where is his wound, she asks, that she may heal it for a moment and then be blissfully enveloped with him in Night:

> *Not of thy wound,*
> *not of thy wound, my hero, die:*
> *let thee and me*
> *together bid life farewell.*

But it is now too late:

> *O cruel one!*
> *Lay'st thou on me*
> *so dire a scourge?*
> *Grantest no grace*
> *for all my pain?*
> *Still art thou deaf*
> *to all my sorrow?*

And with a last appeal to him to wake, if only for a moment, she sinks down, unconscious, on his body, while the orchestra breathes a soft reminiscence of No. 42, to the strain of which, in the second act, they had called upon Death to make them one for ever.

Kurvenal, who had returned to the stage immediately after Isolde, has all this while been gazing in mute despair at Tristan. From behind the scenes there now comes the sound of raised voices and the clash of weapons. The shepherd rushes in to announce the sighting of a second ship. Kurvenal, roused from his torpor, springs up and looks over the battlements. He utters an imprecation, for on this other ship he has recognized King Marke and Melot. He and the shepherd hasten to the gate, which they try to barricade. The steersman of Isolde's ship, rushing in, warns them that it is useless, for Marke is coming with many men. But Kurvenal is now beside himself with grief and rage; no one, he swears, shall enter while he is alive. Hearing Brangaene calling to her mistress to open the gate, he curses her too as a traitor. Then Melot's voice is heard, warning him not to oppose them. Kurvenal, with an angry laugh, blesses the day that has brought him face to face with Tristan's false friend; and as Melot appears in the gateway with a company of armed men Kurvenal hurls himself on him and strikes him dead.

From behind the scenes first Brangaene's voice, then the King's is heard, telling the furious old man that he does not understand; but Kurvenal's only answer is, "Here death alone holds sway: nought else is there to win: wouldst thou have it, come here to me!" He throws himself on the King and his retainers, who have now appeared in the gateway, while Brangaene, who has climbed over the wall at the side of the stage, hastens to the front to deliver a message of joy to her mistress. She finds her prostrate over the body of Tristan, apparently dead; and while she is solicitously tending Isolde the King calls out, "O lies! O madness! Tristan, where art thou?" Kurvenal, now mortally wounded, staggers up to him: "there lies he", he says, "and there lie I". He sinks down at Tristan's feet, groping blindly in his death agony for his master's hand, and stammering "Tristan! Loved one! Chide me not that the true one follows thee!"

51

The tangled threads of the drama pass for a moment into the hands of the old King. "Dead, alas! all are dead!" he ejaculates mournfully. In a passion of futile grief he reproaches his Tristan for once more having betrayed him, for now it is too late for Marke to give him the message of understanding and love and trust that he had come to Kareol to bring. "Awake! Awake!" he cries; "Awake to the call of my woe! Thou faithless-faithfullest friend!" and he bends over the two bodies with a sob.

Meanwhile Brangaene, by her ministrations, has succeeded in

calling Isolde back to the semblance of life. She tells her what
had happened in Cornwall — how she had revealed the secret of
the substituted potion to the King, who, comprehending all now,
had straightway hurried over the sea to yield Isolde up to Tristan.[1] Marke also addresses her, speaking such consolation as his
simple old heart knows:

> *Why this, Isolde,*
> *why this to me?*
> *When clear 'twas revealed*
> *what before I could fathom not,*
> *what bliss to find my friend*
> *was free of all reproach!*
> *With him I loved*
> *then to mate thee,*
> *with swelling sails*
> *I flew on thy track.*
> *But who, bearing*
> *peace with him,*
> *can the torrent of woe o'ertake?*
> *A richer harvest reaped death:*
> *more woe I blindly have wrought!*

But Isolde has already passed to a sphere in which words and
thoughts like these have no meaning. Fixing her eyes — the eyes
now of a visionary — on Tristan's body, she begins, to the melody
of No. 42, her mystical monody of *Verklärung*, of eternal reunion
with him. The poetry of the Liebestod is in large part quite un-
translatable. She does not see her lover as the bystanders do. For
her he is not dead but transfigured, open-eyed, smiling:

> *See ye not*
> *how he beameth*
> *bright and brighter,*
> *lapped in star-shine*
> *high he soars?*
> *See ye not*
> *how his heart*

---

[1] In Gottfried von Strassburg's poem it is Kurvenal who tells King Marke of
the love potion. This dénouement could not be employed by Wagner, who
needed Kurvenal in Kareol.

> *is pulsing brave,*
> *strong and calm*
> *within his breast?*

Or is it, she asks the world, she alone who can see all this, she alone who can hear the great melody pulsing in the air about her, sad and sweet, all-revealing, all-reconciling, streaming from Tristan's being into hers? What and whence are these wonder-tones that envelop her?

> *Are they waves*
> *of breezes fashioned?*
> *Are they clouds*
> *of perfume woven?*
> *How they billow,*
> *thunder round me!*
> *Shall I breathe them?*
> *Shall I listen?*
> *Shall I drink them,*
> *plunge beneath them?*
> *In their odour*
> *die entranced?*
> *In the billowing sea,*
> *in the ocean of sound,*
> *in the world-soul's*
> *depths profound, —*
> *to drown now,*
> *go down now —*
> *swoon in night —*
> *last delight!*

It is the mystical union, at last, for which they had longed. The music is dominated, at the finish, by the motive (No. 31) which, in the prelude to the second act, had been the symbol of Isolde's joy at the thought of reunion with Tristan. Now it becomes the symbol of another union, a more cosmic joy, the ecstasy that throbs "in the world-soul's depths profound":

It broadens out into wider and wider waves of tone as Isolde, lost in her inward vision, sinks transfigured upon Tristan's breast. The last word is given to the motive of Longing with which the opera had begun, outlining itself now through the orchestral texture in the poignant tones of oboe and cor anglais:

No. 60

The Mastersingers of Nuremberg

CHARACTERS

HANS SACHS, SHOEMAKER		Bass
VEIT POGNER, GOLDSMITH		Bass
KUNZ VOGELGESANG, FURRIER		Tenor
KONRAD NACHTIGALL, TINSMITH		Bass
SIXTUS BECKMESSER, TOWN CLERK		Bass
FRITZ KOTHNER, BAKER		Bass
BALTHASAR ZORN, PEWTERER	MASTERSINGERS	Tenor
ULRICH EISSLINGER, GROCER		Tenor
AUGUSTIN MOSER, TAILOR		Tenor
HERMANN ORTEL, SOAP-BOILER		Bass
HANS SCHWARZ, STOCKING-WEAVER		Bass
HANS FOLTZ, COPPERSMITH		Bass
WALTHER VON STOLZING,		Tenor
A YOUNG FRANCONIAN KNIGHT		
DAVID, SACHS'S APPRENTICE		Tenor
EVA, POGNER'S DAUGHTER		Soprano
MAGDALENA, EVA'S NURSE		Soprano
A NIGHT WATCHMAN		Bass

1

THE OPERA-GOER without any first-hand knowledge of the German Mastersingers must not take them at Wagner's valuation. He was writing a lusty comedy, not a specialist treatise, and he exercised to the full the comic dramatist's or novelist's right to use only so much of the historical material lying to his hand as suits his purpose, and occasionally to exaggerate the comicalities of it for his own ends. When he conceived the idea of an opera on the subject in 1845 he could have known not much more about the Mastersingers than he had derived from a reading of Gervinus's *History of German National Literature* (1826); and it is evident from his own account that what mostly interested him at that time in connection with them was the opportunities for fun they presented him with. They caught him on the rebound, as it were, from the deeply serious mood induced in him by his absorption in the ethical milieu of the Lohengrin and Parsifal epics; and just then he wanted nothing more from the Marker and the apprentices and the rest of the Nuremberg crew than material for kindly laughter.

But as the years went on, the subject struck deeper and deeper roots into him. The character of Sachs took on a graver tinge; a philosophy, if not of actual pessimism, at any rate of resignation, slowly spread its grey veil over the central motive of the action; so that just before the first performance of the work (in Munich in 1868), he could write to King Ludwig in this strain: "It is impossible that you should not have sensed, under the opera's quaint superficies of popular humour, the profound melancholy, the lament, the cry of distress of poetry in chains, and its re-incarnation, its new birth, its irresistible magic power achieving mastery over the common and the base." This was a vast expansion and a decided re-tinting of his own first feeling with regard to the work some twenty-three years earlier.

2

His own account of the genesis of the opera, given us in his autobiography, runs thus. During his reading of Gervinus, he says, "I was especially tickled by the title of 'the Marker' and the function he exercised in the Mastersinging. Without knowing very much about Sachs and his poetic contemporaries, I conceived the idea, during one of my walks, of a droll scene in which the cobbler, in the capacity of a popular artisan-poet, makes the Marker sing, and, by the application of his hammer to his last, gives him a lesson by way of punishment for his pedantic misdeeds. For me the whole thing concentrated itself on two points — on the one hand the Marker with his slate covered with chalk-marks, and on the other Hans Sachs holding up the shoes he had managed to finish by 'marking' faults on the soles, each of them indicating that the singer had been 'versungen'.[1] In addition I worked out swiftly, for the conclusion of my second act, a scene in one of the narrow, crooked alleys of Nuremberg, with the neighbours roused from their beds, plunging into a street brawl. And so my whole Mastersingers comedy suddenly sprang into such vivid life within me that, as it was a particularly merry theme, not likely to overexcite me, I felt justified in disobeying my doctor's orders and putting it on paper." The immediate pull of *Lohengrin* was so strong on him, however, that he soon put the comic opera out of his mind.

The street scene to which he refers was a reminiscence of an experience of his own, as a young man of twenty-three, in Nuremberg itself. While staying there in 1835 with his brother-in-law Wolfram he had made the acquaintance, in a local beer-house, of a master carpenter named Lauermann, a grotesque creature who was the stock butt of the local wags. Wolfram had sportively passed off Wagner on him as the famous singer Lablache, visiting Nuremberg incognito; he had heard, it appeared, of Lauermann's wonderful singing and was anxious to hear him and learn from him. The carpenter was gulled one night into giving an exhibition of his art. After the ludicrous exhibition a shindy broke out outside the tavern, and for a little while it looked, says Wagner, as if the whole town would be engaged in a free-for-all fight. The knocking-out of one of the rioters brought the tumult to an end with a suddenness that seemed magical: "within little more than a minute the roaring crowd of several hundred men was quiet, and my brother-in-law and I were able to stroll home arm-in-arm, laughing and joking, through the deserted moonlit streets." The scene was undoubtedly before his eyes when he sketched the closing scene of his second act.

His first Prose Sketch for *The Mastersingers* is dated "Marienbad, 16 July 1845": it is very detailed, running to some twelve pages in the modern imprint. A Second Sketch, equally rich in detail, was made in Vienna in October 1861. As there was no hope at that time of *Tristan* being produced in Vienna for at least another twelve months, Wagner told Bülow on the 17th

[1] The technical term in the Mastersingers' Guild for the failure of a candidate at his trial for Mastership: he had "un-sung" or "mis-sung" himself.

December, he felt he ought to set to work at something new and different. He turned in horror from a "passionate" subject of the *Tristan* type, with all that it would involve in the way of knocking his new ideas into the noddle of a tenor. But by good luck, he said, his thoughts had suddenly reverted to "my old plan for a *Mastersingers of Nuremberg*." He found his memories of that plan astonishingly fresh, and his imagination at once began to play upon it. He had already broached the scheme for "a popular comic opera" to his publisher Schott on the 30th October. The "jovial-poetic" hero of it was to be Hans Sachs; it would be full of drollery, light in style, and easily staged; he particularly congratulated himself on the fact that "this time I shall need neither a so-called first tenor nor a great tragic soprano", the difficulty of finding which rare birds had been the main cause for the long delay in producing *Tristan*.

Schott having shown an interest in the scheme, Wagner sent him a copy of his Second Sketch on the 19th November.[1] Once more, in all innocence, he stressed the simplicity and practicality of the new work; "it will not call for an outstanding tenor — and this, as things are just now, is almost everything — nor for a great tragic soprano, which is a good deal. The leading rôle, that of Hans Sachs, will be written in a convenient bass register, so that it can be sung in any theatre by the best of the baritones or even deep basses." It will all be relatively simple and well within the scope of any small opera company, while the larger theatres will find in it ample opportunities, especially in the choruses, for showing what they can do.

In all this, as was not unusual with him, he was deceiving himself. The *Mastersingers* grew far beyond his first intentions as he became absorbed in it. The orchestral score became the biggest

---

[1] This copy, though it counts technically as a Third Sketch, is virtually identical with the Second.

Sachs, David and Magdalena are the only characters who bear the same names in the First Sketch as those by which we know them now. Eva was for a time simply "The Daughter" or "The Maiden"; then, later, Emma. Similarly Walther von Stolzing was at first only "The Young Man" (later Konrad), and Beckmesser only "The Marker". At a later stage he became "Hanslich", or "Veit Hanslich". Pogner began as "Bogler"; while Magdalena became for a while Kathrine. In the first two Sketches the opening scene was set in St. Sebald's Church.

ever published until then. The opera turned out anything but "light" for the most part; and it called for a first-rate tenor and soprano in addition to the central Sachs. Wagner, in his first enthusiasm, counted on performing the work in the early part of 1862; but the score was not completed until October 1867.

3

For the Second Sketch Wagner sought out more material than had been available to him in 1845. He made a close study of Jakob Grimm's *Ueber den altdeutschen Meistergesang* (1811), a book into which he had probably dipped, however, in the 1840's; and through Peter Cornelius he obtained the loan of Wagenseil's [1] Nuremberg Chronicle from the Vienna Imperial Library. This curious old book was for a long time almost the only source of information about the Nuremberg Mastersingers and their school rules. The famous Chronicle was not published until 1697, by which time the art of Mastersong was well in decline in Nuremberg and elsewhere; Wagenseil based himself, however, on manuscripts of an earlier epoch, and his account of the mid-sixteenth century Masters and their rules is reliable. The bulk of his curious volume is devoted to a history and description (in Latin) of the ancient town of Nuremberg: it is only in the last hundred-and-fifty pages or so that he settles down to set forth (in German) the "Origins, Practice, Utility and Rules of the Gracious Art of the Mastersingers".

From Wagenseil Wagner now made copious extracts, which are today printed in full at the end of his Second Sketch. He jotted down for his own use the names of twelve "old Nuremberg Masters": the list agrees with that of the Masters who appear in the opera, except that there he changes the first name of the historic Fritz Zorn to Balthasar and dispenses with one Nikolaus Vogel, making up the intended round dozen, however, by including Sachs. (He probably left out Nikolaus Vogel for a simple but artful reason which will be suggested later). He copied out with comic gusto the rules — the "Tabulatur" — that governed the Mastersong, the list of the various "faults" for which the Marker debited a candidate with this or that number of points, the list of the Mastersinger "Tones", and the quaint definitions of the various

---

[1] Wagenseil was born in 1633 and died in 1708.

types of rhymes. It was on the basis of all this that he constructed David's exposition of the rules of the Mastersong in the first act of the opera, the faults noted by Beckmesser in Walther's singing and by Sachs in Beckmesser's, and Kothner's formal reading of the Tabulatur to the young knight before he embarks on his "Trial".

As we have just seen, the names of the Masters given in his list of dramatis personae are authentic enough; but the spectator of the opera must not take it for granted that the bearers of those names were in real life merely the uncouth figures of fun he sees on the stage. Wagner, for one thing, follows his own fancy in the trades he allots to them. Wagenseil gives only their names; but Adam Puschman (1532–1600)[1] supplies us with the real occupations of some of them. Wagner makes Kothner a baker; actually he was a clasp or pin-maker. So was Hermann Ortel, who in the opera sinks to a soap-boiler. The historical Ulrich Eisslinger was not, as in the opera, a grocer but a timber merchant, and Friedrich Zorn not a pewterer but a nail-maker. These people were probably not artisans, in the sense in which Wagner employs that term, but well-to-do business men; for Nuremberg was a rich and handsome city, and there was a great demand in it for good building materials, fine metal work, handsome furniture, artistic pottery and so on. Wagner's "tinsmith", "coppersmith", "tailor", "stocking-weaver," etc. are pure fancy; nor is there any historical justification for his making Beckmesser the Town Clerk or for depicting him as a comic and stupid pedant. The melodies of his preserved for posterity by Puschman show him to have been no worse a composer than the majority. (Wagner, following Wagenseil, gives him the forename of Sixtus; according to Puschman it was Sigismondus, abbreviated for ordinary purposes to Six). We possess also authentic specimens of the melodies of Nachtigall, Eisslinger, Kothner, Ortel, Vogelgesang, Zorn, Foltz, a certain Bogner, and, of course, Hans Sachs. Foltz and Nachtigall appear to have had a genuine melodic vein of their own; the former's setting of a poem on the theme of death is a really creditable piece of work.

4

As has just been pointed out, the Mastersingers were by no means the monsters of bourgeois absurdity which the spectators

---

[1] Puschman was a pupil of Sachs.

of Wagner's opera can too easily assume them to have been. They had done much good work throughout the generations, and their rules and faults and definitions were simply the codified results of long experience; it goes without saying, indeed, that no Guild of mere pedantic dunderheads could have earned and kept the respect of intelligent people all over Germany for so long a stretch of time. Their intentions, seen at their best, were a combination of those of, say, the French Academy, the prosodist, the grammarian, the musical Conservatoire, and the adjudicators at a competition festival. A few illustrations will make this clear.

One of the functions of the French Academy is to preserve the purity and uphold the dignity of the French language. The Mastersingers were similarly concerned with the employment of the still rather uncouth German language in its then best forms. They insisted on the use by the candidate of the High German that had become the standard speech of the upper classes and the government offices, and had been put to such fine use by Luther in his translation of the Bible. The dialect of this locality or that was not absolutely barred by the Mastersingers, but it was to be kept within bounds; it must not obtrude itself at points in a poem where it would attract too much and unfavourable attention to itself, and in rhymes it must be used only in conjunction with words from the same dialect, not with words in High German. This was an eminently sensible rule, which must have done a great deal to bring local dialects into conformity with the standard speech of cultivated people, if only by ensuring that the same vowel would have the same sound on all like occasions.

Several of the "faults" enumerated and penalised are quite rightly characterised as such. One of them — referred to in the opera — was "blinde Meinung" (obscure meaning), i.e., saying what one had to say in an irregular or cloudy style. Wagenseil gives as an example "Ich du soll kommen" instead of "Ich und du soll kommen". Browning would thus have been heavily penalised by the Marker for saying:

> *For I am ware it is the seed of act*
> *God holds appraising in His hollow palm,*
> *Not act grown great thence on the world below,*
> *Leafage and branchage, vulgar eyes admire.*

Apart from other small obscurities in this, a "which" should logically come between "branchage" and "vulgar".

It was always a "fault" in the Mastersingers' eyes and ears to play tricks with the language simply to get an easy rhyme or to make the number of syllables in one line correspond to that in another. Shakespeare, for example, would have lost a mark for writing:

> And winking Marybuds begin
> To ope their golden eyes;
> With every thing that pretty bin,
> My lady sweet, arise;

where "bin" has artfully been used instead of "is" to make sure of a rhyme to "begin". The Tabulatur specifies a good many sins of this and kindred sorts against the German language, and is appropriately severe on them; and it is particularly censorious of poetry that does not make its meaning clear at once: the "blinde Meinung" of some modern poetry would have kept the Marker's chalk working overtime. The trouble always is that to insist through thick and thin on general rules of this kind is not to meet a particular case: a thing may be beyond question a technical fault, yet be accepted by us because without it the poet could not have said with the same pungency just what he wanted to say at that particular moment and in that particular connection.

5

In this respect the Mastersingers' rules were calculated to do more harm than good in the long run. They would ensure technical propriety at the occasional cost of individuality; the spirit of the poetic idea would sometimes suffer in order that the letter of the language might be safeguarded. But broadly speaking the Masters of the best period, seen in the light of their own time and place, were proceeding in these matters along the right lines; and it is hardly fair to laugh at them for the exaggerations into which their principles landed them now and then, and to forget how just, in principle, their principles really were. To insist too rigidly on rules, however excellent they may be in theory, is in practice to start sliding down the slippery slope that lands us in pedantry and hide-bound formalism. One of the "faults" the Masters frowned upon was that described as "the soft and hard", that is to say, rhyming a word in which a consonant is by definition hard with another word in which it is defined as soft; for example, "Knaben" with "Knappen", "laden" or "Gnaden" with "Thaten", "Tod" with "Gott", "her" with "Lehr". The purist may say they were mostly right in this; but the poet will plead for a trifle more licence in practice. It is the old story — give the man in office too much power and he will settle down before long into a bureaucrat who is more of a menace than a help to the plain citizen.

There was nothing essentially wrong, again, with the Mastersingers' sifting of rhymes into categories, however comical the names they gave to these categories may sound in the ears of to-day. There were, for example, the "blunt" rhyme, the "clinking", the "orphan", the "pause", the "blow" ("stroke", "percussion"). The "orphan" is an ending that does not rhyme with anything that has preceded it; Wagenseil's example is the hymn "Allein Gott in der Höh' sei Ehr' ". The first verse of this runs thus:

> Allein Gott in der Höh' sei Ehr'
> Und Dank für seine Gnade;
> Darum, dass nun und nimmermehr
> Uns rühren kann kein Schade.
> Ein Wohlgefall'n Gott an uns hat;
> Nun ist gross Fried ohn' Unterlass,
> All Fehd' hat nun ein Ende.

It will be seen that the final lines do not rhyme; and this procedure is repeated in the following verses. These, therefore, said the Masters, are "orphan" rhymes; they have no family ties, no home to go to.

The "pauses", on the other hand, rhyme only at a distance from each other and with a break-off from the adjacent words, as in the following hymn quoted by Wagenseil:

> Ach,
> Was hab' ich, o Herr, begangen!
> Meine Sünden sind zu gross,
> Meine Glieder liegen bloss!
> Herr, nach dir steht mein Verlangen!
> Wach,

Du, mein Gott, und hilf nun mir,
Dass ich bleibe stets bei dir;
Lindre du mir meine Schmerzen,
Denn ich bin von ganzem Herzen
Schwach!

6

All this elaboration of definitions is really, soberly considered, a credit rather than otherwise to the Mastersingers, for it proves that their art had reached a stage of such variety of rhymes and rhythms that the necessity was felt for defining, classifying and organizing them. Their predecessors the Minnesingers had gone quite as far, if not further, in the same direction. It is a phase that always follows, and indeed presupposes, a considerable artistic development; as soon as the creators have demonstrated the variety of which practice is capable the theoreticians step in, sort out the structures and technical devices into categories, and give each of them a label. The Mastersingers' categories are a legacy from the Middle Ages, and, indeed, from Graeco-Roman times, with their passion for verbal hair-splitting, every device of rhetoric being resolved into its constituent atoms and each atom then given a name of its own. The trouble was that as the creative faculty slowly dwindled among the Mastersingers too much importance came to be attached to labels and rules for their own sweet sakes. We have to remember that these "rules" that have come down to us were committed to paper at a time when the Mastersong had entered upon its decline as a living art. And of course it was no business of Wagner's to weigh the historical and other pro's and con's of the matter. All he was concerned with was the opportunities for comedy it presented him with. Wagenseil's solemn enumeration of all the quaintly-named categories had tickled his fancy, and he was determined that other people should share in the fun.

These considerations apply also to the famous "Tones" or "Modes". The names of these amused him immensely; he particularly enjoyed the "Lonely Gormandiser" Tone. And when David reels off the long list of some forty Modes to Walther — the "Hawthorn Bloom Mode", the "Love that Passes" Mode, the "Fresh-gathered Oranges" Mode, the "True Pelican" Mode, and so forth, ending proudly with the "Thread-bright-at-the-end" Mode [1] — we laugh as heartily as the young knight and ejaculate with him, "Heaven help us! There seems no end to the code!"

But it is all quite simple. If we examine any collection of songs, old or new, we see at once that the lines of the poems differ in length, in the number of syllables, in the distribution of the accents, etc., while the melodies differ from each other in respect of the way they begin and end, the extent to which one phrase or more of them is repeated, and where, and so on almost ad infinitum. If we wanted to refer to one of these many variants in such a way that our interlocutor would know instantly which one we meant, we should have to give it a name of its own of some sort, just as horticulturists give fanciful but practicable distinguishing names to the many varieties of the rose. That, in essence, is what the Mastersingers did.

In their further capacities of examiners for a diploma and adjudicators at a competitive musical festival the Masters simply catalogued certain faults that were to be avoided in performance. With these, as with certain other points of their theory and practice, we shall deal as occasion arises in our analysis of Wagner's opera.

7

Wagner had not been the first in the field with some of the elements of the plot of *The Mastersingers*. Sachs had already figured as the hero of a drama, *Hans Sachs*, by a now forgotten dramatist of the name of Johann Ludwig Ferdinand Deinhardstein (1794–1859): the play had been produced in 1827. It is to be presumed that Wagner had read it; but he could have obtained from it very little for his own purposes except the idea of showing the poetic cobbler in love and at variance with his fellow-poets. In Deinhardstein, Sachs is the accepted lover of Kunigunde, the only child of the richest man in Nuremberg, the goldsmith Stef-

[1] As it happens, there was no such Mode as this. In the German it is "die buttglänzende Drahtweise". Nobody has ever been able to say precisely what the "butt" signifies, and after a good deal of discussion it is now generally accepted that it is simply a misprint, in Wagenseil, for "gutt"; for we read elsewhere of a "guttglänzende Drahtweise" ("Well-shining-thread Mode") as the creation of one Jobst Zolner.

fen.[1] Their love has to be kept secret because Kunigunde knows that her father will never consent to her marrying a shoemaker; and she tries her hardest to persuade Sachs to exchange that prosaic profession for one held in more esteem in the best Nuremberg circles. Deinhardstein's Sachs, however, is not at all the humble old cobbler of Wagner's opera: he is young and gallant and well-to-do, evidently a shoemaker in a large way of business. He turns a deaf ear to all Kunigunde's entreaties because he sees nothing to blush for in his line of trade. He has been engaged in it all his life; he has shod half Nuremberg and shod it well. Nor is there any of the humorous diffidence of the Wagnerian Sachs in him; he could easily retire or turn to another trade, he says, but will not do so because he is a fighter, and because he regards a good pair of shoes as no less admirable than the product of any other Nuremberg workshop.

Steffen, unaware of his daughter's clandestine passion, has chosen for her one Eoban Runge, a fop and noodle from Augsburg, who has the distinction of being a senator of his native town. Runge and Sachs soon come into collision, and the former shows himself to be a sneak and a poltroon. But he has assured Steffen (who is proud of being a member of the Mastersingers' Guild), that in Augsburg he enjoys a great reputation as a poet; and this counts with the goldsmith. From Runge Wagner may perhaps have derived a hint or two for his Beckmesser.

But Kunigunde is not Sachs's only trouble. He is perpetually in conflict with the professed Masters. He has no exaggerated opinion of his own poetry, in which he can afford to indulge himself only one day in the week; but poetry is the life-breath of his soul. The other Masters criticise him harshly for not keeping to the rules. One of them plumes himself on having put the would-be cobbler poet in his place at a recent meeting of the Guild: he had exposed so many faults in Sachs's latest poem that the rafters had rung with the laughter of the Masters, and the poor man, according to him, had left the assembly pale and trembling. A second Master praises the first for his frankness: there is no enduring this Sachs who is "always different from the rest of us", who does not appreciate their poetry and their rules, and does all he can to

[1] Sachs's first wife, whom he married in 1519, was a Kunigunde, but her family name was Kreutzer.

avoid their company. When he is accused of flouting the rules his answer always is that the vital thing in poetry is not the form but the spirit that animates the form. One of them hesitatingly admits that the man has some talent. "Talent! Talent!" replies another; "we have no use here for talent. Let him stick to the Tabulatur, avoid the *equivoca,* the *relativa, blind words,* and all the other offences against the rules". It is observance of these, not talent, that makes the poet: "anyone can have talent, but not everyone has the fineness of ear and the solicitousness that enables us to steer clear of errors. Sachs is not solid enough yet; his imagination gets in his way." Here again Deinhardstein may possibly have provided Wagner with a few hints for the apposition of Sachs and Beckmesser.

In other respects Wagner has virtually no points of contact with his predecessor. In Deinhardstein, the shoemaker, angered by Kunigunde's insistence and the ill-will of the Masters, turns his back at last on his beloved Nuremberg and goes out to seek his fortune elsewhere. He falls in with the Emperor Maximilian and his train, who are out hunting; they have lost their way, and Sachs guides them to the city. Neither man is aware of the identity of the other: the Emperor is travelling as a Count, and as the guide does not give his own name Maximilian does not know that he is the Hans Sachs whose poetry he admires and whom he has long been anxious to meet. The play ends, of course, with the Emperor putting everything right when he reaches the city: Sachs gets his Kunigunde, Steffen is reconciled to the thought of a shoemaker for his son-in-law now that Sachs is seen to stand high in the favour of the Emperor, and Runge, his machinations exposed, goes back to Augsburg with his tail between his legs.

8

Wagner may have been indebted for a hint here and there to two or three other German plays and novels of the early nineteenth century. Although there must have been stories from time immemorial of the offering of a maiden's hand as prize in a contest of some kind or other, he may quite possibly have been influenced in the shaping of the central motive of his opera by E. T. A. Hoffmann's well-known tale of *Master Martin the Cooper and his Men.* From the same writer's *Signor Formica* he may have taken the idea of Beckmesser coming to grief through his over-eagerness to pass off some one else's work as his own in order to make sure of winning a prize; and it is on the cards that he may have known Deinhardstein's bright little comedy *Salvator Rosa* (1823), which is a dramatised version of the Hoffmann tale. Deinhardstein's *Hans Sachs* was made into an opera for Lortzing by Philipp Reger and Philipp Düringer: the work was produced in 1840, and Wagner certainly made its acquaintance during his Dresden period. All these odds and ends of fact, however, while necessary to complete the historical record, do not make the *Mastersingers* anyone's work but Wagner's. We are reminded of the research that has proved that this phrase and that of the Austrian national hymn is to be found in this or that popular melody of the period, and of a modern German writer's sensible summing up that Haydn can be credited with the composition of nothing of the hymn except the whole of it.

The poem of the *Mastersingers* was written in thirty days and finished on the 25th January 1862. It was printed towards the end of that year. The prelude was completed by the third week of April 1862. Wagner set to work at the music to the opera about the same time, but often during the troubled years that followed he was either interrupted for long periods or temporarily lost heart for it. The final note of the full score was not written until the 24th October 1867. The first performance was given in Munich, under Bülow, on the 21st June 1868, with the following cast:

HANS SACHS	Franz Betz
POGNER	Kaspar Bausewein
VOGELGESANG	Karl Heinrich
NACHTIGALL	Eduard Sigl
BECKMESSER	Gustav Hölzel
KOTHNER	Karl Fischer
ZORN	Weixlstorfer
EISSLINGER	Eduard Hoppe
MOSER	Pöppl
ORTEL	Thoms
SCHWARTZ	Grasser
FOLTZ	Hayn

WALTHER VON STOLZING	Franz Nachbauer
DAVID	Schlosser
EVA	Mathilde Mallinger
MAGDALENA	Sophie Dietz
THE NIGHT WATCHMAN	Ferdinand Lang

9

The prelude, as Wagner styles it in his score, though he had begun by calling it the overture, opens with the sturdy theme of the Mastersingers in their corporate capacity — a solid bourgeois crew, firm on their feet, very self-conscious and sure of themselves:

No. 1

In the opera the theme represents more particularly what is best in the Guild as transmitted by tradition and typified by Pogner and Sachs, its genuine concern for art according to its lights, and above all its love for, and pride in, the splendid ancient city of Nuremberg. The strain runs its dignified course for twenty-six bars, gathering strength as it proceeds, and closing in the key of the dominant. Then flutes and clarinets strike in more softly with the motive of Walther's wooing; the marking is espressivo:

No. 2

But for the moment Walther and his youthful romantic ardour are only a timid intrusion into the pageantry of Nuremberg and the Mastersingers: they are brushed aside magisterially in a downward swoop of the unison strings, to make way for the brave fanfare — derived from the commencement of an actual Mastersinger melody — that is the badge, as it were, of the ancient and honourable Guild, whose patron saint is King David:

293

No. 3

As if exhilarated by this appearance of the Guild banner, the festal procession now gets thoroughly into its stride with a motive which, in the opera, will be more particularly associated with the Guild as the trustees of the arts of poetry and music; the honest breasts of the Nuremberg burghers are swelling with pride:

No. 4

With a magnificent development of this theme the Masters have had their say for the time being. They pass out of our sight for a while, and first of all there comes into view the young knight from the country, Walther von Stolzing, his boy's heart aching with romantic yearning:

No. 5

which almost immediately finds a fuller and more definite outlet in the theme of his passion for Eva: later in the opera we shall hear it in the final section of the Prize Song:

No. 6 *Dolcissimo*

It merges, by a transition so natural that one wonders whether, in Wagner's original conception, the two did not form part of the same lyrical outburst, into a melody drawn from his Trial Song in the first act: it is youth's cry for the beauty and love of earth in the spring:

The music unfolds itself in more and more luxuriant foliations, till the time comes when the knight in his turn must make way for a group of apprentices that suddenly breaks into the scene. As is only fitting, they have no distinct theme of their own, for so far as Nuremberg is concerned they are insects not yet out of the grub stage; they are only potential tinsmiths and pewterers and cobblers and tailors and what not, possibly also, if the Fates are very kind, Mastersingers some day, entitled, they too, to walk with swelling chests behind the banner of King David; and so, being burghers and Masters only *in posse*, not in *in esse*, the crisp wood wind theme allotted to them is simply that of their graver elders diminished to the scale of their age and mentality — No. 1 with a brisker gait and a perkier manner:

Obviously we need never expect much more from them than a love of chaff and horse-play among themselves and an occasional guying of their grave seniors.

For a moment now and then we get a glimpse in the strings of Walther and his Spring Song, but it cannot make any headway against the gay impertinence of the apprentices, who, after parodying the first of the Mastersinger themes, now subject the second of them (No. 4) to the same treatment. From this they gabble on to a new figure in the 'cellos:

which, it will be seen, combines in the lower part with their own version of No. 4 above it. About this chattering figure we shall have one or two conjectures to make later.

A lively development of this combination of themes, in which the apprentices are obviously making merry at the expense of the Masters — as they must often have done in old Nuremberg — reaches its climax in a couple of bars in which they seem to be dancing with glee:

No. 10

Horns

But into their merriment there suddenly strikes the motive of Walther's yearning (No. 5); the marking is molto espressivo. (The piano arrangements for two hands are necessarily an imperfect representation of the orchestral tissue at this point. They can show only the tail-end of No. 5; as a matter of fact it enters in the orchestra not *after* our No. 10 but during it). This is followed by a blow delivered with the full strength of the orchestra as the Masters sweep the apprentices aside, No. 1 thundering out in the trumpets and trombones. Then Wagner gathers himself up for a last mighty effort. It is the musician, revelling in his craftsmanship, rather than the dramatist or the descriptive writer, that now comes uppermost in him: he has some fine themes on his hands of which he sees the contrapuntal possibilities, and he means to make the most of his opportunity. Three of them, Nos. 1, 3 and 6, he seizes upon and welds into a massive polyphonic whole:

No. 11

col. 8va bassa

Here we have in the upper part the melody of the final stanza of
Walther's Prize Song (No. 6), in the middle part the King David
or Banner fanfare (No. 3), and as a foundation, in the double
basses, bassoons and booming bass tuba, the main Mastersingers'
motive (No. 1). The impudent staccato figure shown in the lower
part of No. 9 makes a passing appearance or two, but broadly
speaking the tissue from now to the end of the overture is woven
out of the dignified motives associated with the Mastersingers
and Nuremberg. There is a comic touch at one point, where the
bass tuba, with a heavy trill on the low A, seems to be shaking its
fat sides with laughter. The climax comes with an imposing statement of No. 3, then No. 4, and finally No. 1. But — a point not always made sufficiently clear in performance — the merry bass of
No. 9 plays about to the last, and it is actually this, in conjunction
with a trumpet fanfare, that has the last word:

In its operatic form the prelude has no formal ending, but runs
straight on into the opening scene.

10

The *Mastersingers* prelude having become a stock piece with
conductors and orchestras, it goes without saying that in nine instances out of ten it is inadequately performed. Many of the finer
points of the score are not brought out because the quiet significance of them has escaped the executants, who are content to
rely upon a general effect of massive sonority. We hardly ever
hear, for example, the bass line in bars 59–70 (entrusted to bassoons, double basses and bass tuba) phrased in accordance with
Wagner's instructions, which he makes so clear that it is evident
he attached some importance to the matter. He has marked the
passage thus in the tuba and bassoons:

It is the custom, again, of some conductors to slow down considerably the King David fanfare theme (No. 3) in its final statement 26 bars before the end of the prelude, following this up with a pumped-up accelerando in the last dozen bars. But if Wagner had wanted any of these violent changes of tempo he would have specified them. All he has asked for at the first point mentioned is a more *emphatic* delivery of No. 3: his marking of it is simply "sehr gewichtig", i.e., molto pesante. Neither then nor later does he indicate any change of speed.

Conductors would do well to make themselves thoroughly acquainted with Wagner's long dissertation on the tempo of the overture in his treatise *On Conducting*. He always attached the greatest importance to tempo; it was his constant complaint in his later years that there was not a single conductor in Germany who could be trusted to find the right tempo for a passage without himself standing at his elbow; and the imagination boggles at the thought of what he would have said of some of the Wagner conductors of the present day. He was particularly severe on those of the tribe who, without any experience of opera, performed this or that excerpt from his works in the light of their feeling for concert music only, without any real understanding of the drama from which the excerpts have been taken.

To the opening and main tempo of the *Mastersingers* overture he gave conductors a clue when he said that it must be that of the corresponding passage in the third act of the opera at the point where Kothner comes forward carrying the banner of the Guild. But the last thing he ever desired was a rigid metronomic time-beating throughout a work or an episode; a tempo should always be subtly inflected from moment to moment, without, however, any violence being done to the basic speed; the music should *sing*, in the way a few of the really great singers have made familiar to us. He had intentionally marked the overture, he says, "sehr mässig bewegt"; i.e., molto moderato but at the same time with animation. The music has to be "kept moving", and "moving" means slighty different things in different conjunctures. When specifying the tempo, Wagner says, he had in mind something like the old allegro maestoso, "and no tempo stands more in need of modification from time to time in a long work than this, especially when the thematic contents are the subject of markedly defined episodic treatment". He shows how easily a steady basic 4/4 can be made to lend itself to this subtle flexibility. Beaten in "vigorously animated" crotchets it can express a lively allegro, as in the eight bars of our No. 5; conceived as a "half-period" resulting from "the combination of two 2/4 beats", as in the diminution which our No. 1 undergoes in No. 8, it can give us the feeling of a "brisk scherzando"; conceived as an alla breve (2/2) it may suggest "the older easy-going tempo andante with its two moderately slow beats", in which sense, he continues, he has employed it during the combination of themes shown in our No. 11; while the upper melody of this, at its first "diminished" appearance "in pure 4/4 beats" (No. 6), can be made to express both tenderness and impulsive passion. For No. 6 a slight easing of the tempo is required; and it was in order to prepare unobtrusively for this that he had marked the preceding bar rallentando. Other little nuances of time and beat are set forth in Wagner's exposition, which should be read and digested by conductors and orchestral players before they attempt the prelude. The overture had gone extremely well, he says, at the first performance under himself in Leipzig; but no sooner did the German Kapellmeisters get hold of it than they made nonsense of it. "Only imagine anything so animated and yet so sensitive and so delicately organised from first to last as the tempo I have indicated for the prelude being suddenly packed into the Procrustes-bed of one of these 'classical' time-beaters! It's a case of 'Get in and lie down: where you are too long I will hack a bit off you; where you are too short I'll stretch you!' and the music strikes up to drown the martyred victim's moans!"

11

The construction of the overture presents us with one or two little puzzles.

It was first performed at Leipzig, under Wagner himself, on the 31st October 1862, at a concert given by him in conjunction with a young protégé of his of that period, Wendelin Weissheimer. As a rule the overture to an opera, like the foreword to a book, is written last; and it was perhaps because Wagner, in his first enthusiasm for his subject, departed from this sound rule that to us of today who know the whole opera so well the "programme" of the overture is not quite as clear as we could wish it to be.

The prelude appears to have been drafted in the early weeks of 1862, when Wagner was living at Biebrich, near Mainz, for Weissheimer tells us in his memoirs that about February or March of that year Wagner showed him "a sheet containing the broad working-out of the initial motive, and, lower down, the second motive in E [our No. 6] and the trumpet passage characterising the Mastersingers [No. 3]. He consequently wrote the prelude before he had composed a note of the text. . . The astonishing thing about the motive in E was the happy accident that later on the words of Walther's Prize Song fitted this wonderful melody precisely. Certainly when conceiving the prelude he had not the remotest idea of that Prize Song in the third act." What was in Weissheimer's mind was probably that in the main the Prize Song as we now have it runs on quite other lines than those of No. 6, which constitutes only an item in the conclusion of the melody. The curious story of the origin of the present Prize Song will be told in full later; all we are concerned with at present is the undoubted fact that the prelude, which has superficially the appearance of being "constructed out of motives from the opera", was conceived and completed before Wagner had begun the formal musical setting of his text. This is established by a letter of his to Minna of the 21st April 1862, in which he says, "Actually I have done nothing of my opera except the overture [*sic*]; but this has turned out very well, and will probably cut out all my other overtures."

We may correlate this passage with one in his autobiography. His pleasant walks in Biebrich in the early spring of 1862, he says, awoke in him once more the desire for work. (By "work" he means musical composition: the poem of the *Mastersingers* had been completed by the 25th January of that year). "Watching one evening from the balcony of my house a fine sunset, lighting up in glory the splendid view of 'golden Mainz' and the majestically flowing Rhine, the prelude to my *Mastersingers* suddenly sprang up clearly in my mind as I had once before beheld it in a troubled mood, as it were a distant mirage, and I proceeded to draft out the prelude precisely as it appears today in the score, that is to say, setting forth with the utmost definiteness the main motives of the whole drama. Then I went on at once to work at the text, composing the scenes in due sequence." Manifestly, then, even while working at the text of the poem, and probably for some time before that, he had decided upon several of his leading motives. This, indeed, was in accordance with his general practice; the musician and the poet in him went hand in hand. When, however, he speaks of having set forth "the *main motives* of the *whole* drama" in the prelude he was obviously generalising very broadly and not entirely in consistency with the facts. The overture contains, for instance, no reference to Sachs, either as poet, as cobbler, or as the wise old man, mellowed by adversity, who has a tender spot in his heart for Eva. The profounder depths of the character did not reveal themselves to Wagner until he had begun to create him musically; and there are good grounds for conjecturing that the theme of "Wahn" (No. 43), which is the very key to the lovable old cobbler's soul, had not so much as entered the composer's consciousness at the time he was writing the overture. Further, there is no reference in the prelude to Beckmesser and what he stands for. Wagner, in fact, had concentrated on what must have seemed to him at that early stage the three seminal elements — Nuremberg and its Masters, the youthful ardour of Walther, and the apprentices and the Folk, who formed the lighter counterpiece to the Mastersingers.

12

But the upshot of it all is a little point that is not quite clear. While there is no reference in the overture to Sachs or Beckmesser, and we hear little more of Walther than is hinted at in the conclusion of the Prize Song and a fragment from the Trial Song, a fair amount of space is allotted to the motive for the 'cellos in our No. 9, which even takes possession, as we have seen in No. 12, of the final bars of the prelude.[1] Does this rather liberal

[1] That is to say, in its operatic form. For concert purposes Wagner had to supply a few more bars of formal close. In the manuscript of the full score of the opera, at the double bar marking the point at which the curtain rises and the prelude runs without a break into the chorale with which the drama opens, he has scribbled a note "for the engraver" which runs thus: "The two bars added in pencil are valid only for the special edition of the prelude for

use of it, one ventures to surmise, represent some first intention or other on Wagner's part in 1862 that was not carried into effect later in the opera itself? For this "motive" — if we can call it that — really cannot be regarded as constituting one of those "*main* motives of the *whole* drama" of which Wagner speaks in *My Life*. After the prelude we hear no more of it until near the conclusion of the opera, when it makes a brief appearance — for no more than three bars — at the end of our No. 1, at the point where the procession of the Masters reaches the platform. Later it crops up in the comic episode of Beckmesser ascending the mound to compete for the prize, where it points the jeering words of the populace:

> *She will never choose him!*
> *If I were the maiden I'd refuse him!* etc.

After that we do not meet with it again until the final two pages of the score, where it dances about in glee as the people shout their last word of homage to "Nuremberg's darling Sachs". This tiny and scarcely-used figure, in fact, is the one chosen to end the opera, as it had been the one chosen to end the overture.

How are we to account for this somewhat strange procedure on Wagner's part? The only possible conclusion seems to be that originally it was designed to play a much larger part than ultimately fell to its lot, and it was with this intention at the back of his mind that Wagner, writing the prelude in advance of the opera, gave it the prominence he did. The commentators, who have to give a name to everything, refer to it as the "Hilarity" motive, though strictly speaking, as we have seen, it occupies so infinitesimal a part of the opera as hardly to warrant its being regarded as a "motive" at all.

To summarise the argument. The full score of the opera runs to 570 pages. It is not until page 485 that the "Hilarity" figure makes an appearance in the opera itself, and that a very brief one. It recurs on pages 504, 505 and 506; after which we hear no more of it until the final page of the score, where, in conjunction with the trumpet flourish (as in our No. 12), it joyously concludes the opera as it had concluded the prelude. My suggestion

concert purposes; in this the double bar must be omitted, while in the opera score the two added bars must be left out, and the double bar holds good."

is that Wagner had planned this conclusion to the whole work even before writing the prelude, with the intention of letting the Folk have the last word as against the Masters. It was only when he came to write the opera proper that he found there was no valid excuse or opportunity for so employing the motive until within a few minutes of the end. Meanwhile, however, it had taken a place in the overture from which there was now no ejecting it without re-modelling the whole piece; so there it had to stay. Few concert room listeners to the prelude associate the "motive" with anything in the opera itself. Those who have read an analysis of the *Mastersingers* recognise it as the snippet of tune to which the people sing "She will never choose him", and therefore associate it in some dim way with Beckmesser, which could not possibly have been Wagner's intention when writing the prelude; as the Marker makes no appearance there as either a personage or a symbol, a jibe at him is surely pointless.

13

The place and period of the action of the opera are "Nuremberg about the middle of the sixteenth century"; and it is as well to have at the back of our minds some notion of what that Nuremberg was like. It was a proud and prosperous city of some thirty thousand inhabitants, very beautiful with its innumerable gable roofs, its many handsome patrician houses, its eleven bridges across the river Pegnitz, its exquisite churches, its magnificent castle, its climbing and winding streets, its many fountains, its triple circle of walls with their close on two hundred towers. No other German town, and few in other lands, could compare with it for beauty: "in all Europe", wrote the sixteenth century Italian traveller Aeneas Sylvius (Pope Pius II), "you will find nothing to surpass it in magnificence and wealth of ornament". "When, coming from Lower Franconia, one perceives this glorious city", he says, "its splendour seems truly magnificent. . . The imperial castle proudly dominates it, and the burghers' dwellings seem to have been built for princes. Indeed, the kings of Scotland would be glad to be housed as luxuriously as the ordinary citizens of Nuremberg." At the time when Hans Sachs lived there the town harboured artists and scientists of the calibre of Albrecht Dürer, Holzschuher (the architect of the old Rathhaus), Peter Vischer (the designer of the exquisite shrine in the church of St. Sebald upon which Sachs must often have feasted his eyes), stoneworkers and art-craftsmen of the quality of Adam Krafft, the great humanist Willibald Pirkheimer, and the explorer Martin Behaim, who constructed the first geographical globe. We may take it for granted that the Mastersingers who were held in esteem in such a town as this were not the purely burlesque figures that Wagner makes of them.[1]

We may fix the time of the action of the opera more precisely at 1560, when Sachs would be sixty-six, for he is shown us as a widower, and his brief widowerhood lasted only about a year from that date. (He was born in 1494 and died in 1576). When the curtain rises we see an oblique section of the interior of St. Catherine's church, a building, by the way, which it is no use the tourist going in search of, for it long ago ceased to exist in its ancient form.[2] The nave is supposed to run crosswise from left to background of the stage, only the last few rows of seats being visible to the spectator. In the foreground is the open space before the choir; this will be closed off later by a black curtain. The service is nearly over. In the last row of seats are Eva and Magdalena; while a short distance from them, at the side, the young Walther von Stolzing is leaning against a pillar, his rapt gaze fixed on Eva, who repeatedly turns towards him with silent gestures: he is conveying his passion in dumb show, while Eva is visibly torn between the impulse to respond in kind, maiden modesty, and respect for the church service.

14

The final bars of the prelude run straight into a noble chorale — the only really first-rate thing in that genre, we are tempted to say, since the great days of German Protestant chorale-writing;[3] it is accompanied by an organ on the stage, and between the lines

---

[1] A general idea of the city may be had from Dürer's engraving of St. Anthony (1519), the background of which represents Nuremberg.

[2] In point of fact, it was the smaller church of St. Martha that was used for the meetings of the Mastersingers in Sachs's day. St. Catherine's did not come into use for that purpose until 1620.

[3] Wagner had made a close study of German chorales and German folksongs before writing the opera.

of the hymn the orchestra breathes softly fragments of the three motives already associated in the prelude with Walther, Nos. 2, 6 and 7: No. 2, however, becomes a flood of passion at the finish, as the congregation rises and makes its way to the door. Eva, followed by Magdalena, slowly comes forward in Walther's direction. He forces his way towards her through the crowd and implores her to tell him his fate: dare he hope, or must he despair? Is it life for him or death, heaven and sunlight or death and hell? He ends with the point-blank question, is she pledged to wed? Eva, to get a chance to reply lucidly to this torrent of enquiries, sends Magdalena back to retrieve first her kerchief, then its pin; but the over-zealous maid returns each time before Eva can open her mouth. The lovers' opportunity seems to have come at last when Magdalena discovers that she has left her prayer-book in the pew and goes back for it; but unfortunately she is with the pair once more just in time to hear the young knight's last question. She curtseys to him, puts him out of his stride by thanking him for the flattering attention he has shown in accompanying Eva thus far, and asks whether Herr Pogner may expect the honour of a visit from him.

Walther, angry at having been frustrated, replies passionately, "Would I never his house had seen!" Magdalena reproves him: he has only just arrived in Nuremberg, and had not Herr Pogner received him in the friendliest fashion; making him free of his house, his table and his cellar? Surely a little gratitude is due for all this kindness? Eva, to the accompaniment of the motive of Walther's wooing (No. 2), explains that the young man is duly sensible of it all, but the fact is that he wants to know whether she is already affianced. Magdalena is shocked at such unmaidenlike bluntness: suppose some one should overhear them? Eva points to the empty church, but even this does not reassure Magdalena. Before she can hurry Eva away, however, she catches sight of Sachs's apprentice David, with whom she herself is in love, entering from the sacristy and beginning to close the black curtains. Apparently the sight of him gives her a sentimental fellow-feeling for the other pair of lovers, and she so far softens towards the knight as to explain to him that, in a sense, Eva is a bride — "But no one yet has seen the groom!" Eva interjects hastily, — though only the song contest on the morrow will re-

veal who has won her hand. By means of rapid question and answer the knight discovers that when the Masters have chosen
the winner of the prize of song the destined bride herself will
crown him and give him her hand.

Eva complicates matters a little by declaring enthusiastically
and not quite logically that it will be Walther or no one. The
scandalised Magdalena points out to her that she had met this
young man for the first time in her life yesterday. True, replies
Eva, but she had fallen in love with him instantaneously because
he is the living image of David, whose characteristic motive now
appears in the wood-wind:

No. 14
Wood Wind

etc.

For the moment this is beyond poor Magdalena's comprehension,
and Eva has to explain that the David she means is not hers, and
not even the sweet singer of Israel who figures with his harp on the
escutcheon of the Masters' Guild — the orchestra, by means of No.
3, tells us who that is — but a better David still, the glorious young
David with golden hair of Meister Dürer's picture, sword at side,
sling in hand, making short work of Goliath. The poetry and the
passion of all this are beyond poor prosaic Magdalena; but the
mention of David has made her quite emotional on her own
account.

David, after disappearing for a moment, has returned with a
rule stuck in his belt and a large piece of white chalk, attached
to a string, in his hand. Magdalena's first coquettish thought is
that he has shut them up in the church to have her all to himself;
but he explains, to the accompaniment of No. 14, which will
henceforth be representative of him, that he has serious business
in hand. He has to prepare the church for a Song Trial at which
the Masters will elevate to their own dignity some novice or other
whose performance is fortunate enough to please them by its strict
observance of the rules. This, Magdalena opines, is a stroke of luck
for the knight. He could not have come to a better place or at a

better time if he wants to qualify for Eva's hand; made, with
luck, a Master today, he can compete for her tomorrow. She will
not dream of allowing him to see them home, as he fain would do:
she will leave him in charge of David, who will do him the service
of coaching him in the rules and procedure of these trials. Walther and Eva bid each other a passionate farewell to the strains
of No. 5, he assuring her that she shall see him again that evening,
and that if his sword does not suffice to win her he will sing her
to his side as a Master among Masters, laying his ardent youth
and his poet's heart at her feet, she vowing to return his love in
full; and the two voices blend in a brief duet on the theme of
No. 6.

Magdalena, rather scandalised and scared by this outburst,
hurries Eva away, leaving Walther to the care of David, who has
been vastly amused at the suggestion that this young lordling
may have the luck to graduate as a Master straight away. Walther,
feverish and brooding, has thrown himself into a high chair which
two apprentices who entered a little while ago, carrying benches,
have just moved from the wall towards the centre of the stage.
Sunk in his own thoughts, he hardly notices what now goes on.
A number of other apprentices have come in, bringing more
benches, which they arrange, according to their lights, for the
session of the Masters. The lovelorn David's thoughts are not with
them and the inexpert attempts they are making to set the scene;
he is thinking how agreeable it would be if he himself were to be
made a Master. The apprentices go about their task gaily but
clumsily, chaffing David all the time; the cobbler's boy and his
rather elderly Magdalena are evidently a standing butt for their
wit.

15

As we have just learned from David, a "Trial" is to be held in
the church that day. "Is there to be a 'Singen'?" Magdalena had
asked him; and his reply had been, "Not today; only a 'Freiung'".
The distinction between a "Freiung" and a "Singschule" was that
the former was of a more preliminary and private character. Can-
didates were heard in the first place and sifted out by the Masters alone, whereas the "Song School" was of a more advanced
character and open to the public. The route to Mastership was a

long and difficult one. Aspirants and practitioners were gradated very much on the lines of the commercial guilds: there were (a) Scholars (beginners) with no knowledge of the Tabulatur, (b) School-friends (those who had a good acquaintance with the rules), (c) Singers (who could sing some half-dozen Master-melodies without faults; this implied a knowledge of the various established "Melodies" and "Tones"), (d) Poets (who could write a song of their own to fit some recognised "Tone"), and (e) Masters (who could turn out not only an original poem but a "Tone" of their own). David, we gather, had got as far as the "School-friend" stage; it is this proud knowledge of his that now enables him to reel off a long list of "Tones" to the dazed Walther.

Of the open Song Schools, we learn from Wagenseil and others, the citizens of Nuremberg were informed by means of four or five tablets, three at least of which were affixed to poles in the marketplace, and one outside St. Catherine's Church. These tablets displayed painted emblems of the Guild and the Mastersong, and were accompanied by posters announcing that "at today's Song School sundry lovers of the art present the Mastersingers with certain prizes to be sung for. First of all there will be sung, in the Free Singing, veracious and proven stories tending to Christian edification"; the songs were to consist of a certain specified number of lines. "In the Chief Singing no song will be allowed that does not conform to Holy Scripture, being taken from the Old or the New Testament"; and here again the number of lines for the day was laid down. "The proceedings will open with the singing of a fine New Song after our fashion." "Whoever wishes to listen, let him come to St. Catherine's Church, where a beginning will be made after the noon sermon."

The singer at the Free Singing had to bare his head, keep his hat or cap in his hand, bow to the Masters, and seat himself in the "Song Chair". Great pains were taken to ensure competence and impartiality on the part of the Markers. In Nuremberg four of these — the most eminent members of the Guild — sat in the box. The singer, before he began, had to announce the book and chapter of the Bible from which his words were taken; and the function of the senior Marker was to follow him from the Bible and note any deviations from the text. A second concentrated on the rules of the Tabulatur, giving the singer bad marks with a

chalk on the desk, according to a fixed tariff, for this or that failure
to comply with them. A third paid particular attention to the
metrics of the versification and jotted down the rhymes; while
the fourth kept a sharp eye on the "Tone" or melody of the song.
All the Markers were pledged to do their work honestly and without personal prejudice. It was laid down that they could either
point out the candidate's faults to him immediately after his trial
or, in some cases, later in private, "so that he might not be derided by the others". To this there was a corollary — the singer
who had done well must not show contempt for the less fortunate
ones. After the session there was an informal convivial gathering
of the Masters, to which the prizewinners were invited. Adam
Puschman, who had had experience of the Mastersong not only
in Nuremberg but in other towns, tells us, among other things,
that the two winners of garlands had the privilege of standing at
the church door at the next session and collecting cash contri-
butions.

Wagner keeps, for the most part, very close to Wagenseil in his
representation of the procedure of the Guild, modifying it a little
only when that becomes necessary for his dramatic purpose; he
has, for example, only one Marker in action, though he makes it
clear, through the mouth of Sachs, that complete impartiality is
expected of him:

> *The Marker must be known to be*
> *above the mere suspicion*
> *of friendship or of enmity.*

This, then, in broad outline, is the strange milieu into which
the romantic young Franconian knight finds himself suddenly
plunged by his passion for a Master's daughter.

16

David has been immensely amused by Walther's parting words
to Eva — that if he cannot win her by his sword he will do so as
a Master. "That's good!" he chuckles. "A Master straight away!
He's got a nerve!" While Walther is brooding darkly in the chair
the others get on with the business of preparing the church for
the meeting of the Masters. They call on David to help them, but
he, like the knight, has his thoughts turned inwards. He is deaf

to their gibes at him — the cobbler's apprentice, according to them, makes his poems with awl and thread and writes them down on raw leather; and speaking of leather, they add glee-fully, how often *they* have tanned his hide!

Still lost in an ecstatic vision of himself as a Master, David sur-prises Walther by suddenly calling out, "Now begin!" "Whatever do you mean?" the young man asks. "That's what the Marker says", David explains: "it's the signal for you to start. Don't you know that? Were you never at a Song Trial before?" Not one where the judges were artisans, says the young aristocrat. And so the dialogue continues. "Are you a 'Poet'?" "Would I were!" "Are you a 'Singer'?" "Would I knew!" "But surely you have passed through the 'Scholar' and 'School-friend' stages?" "The terms are new to me." "Yet you would become a Master at one jump?" "Would that be so difficult?" He begs to be told all about it; and David, delighted to oblige, strikes an appropriate attitude and begins:

> Good Sir! the singer's topmost height
> is not attained in one day's flight.

As for himself, he is lucky enough to enjoy the instruction of Nuremberg's greatest Master, Hans Sachs. For a whole year now the apprentice has been studying cobbling and poetry-making simultaneously:

> When I have hammered smooth the leather,
> vowels and consonants string I together;
> when I have waxed my thread right well,
> what rhymes with what I quick can tell.
> > I ply with zest
> > my bradawl fleet,
> > and learn about rest,
> > and time, and beat,
> > with knees round my last,
> > the slow, the fast,

and everything else embodied in the Masters' lore as set forth in Wagenseil — long syllables and short, clear and dark, hard rhymes and soft, orphan rhymes, pauses, corns, flowers, thorns, and all the rest of it; and at the end he asks triumphantly,

All this have I learned with care and smart:
how far now, think you, extends my art?

for he is proud of his accomplishment. Walther is frankly contemptuous: "Perhaps", he suggests, "as far as a pair of right good
shoes?"

But David is not to be thrown out of his stride by a sarcasm
which, properly taken, can be read as a compliment. Is there not,
rightly considered, the closest analogy between a well-made pair
of shoes and a poem constructed according to the rules of art?
For a Master-song, he says, is constructed, like a shoe, out of certain well-defined materials. A song is made, as the rules prescribe,
of several sections and joins, properly cut and stitched and
seamed and the stanzas well soled and heeled. Then comes the Aftersong, which must be neither too short nor too long, have a melody of its own, and not contain a single rhyme that has already been
heard in the stanzas.[1] Yet even this staggering accomplishment
does not exhaust the list of qualifications required by a Master.
"God help me!" ejaculates Walther. "Must I become a cobbler
then? Tell me rather how to become an artist-singer."

With a sigh that he himself has not yet scaled that dizzy height:

David obliges him with a long list — which is almost entirely Wagenseil in Wagnerian rhymes — of some forty "Tones" that have to
be learned, beginning with the "soft" and "strong", the "short" and
"long" and "overlong" Tones, and so on, and ending with the

---

[1] In the Mastersingers' nomenclature the complete song was a "Bar". It
could run to as many sections ("Gesätze") as the creator of it chose. Each
section consisted as a rule of two stanzas ("Stollen") followed by an aftersong ("Abgesang"). The procedure can be followed, along with Sachs's
comments, in Walther's Morning Dream Song in the third act.

"tawny lion's skin" Tone, the "true pelican" Tone and the "bright-ended thread" Tone. Walther now begins to realise what he is up against. "Good heavens!" he cries, "there seems no end to the code!" But David has the bit between his teeth now, and there is no stopping him. He launches out into a long catalogue of the rules laid down by the Nuremberg Masters for good singing. Words and notes must be clear; the singer must begin neither too high nor too low for his particular voice, having regard to the range of the melody; the breath must be carefully managed so as to last out to the end; there must be no rumbling, no mumbling; liberties must not be taken with the coloratura flourishes of the original:

> *For if you go wrong, or alter one jot,*
> *or lose yourself, or get tied in a knot,*
> > *though in nought else they could correct you,*
> > *for this alone they'll reject you!*

and you will be "versungen". As for himself, he sighs,

> *With all my zeal and diligence*
> *I've not attained this eminence;*

and whenever he makes a fault his master Sachs corrects him, he says feelingly, in the "Kneestrap whack" Tone; and then, if his Lena does not bring him consolation, he sings the "Sad-dry-bread-and-water" strain.

> *So be you warned in time;*
> *give up your dream sublime;*

he concludes; for to become a Master means no less than being both poet and singer.

17

The apprentices, who have been getting into more and more of a mess with their job of fixing up the stage, appeal at this point to David to come and help them out. But there is still no holding the enthusiast. "What and who *is* a poet?" Walther has asked him. To be a poet, David replies, you have first to graduate as a singer, knowing all about the Master Tones; then, if you can take one or two of these and fit words and rhymes to them in proper style you are received as a poet.

By this time the apprentices have had enough of it, and they insist on some attention being paid to the practical business in hand. David, however, has to answer one more question before the knight will let him go — What must one do to be named a Master? "The poet", the apprentice answers solemnly,

> *The poet who, no toil despising,*
> *to words and rhymes he himself has found*
> *a melody adds of his own devising,*
> *he will as 'Mastersinger' be crowned,*

and he sings the final line to the proud melody of the King David motive (No. 3). "Then there is nothing else for it", cries Walther, to the ardent strain of No. 2, "but for me to become a Master, creating my own poem and my own Tone!"

Turning at last to the other apprentices, David finds that they have done everything wrong.[1] He quickly tears their work to pieces; and in its place soon appears a Marker's box — a small platform with a little desk and chair, and a large blackboard to which is attached a piece of chalk by a string; the whole is enclosed in curtains, which are first of all drawn at the back and sides, then across the front. The apprentices, to the merry tune of No. 14, congratulate David at each evidence of his skill. He is a knowing young fellow, they ironically assure him, the pride of Nuremberg, who may perhaps enter for a trial himself some day; for everyone knows how he can sing, and as for technique, does he not already know the "Whack" rhyme and the "Hunger" tune inside out, and — suiting the action to the word — has not his master taught him all there is to be known about the "Hearty Kick" melody? "Laugh if you want to," he tells them, "but not to-day at me." Here is a gallant young knight who means to try his luck. He knows nothing, is neither a Scholar nor a Singer, thinks being a Poet as easy as A B C, yet fancies he can become a fully-fledged Master at the first attempt. So let them rig up the box in good style and put the board where the Marker can get at it easily, for there's going to be some fun. Then he turns to Walther and tries to curdle his blood. Aren't you scared? he asks him.

---

[1] The apprentices have been arranging the scene for a full "Song School", instead of for the more elementary "Free Singing", or "Trial", which is the business for that particular day.

Many a one has the Marker laid low! He will allow you seven faults which he will mark on the board with his chalk; but just one more than that and you can take yourself off, "versungen" and done for. And so, he concludes piously:

No. 16

> Glück auf zum Meis - ter - sing - en!
> Mögt euch das Kränzlein er - schwing - en!
> *Heaven save you from - dis - as - ter,*
> *And make you soon - a Mas - ter!*

and joining hands and dancing round the box the other apprentices sing with him:

No. 17

> Das Blu - men-kränz-lein aus Sei - den fein, wird
> *The pre - cious chap-let of silk - en flowers, we*

> das dem Herrn Rit - ter be - schied - en sein?
> *hope,— Sir Knight, may soon— be yours!*

(This chaplet was bestowed on the successful candidate at the end of a trial).

18

The young imps scatter in alarm and make off towards the back as the vestry door opens and Pogner, a benign and dignified figure, enters accompanied by the acidulous Beckmesser. They go to the back of the stage, which by this time has been fully arranged for the trial. On the right some cushioned benches for the Masters curve towards the centre. At the end of them, in the middle of the scene, stands the Marker's box, while on the left, facing the benches of the areopagites, is the high ecclesiastical chair — the "Singer's chair". In the background is a long bench, *not* cushioned, for the apprentices. Walther, exasperated by their jibes, has flung himself on the front bench. The apprentices, putting on their most respectful look, are standing at the back — all except David, who has taken up a position by the vestry door.

Pogner and Beckmesser enter to a strain associated with the "Freiung" contest (marked A in the next quotation). The episode that follows is based musically, for the most part, on three tiny figures constructed upon what may be called the fishing-rod principle: they can be employed now as a whole, now in sections. They are here shown, for convenience' sake in quotation, as they occur in connected form a little while after the opening of the scene:

Wagner employs any or all of the three figures as the fancy takes him, skilfully weaving them into a symphonic web that makes a continuous musical background in the orchestra to the easy conversation-tone of the characters. Interwoven at times with No. 18 A, B and C are hints of other motives, such as No. 2. The use of this latter may serve to point further the moral so often stressed in our analysis of *Tristan and Isolde*. It has always been convenient, for purposes of exposition, to label No. 2 the motive of Walther's wooing. In the present connection, needless to say, that description does not apply: though it appears in the texture during Pogner's greeting to the knight, there can be no possible reference of it here to "Walther's wooing". That wooing manifestly has to come about in the first place by way of a trial before the Guild; so Wagner sees no incongruity in using the motive as part and parcel of the background to the conversation now in progress.

Pogner and Beckmesser, on their way to the church, have been discussing a matter of great importance to the learned Town Clerk. The rich goldsmith has offered his daughter's hand as chief prize in the song contest on the following day, with the proviso, however, that the maiden herself shall accept the victor willingly. Beckmesser, who is in love with Eva, has a lurking fear that his suit may not be acceptable even if he should win, which he is confident of doing. Pogner tries to reassure him; yet, as Beckmesser logically puts it:

Yet why not this concession make me,
for I confess it troubles me;
if Eva be not bound to take me
what good will all my mastery be?

Pogner, though friendly, is equally logical: "Surely this reflection ought to have occurred to you before; if you are not sure of Eva's approval, why enter for the contest?" Beckmesser sees the point of this, but makes a last attempt to secure his strategical position: will Pogner speak for him with the maiden and tell her what a good, kind, virtuous man he is, and that her father thoroughly approves of him? This Pogner promises cordially to do.

19

Walther now comes forward to greet the goldsmith. The latter is a trifle astonished to find the young knight at a Song School, but Walther glibly explains that he had left his home in the country and come to Nuremberg for love of art: "I forgot to tell you yesterday, but now I must make it known — I want to become a Mastersinger. Accept me, I pray, in your Guild."

Here, however, Wagner seems to have fallen into some confusion. If that had been the knight's purpose in coming to Nuremberg, why, we naturally ask, had he not said so to Pogner when introducing himself at the goldsmith's house on the preceding day? If it had not, then he is fibbing now. The truth appears to be that Wagner was not quite sure how he ought to handle this part of the dramatic action. In the First Prose Sketch (1845) he had outlined it thus: "The young man, son of an impoverished knight, has come to Nuremberg to try to get admission to the Masters' Guild: his reading of the *Heldenbuch*, of the works of Walther von der Vogelweide, etc. has kindled in him a passionate love for the poetic art. He had announced himself to the senior of the Guild and met his daughter; and the two had quickly fallen in love with each other." According to Wagner's first plan, all this was to be made clear to the spectator in the conversation between the lovers in the opening scene in the church. But, as the reader is aware, that conversation runs on rather different lines in the opera. Nothing whatever is said by Walther about his having come to the town to become a Mastersinger: having fallen in love with Eva, it is only after he has learned from Magdalena that the maiden's hand is to go to the victor in a coming contest of song that he decides to become a Master. His later colloquy with David shows that he knows nothing at all about even the commonest terminology of the Guild routine; he does not even know what a Marker is; he is entirely ignorant of the rules of rhymes, Tones, and all the rest of it, and has to ask David to explain just what a Master may be. A young man afire with Minnesinger poetry, who had gone to Nuremberg expressly to gain admission into the Masters' Guild, could not possibly have been so completely uninformed.

In *A Communication to my Friends* (1851) Walther's motive is set forth as in the First Sketch: the young nobleman, inspired by the *Heldenbuch* and the songs of the Minnesingers, "leaves the ruined and impoverished castle of his ancestors to learn the Mastersingers' art at Nuremberg", which, one makes bold to surmise, he would hardly have thought of doing had he not already learned enough about it to inspire him with respect for it. But in the Second Sketch we are told that "Konrad [Walther] had arrived in Nuremberg from his ruined castle only yesterday; *while discussing business with Bogler* [Pogner] he had seen Emma [Eva], and the two had immediately fallen in love." There is no hint here of his having been fired by the old poets with the desire to become a Mastersinger; he had left his home and gone to the rich goldsmith to try to discover some means of re-establishing the family fortunes. He learns later from Kathrine [Magdalena] "that Eva is not actually affianced, but has been destined by her father to be the bride of the winner in the Free-singing to be held on the morrow in the St. John meadow. *His resolution is quickly taken — he himself will get admission into the Guild in order to compete for the prize.*" A few lines further down it appears that, as in the opera, until David begins his exposition he does not even know the names of the Masters, let alone the rules of the craft.[1] In a Third Sketch we are told still more explicitly that what had brought the young knight to the town and to Pogner was business.

[1] In this Second Sketch David, after explaining the functions of the Marker, tells the knight that the present holder of that office, who bears the name of "Hanslich", is regarded as the greatest authority on the rules, a fact which has made him very arrogant. There is no hint of this communication in the opera.

The two dramatic motives, it will be seen, are inconsistent with each other. If Walther had gone to Nuremberg to see Pogner on business, the latter can hardly be expected to take seriously the young man's assurance now that what had really brought him there was enthusiasm for the Mastersingers' art and the desire to become a Master himself; while if that had actually been his prime object it is odd that he should have said nothing to Pogner about it until now. Why then did Wagner not take more trouble to reconcile these little discrepancies and make the matter more self-explanatory to the spectator? The answer seems to be that, as happened once or twice again both in the *Mastersingers* and the *Ring*, he was well aware of the slight confusion but did not regard it as important enough to put himself to a great deal of trouble to clear it up: the spectator would get the general idea, and that was all that mattered; the music would carry it all off.

20

For the moment Pogner does not answer Walther's fervent appeal to be admitted to the Guild; he turns away to give a joyful welcome to two newcomers, Kunz Vogelgesang and Konrad Nachtigall, and to tell them the good news — "this knight, whom I know well, wishes to devote himself to the Master-art." Other Masters drift in, and general greetings and introductions follow. Then Pogner turns warmly to Walther, assuring him of his sympathy and support: "Gladly I helped you to sell your land; now I shall be delighted to see you become one of us."

Beckmesser meanwhile has been standing apart brooding over his own problem. He will make a last attempt, he soliloquises, to influence Pogner; if that fails he will throw in his grand strategic reserve — he will serenade Eva tonight and discover what impression his art has made on her. But suddenly he catches sight of the handsome young Walther in close colloquy with Pogner, and he scents danger in the air. "Who is this? I mislike the man!"

> *What wants he here with his smiling air?*
> *Holla! Sixtus! of him beware!*

He listens with scorn to Walther's thanks of Pogner and his expression of the hope that he may today win Mastership. "Oho! that's good!" he mutters; "a nice conceit he has of himself!" Pogner, of course, makes it clear to the young man that the rules of the Guild must be complied with; but anyhow he himself will stand as his sponsor at today's preliminary trial. (He has not yet realised that Walther is in love with Eva; he is aware only that he desires to become a Master).

By now all the Masters have arrived, including Sachs; and it becomes the duty of the baker Kothner to call the roll. Producing a list, he does so in appropriately official style. First, as the regulations prescribe, he names himself; then he calls in succession on the others, beginning with the head of the Guild, Pogner. Each Master seats himself after answering to his name. When that of Nikolaus Vogel is called out his prentice pops up and says "He's ill!" whereupon the others express sympathy and send best wishes for his recovery. (We may now be permitted to guess at Wagner's reason for omitting Vogel from his list of dramatis personae, though he had copied out, in the Second Sketch, his name along with those of the other eleven mentioned by Wagenseil. He had learned from that old author that the Masters were under strict obligation either to attend the sessions of the Guild or to send a valid excuse for not doing so; and by making Vogel an absentee he both brings in a neat historical touch connected with the rules and enables a charming break to be made in what would have otherwise been the monotony of a continuous calling of eleven names and answering to them). When Sachs's name is called, David jumps up, points to him, and says pertly "He's there!", for which his Master threatens to tan his hide. Beckmesser, for his part, answers to his name with an acid joke at the expense of Sachs, whom he despises both as cobbler and as artist: "always by Sachs", he says, "so that I may learn the rhyme to 'bloom and wax'." [1]

The roll call being completed, Kothner asks if they shall pro-

---

[1] "Immer bei Sachs,
  dass den Reim ich lern' von 'blüh' und wachs'".
The historical Sachs was fond of rhyming about himself in this joking fashion in his poems: for example,

  Daraus ihm Glück und Heil erwachs,
  Den treuen Rat gibt ihm Hans Sachs.

And everyone knows his autobiographical couplet:

  Hans Sachs was a shoe-
  maker and a poet too.

ceed next to elect a Marker. This brings the cantankerous Beckmesser to his feet again: suspecting that the baker wishes to sup-
plant him in the office he acidly offers to retire in his favour. But
Pogner intervenes. A little thing of that sort, he says, can wait until after he has told them something of importance. Tomorrow,
he reminds them, is Johannistag — Midsummer day — when the
Nurembergers are wont to hold a festival in the meadows outside
the town, in the course of which the Masters regale the folk with
song, and a grand Song School is held at which prizes are com-
peted for. One thing saddens him, however. Travelling recently
through the German lands he had been grieved to find that everywhere, among princes and peasants alike, the burgher is held in
low esteem. He is charged with thinking of nothing but trade
and gold, whereas they in Nuremberg, at least, have taken art
under their protection. As God has made him a man of wealth,
he proposes to remove the stigma from his dearly-loved town by
giving all his goods and gold to the winner in the Johannistag
Song School, with the hand of his daughter Eva into the bargain.
The generous offer is applauded enthusiastically by Masters and
apprentices. But Pogner has not yet finished: the Masters, it is
true, are to choose the prize winner, but the maiden herself shall
be free to take him or not, according to her fancy.

21

Pogner's Address, as it is generally styled, is constructed musically upon (a) a rich symphonic development of a motive:

No. 19

always associated with the joyousness of Midsummer day, and
(b) the dignified motive of the Guild (No. 4).

The Masters are a trifle damped, as Beckmesser had been, by
the final clause of Pogner's offer. As they reasonably point out, it
"leaves them in the maiden's hands"; what validity will their
award of the prize have if she is to be free to reject the victor?
But Pogner has an answer to this: his daughter can indeed throw

the man over, but in that case she can take no other lover; the fortunate man must be a Master or no one. Sachs now comes into the forefront of the action. Rising from his seat, he suggests a simple way out of the difficulty. The mind of woman, he says, is like that of the folk, unschooled, but sound in its instincts and intuitions. So why not leave the decision to the folk, who may safely be trusted to choose just as the maiden herself would do?

At once the Masters are up in arms. The proposal is outrageous, they cry; if the folk are to be given the decisive word, what will become of art? Sachs explains patiently. No one is more loyal to the rules of the Guild than he, he says. Still, it would not be a bad idea if just once in the year the Masters were to overhaul their rules, lest they should come to cling too blindly to the letter and lose the spirit. After all, nature is the best guide in everything, as those will tell them who have no technical knowledge of the Tabulatur — a revolutionary sentiment received glumly by the Masters but warmly applauded by the apprentices, who jump up and rub their hands. (Here Wagner is speaking, through Sachs, in the first person: he had always maintained that the opposition to him came mostly from the "Guilds" of critics, professors and so on, and that the ordinary listener, with a mind unclouded by theory and unbefuddled by learning, never had any difficulty in understanding and liking him).

Sachs continues earnestly:

> *Believe me, ye ne'er would rue it,*
> *if on Midsummer's day each year*
> *ye asked no more the people here,*
> *but from your Master-cloud-land broke*
> *and went yourselves towards the folk,*

letting *them* decide by the evidence of their own ears what was good and what bad.

When Pogner had said to the company:

> *A lifeless gift I offer not;*
> *a maiden helps to cast the lot:*
> *the prize the Masters shall declare:*
> *but for the rest 'tis only fair,*
> > *whome'er the Masters choose*
> > *the bride may still refuse,*

he had been accompanied by a quiet passage in the violins:

No. 20 Scherzando, dolce

which is one of the minor puzzles of the *Meistersinger* score. Wagner has marked it scherzando. Why? It bears the same marking when, a trifle later, it passes to the oboe as Pogner says, in reply to Beckmesser's angry objection that if the maiden is to have free choice the Masters might as well be left out of the game:

> *Nay, nay! Why so? Let me explain!*
> *any man who the prize shall gain*
>   *the maid may throw him over,*
>   *but take no other for lover.*
> *A Mastersinger he must be,*
> *one crowned by you, or nobody.*

Why, we ask again, the "scherzando"? Is Pogner pulling their leg? We do not dispose of the difficulty by saying, as some commentators do, that No. 20 has no actual existence of its own but is merely a flourish, thrown off *en passant*, from the motive of the Masters (No. 4, bars 3 ff.). That fails to explain why twice, when Pogner is imposing his curious proviso on his offer, it should be just this figure that the orchestra should use to point his words, and that each time it should be marked scherzando. Has he perhaps seen some reason, after his colloquy with Walther, for guessing that the problem of the coincidence of the Masters' choice with the maiden's choice will solve itself in a way that none of the others suspects? It is curious, again, that No. 20 should be drawn upon once more when Sachs says:

> *then let the folk the judges be;*
> *with the maid, I'm certain, they will agree;*

and later, when he urges that the judgment of the folk should be trusted, the flute and oboe give out No. 20 again, and once more it is marked scherzando. That the figure had, for Wagner, some special inner connection with the verdict of the folk and the choice of Eva seems indicated by the fact that it does not appear in the score again until the last few minutes of the opera, when, as we shall see, it is once more associated with the folk as the final arbiters in matters of poetry and song.

22

Sachs's approval of the popular judgment, of course, is rank heresy in the ears of the Masters. They are up in arms at once. Kunz Vogelgesang admits that Sachs means well, but that is all there is to be said for him. For Nachtigall, when the mob speaks it is time for a Master to be silent. Kothner sees nothing but the ruin of their art ahead of them if they make it dependent on the likes and dislikes of the people. Beckmesser, cantankerous as usual, says the proposed New Order would be a fine thing for the cobbler-poet, who for the most part can turn out nothing but street songs; and even the big-hearted Pogner thinks his colleague is going a trifle too far and too fast. So he brings them all back to his original proposition: do the Masters accept it or not? The winner, of course, says Kothner thoughtfully, will have to be a bachelor, he being presumably a bachelor himself. But why not a widower? snaps Beckmesser; why not Sachs? The old cobbler disclaims any ambition of that sort, and at the same time gets a shaft through the Town Clerk's armour — the wooer will have to be younger than either of them if little Eva is going to accept him. This reference to his age adds to Beckmesser's ire.

As the discussion looks like becoming acrimonious, Pogner, in virtue of his position as head of the Guild, recalls them to the business of the day. They have come to the church for a trial; and he himself wishes to commend to them a young man who is anxious to become a Master. Walther steps forward and bows to the company, to the accompaniment of the proud motive of himself *in propria persona*:

No. 21

Beckmesser, scenting trouble, suggests that it is too late now for a trial that day. Some of the others are inclined to caution — an aristocrat presenting himself for Mastership is a novelty, and there is no knowing what a dubious innovation of that sort may lead to. Kothner insists that anyhow the young man must undergo the regulation trial. Pogner agrees with him that the rules must be observed; whereupon Kothner puts to him the prescribed questions about the candidate. First of all, is he a freeman of honourable birth? Pogner will go bond for that: the young man is Sir Walther von Stolzing, a Franconian knight, the last scion of an ancient line, who has come to Nuremberg with the desire to become a burgher. (A burgher, be it observed, not a Mastersinger, as Walther had assured Pogner only a few minutes earlier. Wagner is still careless about reconciling his varying accounts of Walther's motive in the Sketches and in the poem). "This Junker breed is good for nothing!" growls the democratic Beckmesser. But for the others Pogner's word is good enough, while Sachs points out that in the Mastersingers' articles it is laid down that no distinction shall be made between lord and peasant, the only thing that matters being art.

23

From this point onwards the action of the scene follows the historic rules of the Guild. First of all Kothner calls on the candidate to name the Master under whom he has worked. Walther replies in a long lyrical passage commencing thus:

No. 22

He tells how one winter's day he had been thrilled by the reading of an ancient book that sang of the loveliness of spring; the author was the poet whom he names as his Master, none other than Wal-

ther von der Vogelweide. "A right good Master!" Sachs interjects.
"But long since dead", objects the peevish Beckmesser; "what instruction could *he* give him in our rules?" And where did you
study after that?" is Kothner's next question. "When the frost had
passed away", replies Walther in a second stanza to the melody
of the first, "and summer sang its roundelay, in the woods I saw
and heard what the old book described: there it was I learned my
singing." This is too much for Beckmesser. "Oho! so you got your
melodies from the finches and the titmice?" Vogelgesang tells him
that he must at least admit that so far the young man has turned
out two very decent stanzas; and Beckmesser, always apt at small
repartee, turns on him with a savage "I suppose you praise him,
Master Vogelgesang, because he learned his song from the birds?
(Wohl weil vom *Vogel* er lernt' den *Gesang*)".

Kothner now begins to have his doubts. "Should we go on?" he
asks them; "I fear the knight has done for himself." It is left to
Sachs, as usual, to say the sensible thing: "that we shall soon find
out; if his art is good, what does it matter where he learned it?"
So Kothner asks the young man if he is prepared to sing them
then and there a true Mastersong, in which words and music shall
both be his own. (Wagner's sly reference to his own case is obvious here).

For answer, Walther plunges into an aftersong with a new melody, commencing in a new key but finishing in the main one:

No. 23

Everything he has seen and heard and read, he says, has turned
to music within him; and if it is a Mastersong they want he will
do his best to satisfy them. The others are puzzled, for all this is
new and strange to them; but they decide to let him try his luck.
Wagner has woven the whole long episode into a single musical

pattern by a ceaseless play of the orchestra upon some of the main elements of Walther's lyrical preamble.

24

The trial proceeds according to the rules of the Guild. Beckmesser, the Marker for the day, goes with a hypocritical show of reluctance into the box: his chalk, he fears, is going to have its work cut out! As in duty bound, he explains to the candidate that he will be allowed seven faults, all of which will be chalked on the board. If he makes more than seven he will be pronounced "versungen". The Marker's ears, he says,

> *are keen;*
> *but as your nerves, if he were seen,*
> *might be depressed,*
> *he leaves you at rest,*
> *and hides him in his lair:*
> *so heaven have you in its care!*

He pokes his head out with a malicious leer, then draws the curtains to. The acid, niggling nature of the man is defined for us from the outset in his characteristic motive: [1]

Kothner makes a sign to the apprentices, who take down from the wall the board containing the "Leges tabulaturae"; they hold it up in front of him and he reads out the rules to Walther. A Mastersong must be made according to a plan. Each stanza must consist of two strophes sung to the same melody, and extend to several lines rhyming at the ends: then must come the aftersong, having another melody than that of the strophes: not more than four syllables in succession must have been used by any other Master in a previous song; and giving back the board to the ap-

---

[1] It is possible to see in this, as some commentators do, a sort of degradation by Beckmesser of the dignified theme of the knight (No. 21).

prentices, who hang it up again, he bids Walther seat himself in the singer's chair. Wagner makes delightful music out of the reading of the rules; especially piquant are the conventional coloratura flourishes that adorn the ends of the phrases — a feature of the Mastersong — which are imitated with great zest by the orchestra.

"In this chair?" the young romantic asks with a shudder; this is not at all his notion of the freedom due to a poet and musician. But Kothner insists — "That is the rule" — and the young man takes his seat, remarking aside, "For you, beloved!" "The singer sits!" Kothner calls out loudly to the Marker, and from within the box comes the regulation order, "Now begin!"

Walther's trial song is an inspiration of the moment, evidently, for he fastens on the "Now begin!" as a kind of poetic motive and embroiders upon it. "So cried the spring through the land", he says:

No. 25

and the forest heard it and responded, the whole glad earth rejoicing in the liberation of spring:

No. 26

The lovely song is filled with the ardour of youth; but apparently it sins grievously against the Nuremberg rules, for the sound of vigorous scratchings on the board comes from the box. Walther is perturbed, but masters himself and proceeds with a description of gloomy old winter cowering and snarling in its lair, listening enviously, bent on turning this song of the gladness of earth into one of sadness: whether Walther intends it or not, his song of wintry petrifaction and spring renewal is symbolical of the pedantic Masters and himself. Now all on fire, he rises from the chair — a capital crime according to the rules — and launches out into a paean to youth and spring and love. One feature of the song, the soft murmur of spring:

No. 27

has to be specially noticed, for, as we shall see later, it struck deep into the poetic and still young heart of old Sachs.

The curtains are flung violently aside and Beckmesser's head appears. "Have you finished?" he asks harshly. "Why?" says Walther. "Because there's no more room on my board!" and the Marker holds it out, showing every inch of it covered with chalk marks. The Masters break into loud laughter, to the accompaniment of a derisive figure:

No. 28

in the orchestra.

Walther tries to make them understand that he has another stanza to sing, this time in praise of his lady. But Beckmesser, cutting him short, steps out of the box and invites the Masters to inspect the board in detail. Never has he listened to such an exhibition of incompetence, he says — "cloudy meaning", mistakes in quantity and time, "too short", "too long", "faulty rhyme", the melody a nonsensical mixture of the "Adventure" Mode, the "Blue-knight-spur" Mode, the "High fir-tree" Mode, the "Proud stripling"

Mode, and heaven knows what; all the faults, *mutatis mutandis,* of incompetence and plagiarism and bad taste which the critics and professors used to try to fix on Wagner himself. The other Masters agree with Beckmesser; Kothner's special grievance is that the singer in his enthusiasm had risen from the chair before receiving permission to do so.

25

One alone among them keeps his head. Sachs, whose interest in the song had manifestly increased the more he heard of it, now comes forward. The serious, even mournful side of the nature of the shoemaker who is also an artist and a philosopher is expressed in a little phrase in the orchestra of which we shall hear more later:

No. 29

But this gives way at once to the motive of Sachs's Benevolence, as it may be called:

No. 30

as he gives the company his own view of what they have just heard. The song, he says, is undoubtedly novel in substance and form, but he has not found it, as they have done, wild or confused. True it had not run along the lines laid down by the Masters, but its course for all that had been steady and sure. And he gives the Guild some good advice:

> *Before you try to measure*
> *what does not with your rules agree,*
> *forget the laws you treasure,*
> *ask first what its own rules may be!*

Beckmesser's derisive reply to this is the traditional one of the academic — "To tell the poet that he should sing just as he feels, regardless of rules, is to throw the doors of art wide open to the common herd. Sing to the people in the street and the market-place in this style if you like, but here among *us* nothing is permitted that runs counter to the rules."

Sachs tells him, in effect, that what *he* needs is a new pair of ears. Anyhow, since he is so concerned for the sanctity of the rules, let him remember the one that lays it down that the Marker must be above all suspicion of friendship or enmity towards a contestant. How does Beckmesser come through that test? Since he is going a-wooing, would it not be only simple human nature in him to do what he can to shame his rival before the School?

Does Sachs, perhaps, half-suspect *why* the knight is so anxious to be accepted as a Master this very day? It may be so. Anyhow Walther seems to be sensitive to the unspoken nuance of suggestion, for he "flames up", as the stage directions put it. The others think that Sachs has "gone too far"; Kothner reproves him for "being personal". Beckmesser, feeling that the best defence is attack, rounds on Sachs. Let the cobbler stick to his last, he says; since Sachs took to poetry his shoemaking has deteriorated. "Just look at this shoe of mine", he cries; "see how loose it is; hear how it cracks!"

> *This stuff he loves to scrawl,*
> *for me he may keep it all,*
> *his histories, plays, and his farcical muse,*
> *if tomorrow he'll bring me my new pair of shoes;*

and a figure suggestive of the cobbler hammering away at a shoe is reiterated by the orchestra:

No. 31
Animato

Sachs scratches his head in humorous discomfiture: no one, he
says, objects to his scribbling a bit of doggerel on the soles of a
donkey-driver's shoes; can't he be permitted, then, to decorate
the Town Clerk's in the same harmless way? The trouble is that
so far he hasn't been able to think of a couplet worthy of so august a subject. Possibly it may come to him if he hears the remainder of the knight's song; so he suggests that he shall be allowed to continue.

26

The Masters protest that they have had enough of it, but Sachs
gives the knight a bit of sensible advice — "Sing on, just to annoy
the Marker!" So Walther mounts the chair once more and breaks
into the final section of his song, which describes the screech owl
and the raven, the magpie and the crow, making the woodland
hideous with their raucous voices — for all the world like so many
Masters — until a bright and beautiful bird soars up into the blue
above him, inviting him to join it in its flight, and filling his heart
with joy and his throat with song:

> *towards the light*
> *I take my flight,*
> *from the city dead,*
> *with wings wide spread,*
> *to the hill of my desiring,*
> *to the Vogelweid' so green, so free,*
> *where Master Walther sang to me;*
> *and there my voice I raise*
> *to sing my lady's praise;*
> *forth it flows,*
> *unheeding croaks of Master-crows,*
> *the song of love's sweet spell!*
> *Farewell, ye Masters, farewell!*

But the croaking crows and chattering magpies of the Guild
are not so easily silenced. Throughout the big ensemble that
terminates the act the Masters keep up a machine-gun fire of
disparaging comment as Walther sings. Beckmesser trots from
one to another of them, exhibiting the board with its scoring of
not a mere seven but more than fifty faults; and this presumptu-

ous young lunatic wants to qualify as a Master! The apprentices, including David, are delighted to join in: they link hands in a ring and dance round the box, singing their merry motive of the Silken Chaplet (No. 17). It is all wrought into one massive choral structure, with the angry Walther going on indomitably, his song soaring above the turmoil. Sachs is barely audible, but what he is saying is that the knight is a true poet and singer who can hold his own against the rabble of Masters.

At last Beckmesser is heard inviting the others to register their final verdict. They raise their hands *en masse* (except Sachs) and declare the knight "versungen und verthan". Walther, with a proud contemptuous gesture, leaves the chair and stalks out. The hullabaloo increases; the apprentices take possession of the Marker's box, and even jostle the august persons of the Masters as they leave. Finally Sachs alone, apart from the apprentices, remains in the church. We hear for a moment No. 26 in the oboe, as if this passage from Walther's song were still humming in the old cobbler's head; but it yields to No. 17 and then to a comically pompous strut of the motive of the Masters (No. 1) in the bassoons. Sachs sums it all up in a gesture of humorous discouragement, turns on his heels, and, as the apprentices make merry with the singer's chair, leaves the stage as the curtain falls.

27

The second act is Wagner's most dexterous achievement in the way of dramatic structure; the action is kept always moving, and piece fits into piece with such perfect neatness that it is only after close analysis of it all that we realise the skilled craftsmanship of the carpentry.

The act opens with a joyous orchestral prelude on the Midsummer day motive (No. 19), now gay with trills and glissandi and bubbling over with high spirits in little turns like these:

As the curtain rises we see a group of apprentices closing the shutters of the houses on one side of an alley and looking forward happily to the morrow's festival:

No. 33

Jo - han - nis - tag! Jo - han - nis - tag!
Mid - sum - mer's day! Mid - sum - mer's day!

Blu - men_ und_ Bän - der   so__ viel man mag!
Flow - ers_ and_ fa - vours   ma - ny and gay!

while David, engaged in the same task on the opposite side, is wishing that the silken chaplet to be awarded in the contest might be his (No. 17).

Along the foreground of the scene runs a street in Nuremberg, from the middle of which branches a narrow alley, winding crookedly towards the back. This presents the spectator with two corner houses — a handsome one (Pogner's) on his right, with steps leading up to it and embrasures with stone seats along its front, and a humbler one (Sachs's) on his left. At the right-hand edge of the stage, close to Pogner's house, is a stately lime tree; at its base are green shrubs, and in front of it a stone bench. The door of Sachs's house is overhung by an elder tree. The entrance to the house is from the front street; a divided door leads straight into the workshop; on the alley side of the house are two windows, one to the workshop, the other to a room beyond. It is a beautiful summer evening, night gradually closing in as the action develops.

The apprentices are teasing David as usual when Magdalena arrives, bringing him a basket of dainties. She asks him eagerly how the knight had fared that afternoon at the Song School; and when she learns that he was "versungen und verthan" she peevishly snatches back the basket and goes into Pogner's house in great dejection. The apprentices, who have seen and heard it all, make merry once more at poor David's expense. In his rage he is about to attack them when Sachs comes up the alley. The boys scurry away: David protests that it wasn't he who began the row, and his master orders him to go in, lock up, bring a light, and put the new shoes on the last. As they enter the workshop and pass on through the inner door Pogner and Eva appear in the alley, returning from their evening walk. David emerges from the inner

room, places a light by the shop window, and sets Sachs's work
out there.

Pogner has half an idea to look his friend up, but thinks better
of it: evidently something is troubling him. He appears to be in
some doubt now whether he has acted quite wisely in the matter
of the prize; he would like to talk it over with his old friend Sachs,
but is not sure that any advice at all would be helpful just now.
To tranquil music he bids Eva, who also seems to have something
on her mind, sit down with him on the bench under the lime tree.
To a new motive in the orchestra, henceforth to be associated
with grand and dear old Nuremberg:

No.34

he drinks in the soft evening air with satisfaction; tomorrow, he
says, promises to be fine. Does not his daughter's heart rejoice, he
asks her, at the thought of the festival, when she will crown the
one who has proved himself Master? "Dear father, *must* it be a
Master?" she asks. "For sure", he replies; "but", speaking more
prophetically than he knows, "a Master of your own choice."

Eva, with a sigh, agrees with him as to that. She calls out to
Magdalena, who has appeared at the door of the house and is
beckoning to her, that she is coming, and then reminds her father
that supper is waiting. "But no guest?" he asks with a touch of ir-
ritation; and when she replies "Perhaps the knight?" he looks at
her wonderingly. Did her father see him that afternoon? she asks.
"Yes, but I was not pleased with him." Then it begins to dawn on
him what is behind her curiosity with regard to Walther; he taps
his forehead and asks himself whether, maybe, he has not been
a trifle dull-witted until now.

She makes him precede her into the house, and manages to
have a word with Magdalena behind his back. She learns of Walther's failure. Her first impulse in her distress is to go to kindly old
Sachs and ask for first-hand news about it all. But the maid restrains her: her father is sure to notice her absence, so it will be
wiser to wait until supper is over. Besides, Magdalena has "some-

thing to tell her", a "secret message" from "somebody". "Sir Walther?" Eva asks eagerly. "No, Beckmesser!" With a contemptuous
shrug of her shoulders at this unimportant piece of news Eva goes
into the house, followed by the maid.

28

Street and alley are both empty now. Sachs, in indoor clothes,
comes back into his workshop from the inner room. With the
Cobbler motive (No. 31) in the orchestra punctuating his remarks he tells David, who is still at the bench, to place the table
and the stool at the door of the shop, where Sachs can work in the
fresh air, and then "get off to bed; sleep off thy folly, and tomorrow have a little more sense". David goes off to his own room,
which is on the alley side. Sachs sits down, takes up his tools, lays
them down again, and leans back with his arm resting on the
closed lower half of the door.

The orchestra, with softly-breathed reminiscences of No. 26
and No. 27, shows us where his thoughts are: they have gone
back to Walther's song before the Guild and the glowing sense of
the loveliness of youth and spring it had brought him. He revels
for a moment in the scent of the elder tree above his head, and
then humorously reproves the poet in him for standing in the way
of work. Making an attempt to drive poetry out of his head he
takes up his hammer and sets to work noisily at the shoe — Beckmesser's — on the last. But in vain; No. 26 and other snatches
from Walther's melody pass through one transformation after another in the orchestra as he recalls that ardent song of love and
youth and the beauty of earth. From the heart that song had
come, and to the heart it had gone. The old man plays, as the
historical Sachs was so fond of doing, on his own name and the
homely wax of his trade that rhymes with it: one may roughly
render the final quatrain of his monologue thus:

> *The bird who sang today*
> *I warrant knows the singer's knacks well!*
> *Masters may say him nay,*
> *but this I know, he pleased Hans Sachs well!*

and, like the philosopher he is, he puts poetry out of his mind for
the time being and begins working cheerfully at the shoe.

335

Meanwhile Eva has come into the street. She goes to the shop door and greets him. He is very glad to see her. Over two gracious motives in the orchestra:

No. 35

No. 36

that keep weaving the loveliest of symphonic patterns, the pair engage in a long fencing bout. Eva fishes for information about the knight, but dares not ask outright what she desires to know: wise old Sachs reads her thoughts, but will not let her see that he does so. The new shoes he has made for her, she begins by saying, are very fine, but she hasn't worn them yet. "Tomorrow, of course", he suggests, "as bride?" "No doubt, but who will the bridegroom be? How do you know I shall be a bride?" "Well, everyone knows that." "What everyone knows, no one knows. Is this the best Sachs can do? I thought he knew more." "What ought I to know, then?" "Ah, friend Sachs, I see now that pitch is not wax! I credited you with more shrewdness." "My child, I know all there is to be known about pitch and wax. I waxed the silken threads of your shoes to make them dainty; but now I must work in pitch, to harden the thread for a rough man's use. Need I name him? The shoes are for Beckmesser, who hopes that all will acclaim him as singer and wooer tomorrow."

> *Then use the strongest pitch you can:*
> *may he stick, and I escape the man!*

she cries; and the verbal duel continues.

She ought not to be so uppish, he tells her; good single men are scarce. "But why should a widower not succeed?" "My child, he would be too old for thee." "Too old? what counts in this case is art; let him who understands it woo me." "You jest!" "No, it is you who are shuffling. God knows what maid Sachs holds in his heart now, but for years I have thought it was I. You carried me in your arms, but only, I see now, because you had no child of your own." "Once I had wife and children too", he replies gravely; "but they are dead, and you have grown tall and fair." "I thought I should be wife and child to you. But now I see how it is; Master Sachs would not grieve if tomorrow Beckmesser were to carry me off under his very nose." "How can I stop him? It all rests with your father." "Oh, you Masters! Where do you keep your brains? Yours seem to have left you." "Yes, yes, mine's a poor addled head":

> *I've had much care and fret today,*
> *and all my wits have flown away;*

to which the orchestra gives point with No. 29.

This remark of his gives Eva the opening she has been manœuvring for. "Was it in the School?" "Yes, at a trial that went not well." "Ah, Sachs, had you but told me *that* I should not have wearied you with my chatter. But tell me now, who was at this trial?" "A knight, my child (No. 21), lamentably untaught." "A knight, eh? was he elected?" (No. 28). "No, they were against him to a man."

29

At this point Magdalena slips out of the house and calls softly to Eva, warning her that her father is asking for her. But she only turns the more eagerly to Sachs. "Is it hopeless? Why? Did he sing so badly that he will never be a Master?" "Never, anywhere! for the Master born will always fare worst at Masters' hands." Another urgent call from Magdalena goes unregarded. "But tell me, did he win any friend at all among them?" "Impossible! All felt too small beside him. He has too much pride: let him see the world a little. Why can't he leave us in peace to what we have learned with so much toil and smart? If he wants to kick over the traces let him go somewhere else to do it!" At this, Eva loses her temper. "Aye", she cries, to the accompaniment of the Derision motive (No. 28):

Aye! elsewhere then he'll fortune find,
whate'er a nasty jealous man says —
where hearts are generous and kind,
far from all spiteful Master Hanses!
Yes, Lena, yes! I'm coming, dear!
Small consolation is there here!
It smells of pitch, God save us from harm!
Let him burn in it and keep himself warm!

She leaves him in a rage and goes over to Magdalena. "I thought as much", says Sachs to himself, looking thoughtfully and tenderly after her, while the Care motive (No. 29) wells up once more in the strings. "Now to find a way!" He closes the upper half of the door, so that only a glimmer of light comes through it, and he himself is almost invisible.

On the other side of the stage Eva and Magdalena engage in excited talk. Eva tells the maid to go to bed and cease worrying her; but Magdalena insists on giving her the commission she has received from Beckmesser. She is to persuade her mistress to be at her window when it gets dark, to hear him try out the song with which he hopes to win her hand the next day. "This is the last straw!" cries poor Eva. "Oh, if only *he* would come!" she wails; and that motive No. 29 was for Wagner the symbol not only of Sachs's cares but of care in general, Eva's and humanity's, is shown by his employing it again in some peculiarly poignant forms in the present connection. (Occasionally, indeed, his motives must have had for him psychological connotations that escape us: how, for example, are we to account for the persistent use of the Cobbler motive (No. 31) in the orchestra during the closing passage of this dialogue between the two women?)

Eva has heard footsteps which she takes to be those of Walther. In vain does Magdalena try to induce her to go indoors before her father notices her absence. "Go thou to the window in my stead", she tells Magdalena, still listening in the direction from which she had heard footsteps.[1] The idea of appearing at the window

---

[1] Wagner's handling of the change-of-clothes motive is not entirely lucid, and the variants between the Sketches and the poem show that it constituted something of a problem for him. The difficulty had arisen through the insertion in the opera at the last moment of the long conversation between Sachs and Eva, an episode for which there had been no provision in any of

dressed up as her mistress appeals strongly to Magdalena: David, who sleeps on the alley side, is sure to hear the serenade, and it will make him jealous and perhaps bring him to proposal point. She manages to draw Eva towards the door, but just then Walther turns the corner, and Eva runs to meet him with a glad cry. The orchestra whips up the excitement of anticipation very much as it does just before Tristan's entry in the second act of *Tristan and Isolde.*

30

The impassioned dialogue of the lovers begins to the accompaniment of No. 36, now, however, in a more fiery form. Beside herself with joy, Eva greets the knight as her destined own, her poet and her friend. "Friend indeed", he replies, "but not poet, for as poet they have rejected and derided me, and so I have lost your hand." They go despairingly over the old ground again — she swears she will accept no one but him, but how are they to evade the hard conditions laid down by her father? He had sung his heart out at the trial, he says; but those accursed Masters, those hide-bound pedants and poetasters, had spurned him! Only one thing is left to them — flight together to freedom, into a world where he will be a Master by the grace of God. At the very thought of his enemies he sees red: the orchestra executes a wild fantasia upon the Derision motive (No. 28) as in his imagination he still sees and hears them all about him:

> *Markers beset me,*
> *torment and fret me;*
> *round me they're flocking,*
> *gibing and mocking:*
> *Markers from boxes,*
> *cunning old foxes,*
> *up from the highways,*
> *down all the byways. . .*

---

the Sketches. The slight confusion which this insertion introduced into his original plan, and the not wholly convincing devices by which he sought to remedy the confusion, are of considerable interest to the student of his dramatic technique. To go over the whole ground critically here, however, would delay us unnecessarily. The reader will find a full discussion of the matter in my *Life of Richard Wagner*, III, 159–163.

insult thee and flout thee,
dance about thee,
snuffling and screeching,
thy hand beseeching:
a Master takes thee,
wretched bride he makes thee,
trembling and weeping;
round thee they're creeping!
And I must bear it,
may not pursue them,
may not strike my good sword through them!

At the height of his delirium the horn of the Night-watchman is heard not far away — a single note that strikes into the tissue of both the music and the action with extraordinary dramatic effect. Walther's first impulse is to draw his sword and cut his way through a danger which he senses but does not comprehend; but Eva lays her hand on him soothingly, and in an instant the music softens to the melody of the Magic of Midsummer eve:

"It was only the Watchman you heard", Eva tells him; "conceal yourself under the lime tree until he passes." Magdalena calls to her to make haste; and as the orchestra gives out quietly the tender Love motive (No. 6) she follows the maid into the house, giving Walther, as she goes, what seems to be an assurance that she will elope with him.

As he conceals himself the Watchman comes slowly down the alley, reaches the street, turns the corner of Pogner's house, and gradually passes out of sight, singing the simple traditional warning to all good citizens to look out for fire and evil-doers:

Hearken to my words, good people;
strikes ten from every steeple;
guard well your fire and eke your light,
that no one may be harmed this night.
Praise the Lord of all!

No. 38

Hört ihr Leut' und lasst euch sa - gen, die Glock' hat
Heark-en to my words, good peo-ple; strikes ten from

zehn___ ge - schla-gen;
ev' - ry stee - ple;

He sings it on a key-basis of F major, and then startles us by
blowing on his horn a booming G flat. (In the old Germany that
still survived in Wagner's young days the Night-watchman still
went his rounds, waking the citizens up to assure them that it
was all right to go on sleeping. Wagner must often have heard
the call and the horn blast as a boy. Perhaps the words and the
melody were to some extent the same everywhere, for a night-
watchman's song of the mid-sixteenth century has come down to
us that begins thus:

No. 39

Lost ir herrn und lasst euch sagn, es hat vie - re ge-schlagn.

The similarity between the melody and the words of this — "Hear
me now, it has struck four" — and those of Wagner's Night-
watchman is too close to be accidental).

31

A quiet enunciation of the Cobbler motive in the violas tells us
that Sachs has been listening and taking notice of it all. He
withdraws his lamp and opens his door a little further: "This is
getting serious", he remarks; "an elopement on foot? That mustn't
be. I must keep my eye on them."

Walther, behind the lime tree, is surprised to see, as he thinks,
Magdalena approaching him; but as No. 6 unfolds itself he perceives that it is Eva, who throws herself on his breast. Now, he
says, he no longer doubts that he has won the Master-prize! They
prepare to make their dash for freedom. It is time now for Sachs
to act. He places his lamp behind a glass globe, and as the lovers

turn into the alley he opens the shutter again, so that a beam of light shoots steadily across the road. Eva and Walther, thus suddenly made visible, withdraw hastily into hiding, and to add to the tension of the situation the harsh G flat of the Watchman's horn strikes in again from a distance. There are only two routes open to the lovers, the way by the street — which Eva does not know very well — and that through the alley. Walther is sure he has only to appeal to Sachs and all will be well, for the cobbler is his friend; but Eva assures him that he is nothing of the kind: "he had nothing but evil to say of you." "Sachs too?", says Walther; "then out goes his light!"

But before he can go towards the shop to carry out his purpose the sound of a lute being tuned is heard. Beckmesser had crept down the alley in the wake of the Watchman: now he seats himself on a stone bench between the two windows of Sachs's house and looks up enquiringly at Pogner's windows. For a moment it seems to Walther that the coast is clear, for Sachs has withdrawn his light a little, closed the lower half of his door, and placed his work-bench right in the doorway. The lute has given the cobbler a brilliant idea: he sees now how both to check the imprudent plan of the lovers and have some fun of his own with Beckmesser. When Eva tells Walther that a newcomer has appeared in the alley, and that he is none other than the Marker, Walther is for paying off his score against him at once. The anxious Eva holds him back: her father will be roused if there is any commotion in the alley: Beckmesser will merely sing a song and go away, and then the coast will be clear. So the pair withdraw further into the shadow of the bushes by the lime tree.

Beckmesser, not seeing the expected figure at the window, begins strumming his lute impatiently:

No. 40

unconscious of the trouble that is brewing for him, a hint of which we get from a whisper of the Cobbler motive in the orchestra. Before he can begin his serenade, however, Sachs hammers on his last and trolls a hearty "Jerum! Jerum! Hallo-hallo-he! Oho! Tra-lalei!":

No. 41

and then launches into a ditty in popular style:

No. 42

the burden of which is that when the Lord drove Eve out of Paradise for her fault He took pity on her poor feet and sent an angel after her with instructions to make her a pair of shoes, and one for innocent barefoot Adam into the bargain.

32

Then the rich comedy begins. Sachs, in reply to Beckmesser's protests, explains that he has to work late to finish the pair of shoes in which the Marker is to go singing and wooing on the morrow. There is no stopping the jovial cobbler: a second verse, which Eva and Walther have a suspicion refers to themselves, tells of the responsibility of mother Eve for angels like him getting no rest, for they have to sit up to all hours shoe-making:

> *If you'd been more discreet,*
> *no stones would hurt our feet:*
> *but for that little slip you made*
> *I now must ply my awl and thread;*
> *and since poor Adam fell with you,*

I ply my wax and sole my shoe!
But were not I
an angel from on high,
devil make your shoes, I'd cry!

In the final stanza Sachs asks mother Eve (and through her the descendant and namesake of hers who is in hiding across the road) to feel for the cobbler in his woe; for are not all his works trodden upon and ruined past repairing?

Did not my weary soul
an angel oft console,
and call me up to Paradise,
I'd leave this world which I despise.
But when with him to heaven I go
this world of care I leave below;
peace fills me through,
Hans Sachs is shoe-
maker and a poet too.

As he begins this stanza we hear in wood wind and horns a countertheme to the melody of No. 42 that symbolises the heartache of the sensitive old poet in Sachs over the evil and misery of the world; it becomes of prime importance later in the orchestral prelude to the third act:

No. 43

Beckmesser is in despair: how is he to sing to his beloved — Magdalena has just appeared at the window in Eva's clothes — if this noise goes on? Eva, indeed, may even imagine that Sachs's ribald song is *his* serenade! He and Sachs discuss the situation. The shoemaker, for his part, pleads that he must get on with his work: has not the Marker, indeed, already reproached him publicly for giving more time to his poetising than to his cobbling? Beckmesser tries a combination of diplomacy and flattery: will not so excellent a judge as Sachs just listen to his song and tell him what he thinks of it?

Still of my shoes you're thinking solely,
while truly I'd forgot them wholly.
Of cobblers you're the best, I swear;
as critic you're beyond compare.
Your judgment mightily I prize;
this song, then, prithee, criticise,
with which tomorrow, when I chant it,
I'll win the maid, if God but grant it.

Finally, after much argument, they arrive at a compromise. Beckmesser is to get on with his song, Sachs with his work. But if he is to mark, obviously it can't be with chalk: the shoes will never be finished that way. So why shouldn't he combine the functions of cobbler and Marker? Why not score the faults, if any, with his hammer? His professional pride making him feel safe on that score, Beckmesser agrees. He tunes his lute, but in his agitation screws the D string up too high. He corrects it and begins his serenade.

It is impossible to follow Wagner's words faithfully and at the same time throw the stresses on the same wrong syllables as in the German. In another language only the absurdity of the general effect can be conveyed, something in this fashion:

I see the dawning daylight,
that imparts great pleasure;
it doth my heart so excite,
promising soon rapture,
I do not think of dying,
rather of trying
to secure a young bride;

and so on:

No. 44
Moderato

Den Tag seh' ich_ er - schei-nen, der mir wohl ge_ fall'n tut:
I   see the dawn-ing day-light that im-parts great pleas-ure.

The whole thing is a burlesque by Wagner of the type of song in which the melodic stresses fall with mechanical regularity on the strong beat of the bar, regardless of whether the accompanying word or syllable calls for accentuation or not.

Sachs's hammer marks three faults in the first four lines of the song, and Beckmesser angrily asks him what is wrong. Would it not be better, says the shoemaker, if instead of:

No. 45

Da fasst mein Herz sich ei - nen.___ gu-ten und fri-schen
It doth my heart so ex - cite,___ pro - mis-ing soon rap-

he had proceeded something like this?

No. 46

Da fasst mein Herz___ ei -nen gu-ten, fri - schen
It doth my heart___ so ex - cite with pro - mise

Sachs, in fact, would handle the words, for musical purposes, with the rhythmic freedom with which Hugo Wolf and other moderns have familiarised us, making the vital words coincide with the strong beats. But in that case, Beckmesser asks testily, what becomes of my rhyme of "sich einen" and "erscheinen"? They argue this technical point for a moment, and then the Marker continues as best he can, for the further he goes the more faults the shoemaker marks, till in the end we can hardly hear the song for the hammer-strokes; we perceive, however, that it is liberally larded with the coloratura flourishes of which the Masters were so fond. Matters are not improved by the exasperated Beckmesser losing both his head and his wind, so that he commits more and more offences against good song and good speech as he goes on. In vain does he protest:

> *Now art's the thing;*
> *he who can fling*
> *his soul into his throat and sing*
> *a song both learnéd and loving*
> *will win the maid for his darling,*
> *and be by hér belóved.*

33

By this time the shoes, thanks to the faults that have been scored on them with the hammer, are quite finished, and Sachs holds them up in glee; but regardless of the shoemaker's reminder that

> *Good song keeps time*
> *and proper rhyme;*
> *when Town Clerks clean forget it,*
> *upon their soles do I set it,*

Beckmesser, now quite out of breath and shaking his lute furiously at Sachs, keeps rambling on to the tune of No. 44:

> *I knów the rules perféctly,*
> *I kéep excéllent time;*
> *but tó sing incorréctly*
> *for once were no great crime,*
> *when mý heart quákes withín me,*
> > *trýing to win me*
> *the faír maidén I wóo.*

All this long while the lovers have been watching and listening, half-wondering, half-amused: Walther asks Eva if he can have gone mad, or is it all a dream, for he has the feeling that he is back in the School again, or in the singer's chair.

But the end is near. The hullabaloo has wakened David, who looks out and sees, as he imagines, his Magdalena being serenaded by a stranger. He comes out armed with a cudgel. Magdalena signs frantically to him to go away; Beckmesser thinks Eva is signifying her displeasure with his song, and he flings himself into the sorry remnants of it with the energy of despair. David collars him and begins to thrash him. By this time the neighbours also have been aroused, and now they begin to pour into the alley and the street. Seeing two men fighting they automatically take sides, as crowds will do, without understanding or caring anything about the rights and wrongs of the squabble. Guild rivalries and jealousies come into play: the cobblers swear it is the tailors, the tailors the cobblers; the locksmiths, the butchers, the bakers, the weavers, the tanners, the grocers, the joiners, the tin workers, the glue boilers, the wax makers, the flax weavers, soon are all in it, acting on the Irishman's sound precept for behaviour in a free-for-all — "wherever you see a head, hit it".

The women look out of their windows, and seeing their husbands and brothers being assaulted scream blue murder and start emptying cans and buckets of water on the milling crowd. The apprentices, of course, have been in it joyously from the beginning; now the journeymen rush in with clubs and take a hand in the game. Finally the dignified Masters and grave elderly citizens come in and exhort the madmen to stop before they are all murdered. All Nuremberg seems to be jostling and shouting in the streets.

34

Sachs, meanwhile, has extinguished his light and closed his shutters so that, without being visible himself, he can see through a chink the lovers by the lime tree. They have been watching the turmoil with increasing anxiety. Walther draws Eva to him and wraps his cloak round her, and they take cover as best they can in the bushes by the tree. More and more respectable citizens, roused from their sleep, come out in their night attire: Pogner appears at the window where the pseudo-Eva is weeping and wringing her hands, and, under the impression that it is his daughter, drags her back into the room. At last Walther draws his sword, clasps Eva in his left arm, and decides to cut his way through the mêlée; but when they reach the middle of the alley Sachs darts out, scatters the combatants with his strap, seizes Walther by the arm, and pushes the half-fainting Eva up the steps of her father's house, saying "In with you, Mistress Lena!" She is received and taken away by Pogner, who, what with the darkness and the change of costume, believes she is Magdalena. Then Sachs turns his attention to David, who is still, as he has been throughout, hard at work on Beckmesser. The Watchman's horn strikes in once more, and at the sound of it the crowd breaks up and flees in panic: the women disappear from the windows, the house doors are hastily closed. Sachs seizes David, gives him one with his strap and kicks him into the shop; Beckmesser picks himself up and staggers out with the others. All this while Sachs has not relaxed his hold on Walther; now he hustles him into the shop and closes the door.

When the Watchman enters he can scarcely believe his eyes and ears; he finds the place empty and as quiet as the tomb. He sings his ditty again in a quavering voice, this time making it eleven o' the clock; and once more he blows his discordant G flat against an F major harmony as he walks away slowly down the empty alley, which is now bathed in soft moonlight. An immense peace seems to have descended upon the town: the strings give out softly the motive of Midsummer eve Magic (No. 37), which is followed by quiet echoes of a motive that has played a great part in the texture during the cudgelling of Beckmesser and the accompanying riot:

The peace deepens, the last word being given to a tender little thought for Beckmesser, whose attempt at a display of Mastership seems to peter out, like the poor singer himself, in a sort of sore and sorry limp:

The slow-moving Watchman turns the corner and disappears from sight at the exact moment of the falling of the curtain.

35

In the third act Sachs — not the cobbler or even the Master but the wise and humane old poet — comes into his own; even Walther and Eva now become subsidiary characters. Perhaps the most remarkable thing in connection with the opera is the way the character of Sachs developed silently within Wagner in the course of the years. In the First Sketch of 1845 the shoemaker-Master had in him something of the aggressiveness and irritability of the Sachs of Deinhardstein. There Wagner had shown him on terms of hostility, secret or avowed, with the whole Guild. In the trial scene in the first act he had been the "keeper of the rules" for

the day, in which capacity he has to read them out to the young
aspirant for Mastership: this he does "with a touch of irony", and
his behaviour every now and then strikes the other Masters as
"suspicious". He "speaks sharply to the young man, so that the latter is a little abashed and anxious", though as Walther's song proceeds Sachs "looks at him sympathetically and at the Marker with
irony". When the Masters declare themselves outraged by the
song he turns on them, makes merry at their expense, and chal-
lenges the Marker to contribute a song of his own which *he* will
take pleasure in marking. All through the work, in the First
Sketch, there is a touch of personal frustration and bitterness in
Sachs; when he hits out, as in the serenade scene with Beckmesser in the second act, it is to hurt.

Wagner, again, had seen him at first too much in terms of not
only the artistic but the social and political and religious milieu
of the divided Germany of the sixteenth century. In what is now
the famous monologue upon life and art in the third act of the
opera Wagner had made him, in 1845, lament that German poetry was coming to a degenerate end: "am I, a cobbler, the only
man left who breathes the spirit of the great German past?" This
note of personal exasperation disappears from the final work;
Sachs now bemoans not his own lack of recognition as a poet but
the folly of humanity in general, a humanity, however, which he
loves deeply and would fain lead to higher things. Furthermore,
when, in the Sketch of 1845, the young man comes into the room in
the third act and Sachs questions him about his poetic ideals and
looks through some of his poems, his advice to him is couched in
terms of the German situation of his own day; "Sachs reflects for
a time, then turns to the young man again. 'You are a poet; yet
you will not prosper in the present time'. He depicts with melancholy humour the times they live in, the impending disappearance of the last sad remnants of the old art of Mastersong. 'Look
at me; I would have found it impossible to carry on had I not
been able to occupy my mind with these thoughts. That is why
I am a cobbler, and, believe me, this cobbler is the last poet of
the old German song-craft.' The young man protests energetically.
Sachs: 'Believe me, for a long time to come men will not be interested in poetry. They will fight with other weapons than songs

— with reason, with philosophy, against obscurantism and super-
stition,[1] aye, with the sword men will defend these new weapons.
In that fight you, who have such beautiful and noble sentiments,
ought to take your part; in this way you will achieve more than by
the exercise of a gift which no one thinks anything of today. And
when centuries have gone by and a new world has come into being, perhaps men will turn back and glance at what they once
had; then, perhaps, they will return to Hans Sachs, and he will
point them still further back, to Walther [von der Vogelweide],
and Wolfram, and the *Heldenlieder.*' *The Young Man:* 'Advise
me, then, what to do.' *Sachs, cheerfully:* 'Return to your castle,
study the writings of Ulrich von Hutten [2] and the Wittenberger,[3]
and then, if it be necessary, defend with the sword what you
have learned.' 'Very good, Meister! But now I need a wife!' 'You
shall have one. Leave that to me'".

None of this political and religious motivation is carried over
into the Second Sketch, a fact on which we can congratulate ourselves today. Between 1845 and 1861 the character of Sachs had
developed within Wagner on other and more broadly humanistic
lines; the shoemaker-poet is no longer the specific product of the
epoch of Luther and Hutten but a universal type of poetic ardour,
understanding of the world of men, and resigned toleration,
flecked with humour, of its weaknesses.

36

Had Wagner written the music of the opera in 1845 he could
not have presented us with such a Sachs as the one we see in the
orchestral prelude to the third act. The composer has left us, in
a letter of 1869 to King Ludwig, the clue to the sequence of
moods in the music. As we have seen, in the third stanza of the
Cobbling song in the second act Wagner had introduced a countertheme (No. 43) to the main melody: this, he says, is "the bitter
lament of the resigned man who shows the world a cheerful, energetic countenance; that cry from hidden depths had been understood by Eva, and so profoundly was her heart pierced by it

---

[1] The reader will remember that Sachs was a contemporary of Luther.

[2] One of the leaders of the German Reformation.

[3] Luther.

that she would fain flee away, that she might hear no more of that song which on the surface was so cheerful."

The spectator may reasonably ask how we are to read Eva's thoughts to that extent; is not Wagner expecting us to take for granted, on his bare word, something that we should not have been able to deduce from the stage action itself? The answer is "No, or at all events not entirely": the clue *is* there in the poem, though even the most attentive listener in the theatre is certain to miss it; and for this Wagner himself must be held responsible. After the final words (quoted on page 344) of the Cobbling song — "Hans Sachs was a shoemaker and a poet too" — the full orchestra had given out the main melody (No. 42) fortissimo, with trumpets and trombones in full blast, the countertheme also (No. 43) asserting itself fortissimo in the horns. It is against this tornado of sound that Eva has to say "That song grieves me, I know not why!" There is the minimum chance of her being heard at all at the pitch at which she is singing, and hardly the ghost of a probability of the spectator catching the words. The stage direction in the score is that she is "greatly agitated"; but the audience is hardly likely to perceive this, in the first place because she is tucked away at the side of the darkened stage, and in the second place because at that precise moment Beckmesser looks up at Pogner's house and cries "The window opens!", and Magdalena appears at it in Eva's clothes: naturally the eyes of the audience turn at once in that direction.

While the orchestra is proceeding with No. 42 and Beckmesser is ejaculating "Good God! 'Tis she!" the lovers, in their hiding-place, have the following little dialogue:

Eva:　　That song grieves me, I know not why. Let us hasten
　　　　　away!
Walther:　(half-drawing his sword): Aye, now, with my sword!
Eva:　　No! Forbear!
Walther:　(withdrawing his hand from his sword): Scarce worth
　　　　　the while.
Eva:　　Yes, patience is best. O friend in need! That I should
　　　　　cause thee such trouble!

Naturally, after what has immediately preceded these last words, the casual reader of the poem takes them to be addressed to Walther. But obviously they apply to Sachs: *he* is the friend who, as she now sees, has divined Eva's need and suddenly come to her help; he it is whom she regrets having drawn into the tangled web of her own troubles. Wagner is manifestly carrying further the psychological motive that began with the "greatly agitated" and "That song grieves me, I know not why." But he has presumed too much on the spectator's hearing all these words, and, assuming him to have done so, on his reading into them, in that fleeting fifteen seconds or so, the wealth of meaning they had for the composer.

However, since he has made that meaning clear to us in his analytical note on the prelude to the third act, we can only accept it with gratitude and read it into the scene in the second act the next time we see the opera on the stage. We are reminded of Lord Burleigh's silent shake of the head in Sheridan's *The Critic:*

Sneer: He is very perfect indeed! Now pray what did he mean by that?

Puff: You don't take it?

Sneer: No, I don't, upon my soul.

Puff: Why, by that shake of the head he gave you to understand that even though they had more justice in their cause, and wisdom in their measures — yet, if there was not a greater spirit shown on the part of the people, the country would at last fall a sacrifice to the hostile ambition of the Spanish monarchy.

Sneer: The devil! Did he mean all that by shaking his head?

Puff: Every word of it — if he shook his head as I taught him.

Sneer: Ah! there certainly is a vast deal to be done on the stage by dumb show and expressions of face; and a judicious author knows how much he may trust to it.

37

To return to the prelude to the third act. The 'cellos having given out No. 43, it is taken up in imitation by the violas and then the violins, and woven into a texture of profoundly sorrowful meaning. Then the key shifts to G major, and horns and bassoons, with a passing intensification of the harmonies in trumpets, trombones and tuba, give out a theme:

No. 49

which, says Wagner, is "the solemn song with which Sachs greets Luther and the Reformation; it had won the poet an incomparable popularity". (We shall meet with it again later). After the first strophe", Wagner continues, "the strings take up once more single fragments of the Cobbling song, as though the man were turning his gaze from his handiwork heavenwards and losing himself in tender reveries." (Reiterations of phrases from the song, gradually soaring up into the higher reaches of the violins). "Then, with increased sonority, the horns continue the [Luther] hymn with which Hans Sachs, on his appearance at the festival, is greeted by the whole of the Nuremberg folk in a thunderous unison outburst. Next the first motive of the strings [No. 43] recurs, in a massive expression of the perturbation of a profoundly-stirred soul: finally, allayed and calmed, it attains the utmost cheerfulness of a benign and blissful resignation."

Before quitting the prelude let us give a glance at a little chronological difficulty connected with it. In May 1862 (not long after he had started work on the music of the opera), Wagner wrote to Frau Wesendonk that the idea had just come to him for the orchestral introduction to the third act. The emotional climax of this act, he says, will be the moment when Sachs stands up and is acclaimed by the whole assembly. "The people sing in solemn style the first eight lines of Sachs's poem on Luther: the music for this is already written. Now in the prelude to the third act, where, on the rising of the curtain, we see Sachs brooding in his chair, I am making the bass instruments play a soft, subdued, profoundly melancholy passage that bears the imprint of the deepest resignation". (This is our No. 43). Wagner goes on to describe the further course of the prelude. Now why is there no mention here of this motive appearing earlier as a countertheme to the third stanza of Sachs's cobbling song in the second act? The inference would appear to be that the idea of introducing it there had not yet occurred to Wagner — that so far from the motive having been transferred from the song to the prelude (as we have always supposed to have been the case), Wagner conceived it first of all in connection with the prelude, and only later, perhaps when he was at work on the second act, had the idea of inserting it in the cobbling song. It would be interesting to know what light, if any, Wagner's musical sketches throw on the matter.

38

The curtain rises, showing Sachs's workshop, with a half-open door in the background leading to the street. (It is one of the marvels of stage setting that the humble cobbler's workshop here looks larger than the whole house had done in act two. Sachs, we feel, must have been in an enviably large way of business — and with no one but David to help him! — to keep up an establishment of this size). On the right of the room is the door to an inner chamber. On the left, a window overlooks the alley; it has flowers before it; beside it is Sachs's work-bench. He is seen sitting in a large armchair by the window, absorbed in a big folio volume that rests on his knees: the sun shines brightly on him. It is the morning after the second act.

To the bright little tune of No. 14 David comes jauntily up the street and peeps in at the door. He is a trifle abashed when he sees the Master, but is reassured when it looks as if the latter had not noticed his entry. He carries a basket which he deposits on the work-bench at the back by the door; he draws from it flowers and ribbons, lays them out on the table, and, from the very bottom of the basket, extracts a sausage and a cake. These he is going to eat when Sachs, who still has not observed him, turns over a page of the folio noisily. David hurriedly puts the food out of sight and reports for duty: the shoes, he says, he has taken to Herr Beckmesser's house. He stops his chatter when he becomes aware of what looks like calculated silence on his master's part, which his guilty conscience puts down to displeasure over his rowdy behaviour last night.

He approaches Sachs humbly and begs for forgiveness: "can a prentice always behave as he should?" Can Sachs blame him for sticking up for his Lena as he did? She is so good to him, looks

355

at him so tenderly, consoles him when he has had a thrashing, brings him titbits when he is hungry. But yesterday she had first of all hurt him by snatching a basket of food out of his eager hands; and afterwards when he found another man serenading her he lost his temper, he confesses, and gave the fellow a hiding. But today Magdalena has explained everything and has sent him nice flowers and ribbons; and he, for his part, is willing now to pass the sponge of oblivion over last night's unorthodox proceedings.

39

Perhaps this scene had been rather better handled in some respects in the Second Sketch than it is in the opera. In the First Sketch David did not make his entry after the rise of the curtain and find his master there already, reading; he was in the room with him from the first, at work on a pair of shoes by the window. During Sachs's long reverie Magdalena called languishingly, from outside, "David!"; and he signified his annoyance over her conduct last night by "reproachful gestures". But when Wagner came to draft his Second Sketch, fifteen years later, he seems to have realised that a bit of explanation was called for at the opening of the third act.

The spectator may be expected to remember that the previous night's darkness had been so complete that not only did Walther believe at first that the woman in Magdalena's clothes who approached him was really Magdalena, not only did Beckmesser believe that the woman in Eva's clothes at the window was really Eva, but Pogner himself had mistaken the figure for his daughter when he dragged her back into the room, and had then gone down to the street door and cried "Ho, Lena! where art thou?" It might strike the spectator as a little odd, then, that David should have seen at once, when he opened his own window, that it was not Eva but his own Magdalena who was being serenaded; and stranger still that he does not recognise Beckmesser even while he is cudgelling him. (This is evident enough from the text of the opera: not only are we nowhere given the smallest hint that the apprentice knows his victim to be the Marker but the few words he addresses to him are such as no prentice in Nuremberg would ever have dared to use to one who was Master, Marker and Town

Clerk. "Who's that up there?" David had cried at the first sight of the figure at the window. "Upon my word it's Lena. Good Lord! she has given him an assignation. This is the man she prefers to me!"; and when he falls on the serenader it is with the remark, "To the devil with you, you damned churl . . . I'll break every bone in your body!" And Magdalena screams to him from the window, towards the end of the mêlée, "Listen, David: it's Beckmesser!").

It is evident enough that at some time or another between the Sketches and the final poem Wagner felt himself in a little difficulty as regards all this, and tried to put it right. In the Second Sketch he does a little explaining. When David slinks into the room at the opening of the third act he apologises humbly to his master for his disgraceful conduct the night before; "he confesses", says the Sketch, "that he had 'intentions' with regard to Frau Magdalena", who had been very kind to him in many ways. "Then he had seen a coxcomb serenading her — for in spite of her clothing he had recognised Frau Magdalena. Thereupon he had seen red, and when he further became aware that his rival was the Marker who had behaved so vilely to Sachs the day before [at the Song School], he just had to give him a thrashing. Now he begs forgiveness." That is not a very plausible explanation, all things considered, but at least it is an explanation of sorts. Yet when Wagner came to write his poem he cut out the passage relating to David's recognition of Beckmesser. "When I found", says the apprentice in the poem,

> *at nightfall another sneaking round,*
> *who sang to her, and howled like mad,*
> *well! such a drubbing he's ne'er had.*
> *Should I be blamed if others choose to fight?*
> *Besides, for our love 'twas a godsend quite;*
> *and Lena has explained the whole affair,*
> *and today sends me flowers and ribbons to wear.*

Here, it will be observed, he says nothing at all about having recognised Beckmesser from the first and chastised him not only for coming courting Lena but for his impudence to Sachs, nor, for that matter, does Beckmesser himself, in the poem, ever drop the least hint, either during the fight or in his colloquy with Sachs in the third act, that he knew his assailant to be the cobbler's apprentice. Yet if we grant that the darkness made this mutual recognition impossible, how are we to account for it not having been too dark for David to recognise Magdalena at the window? The whole thing is yet another instance of Wagner's conceiving an episode in different terms at different stages of his work upon a subject, and failing to smooth out all the discrepancies when he came to give his poem its final form.

40

To resume our account of the scene at the commencement of the third act. Sachs's continued silence terrifies David. It is ended by the shoemaker suddenly closing the folio with a bang that brings David to his knees in front of him. But when he speaks it is with a friendliness that astonishes the apprentice: how came these lovely flowers and ribbons here? he asks. David reminds him that it is Midsummer day, when everyone adorns himself in his best. So last night was "Polterabend"? (the evening of licensed rowdiness) the Master asks abstractedly. Then, pulling himself together, he bids the boy repeat his verses, if he knows them. David, delighted that all is going so well, begins to reel the lines off, but, with his mind still on last night, sings them to the tune of Beckmesser's serenade (No. 44).[1] Sachs calls him sharply to order, and David now sings quite correctly, to a simple melody in folk-style, a little song about the good St. John by Jordan's strand, baptizing all comers, among them the child of a German woman, to whom the Saint gives the name of Johannes:

No. 50

---

[1] In the First Sketch this episode had been handled very differently. There Magdalena calls to him from outside, and to annoy her with an affectation of indifference he starts singing Sachs's Cobbling song of the previous night.

When the pair get back to Nuremberg, however, what was Johannes by the Jordan becomes, on the banks of the Pegnitz, plain Hans, which, by an odd coincidence, is the name of the master to whom David now cajolingly offers the flowers and the ribbons, the cake and the sausage. He even suggests that Sachs should compete for the hand of the bride that afternoon; if he does, he assures him, Beckmesser won't stand a chance against him. Sachs puts the question aside with an indulgent smile and sends him away, bidding him dress up in his best clothes for the coming festival. David kisses his hand with emotion, and goes out quite overwhelmed by the unexpected mildness of his master; the least he had expected for his riotous behaviour the night before had been a taste of the strap.

41

Sachs, with the folio still on his knees, takes up again the broken thread of his meditations. The Renunciation motive (No. 43) comes out softly, first in the 'cellos and basses, then in a solo trombone, as he begins his famous "Wahn! Wahn!" monologue.[1] The burden of it is a lament over the folly of men, who will not live in peace together, but brother falls on brother "in aimless, frantic spite":

> *Nought does he know*
> *but grief and woe:*
> *he flies in fear*

"Sachs is at first startled and vexed. But the thought of the popularity he has acquired delights him; he lets David continue and himself sings with him." There is nothing of this in the Second and Third Sketches.

[1] There is a footnote in the orchestral score at this point: "If there is not a first-rate trombonist who can play the passage tenderly and legato it should be entrusted to a horn player."

"Wahn" means all kinds of things in different connections — according to the dictionaries "erroneous or false opinion", "illusion", "delusion", "hallucination", "error", "monomania", "folly", "madness" etc. Only two monosyllables are available for the English translator of the monologue — "craze" and "mad". "Craze! Craze! Everywhere craze!" conveys the literal meaning of Sachs's opening line very well, but "craze" has a touch of awkwardness about it when sung. "Mad" is perhaps better, if the listener understands it not in the sense of insanity but of folly in act and thought. The Italian version gives "follia", which carries the right shade of meaning but compels Sachs to sing three syllables where there is only one in the German.

yet deems he is pursuing;
hears not his own wild cry of pain
when his own heart he rends in twain,
but glories in his anguish.
What name were fit for this?
The ancient madness 'tis
that runs through all our striving,
to folly ever driving!

His dear old Nuremberg has been free of this madness:

Thy peaceful ways pursuing,
serene thou dost abide,
far from the clash of nations,[1]
dear Nuremberg, my pride;

But last night the universal madness had broken out there, and
why? Because, forsooth, some sprite or other had flitted through
men's minds: two lovers had tried to make for freedom and a
cobbler in his workshop had happened to give a tug at the strings
of folly: a riot had broken out:

and madness with madness vieing,
the cudgels soon are flying;
each madman must belabour
his own best friend and neighbour:
God knows how that befell!
Some goblin wove the spell!
Some glow-worm sought his mate in vain;
'twas he who brought this bitter bane!

Was it the elder's scent? Midsummer eve? But now, God be
praised, Midsummer day has dawned; so let Hans Sachs turn, if
he can, this evil to good, direct folly to a noble end.

We may be permitted to ask, as a simple matter of dramatic
consistency, why Sachs should now be taking the trifling events
of the previous night with such tragic seriousness, seeing in them
a symbol of the evil that is at the core of the cosmos. The answer
seems to be that Wagner had still not purged his mind of the original conception, with all that it implied, of Sachs as a definite

---

[1] Literally "in the centre of Germany".

historical character, lamenting not only the decline of poetry in his day but the strife of political and religious parties in the Germany of the period of the Reformation. In the First Sketch Wagner had made the subject of Sachs's broodings, when poring over the folio, the bitter thought, "Has an end really come to the divine art of poetry? Am I, a cobbler, really the only man left who breathes the spirit of the great German past?" This motive does not appear in the present poem; we are given no clue at all to Sachs's thoughts in the opening scene. The motive had, in fact, already been discarded in the Second Sketch, where it is made clear to us that what the shoemaker had been brooding over when turning the pages of the old world-chronicle was the ineradicable unfriendliness of man to man.

"Sachs", says the Second Sketch at the point where the monologue is reached, "remains for some time with his arm resting on the closed folio, sunk in reverie. He had been searching the world-chronicle for similar crazy proceedings that might explain for him the nature of the *Wahn* that so often takes possession of mankind and urges it on to the maddest deeds, so that men attack each other without any reason, seek out and shun each other, make war on each other, persecute one another, without a single one of them being any better for it all in the end. He discovers that all the books are at one on this matter; everything in the world is filled through and through with unreason [*Unsinn*]. This time, no doubt, it was because of Midsummer eve: a glow-worm failed to find its little mate; in its alarm it flitted through many a weary human brain; it set sparks crackling there; the world breaks into flame; the heart awakes and throbs and rages; fists are clenched, cudgels are seized, and it takes a rain of blows to put out the world-conflagration! A goblin's fit of insanity!"

Obviously all this grave philosophising, with its talk of a world-conflagration, developed from Wagner's original conception of Sachs and Nuremberg in the setting of the Germany of the sixteenth century, torn by political and religious hatreds: it is straining dramatic probability a little too far to make it appear that the Sachs who, the night before, had played the joyous part he did in the harmless baiting of a comically bad singer, should this morning see it all as a symbol of the universal and eternal human woe.

But what does it matter to us now if Wagner made a slight

mistake in dramatic psychology, when the mistake has brought us words of such wise humanism and music of such heart-searching beauty as the "Wahn! Wahn!" monologue?

42

The first section of it, in which Sachs muses on the innate and universal folly of mankind, is based upon that sorrowful motive of Resignation (No. 43) which had first appeared in the second act as a countertheme to the cobbling song, and had served to introduce the prelude to the third act. As the old man thinks with a glow of pride of the general tranquillity of his own beloved town the Nuremberg motive (No. 34) comes to the forefront. Then we hear reminiscences of the music of the ensemble at the end of the second act as Sachs recalls the tumult of the night before, when for a moment the quiet town seemed to be caught up in the general madness of the world. But this temporary fret yields place to the Magic of Midsummer's eve (No. 37), which touches with tender beauty even the echoes of the cudgelling scene that flit through the cobbler's mind as he speaks of the havoc wrought by the "glow-worm" that had flitted from brain to brain in frantic search of its little mate. "That", Sachs muses tenderly, "was Midsummer's eve; but now has dawned Midsummer's day"; and with a great crescendo that is one of the most thrilling moments of the whole score the monologue settles into its final stage. Through an orchestral tissue woven out of the Midsummer day motive (No. 19) in conjunction with that of Nuremberg (No. 34) the old cobbler turns with a mixture of philosophy and humour to the business he has set himself for the day, that of drawing all the tangled threads together and weaving a new pattern of human kindliness out of them:

> *We'll see now how Hans Sachs intends*
> *turning this madness to his ends,*
> *that good may come of ill;*
> *for if it plagues us still,*
> *e'en here in Nuremberg,*
> *let's make it do such work*
> *as needs a touch of madness in it;*
> *and so let one who's mad begin it!*

How that end is to be achieved will soon be made apparent, by no less an agency than the would-be cunning and folly of the one disturbing element in the picture, Beckmesser.

43

As the last strains of the monologue die away, with the orchestra throwing out the Midsummer day motive in peal after joyous peal, Walther emerges from the inner room. He is warmly greeted by Sachs, who enquires how he has slept. "A little, but soundly", replies the young man, who is obviously in a subdued mood this morning, for he had had a dream so beautiful that he hardly dares recall it, lest it should slip away from him. To the accompaniment of the motive of Sachs's Benevolence (No. 30), which had played so large a part in the dialogue between him and Eva in the second act, the cobbler assures him that it is precisely the poet's function to give expression and form to dreams, which are the best things in us. "Did your dream", he asks, "give you any hint of how you might become a Master?" The knight tells him, however, that after his reception by the Masters the day before he had given up all hope in that direction.

Sachs reproves him gently but earnestly. He himself, he says, has not abandoned hope; had it come to that pass he would not merely not have frustrated the young man's flight but would have kept him company. Walther must not judge the Masters too harshly; they may be narrow in their views, but at bottom they are honest souls who mean well. And was there not a certain amount of justification for their behaviour at the trial yesterday? For the knight's song had been, to say the least, a trifle unusual:

> *Your song the Masters somewhat scared,*
> *and with good cause, for on my word,*
> *if maids hear songs so hot and glowing*
> *what they'd be up to there's no knowing!*

The calm joys of wedded life call for other words, other melodies. "Yes", Walther retorts drily, "so I gathered from last night's affair; the alley resounded with them." "Aye, aye", Sachs chuckles, "and no doubt you heard me beating time to them!" But, he continues more seriously, "put all this out of your head now and think of making a Mastersong." The young man objects that were he to

achieve a beautiful poem and melody the Masters would only declare them not a Mastersong. Thereupon the wise old man gives
him, to a new motive:

No. 51
Tenderly

Mein Freund, in hol - der Ju - gend-zeit, wenn
My friend, in youth's en - chant - ed days, when

uns von mächt'- gen Trie - ben
warm the blood is flow - ing, etc.

some wise counsel as to the difference between life and art. The
burden of the lesson is that "inspiration" is all very well in its way,
but it is not the whole of art. In youth the warm blood makes
every man something of a poet: "'tis Spring that sings, not he".
The testing time for the artist comes later — in the summer, au-
tumn, and finally winter of life, when work is hard and cares accumulate, and the heart tends, in self-defence, to harden: if *then*
a man can fashion a lovely song, he is a real Master.

Walther, now all afire, protests that he is in love with a maid
whom he means to woo and win. "Then submit your mood", says
his mentor, in effect, "to the discipline of art: learn the Master-
rules, by doing which you will not fetter your imagination but
give it stronger and surer wings." "But what are these rules?" asks
the impatient young poet, "which you praise so highly? By whom
were they made?" Sachs's reply is warm with the wisdom of age
and experience:

> *By Masters whom the world had wasted,*
> *who life's embittered draught had tasted:*
> *with pain and sorrow mated,*
> *a vision they created*
> *of youth's first madness,*
> *its love and gladness,*
> *to give their souls the old free wing,*
> *and feel again the joy of Spring.*

"Yet how", asks Walther,

Yet how can dreaming age recapture
the vanished Spring and all its rapture?

Sachs's reply is:

It takes a draught whene'er it can:
so let me, a soul-thirsty man,
teach you the rules as I know them;
then with new meaning endow them.

"See", he continues, "here are pen. ink and paper. Dictate your morning dream to me, and I will take it down." But Walther needs yet another lesson in the psychology of the artist, which Wagner, speaking through Sachs, proceeds to give him. "To think of your rules", the young man had objected, "is to make me forget my dream." Sachs's reply is, in essence, Wordsworth's tracing of poetry to emotion recollected in tranquillity:

Sachs: Then call the poet's art to aid;
          it oft recalls what from memory's strayed.
Walther: Then 'twere no dream, but art alone?
Sachs: Good friends are they; the twain are one.
Walther: But how can I your rules obey?
Sachs: Make rules of your own, then sing away!

It is the artist Wagner speaking *in propria persona.*

44

Standing by the work-bench beside Sachs, who takes the words down as they fall from his lips, the knight launches into what will ultimately become the Prize Song, but at this stage is known to the German commentators as the Interpretation of the Morning Dream:

No. 52

Moderato

p dolce

Mor - gen - lich leuch - tend in ro - si - gem
Bright in the sun - light at dawn of the

Schein, von Blüt und Duft ge-schwellt die Luft,
day, when fra-grance rare filled all the air,

The first stanza consists of seven lines, rhyming thus, $1 + 6 + 7$, $2 + 3$, $4 + 5$ ("Schein", "Duft", "Luft", "Wonnen", "ersonnen", "ein", "sein") — a good metrical scheme, with the two inner rhymes held in the strong armature of the first and the two last.

That, Sachs tells him approvingly, was a "Stollen" in the nomenclature of the Mastersingers; let him follow it up with another on the same pattern. "Why the same?" Walther asks. A modern teacher of "musical form" would reply: "In the first place to impress your opening, with its main idea, firmly on the mind of the listener, in the second place, by the slightest of divergences from it, to achieve a certain necessary unity-in-variety and pave the way for a transition to a new idea." Sachs says much the same thing in the imagery of his own day, combining homely humour with sound aesthetics: "to let men see that you have chosen a bride like yourself." So the young man, whose first impulse had been to take a new flight straight away, disciplines his inspiration as ordered, keeping it on a level wing until it shall be time to make an effective swerve. His second "Stollen" is constructed on the same metrical pattern as the first, with the rhymes "Raum", "Frucht", "Wucht", "Prangen", "Verlangen", "Saum", "Baum". It tells how in the garden of the young man's dream stood a tree laden with golden fruit; and it ends not in the key of the tonic, as the first "Stollen" had done, but in that of the dominant. This procedure, Sachs tells him, would hardly be approved of by the Masters, but it is quite right in *his* eyes. And now let him make an "Abgesang" ("Afterstrain"). "Why?" Walther enquires. Because, the older poet informs him, pursuing his homely metaphor of the two "Stollen" standing in the relation to each other of bridegroom and bride, it is now necessary to think of the children; just as these are like the parents yet unlike, so the "Abgesang" must resemble the two "Stollen" yet differ from them, carrying on the idea but having a shape and rhymes and tones of its own. In other words, a "development section" is now called for.

So Walther fashions a new stanza, this time of eleven lines, with the rhymes pairing thus, $1 + 5$, $2 + 4$, $3 + 6$, $7 + 8$, $9 + 10$, with the final line standing apart from the others in unrhymed self-assured isolation.[1] This "Abgesang" is sung to a new melody

---

[1] Actually it rhymes ("Lebensbaum") with the final "Baum" of the second "Stollen" and the "Lorbeerbaum" ("laurel tree") of the twenty-fifth (the

which we have already met with in the overture and elsewhere as the Love motive (No. 6); now, however, it is in 3/4 time, and the words describe what befell the dreamer beneath the tree — a vision appeared to him of a maid more fair than tongue can tell, who took him to her breast and pointed out to him, with a smile, the object of his heart's desire, the lovely fruit upon the tree of life. The close is in C major, the key of the opening of the song, thus rounding off the curve of the whole.

Sachs, who had begun by giving a lesson in the interpenetration of matter and form, is now receiving one. Though deeply moved by the song, he confesses that while the complete "Bar" is satisfactory he finds the melody "a trifle free": not, he hastens to add, that *he* regards that as a fault, but freedom of this sort makes it a little difficult to retain the melody in the mind, and the ancients of the Guild do not like anything of that kind. It is Wagner himself once more defending himself against the contemporary charge that his "free" melody was not melody at all. However, Sachs continues, the young man must now compose a second "Bar" to make the first one quite clear; "for really your song, well as it is rhymed, leaves me in some doubt as to how much in it is your dream, how much your art."

So Walther sings a second "Bar", symmetrical with the first, i.e., having two "Stollen" and an "Abgesang", all three metricized and rhymed on the plan of their predecessors; and this second "Bar" tells how, when morning gave place first to evening, then to night, two stars appeared and beamed softly on the dreamer, the murmur of a stream stole on his ear, the stars broke into a dance among the leaves and branches, and "not fruit but a starry host hung from the laurel tree". The musical form of this second three-limbed "Bar" is that of the first one, with a tonic close to the first "Stollen", a dominant to the second, and a clinching tonic again to the third.

45

More profoundly moved still by the youthful fire and beauty of it all, Sachs suggests a third "Bar", which would make the

last) line of the next and concluding strain of the song; but these subtleties, though obviously factors in Wagner's poetic idea and technical design, are not likely to be perceived by the casual listener in the theatre.

poet's interpretation of the dream clear beyond all doubt to him. But Walther brushes the invitation aside: "How could I do that? Enough of words!" (Wagner, of course, like a good dramatist, is keeping the third section of the song up his sleeve for a later occasion, when it will be twice as effective as it would be if put before us now and merely repeated towards the end of the opera).

Sachs is wise enough to see that it would be tactless to press the young poet further just then. He rises and goes up to him; "then let us have word and deed at the proper time", he says. "But don't lose the melody, for it seems to me the very thing for poetry; and if you sing it later before them all, don't forget your morning dream." As Walther does not quite understand this, Sachs explains further. "Your trusty squire followed you here with your bag and baggage, including the clothes you will wear at the marriage feast. Some dove, surely, must have brought him to the nest where his master lay dreaming. So back to your chamber; we will both of us array ourselves in our best, for there is notable work ahead of us." Walther grasps the friendly old man's hand. Sachs leads him quietly to his room, opens the door for him respectfully, and follows him in.

The build of this scene seems so natural, the sequence of episodes and the flow of conversation so easy, that it all has the appearance of a happy improvisation of the moment. Yet manifestly it had cost Wagner a great deal of thought, for in the Sketches it had been handled quite differently. In the First Sketch Walther, entering the room immediately after the departure of David, had been gently reproved by Sachs for his rash attempt at elopement with Eva. The knight confesses his error, but asks what he is to do now. Is he to stand idly by and see his beloved carried off by his enemy Beckmesser? "That mustn't happen", replies Sachs. "But you will have to win her in the contest: leave it to me." How different the kind old cobbler is, Walther says gratefully, from those tiresome Masters who treated him so badly! He had thought to find the love of art in them, but how woefully he had been disappointed! The Sketch continues thus: "*Sachs:* 'What have you written so far?' 'Hero-songs; praises of the great Emperor; look; look!' 'No Minnesongs?' 'Here is my latest.' 'Give it me.' Sachs reads it through attentively. (The orchestra plays the melody). Sachs remains for a time sunk in reflection; then he turns to the

young man: 'You are a poet!' "; after which the dialogue continues
as on page 350. After Walther's declaration that he "needs a wife"
and Sachs's assurance "You shall have one; leave that to me", the
Sketch continues thus: "The Beloved enters to discuss the question of her shoes. Terzett. She begins to overwhelm Sachs with reproaches, but the young man defends him. Sachs consoles them
both and hints at a happy outcome: he tells them the part each
must play. They thank him and promise obedience. The three go
out by different exits"; whereupon Beckmesser enters.

<h2 style="text-align:center">46</h2>

In the Second Sketch, after Sachs's monologue, Walther enters
and reproaches him for having hindered his flight the night before. Sachs explains that things like that are not done in respectable circles in Nuremberg; while he is on the knight's side he
wants to be sure that his love for the maiden is genuine and that
it will last. Walther turns away from him impatiently. The old man
had noticed that it was daylight before the other had gone to rest,
and Walther explains that, being unable to sleep, he had spent
the time writing a poem to his beloved. He produces it and hands
it to Sachs, and while the latter is silently reading it the orchestra
plays the melody softly. (We may take it, from this, that the poem
was a short one, or that the cobbler did not read it all; for we
cannot imagine his doing so in silence for anything like the time
occupied by the present singing of the Morning Dream song).
Delighted with the poem, he promises Walther that the "Wahn"
started by some kobold or other the preceding night shall today
turn to his advantage. "How?" asks Walther. "By diverting the
minds of men for a little while from their dull beaten track", says
Sachs. "Come into the other room with me; I am going to dress for
the festival, and we will have a talk about it all." Both go into the
inner room, and while they are out, Beckmesser enters.

Evidently, then, the plan for the present superior handling of
the scene did not occur to Wagner until he was actually at work
on the opera. But the curious history of the Prize Song does not
end here.

In March 1862, shortly after he had begun work at his score,
Wagner, in a letter to Mathilde Wesendonk, quoted the opening
lines of the Prize Song as it stood in the original poem:

> *Fern*
> *meiner Jugend gold'nen Toren*
> *zog ich einst aus*
> *in Betrachtung ganz verloren:*
> *väterlich Haus,*
> *kindliche Wiege,*
> *lebet wohl! ich eil', ich fliege*
> *einer neuen Welt nun zu!*

"I have fitted these lines", he said, "to a melody already in my head", and he quoted the first few bars of the music:

No. 53

As the reader will be aware, the music of the present Prize Song runs on entirely different lines from these. Nor have the words of the song, in that first form, the smallest connection, either in metre or in meaning, with those in the opera.

As time went on, the Prize Song, and its forerunner, the Morning Dream Song, and the stage situation in which the latter was to be floated, all took quite other shapes in Wagner's mind. In October 1866 he wrote to King Ludwig, "I am now well into the [music of the] third act, and one of these days I shall have to write the words of Walther's Prize Song [i.e., the Morning Dream Song], the melody of which is already finished." The popular belief that Wagner's way with an opera was first to put together a "book" and then "set it to music" is quite mistaken. Here we have two instances of his writing the music first and finding words for it later — for, as the reader will have observed, the melody of 1862 which he had quoted for the benefit of Frau Wesendonk had been complete in his head before he "began to make lines to fit it". Precisely the same thing happened in 1866 in connection with the present Morning Dream Song. "Melody of the Prize Song, without text", is one of the jottings in his private "Annals". The entry was not made until near the end of the year, but it relates to the previous September, by the 28th of which month the melody was fully sketched and dated. He did not trouble at the time about the words, but went on tranquilly with the composition of his third act: pages 19–22 of his Composition Sketch, we now know, present a curious spectacle — the broken dialogue between Sachs and Walther is complete, words and music, while the Morning Dream melody is written out in full, but without any words. These were not ready until Christmas of that year.

One other curious feature of this scene may be noted here. We have heard (page 368) Sachs telling Walther that his clothes have been brought to the house by his "trusty servant" — "some little dove must have shown him the nest where his master lay dreaming". Why the "little dove" (*Täubchen*)? The explanation is that in the poem of the Morning Dream in its original (and later discarded) form the Beloved had appeared to the knight, in his dream, as a dove. Obviously only Eva knows where Walther had gone after their separation the night before, and only she can have told the servant where he was to be found. A jocular allusion to her as the *Täubchen* on Sachs's part would therefore have been quite in order in the earlier scheme. But there is no dramatic reason why this image of her should occur to him in the present poem, for there is no allusion to her as a *Täubchen* in the Morning Dream as Walther now sings it. Presumably the image had stuck in Wagner's mind, and he carried it over from the old to the new version without giving the matter any thought. The user of the Schott score of the opera misses the point, because Mr. Frederick Jameson has translated the passage "some *bird*, sure, must have shewn the nest wherein his master dreams". *Täubchen*, by the way, carries a double meaning, upon which Sachs is slily playing; colloquially it is a term of affection — "lovey" or "duck".

47

To resume our analysis of the opera.

As soon as Sachs and Walther have left the room Beckmesser comes in, and the delicious scene begins in which he unwittingly sets a trap that will snap decisively on him a few hours later. The devising of that trap cost Wagner a good deal of hard thinking. Beckmesser was to catch sight of the manuscript of what he naturally took to be a song by Sachs, and by some means or other be led to pass it off as his own at the contest, to his utter and final discomfiture. The problem before Wagner was a double one — how to give the utmost plausibility to those means, and how to manage it that our sympathies did not turn against Sachs. Let us first of all see how the action runs in the opera as we now have it.

Beckmesser comes in showily dressed, but obviously in poor shape physically after his experience of the night before. He is accompanied graphically in the orchestra by cunning interweavings of the theme of his serenade (No. 44), the Cudgelling motive (No. 27), the Marker motive (No. 24), etc. The music not only depicts his physical twinges but shows us that he is living over again, in imagination, the painful events in the alley. It is all set forth for us in the detailed stage directions for the long episode in dumb show.

He peeps round the door before venturing in. He limps forward, but, feeling a sudden twinge, gives a convulsive quiver and rubs his back. At the next step he takes his knee hurts him, and he rubs this. He sits down on the cobbler's stool, but at once starts up in pain. Perspiration breaks out on his brow as he visualises all he went through last night. He staggers about blindly in all directions, trying to escape from an invisible David. At last he steadies himself by holding on to the table; then he goes to the window and looks up at Pogner's house, trying to find consolation in the thought of Eva. But this brings up memories of Walther, and in a fit of jealous rage he beats his forehead. Once more he hears the derisive laughter of the women in the alley; he slams the window angrily and turns mechanically to the table, his worried mind occupied with the new song he will have to compose for today's contest, the one he had intended for the occasion having come so sadly to pieces.

The manuscript left there by Sachs catches his eye: he picks it up inquisitively, runs a rapid eye over it, and finally bursts out wrathfully, "A wooing song! By Sachs! Ha! now all's as clear as day!" He smells rivalry and treachery in the air: so that is what the artful cobbler had been up to all the time! Now he understands why the old rascal slaughtered his serenade and got him thrashed last night; it was to get a rival out of his way today.

As Sachs comes in in holiday attire Beckmesser hastily crams
the paper into his pocket. For a little while the two fence with
each other; Beckmesser is irritable and rude, the cobbler ironic
and polite. The Marker charges him with engineering the shindy
of the evening before in order to ruin his chances today: Sachs's
jocular reply is that as it was Beckmesser's wedding eve the usual
jollification was quite in order. The Marker now loses his temper
completely. A new motive appears — that of Beckmesser's Indignation:

No. 54

as he traces all his misfortunes to his supposed rival for Eva's
hand. It was Sachs who had cunningly persuaded Pogner to put
that clause about the maiden's consent into the offer of the prize,
hoping she would fall into *his* hands. It was Sachs who with malice aforethought had ruined his song:

> *That's why! That's why!*
> *And blind was I!*
> *He tried to stop my song last night,*
> *He banged and bawled with all his might,*
> *to keep back from the maid*
> *another man's serenade.*
> *Aye, aye! Ho, ho!*
> *Was it not so?*
> *You sat there in your cobbler's den,*
> *and called your friends up, boys and men,*
> *to beat me black and blue,*

> *and clear the course for you!*
> *Oh Lord! Oh Lord!*
> *My back they've scored,*
> *and shamed me 'fore the maid adored;*
> *they did so swipe and switch me*
> *that no tailor, sure, could stitch me!*
> *To treat a man so!*
> *My hide to tan so!*

and so on at great length, in the finest piece of vituperation in all opera.

Taking up the theme of No. 54, Sachs replies quietly that he is mistaken: "believe what you like about me, but at any rate calm your jealous fears. I am no wooer, and not your rival." The furious Marker gives him the lie direct. A dialogue of the swiftest and neatest give-and-take ensues. As proof that he is right, Beckmesser produces the manuscript, with the ink hardly dry on it. Perhaps, he surmises sarcastically, it is just a biblical song? Sachs waves the suggestion aside. Then what?

> *Oh Sachs, for all your virtuous pose,*
> *for craft you'd run the devil close!*

Maybe, the cobbler replies quietly:

> *Maybe, but yet I was never known*
> *to pocket things I did not own:*
> *and so that you may not be called a thief,*
> *no longer 'tis mine — I give you the leaf.*

Beckmesser can hardly believe his ears. But is there not a catch in this generous offer somewhere? What is the use of the gift if Sachs remembers the song?

Beckmesser: *Perhaps it's all well fixed in your mind?*
Sachs: *No fear need you have of me, you'll find.*
Beckmesser: *You give me the leaf?*
Sachs: *To save your good name.*
Beckmesser: *To use as my own?*
Sachs: *Pray feel no shame.*
Beckmesser: *To sing if I like?*
Sachs: *By all means try.*

Beckmesser: And if I succeed?
Sachs: None more surprised than I.

Beckmesser is overwhelmed by this generosity. After the hammering he has had, he says, he doesn't feel equal to writing a new song today, and one by Sachs is sure to be first-rate. Let them be friends for life! Then a new suspicion worms itself into his mind, and he exacts a promise from Sachs:

> *Yet one thing swear —*
> *if the song you should hear anywhere,*
> *you'll promise to make no remark,*
> *not claim it as yours, but keep it dark?*

Sachs: *I swear it: may I punished be*
              if e'er I mention the song is by me.

Beckmesser rubs his hands with satisfaction: now he feels perfectly safe. Sachs gives him a final piece of friendly advice — to study the song well before singing it, for it isn't easy, and he may come to grief over both melody and words. His old belief in himself fully restored, Beckmesser assures him that all Nuremberg admits he hasn't a superior when it comes to tones and modes. And now he must not fritter away any more time here; he must be off to con the song. Buttering his dear friend Sachs with compliments and protestations of undying affection:

No. 55

he cavorts to the door, imagines he has forgotten the poem, rushes back anxiously to the table, finds the manuscript is in his hand, embraces Sachs again, and at last limps out. Sachs gazes thoughtfully after him, smiles sardonically, and looks forward with satisfaction to the time when the foolish fellow's sin will find him out. The long scene is an incomparable scherzo, equally symphonic and dramatic.

49

Let us now glance at the slow process by which Wagner arrived at the present dexterous handling of the scene.

In the opera, Walther's song is taken down on paper by Sachs, whereas in the First Sketch the young man had brought with him a copy of his latest poem to show the cobbler. It is this manuscript, left on the table at their exit, that catches Beckmesser's eye when he comes into the now empty room. In the opera he arrives boiling over with rage against Sachs for his behaviour the night before, while to the pains of the cudgelling he had received there is now added the suspicion that the cobbler, judging from the freshly-written poem in his handwriting on the table, intends to enter the lists for Eva's hand. This line of procedure had not at first suggested itself to Wagner; for in the Sketch "the Marker comes in diffidently: he is in great distress, for now he is convinced that last night his chances with the maiden had been ruined. He wants to make sure of Sachs, for he knows how great his influence is with the people."

It was at this point that Wagner's difficulties began. How was Beckmesser to be caught in a trap entirely of his own setting? Was he to be shown as fully deserving all he got later, or was he to be the victim to some extent of Sachs's craft and malice? Wagner's first idea took the following form: "The Marker catches sight of the song on the work-table, reads it, and finds it will suit him. He is in doubt whether to pocket it or not: when Sachs enters he slips it hastily but involuntarily into his breast. He is embarrassed. He feels that he cannot make use of the song without Sachs's permission; hence the milder tone he now adopts. At last, his conscience getting the upper hand, he confesses the theft and is presented with the song by Sachs." "Perhaps", Wagner adds in a parenthesis, "Sachs can make out that he has no idea whose the song is — it might be the young man's, who by this time is over the hills and far away. 'It seems to be a magical song! If only the melody were there with it! Take good care to find the right tune!'"

But in a parallel column Wagner sketches an alternative pro-

cedure, in which the cobbler plays rather maliciously on the
Marker's weaknesses. When Sachs re-enters the room he is astonished, or professes to be, to find the Marker there. Is there anything wrong with the new shoes? he asks innocently. Thereupon
Beckmesser vents his gall on him for the trick of the night before. Sachs defends himself humorously. Then the Marker tries
a smoother tone: his wooing song had been ruined, and how is he
to find another? Taken in by Sachs's friendliness he becomes
more and more confidential: he has no doubts as regards his own
powers, but he mistrusts the maiden and the folk, who understand nothing of the art of the Masters. In the end Sachs offers
him a song of his own, which, written in the days of his youth,
is not known to anyone in the town. Beckmesser is at first suspicious of a trap: suppose, in the event of the song bringing
him success at the contest, the cobbler comes forward and
claims it as his. Sachs reassures him on this point: he is an old
graybeard, a widower for some years: is he likely to be so foolish
as to want to marry again? It ends in Beckmesser, his suspicions
allayed, going off with the young man's song in the belief that it
is one by Sachs; and as he departs, the latter maliciously instructs
him how to sing it.

50

In this version, then, Sachs deliberately deceives Beckmesser.
After riper reflection Wagner must have seen that this would
alienate the audience's sympathies to some extent from the cobbler; so he went back, in essentials, to the first of his two alternative plans, dexterously making the Marker fall into a pit of his
own digging, with Sachs assuredly not pushing him in, but as assuredly doing nothing to hold him back. Thus both characters
are rescued so far as dramatic psychology is concerned. In the
opera we do not censure Beckmesser for his hasty pocketing of
the song in the first place, and in the second place for his willing-
ness, when it is turned over to him, to palm it off as his own, because he is throughout a figure of farcical fun, against whom, by the
conventions of the theatre, the ordinary laws of good behaviour
are not so sternly invoked as they are against more serious characters. Sachs, however, must not be allowed to lapse from normal
standards of honour; so it has to be not he who hangs Beckmesser

but Beckmesser who hangs himself, Sachs merely letting him have the rope he is so keen on getting. From first to last, in the admirable scene as we now have it in the opera, the cobbler does not say a single untrue thing about the song or his own share in it; he is speaking no more and no less than the simple truth when he admits that the handwriting is his, with the ink still fresh, and tells the Marker he can have the document if he wants it.

This is the really artful touch on Wagner's part. Sachs does not present Beckmesser with the *poem*, but with the bit of paper on which it is written: what he says is "Behaltet das Blatt, es sei euch geschenkt" ("Keep the sheet; I make you a present of it"). All he does is to present Beckmesser with a bit of his own property, the scrap of paper; if the schemer chooses to make the false inference that because the writing is Sachs's the poem is Sachs's, that is the man's own affair. It is Beckmesser who, in his haste and greed, picks out the card the conjuror wanted him to draw. The English translators, myself included, somewhat obscure the matter when, to avoid the repetition of the word "sheet", they make Beckmesser ask "You give me the song?", to which Sachs replies, in effect, "Yes, so that you won't have theft on your conscience." But what Beckmesser really says to him, in the German, is not "You give me the song?" but "You give me the leaf?", which Sachs can do without having anything on *his* conscience. He is not making himself an accomplice in an infringement of literary copyright, but merely presenting Beckmesser with a bit of his own legal property, to wit, a sheet of paper with some words on it in his own handwriting. With the whitest conscience in the world he can assure the Marker that at no time and in no place will he claim the song as his. The cobbler's reputation remains as pure as driven snow; Beckmesser, for his part, leaves the court, as an Irish judge said of a lucky defendant, without a stain on his character beyond those on it when he came in.[1]

[1] In *A Communication to my Friends* (1851) Wagner gave his readers an outline of the story of the new opera he was planning. This is in the main a swift summary of the First Sketch; but manifestly he was still doubtful, after six years, how to manage the episode of Beckmesser and the manuscript, for this is how he now describes it: "The next day the Marker comes disconsolately to Sachs and begs of him a new song with which to woo the bride. The cobbler gives him a poem of the young knight's, pretending not to know how it had come into his possession; he warns him, however, to be

51

The scene that follows in the opera is also a later invention of Wagner's. Originally, as we have seen, he had made Eva appear earlier in the action and sing a trio with Walther and Sachs; later he cut out that episode entirely and delayed her participation in the drama until after the departure of Beckmesser. She now enters, from the street, in splendid attire, for she is dressed for the festival; she is pale and sorrowful-looking, however, and she comes towards the old man slowly, accompanied in the orchestra by the gracious motive (No. 35) that had served as background to their colloquy in the second act. Her anxiety is depicted in a new motive:

No. 56

first breathed in the soft tones of the wood wind, which runs symphonically through the dialogue that ensues.

Sachs congratulates her on looking so smart; but her heart, she assures him, is anything but as gay as her dress. Can't he guess where the shoe is pinching her? Their dialogue, like their former one in the second act, is a fencing bout. Everything she says has another meaning than the literal one: she is fishing for information about the knight, but will not say so openly; while Sachs affects to take everything she says quite literally, though he is perfectly aware of what is unspoken in it. Ostensibly she is complaining about the fit of the new shoes he has made for her; but what is really pinching her is not the shoes but the uncertainty about Walther. The odd thing about these shoes, she says, is their contrariness; when she stops they would go, and when she wants to go they stop. The reference is plainly to her love and the frustrated elopement. Cannot Sachs do something about it? At his bidding she puts a foot on the stool, and he examines the shoe.

careful to find a fitting melody to which to sing it." This "pretence", it will be seen, evades the ethical problem of how Sachs is to plant the poem on Beckmesser without himself incurring the charge of trickery. Evidently Wagner was content just then to leave this knotty problem to solve itself later.

"It's too wide, you see." "Nonsense, my child; that's pure vanity; the shoe fits close." "Just so; my toes are pinched most shockingly." "Here, on the left?" "No, on the right." "The heel?" "No, the instep." Then, in a flash of petulance, "Ah, Master, do you know better than I where the shoe pinches?"

Just then, to a mighty surge in the orchestra of the motive of the Magic of Midsummer eve (No. 37), Walther, in splendid knightly array, appears at the open inner door. Eva gives a cry, but does not move, her foot remaining on the stool all the while as she gazes at him. Walther is also immobilised, spellbound at the unexpected sight of Eva. Sachs has his back to the door; he knows well the cause of Eva's cry, but he does not look round, pretending to be professionally intent on the shoe. He takes it off her foot, saying he will ease it on the last, and goes to the bench with it, still betraying no recognition of the new situation. Eva does not move. At work on the shoe, Sachs grumbles about the hardness of the cobbler's life, always at work, day in, day out, early and late. He has a plan in his mind, he tells her. No more cobbling for him; he will woo her today, hoping to have better luck as singer than as shoemaker. Had not she herself suggested this the previous day? "Well, well," he goes on, as she makes no reply. "I see what your answer is — 'Stick to your shoes! If only I could hear a song while I work! I heard a lovely one today; I wonder if there is a third verse to it?"

Walther, his gaze still riveted on Eva, breaks into the third section of the Dream Song, for which we, like Sachs, have long been waiting. Metrically and melodically it is made on the pattern of the two previous ones. The poetic content of it is the completion of the vision seen in his dream — the dancing stars had lighted on the head of the Beloved, her eyes had become two suns of beauty, and she had crowned his head with a wreath and filled the poet's breast with the rapture of paradise.

52

"My child", Sachs had remarked to Eva after the first "Stollen", "that is a Mastersong!" When it is over he returns with the shoe, fits it on her foot, and plays once more with the literal and the veiled meaning of it all: "Let's see if the shoe fits now. I think I've managed it at last. Stand up and try it. Does it pinch you still?"

Eva bursts into passionate tears, falls on his breast, and clings sobbing to him. Walther goes up to him and presses his hand, his heart too full for words. Mastering himself, Sachs tears himself away as if displeased—leaving Eva resting unconsciously on Walther's shoulder,—and, as usual with him, finds relief in homely, half-serious, half-humorous disparagement of his craft. But here again there is something unexpressed at the back of his words.[1] What a life is the cobbler's! he grumbles:

> *Were I not a poet too,*
> *henceforth I'd never touch a shoe!*

For a shoemaker is a drudge, a slave at everyone's beck and call, abused by everyone for his bad workmanship. If he happens to be a poet as well, he gets no peace: if he is a widower into the bargain, everyone imagines he is a fool. The maidens would take him, for better or for worse, when younger men are scarce; but in the end

> *the smell of pitch they catch,*
> *and call him fool, rascal and wretch.*

For the first time we see right into the kind old heart, realise how profound is his love for Eva, how nobly and unselfishly he has worked for her happiness.

He ends by railing at David for not being there: the fellow thinks of nothing but his Lena and his stomach! And he makes as if to go in search of him, leaving the lovers to each other. But Eva falls into his arms, and, in a great cry that is one of the blinding emotional high lights of the opera, hails him, to his own motive of Resignation (No. 43), as the friend in need for whom she cannot find adequate words of thanks. The orchestra accompanies her with a theme curiously suggestive of *Tristan and Isolde*:

No. 57

[1] His melody is that of his cobbling song in the second act (No. 42), but it is accompanied in the horns by the melancholy motive (No. 43) of Sachs's heart-ache. This, however, the piano scores cannot show.

as she pours out her gratitude to him: he had wakened her, she says, when a child; he had watched over her as she grew to womanhood; and now he wakens her to a new free life; through him she is born anew. She deserves a scolding from him: had her choice been free it was he whom she would have chosen for husband: and No. 57 rises to new heights of expression as she says:

> But now my will is dead;
> no more I may rejoice;
> and if today I wed,
> I am bereft of choice;
> that were to catch me in a net!
> E'en you, my Master, would regret!

No. 57 becomes frankly a quotation from the opening of the *Tristan* prelude as Sachs reassures her:

> My child, of Tristan and Isolde
> the grievous tale I know;
> Hans Sachs was wise, and would not
> through King Marke's torments go.
> 'Twas time to find the proper groom,
> or I at last had met my rightful doom.

He turns from half-grave to wholly gay as Magdalena enters through the shop door and David from the inner room, each of them beflowered and beribboned for the festival; and the motive of Eva's anxiety (No. 56) becomes all innocent joy as the cobbler demands the attention of them all. To the strain of the chorale from the church scene in the first act he summons them to a christening. It is the custom of the Masters, he reminds them, when a Mastersong is born, to give it a name by which it shall always be known. Well, the young knight here has created a Master-melody, to which he, Hans Sachs, and Eva Pogner are to stand godfather and godmother, with David and Magdalena as

witnesses. But as by Nuremberg law no apprentice can be a witness, and as David has sung creditably today, he makes the boy
a journeyman. The delighted David kneels down, and receives
the accolade in the form of a smart box on the ear.

Sachs names the new song, in true Mastersinger fashion, "the
Morning Dream's Interpretation", and bids the young godmother
say the appropriate thing about the infant. She does so by launch-
ing the great quintet:

No. 58

She sings of the joy this day has brought her, the day when her
lover shall prove himself Master and win the highest prize. The
more prosaic David and Magdalena are lost in astonishment that
the former is an apprentice no longer, and they dream of a day
when he too shall be a Master, with Lena as bride. Walther, to
the melody of No. 52, sings of the felicity of the discovery that
his Morning Dream has come true. Sachs, for his part, once more
lets us see into the depths of his kind and philosophical old soul:

> *To the maiden dear I'd fain*
> *sing my song of sadness;*
> *but must hide my heart's sweet pain,*
> *wear a mask of gladness.*

For him the message of the Dream is clear:

> *Love and youth that never dies*
> *bloom but through the poet's prize.*

His one thought now is for the lovers whom he had saved from the consequences of their folly the night before and brought within sight of triumph and happiness.

The noble quintet finished, he turns abruptly to practical affairs. Eva he sends off to her father, Magdalena with her; and bidding David see that the shop is properly locked up he takes Walther away with him to the festival.

53

During the change of scene on the stage the orchestra develops the Nuremberg motive (No. 34) at some length. Horn and trumpet fanfares ring out from afar, and the motive of the Mastersingers (No. 4) blends with that of Midsummer day (No. 19). All Nuremberg, we feel, is *en fête.*

When the curtain rises again we see an open meadow outside the town. Across the stage winds the little Pegnitz river, which is bringing boat-loads of men, women and children to the festival, all in their holiday clothes. On one side of the stage is a raised platform with chairs and benches on it; it is decorated with the banners of the Guilds that have already arrived, and as the others come in their banners also are added to the number, so that finally they enclose the platform on three sides. In the foreground and at the sides of the stage the populace is lying about or making merry outside tents and drinking-booths. The prentices, arrayed in their best, adorned with flowers and favours and carrying slender be-ribboned staves, act as heralds and marshals for the procession that now appears; they conduct the members of each Guild in turn to the platform; there the respective banners are planted, after which the burghers and journeymen break up and make for the booths.

At the point when the curtain rises it is the Shoemakers who are arriving, singing — to the accompaniment, of course, of the Cobbling motive (No. 31) — to their patron, St. Crispin, who taught the world how to be comfortably shod. The fanfares ring out again (this time on the stage): the town trumpeters and drummers, lute-makers, and journeymen with toy trumpets are all showing what they can do. The Tailors come in with their appropriate banner flying: they tell, with goat-like trills,[1] the heroic

---

[1] There is a traditional German association of tailors with goats.

tale of how, when Nuremberg was once beleaguered and famine threatened, a tailor appeared sewn up in a goat-skin, who walked boldly out on the battlements with many a skip and caper and put the astonished enemy to flight: "who'd think a tailor could rise to such heights?" In the course of the narration Wagner slyly turns to his own purposes a passage in one of the most popular Italian opera arias of the day, the "Di tanti palpiti" from Rossini's *Tancredi.* The Tailors are followed by the Bakers, who sing the praises of bread as the dispeller of hunger; and these by the Cobblers, who are no less lyrical in praise of leather.

A gaily decorated boat brings to shore a number of young girls in rich peasant finery; the prentices, with a glad cry of "Maidens from Fürth!", run to help them to land, and all break into a rustic dance over a drone bass:

No. 59

the prentices contending with the journeymen for the girls. David, conscious of the dignity of his new standing as journeyman, views it all with disapproval: let them look out if the Masters catch them! he says. But in the end he too seizes a pretty girl and joins the dance; he breaks away from her in fright for a moment when the prentices tell him that his Lena is coming, but sees that he has been fooled and throws himself into the dance again more ardently than ever.

It comes to a sudden end with a cry of "The Mastersingers!" from the journeymen on the bank who have been looking towards the town. The apprentices and the folk prepare to receive the Masters, who come in, in solemn procession, to the dignified music of the opening of the prelude to the first act: at the sight of Kothner, who carries the banner on which King David is depicted with his harp, the people cheer and wave their hats. Pogner leads Eva by the hand: richly dressed, and accompanied by Magdalena and a bevy of maidens, she is shown to the place of honour. When the muster on the benches is complete the fanfare rings out once more, and the prentices come forward ceremoniously and call "Silentium! Not a word! Be ye all as dumb!" Sachs rises in his place. All raise their hats and caps and press forward, pointing to him; and with a general cry of "Begin!" the whole assembly thunders out the song to the words of which the historical Sachs had hailed Luther and the Reformation:

> *Awake! full soon will dawn the day!*
> *I hear within the coppice gray*
> *a rapture-laden nightingale,*
> *his song resounds o'er hill and dale:*
> *the night expires in western skies,*
> *the new day in the east doth rise,*
> *the red dawn floods the fields with light,*
> *and puts the gloomy clouds to flight.*

At the conclusion of the mighty chorus the people, to the music always associated with the Masters, break into jubilant praise of "Nuremberg's darling Sachs".[1]

---

[1] Sachs's poem falls, after the manner of its epoch, into a regular succession of iambics:

> Wacht auf, es nahet gen dem Tag,
> ich hör' singen im grünen Hag, etc.

Wagner, of course, could not affront the modern ear with what it would regard as a misaccentuation of the second syllable of "singen"; so, as the reader will perceive from the above musical quotation, he shapes his soprano part in such a way as to ensure that the first syllable of the word gets a stronger

54

One man alone in the joyous company has care in his heart. The torrent of sound dies away suddenly to a pianissimo as the strings alone give out the motive of Resignation (No. 43). Immobile, sunk in thought, Sachs's gaze all the while has been over the heads of the crowd. Now he turns to them with a kindly glance. Beginning in a voice tremulous with emotion, but growing firmer as he proceeds, he thanks them for the honour their love has prompted them to do him. To the accompaniment of the motive of Benevolence (No. 30), which had originally been heard in the first act, at the point where Sachs pleaded with the Masters for Walther, and had figured again in the colloquy between him and the knight in the earlier part of the third act, he tells them that today he is to be their spokesman. They prize the art of song indeed, he says, and one among them, "a Master rich and high-souled", today shows such love for it that he offers daughter, land and treasure as prize in the coming contest. Let all who wish to try for it be noble and pure of heart, for never has so great a prize been known before, in ancient times or modern. Pogner, deeply moved, presses his hand and thanks him: his old cobbler friend alone knows what a load had been lying on his heart of late.

Then Sachs turns to the Herr Marker, who, all this while, in an agony of apprehension, has been taking the poem from his pocket, furtively trying to memorise it, and wiping the sweat from his brow: do what he will he cannot fix the difficult thing in his mind. "Well, my friend, you're not committed to it", Sachs tells him. "Too late!" replies poor Beckmesser: "my own came smash, thanks to you." Blaming the cobbler for all his troubles, he

---

accent than the second. But in the inner parts he is less careful, and one jibs at the stressing of "-gen" at the expense of the "sin-" in these: the tenor part, for instance, is phrased thus:

No. 61

Ich hör' sin - gen im Hag

The critical Sachs of the opera would have given Beckmesser's shoe several reproving hammer-strokes for false accents of this kind.

still entreats his help. He is confident he can beat all comers if only Sachs does not compete. But this new song! No one will understand it; so will Sachs use his popularity with the crowd and tip the beam in his favour?

55

Kothner, coming forward, proclaims the session open: bachelors first, and the older before the younger; so let Herr Beckmesser begin. The prentices, to the accompaniment of their impudent No. 8, conduct the singer to a small mound of turf they have beaten up in front of the platform and covered with flowers. Beckmesser, after many a stumble, manages to scramble to the top of it, the people all the while commenting unkindly on his awkwardness: this, surely, is not the man for the maiden; he may be an ornament to the Town Council, but as wooer he is a comic loon! Once more the prentices call out "Silentium!", and Kothner launches the official "Now begin!" Beckmesser, who has managed at last to find a firm footing on the mound, bows clumsily first to the Masters, then, with a leer that is meant to be ingratiating, at Eva, who averts her eyes from the grotesque spectacle. He tries to collect his thoughts with a prelude on his lute, but the orchestra replies with an ominous thumb-nail sketch of himself as the one-time all-powerful Marker (No. 24).

At last he begins to attempt to sing the song he had so rashly accepted from Sachs. It is an even more ludicrous performance than his serenade in the second act: the knight's poetry becomes utter balderdash in his mouth, though he takes a furtive peep at the manuscript every now and then; for the melody he falls back on tags from his earlier song. The Masters and the folk can hardly believe their ears: has the man gone out of his mind? they ask each other as they repeat some of the more absurd of his lines. He breaks into a cold perspiration, mops his brow, and has another try; but after his first "Abgesang" the crowd bursts into loud laughter.

He gives up. Leaving the mound he goes up to Sachs in a fury:

> *Accursed cobbler, this is your snare!*
> *The song is not my own, I swear:*
> *'twas Sachs, to whom you bow the knee,*

> *your precious Sachs, who gave it to me.*
> *Has he not shamed me quite enough,*
> *but must palm on me his wretched stuff?*

and he rushes out madly and is lost in the crowd.

Kothner and the others call on Sachs to explain how Beckmesser's song can possibly be his: "a scandal!" says Konrad Nachtigall reprovingly; "an extraordinary thing!" opine Hermann Ortel and Hans Foltz. Sachs, who has quietly picked up the manuscript Beckmesser has hurled at him before leaving, assures them that the song is not by him; *his* modest muse could never rise to such heights. Let Herr Beckmesser tell them, if he cares to do so, how he came into possession of it. The others are astounded at this assurance that the song is a good one. Sachs explains that it merely wants singing properly, with the right words and the right melody; and he calls on a witness to prove his point, if there be one present who is prepared to do so.

56

Walther steps forward and salutes the Masters and the folk with knightly courtesy; all look at him in silence, but sympathetically.

> *Bear witness this song is not by me;*
> *and sing it so that all may see*
> *my praise of the song*
> *was not a whit too strong,*

Sachs tells him. Walther ascends the mound with firm steps, and Sachs hands the manuscript to Kothner for him and the other Masters to follow from. The knight now converts the Morning Dream song into the Prize Song: the meaning and the shape of it are essentially the same, but after the sixth line it takes a new turn both verbally and musically.

Wagner's original intention had been that the Prize Song should be simply a repetition of its predecessor. His sense of the theatre made it clear to him later that this would result in monotony, if not in actual anticlimax; and yet the situation demanded that what is now sung shall correspond literally with what is on the paper, so that the Masters can see for themselves that Sachs was speaking the truth when he said that the words and the melody were alike good, with the present singer as the only possible author of them. A letter from Cosima to King Ludwig in the early part of 1867 shows how Wagner tackled and solved this problem. He had "lately come to the conclusion", Cosima wrote, "that it was absolutely impossible to have the same poem sung twice in the same act. It must be the same yet different, clear and concentrated; moreover, it would have gone against the grain with Walther to repeat before the Masters and the folk the intimate happenings in Sachs's room. This difficult problem, which has kept him uncommonly busy during the last few days, has in my opinion been solved with wonderful success. . . ." The discovery by the Masters that the song is *not* the one on the paper is now side-stepped in the simplest way imaginable. When Walther has reached the sixth line, Kothner, overcome by emotion at the beauty of the song, involuntarily lets the manuscript fall from his hand. No one picks it up; all are too intent on the song and the singer for that. Walther, according to the stage directions, perceives this, and now boldly goes on to re-shape his lay as the inspiration of the moment dictates. The effective little point is almost invariably missed in the theatre because the eyes of the audience are naturally fixed on the tenor: the spectator who does not know all that is involved does not see Kothner let the manuscript fall, or, if he does so, does not grasp the meaning and the implications of it all.[1]

Now and then Masters and people interject a naïve admiring comment on the song:

> *Ah yes! I see it improves a song*
> *to sing it right instead of wrong;*

> . . . .

> *'Tis strange and daring, that is true;*
> *but rhymed quite well, and vocal too!*

[1] In the original edition of the orchestral score the stage directions are merely "at this point Kothner, who has been following from the manuscript with the other Masters, involuntarily lets it drop; he and the others now merely listen, absorbed, to the remainder of the song", and that is how the direction appears also in the earlier piano scores and translations. A succeeding sentence — "Walther perceives this, and, without betraying that he has done so, now continues in freer style" (i.e., with changes in words and melody) — was added by Wagner in a later imprint of the poem.

and so on. At the conclusion of it the people unanimously award Walther the prize, and the Masters confirm their judgment: Pogner turns to Sachs with a warm word of thanks for having lifted a load from his heart.

57

The knight is led to the steps of the platform, where he falls on one knee before Eva, who crowns him with a wreath of laurel and myrtle; then both of them kneel before Pogner, who gives them his blessing. Sachs turns in triumph to the assembly: "Was I not right? Was not my witness well chosen?" The Masters call on Pogner, as the senior of the Guild, to confer Masterhood on the young man; the goldsmith holds out to him the gold chain with three large medals on it, and dubs him Master in the name of King David. But Walther turns away impetuously. He does not want their Masterhood; the only reward he values is one that Eva alone can bestow. In perplexity and embarrassment everyone looks towards Sachs, who advances to Walther, takes him meaningly by the hand, and, to the accompaniment of the various motives associated with the Guild, reads him a little lecture. Let him not disdain the Masters, but honour their art. It is not lineage, wealth, weapons that have served him, but his art. The Masters have tended their own art lovingly and well, and have kept it noble and German in soul through difficult days. An evil day may dawn, when Germans shall be no more one: then,

> *if foreign kings should rule our land,*
> *no prince his folk will understand,*
> *and foreign mists before us rise*
> *to dupe and blind our German eyes;*
> *the good and true were lost for aye*
> *if German art we should betray.*
> *So heed my words:*
> *honour your German Masters,*
> *if you'd forefend disasters!*
> *Let us but take them to our heart,*
> *though should depart*
> *the might of holy Rome,*
> *no harm will come*
> *to holy German art!*

The whole assembly repeats the final words in chorus. Eva takes the wreath from Walther's brow and places it on Sachs's, who takes the chain from Pogner's hand and hangs it on the knight's neck. In a final tableau Walther and Eva stand one on each side of Sachs, before whom Pogner bows the knee in homage, while all the other Masters hail him as their chief; the people wave hats and kerchiefs, and the prentices dance and clap their hands, to a general cry of "Hail! Sachs! Nuremberg's darling Sachs!"

In the First Sketch (1845) Sachs had merely admonished Walther to honour the Masters and their art; the lines "Though should depart the might of holy Rome" etc. were added in 1861, at a time when the long-suppressed impulse towards German unity was moving at last towards realisation.

It is interesting to learn, from a letter of Cosima's of January 1867 to King Ludwig, that when Wagner was completing his score he planned to end the opera with the Prize Song and its jubilant reception by the assembly: "Sachs's big address, he contended, was not really part and parcel of the matter, but rather a speech of the poet to the people"; so he proposed to omit it. But Cosima protested vehemently against this; and Wagner, she says, "thought it over, though naturally he remained of his own way of thinking." In the end he gave way to her, and worked out the "address" in full between two and three o'clock of the morning of January 28th, after Cosima "had been talking to him the whole day about the conclusion of the work". Perhaps, on the whole, Wagner would have been wiser to have "remained of his own way of thinking about it".